An Economic and Social History of Western Europe Since 1945

ANTHONY SUTCLIFFE

Longman

London and New York

HC
240
.S824
1996

Addison Wesley Longman Limited
Edinburgh Gate
Harlow, Essex CM20 2JE, United Kingdom
and associated Companies throughout the world.

*Published in the United States of America
by Addison Wesley Longman Inc., New York.*

First published 1996

ISBN 0 582 23646 0 CSD
ISBN 0 582 23645 2 PPR

British Library Cataloguing-in-Publication Data

A catalogue record of this book is
available from the British Library

Library of Congress Cataloging-in-Publication Data

Sutcliffe, Anthony, 1942–
  An economic and social history of Western Europe since 1945
Anthony Sutcliffe.
     p. cm.
  Includes bibliographical references and index.
     ISBN 0–582–23646–0. — ISBN 0–582–23645–2 (pbk.)
     1. Europe, Western—Economic conditions—1945- 2. Europe,
Western—Social conditions. I. Title.
HC240.S824 1996
306'.094'09045—dc20   96—8269
                                                              CIP

Set by 7 in 10/12p Baskerville
Produced by Longman Singapore Publishers (Pte) Ltd.
Printed in Singapore

In memory of Roger Smith

Contents

The publishers would like to thank the following for granting permission to use copyright material: Editions la Découverte, Paris for Figure 11.3 and Hodder Headline (Edward Arnold) for Figure 2.1.

Preface

As the end of the second millennium of our era approaches, interest in the recent history of western Europe is growing. With European integration proceeding apace, more of us need to know how it has come about, and what its implications are. More students find themselves taking survey courses which deal exclusively or in part with western Europe. Many of us now feel the need to set the history of our own time in a European as well as a national perspective.

To write a history of the economy and society of western Europe since the war for such a varied readership is a tall order. Fortunately, this series already includes a political history of post-war Europe by Neil Urwin. *Western Europe Since 1945: A Short Political History* has run to four editions since it was first published in 1968. Urwin's historical frame is similar to ours and the two books are complementary. Indeed, those accustomed to economic history surveys may be surprised by the presence of political history in what follows. There are two main reasons for this. First, the association of economic *and* social history in one account creates a very broad historical arena within which political changes cannot be ignored. Second, so great has been the role of government in economic and social affairs since 1945 that political factors have to be made explicit.

The structure of this book is an attempt to reconcile the presentation of national and continental experiences. Western Europe is understood as a large, sub-continental region, the birthplace of industrialisation in the late eighteenth and nineteenth centuries, but with broad areas still almost unaffected by it in 1945. The main industrialised area, centred on Britain, Belgium, France and Germany, is designated here as the 'core'. The non-industrialised or industrialising areas form two 'fringe' zones to the north, in Scandinavia, and in the Mediterranean south. There is a tiny western 'fringe', composed of Ireland. Not all the national economies are treated in detail – Switzerland, Ireland and Austria are the main exclusions – but the remainder are grouped within the two fringe zones and the core.

Within this framework it has been possible to discuss the economic fortunes of fourteen western European countries in some detail. However, no attempt has been made to adopt the same agenda for each. The national accounts emphasise features or episodes that are significant for those countries, or for western Europe in general. For instance, the comprehensive reconstruction of western Germany under Allied direction secures extensive treatment because of its importance not only for the economic revival of Germany but for that of western Europe as a whole. In France, the modernising role of Charles De Gaulle from the 1940s to the 1960s secures repeated attention. In Britain, the theme is one of relative economic decline until the 1980s. In this way, the fortunes of each country contribute to the economic and social history of western Europe which is the central concern of the book.

Social history, which is dealt with on a continental scale in two long chapters, is not given distinct national treatments. Important developments, such as the rise of a youth culture, are discussed in relation to countries and periods of time where they were most visible, or from where they exercised continental influence. The emphasis is on change and human experience, not on structures and continuity.

This book is based on part of Towards a New Europe, a First Year course taught by the Department of Economic and Social History at the University of Leicester. The course is followed by students from several departments in the Faculty of the Social Sciences and the Faculty of Arts, most of whom have not previously encountered the discipline of Economic and Social History. Several of my Leicester colleagues have taken a very helpful and generous interest. Derek Aldcroft, now of Manchester Metropolitan University, whose work on European economic history has been the touchstone for this book, has been a constant source of ideas and reactions. He has read the book in several drafts, and pointed out numerous errors and weaknesses. I have tried to deal with all of these, but he is not, of course, responsible for the faults that remain. Francesco Galassi is a true world historian who has helped me greatly with novel perspectives and striking examples. Philip Cottrell's grasp of the international economy has also been of great value. His comments on part of the draft have led to a large number of detailed and even structural improvements, but he is not responsible for any surviving errors, repetitions, and lack of precision. Sally Horrocks and David Williams have lent me books from their collections. David Nunn, a Leicester undergraduate with the unusual distinction of having met Albert Speer, volunteered to make a special trip into town to buy me a rare copy of Mandy Rice-Davies' novel, *Today and Tomorrow*, which he had glimpsed in a second-hand bookshop. In producing the manuscript, Lynne Haynes and Gillian Austen have been a constant support.

Western Europe is a small, western extension of the continent of Europe. Europe as a whole is not a large continent. It stretches eastward for more than four thousand kilometres from the Atlantic to the far side of the Ural Mountains. Of the seven continents conventionally delineated by geographers, Europe is the sixth in area; only Australia is smaller. It is, moreover, not an obvious continent, being the western peninsula of the huge Eurasian land mass which runs from the Pacific Ocean to the Atlantic. Had the geographers who first defined the continental system not been Europeans, Europe might not have been regarded as a separate continent. However, Europe's racial and cultural identity has been persuasive and the continent's small area has encouraged a social and economic homogeneity which has not been a feature of most of the other continents until very recent times.

Europe engendered the great creative force of today's world, industrialisation. As industrialisation spread across Europe in the nineteenth century, moving from west to east, and from north to south, the prospect of a unified, continental economy began to emerge. In the twentieth century war and economic nationalism postponed this result. From 1945 the idea of economic integration revived in Europe, but by 1948 new impediments had replaced the old. In different political circumstances Europe might have developed as a single economic unit, and it may yet do so. However, during most of the period covered by this book, the eastern part of Europe was almost completely isolated economically from the west by the aspirations of Communism, which controlled it politically and militarily, to develop a non-capitalist economic system. The area thus cut off lay, in Churchill's perception of 1946, east of the north–south line from Stettin to Trieste.

Stalin's creation of the 'Iron Curtain' in 1947 and 1948 assigned some two-thirds of Europe to Communism. This great swathe of territory was, however, much more backward economically than capitalism's share to the West. The fact that exchanges of goods, services and people across the Iron Curtain were too restricted to

allow significant economic and social cooperation may not have
detracted greatly from economic development in western Europe,
which continued to look towards North America and to its
imperial territories. But what might western Europe have become
if that great eastern market had been open to it, with higher living
standards there than Stalin and his successors could ever provide?

Even deprived of the East, western Europe remains a large,
populous and productive region. Its population by the mid-
twentieth century was comparable to North America's. With most
North Americans descended from European stock, two great,
compatible continents faced each other across the Atlantic Ocean,
jointly forming the core of the West. The most obvious difference
between North America and western Europe is the latter's division
into a large number of nation states. These need not in themselves
have hindered economic and social integration but the emergence
of numerous languages dating from the early Middle Ages, a
variety of legal provisions, and, eventually, a number of barriers to
trade designed to raise revenue or encourage domestic industries,
were obstacles to exchange of all sorts. During the nineteenth
century, under Britain's leadership, barriers to trade within
Europe were reduced, while internal tariffs and other discouragements were removed as part of the great movement of national
unification which, among other results, produced the modern
Germany and Italy.

Western Europe's progress towards a free-trade economy was,
however, halted by the First World War. The war was the product
of various rivalries between the main European states. Economic
competition was only one of these, and after the war the United
States, the British Empire and Europe sought to return to the
pre-war situation with currency stability backed by gold and free
international trade. In practice the economic troubles of the 1920s
and early 1930s undermined this agreement. With Europe's
biggest economy, Germany, seeking autarky after 1933, France
defending its *franc Poincaré* at the expense of output, and Britain
leaving the gold standard in 1931 and turning towards
'Commonwealth preference' in 1932, western Europe moved
towards economic nationalism. The new policies helped to reduce
unemployment almost everywhere (except France) by 1939, but
world trade was severely restrained and the danger of war became
much more acute.

After 1945 a very different picture emerges. The growth of the
western European economy is much faster than ever before.

Meanwhile, economic protectionism is gradually abandoned and progress is made towards the world-wide reduction of trade barriers, the easing of international payments, and the economic integration of western Europe on a scale which by 1996 is well on the way to the creation of a single western European economy. Greater exchange between the western European countries and the greater specialisation which tended to result were not the only factors in European economic growth but it is here that the contrast with the inter-war years is the most striking.

The development of an industrialised western European economy and society after 1945 justifies the structure of this book. At the end of the war a dislocated Europe looked to the United States for funds, advice and markets. An American vision of European countries trading freely among themselves and with the rest of the world was reinforced by the integrationist view of many in Europe who feared a further war. When West Germany emerged once more as Europe's biggest economy in the 1950s, it did so not as a threat but as Europe's most enthusiastic economic cooperator and increasingly as the European economy's biggest stabilising force. By 1957, when the European Economic Community (EEC) was set up, integration was well under way. Social integration followed multiple paths, but rising and converging living standards tended to produce a western European civilisation which all could recognise. This is a lively, rapidly moving story, unique in economic and social history, and in this account we shall be stressing events as well as structures and trends.

Terminology

In 1957 the Treaty of Rome set up the European Economic Community (EEC). In the 1960s the term 'European Community' (EC) came into general use as a broader alternative to 'European Economic Community'. In 1992 the Maastricht Treaty set up the European Union, an organisation of several components, including the European Community, whose name was formally altered from 'European Economic Community' at this time. In this book, the term 'European Economic Community' (EEC) will generally be used until 1992, and either 'EC' or 'EU', as appropriate, thereafter.

Nottingham
26 February 1996

Western Europe Since 1945

Figure 0.1 *Map of western Europe in 1950, showing national boundaries*

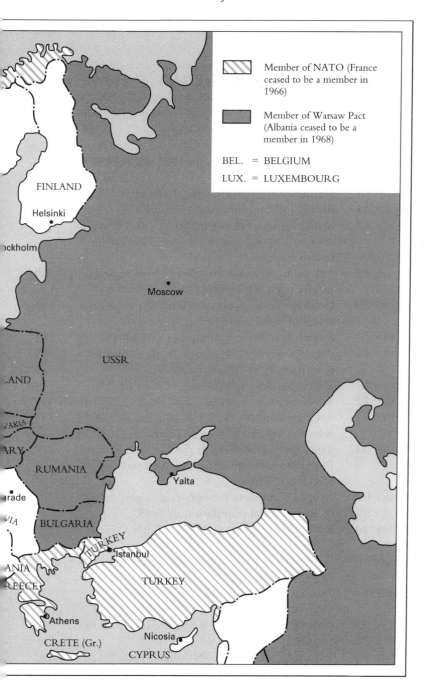

Member of NATO (France ceased to be a member in 1966)

Member of Warsaw Pact (Albania ceased to be a member in 1968)

BEL. = BELGIUM

LUX. = LUXEMBOURG

FINLAND

Helsinki

ockholm

Moscow

USSR

AND

AKIA

ARY

RUMANIA

Yalta

rade

IA   BULGARIA

TURKEY

ANIA   Istanbul

REECE   TURKEY

Athens

CRETE (Gr.)   Nicosia

CYPRUS

List of Figures

List of Abbreviations

CAP   Common Agricultural Policy
CIS   Commonwealth of Independent States
CMEA   Council for Mutual Economic Assistance (Comecon)
EBRD   European Bank for Reconstruction and Development
EC   European Community
ECA   Economic Cooperation Administration
ECSC   European Coal and Steel Community
EDC   European Defence Community
EDF   Electricité de France
EEC   European Economic Community
EFTA   European Free Trade Association
EIB   European Investment Bank
EIF   European Investment Fund
EMS   European Monetary System
EMU   European Monetary Union
EPC   European Political Community
EPU   European Payments Union
ERDF   European Regional Development Fund
ERM   Exchange Rate Mechanism
ERP   European Recovery Programme
EU   European Union
FAO   Food and Agriculture Organisation (of the United
            Nations)
GARIOA   Government and Relief in Occupied Areas
GATT   General Agreement on Tariffs and Trade
IBRO   International Bank for Reconstruction and
            Development
IMF   International Monetary Fund
ITO   International Trade Organisation
NATO   North Atlantic Treaty Organisation
OECD   Organisation for Economic Cooperation and
            Development
OEEC   Organisation for European Economic Cooperation

SNCF	Société nationale des chemins de fer français
TVA	Tennessee Valley Authority
UNRRA	United Nations Relief and Rehabilitation Administration

CHAPTER ONE

The Reconstruction Challenge: Western Europe, 1945–c.1952

The potential participants in reconstruction

In Germany they soon came to call the last day of the war in Europe, 8 May 1945, *Stunde null* (zero hour). In their gloomy sense of 'zero hour', everything had broken down, while the future offered nothing that they could discern (see Leiwig, 1988). Meanwhile, there were parts of Europe where life had been little touched by the war. Neutral Sweden and Switzerland had even prospered, mainly by supplying Germany on favourable terms of trade and welcoming rich or talented refugees. Spain's acute problems were largely the result of its own Civil War (1936–39), and its wise refusal to join the Axis struggle spared it further military suffering. Britain's total mobilisation for war production left it with serious economic problems but its role as the great European leader of the anti-Axis effort renewed its nineteenth-century stance as an example to the whole of the continent. Finally, the United States, by far the biggest contributor to the western war effort, had reinforced its economy and had made clear its determination to inspire European reconstruction after the war.

We now know that western Europe would recover surprisingly quickly from what Aldcroft has described as 'a shambles' (Aldcroft, 1993, 108). In 1945, however, no one could be confident that the recovery would be rapid, or even that there would be a recovery at all before some new disaster took place. Human and material losses had been much greater than in the First World War, and the growing attacks on civilian populations as the war dragged on had been demoralising and dislocating in their effect. Hitler's desperate defence of the Reich had reduced Germany to a level of

1

devastation and suffering which recalled the darker descriptions of the Thirty Years' War (Beck, 1986, 172–97). The number of deaths caused by the war in Europe is estimated at about 40 million, and over 30 million Europeans had been transplanted or dispossessed. Most countries suffered a large fall in GNP between 1938 and 1946. In many countries, exports had dropped almost to nil by 1946. Meat production declined by one-third and bread output fell to 60 per cent of pre-war (Aldcroft, 1993, 112). Malnutrition was serious in the occupied countries. With the American contribution to reconstruction not yet clear, there was much talk of growing chaos and discontent, followed by another war.

For the victor countries, the end of the fighting was the prelude to a period of continuing effort in which a transition to peacetime conditions involved important decisions and new initiatives. Much more than the neutral and liberated countries, they could lead the way towards new international arrangements. The strongest leader by far was the USA. There were, however, two big problems. One was the role and objectives of the Soviet Union. The other was the future influence of National Socialism.

Annihilating National Socialism

National Socialist ideology and policies are now so fully discredited that their influential role in a great European Fascist revolution, beginning in Italy in 1923, is often not recognised. This movement had its intellectuals, its newspapers and journals, and its artists, as well as its soldiers, brawlers and politicians. The National Socialists sought nothing less than a revolution which would first of all transform Germany, then incorporate foreign territories where large German communities lived, and then absorb such parts of Europe, like the Netherlands, as the Nazis felt worthy of inclusion in their New Order. Ideas and policies were also developed to deal with other parts of Europe which would be either exploited or virtually exterminated, like eastern Poland.

Although the general concept of German superiority over other peoples had matured by the later 1930s, no detailed planning had been done for the development or exploitation of likely new territories. Certain areas with Germanic minority populations or traditions were earmarked for incorporation into the Reich, but little thought had been given to the planning implications. The collapse of Poland in September 1939 prompted urgent efforts to plan the germanisation of western Poland on the basis of new communications, a new urban structure, the eradication of the Polish agricultural system, and the expulsion of part of the Polish population (Ward, 1982, 93–103). Work on the planning of occupied areas continued, mainly under the direction of the *Wehrmacht* (armed forces), until 1942, when the Russian revival forced the Germans to concentrate on defence rather than continental planning and dreaming.

Meanwhile, several ministries, culminating in the Ministry of Armaments and War Production developed by Albert Speer between 1942 and 1945, worked on the economic aspects of Germany's New Order in Europe. This funnelled massive supplies of primary and secondary materials to Germany at artificially low prices. Most of these were war materials, and they included armaments produced by local firms in the occupied areas. Some progress was also made towards securing the production of consumer goods within the occupied territories, for export to Germany and even to other parts of the German system (Milward, 1970b, 276–80). Albert Speer hoped to set up a series of European cartels for coal, iron ore, electricity and so on, following proposals and initiatives of the large German banks and industrial firms which dated back to 1940 in some cases (Mommen, 1994, 62–3). These would be extensions of the German structure of war production, and would involve the lifting of all tariff barriers in the context of a continental production plan. Speer told his interrogators in 1945 that he expected Sweden and the other neutral countries to join this system (Milward, 1970b, 147).

This German approach to the reorganisation of Europe had something in common with the Allied one after 1945, even though its principles and the resulting policies were very different. Domestic programmes were mostly the work of national ministries, the SS, and the National Socialist party, while the planning and treatment of the occupied territories were largely the work of the *Wehrmacht.* Party members, SS members and industrialists could exercise some influence on the general formulation of policy but the process was not consultative in the formal sense. When it was the Allies' turn to take on new territories, from 1945, the Army (American, British and French) was likewise the main agent on the ground, while a wide variety of participants shaped the policies at government level. German and American pluralistic decision-making ironically had more in common with each other than with British and French centralism.

When Germany surrendered in 1945, the Allies took the horrific power of National Socialist thinking very seriously. It had, for instance, sustained the German forces in a hopeless defence which lasted until most of them had been overrun. Interrogated prisoners had generally expressed support for, and confidence in, the regime. National Socialism had sustained millions of Germans in the execution or observation of brutal acts and had given them the ideology to justify them. A resistance movement in occupied Germany could not be ruled out, and popular support for underground Nazi activity seemed possible. The association of German nationalism and National Socialist ideology which was Hitler's biggest political achievement could easily remain a potent force after the war, so that even if order were restored soon after the surrender, it could revive almost unaltered once circumstances favoured it again.

This spirit was present in Hitler's New Year's Day radio speech to the German people in 1945, when he looked forward to the reconstruction 'in a few years' of everything that the enemy had destroyed. This achievement would be the result of the 'super-human' and 'heroic' efforts which only the German people could generate. The work would go on until, one day, the objectives of Germany's enemies would be abandoned. This product of the German spirit and the German will would, Hitler concluded, go down in history as 'the miracle of the twentieth century' (Hohlbein, 1985, 6). The idea that Germany would be rebuilt 'more beautiful than before' dated back, in Hitler's speeches, to 1942, but to suggest that the work would go on during the war, and that it would persuade Germany's enemies to abandon their military efforts, implied a continuing National Socialist movement. The idea had something in common with Marshal Pétain's assertion in June 1940 that a reinvigorated France could so impress the Germans that they would leave of their own accord. Unrealistic though Hitler's ideas sounded, they could not be discounted as the Allied victory approached, particularly in view of the mysterious 'miracle weapon' promised by German propaganda.

The Allies had decided to remove this danger by rooting National Socialism out of Germany. This meant arresting and punishing the Nazi leaders, 'denazifying' German society by demoting large numbers of party members, officials, and politicians, banning all public expressions of Nazi views, destroying or sequestering Nazi literature, cleansing school and university programmes, and removing party insignia from such buildings as still stood. In the early stages of the Occupation, Allied personnel were banned from speaking to Germans so that they could be made to feel their pariah status. Films about concentration camps were shown in the surviving cinemas to the local population, who were forced to attend in order to secure their food rations.

At first, many German people were too dazed by the collapse of the Reich and the devastation in the cities to understand that the Allies were aiming at a national revolution in thought and attitudes, as ambitious as Hitler's had been. With about 5 million party members, denazification was a slow process; it was still going on in 1948. However, one thing was clear. Germany would not be allowed to generate its own reconstruction ideology, however many liberals came to the surface and offered to take on the task. They would be allowed to share in government and economic revival, as did Konrad Adenauer and Ludwig Erhard, but at first their role would be a subordinate and supervised one. Even as late as 1949, just before the German Federal Republic was set up, rather earlier than had been expected, the senior Germans of the day were still working under Allied tutelage. Germany did not direct its own reconstruction before 1949, and did not even have a major influence on it. The result was a large gap which was filled by the Allies, and principally by the USA. As Germany was still the biggest country, and potentially the largest economy, in Europe, the absence of a German contribution left the way clear for a huge American influence on the reconstruction of Europe as a whole.

The voluntary exclusion of the Soviet Union

As Allied soldiers marched through the ruined cities of western Germany in 1945, they probably concluded that the core of European destruction must be here. In fact, most of the fighting had taken place in eastern Europe, with widespread destruction in western Russia as far as Leningrad, Moscow and Stalingrad where the Soviet line had held firm in 1942. As the war ended, there were still hopes that the USSR would join the western Allies in a concerted programme for the rebuilding of Europe. This would presumably have included an alliance of American capital and Soviet labour to rebuild Russia, and would have rivalled the reconstruction of western Europe.

Stalin, however, chose a different course, incorporating eastern Europe, including part of Germany, into the Communist world.

Insofar as this was a rational decision, it was probably designed to build up the economic strength of Communism rather than dilute it in a pan-European economy which would inevitably be dominated by American capital and expertise. The descent of the 'Iron Curtain', as Churchill called it in a big speech at Fulton, Missouri, on 5 March 1946, was total by 1948, and it cut Stalin's world adrift on the aimless voyage towards the collapse of European Communism in 1991. None of that sad Odyssey is the concern of this book, and the reconstruction story of this chapter is that of western Europe alone. Indeed, the term 'western Europe' came into general use in 1947/48 to signify 'non-Communist Europe' (De Jouvenel, 1948, 16).

The USA

The voluntary exclusion of the USSR from western European reconstruction allowed the USA to play the leading role. The origins of this role dated back to December 1940, when a Roosevelt press conference had used the metaphor of 'the garden hose' to explain that the United States intended to help put out Europe's house fire, provided that it got its hose back later (Stettinius, 1944, 1). On 11 March 1941, Congress approved the Lend-Lease Act after a vigorous national debate in which the disturbing idea of indirect involvement in a second European war, and rearmament at home, had been justified on the grounds that hostilities could well reach America later on.

The Japanese attack on the US naval base of Pearl Harbor, at Honolulu, on 7 December 1941, had then launched the USA into a naval war in the Pacific but it was Hitler's rash decision to honour an Axis treaty pledge and declare war on the USA a few days later that drew the Americans into a world war. Already non-belligerent supporters of Britain, the last anti-Fascist outpost in Europe, they found themselves in alliance with the Soviet Union, under German attack since May 1941. The USA decided on strategic grounds to take a direct part in the war in Europe, which they and Britain came to regard as the crucial theatre of the Second World War. With China also drawing on Lend-Lease support, the Americans shaped the concept of 1,500 million people fighting together against aggression, and began to refer to them as the 'United Nations' (Stettinius, 1944, 5).

From the first the United States assumed that they and their allies would win the war. They also aimed to secure the utter defeat of their Axis enemies, rather than a negotiated peace which might leave the Fascist and Japanese-imperialist regimes still in existence, in however reduced a form. They wanted to avoid the survival of national and international conditions which might lead to a later conflict, much as they had after the First World War. The US government presented its European and Asian enemies to the American people and to its friends as a world conspiracy of evil which had to be destroyed, root and branch. This meant that something had to be put in its place after the war, with the USA again taking the lead. Participation by the Soviet Union in the ordering of the post-war world would have complicated the American task, but the compromise solution of a division into spheres of influence both simplified and limited it.

Planning for the post-war world could therefore begin very quickly, in early 1942. It built on a statement of broad principle, the Atlantic Charter, drawn up from August 1941 on the basis of early discussions between Roosevelt and Churchill. The Atlantic Charter set out the principles on which the post-war world would be based. Essentially these were freedom, democracy, and a prosperous economy based on free exchange. Britain pressed the USA to start work immediately on planning a post-war system of stable exchange rates and smoothly running international payments. US discussions took place at the highest levels, under the direct guidance of President Roosevelt, who was mindful of the strengths and the weaknesses of President Woodrow Wilson's efforts to create a better world after the First World War and wanted to follow his example, though with much greater success.

Washington committees, while uncertain about precise reforms, were prepared to envisage radical change. So were citizens' advisory groups like the Council on Foreign Relations which clearly stated in 1942 that the USA should be prepared to create completely new institutions in all areas affected by the war:

> Americans are inclined to believe that the period at the end of the war will provide a tabula rasa on which can be written the terms of a democratic new order. The economic and political institutions of 1939 and before are clearly in suspension and need not be restored intact after the war.

US planning, with which Britain and Canada were in general agreement, sought to create a world without wars, with harmonious relationships between countries, and international institutions to provide the framework for those relationships and to resolve any disagreements. The danger of major international grievances would be minimised by the creation of a prosperous world economy (Hansen, 1945, 8). No reduction of national sovereignty was ever envisaged, so the world would continue to be divided into independent states, of which the United States would be the most powerful. International cooperation was thus seen as the way forward, and a framework within which countries could prosper was essential. New arrangements for the world economy therefore had a high priority.

It was clear that the countries of Europe would have to take their place within this framework. They would have no position of privilege (and even Britain, which would claim a 'special relationship' with the USA after the war, did so mainly on military grounds relating to the Cold War). Nevertheless, as an economic cluster of mainly advanced countries which, taken as a whole, was comparable in terms of economic strength with North America, Europe was seen by the Americans as crucial to the construction of the post-war world. It was also bound to prosper if the post-war structure were set up successfully. Europe therefore had to be involved in American planning and, during the potentially difficult post-war years, Europe would justify American economic support, and probably more than less industrialised countries elsewhere, such as South America. Europe's future position, if not a privileged one, would associate it closely with the world's most powerful country. To take up this position fully, though, the European countries would have to be closely associated among themselves.

These general objectives were clear enough by 1942–43. However, the agreement of general principles was not accompanied by much detailed planning for Europe because the USA was preoccupied for a while by its war with Japan in the Pacific. The emergence of the USA as the major Allied force on the ground in Europe did not come about until the D-Day landings in 1944. Only then did the American public direct much attention to the European campaign.

Even when the US planners started detailed work on Europe in 1944, their methods produced more diversity than clarity. US planning was highly decentralised, with a variety of Federal departments, together with the armed forces, allowed to conduct a planning debate and to issue reports and recommendations. This pluralistic planning procedure had been a feature of the Roosevelt New Deal after 1933 and it continued into wartime planning without interruption. Final decisions rested with the President but their application by the armed forces and government departments could greatly distort them.

The result was to a large extent an extension of New Deal philosophy, methods, and even policies to western Europe This meant creating greater economic efficiency through planning, and the encouragement of social change to bring about a society which would be both stable and receptive of modernising ideas. Vice-President Henry Wallace and his followers were an especially strong influence in this respect (Harper, 1986, 4). Meanwhile, the Secretary of State, Cordell Hull, wanted to release the forces of US capitalism abroad. The State Department remained inspired by President Woodrow Wilson's Fourteen Points, the largely abortive American programme for a peaceful world after the First World War. Later Cordell Hull came to support the idea of free trade (Harper, 1986, 7).

By 1945, however, detailed planning had not proceeded very far. German resistance was so tenacious that the war seemed likely to last into 1946 and even longer. The rapid Allied advance on Berlin from both east and west in 1945 was a pleasant surprise for the American planners but it left them without detailed arrangements for Germany and Italy, as for Europe more generally.

Of course, Britain had not been through the equivalent of a New Deal in the 1930s, though it had set up a national and imperial reconstruction programme in 1942. The Mutual Aid Agreement (Lend-Lease) of February 1942 between the USA and Britain looked forward to an expanding, stable, post-war world economy in which all barriers to trade would be eliminated (Hancock and Gowing, 1949, 543). The two countries would not only cooperate during the war, but also in the reconstruction phase. In autumn 1943, talks took place with the Americans on a wide range of aspects of the international economy, including the relationship between money, trade, international payments, and national production. These led to the Bretton Woods conference in the summer of 1944, and the Bretton Woods Act, 1945.

By 1942, when the Beveridge Report on social insurance appeared, British opinion welcomed the prospect of a society based on full employment and social welfare aims, which had much in common with the New Deal concept. In fact, William Beveridge referred deliberately to the Atlantic Charter on p.7 of his report when he included 'Freedom from Want' in a sub-heading and explained its significance two years later (Beveridge, 1942, 7; Beveridge, 1944, 17). In Britain this new vision was presented as a reward to the masses for their part in the war effort, but those in government saw it as dependent on the achievement of full employment. For a country heavily reliant on exports, as Britain had become, full employment required a buoyant world demand for British goods, and particularly in the dollar area. The USA, on the other hand, was potentially self-sufficient and inclined towards protection, but was reluctant to allow the world to return to the ruinous and dangerous international competition which had marked the 1930s. The result was an Anglo-American understanding that the dollar and sterling areas would combine to lead the world, including the Soviet Union if it wished, into a productive economic system based on free exchange. It would rest on a firm monetary basis. National states would be strongly democratic. New international institutions would guide and stabilise the whole system.

The underlying economic theory was largely the work of a British economist, John Maynard Keynes, whose most influential book, *General Theory of Employment, Interest, and Money*, had been published in 1936. Keynes joined the Treasury in 1940. He was later sent to Washington by the British government to help coordinate work on the post-war system, and he became very influential there (see Peden, 1988, 44–9). Keynes showed that the trade cycle could be levelled out, partly by monetary and fiscal means, allowing full employment and maximum output to be achieved. This approach became orthodoxy in Britain during the war and it secured much respect in the USA.

New institutions

During the last two years of the war, the United States directed the creation of the institutions which would allow the new world system to function. These fell into three main areas: money, trade, and international disputes.

The first Allied conference on long-term economic problems was held in May 1943. It concentrated on food supply, and led to the creation of the Food and Agriculture Organisation of the United Nations (FAO) at the end of 1944, with Britain a founding member. The United Nations Relief and Rehabilitation Administration (UNRRA) was set up in November 1943 to organise supplies in liberated areas. Britain contributed a total of £155 million during the period of operation of UNRRA, though the USA contributed 72 per cent of the total funds distributed (Hancock and Gowing, 1949, 542). It was the main US organ of economic aid from the end of the war until June 1947, when it was wound up, having contributed principally to eastern Europe and to three western European countries threatened by Communism – Greece, Italy and Austria (De Jouvenel, 1948, 22). The desire to spare the world further armed conflicts was reflected in the United Nations Organisation, set up in 1946. The avoidance of future wars was clearly fundamental to the new world of prosperity and full employment.

The currency problems which had bedevilled the 1930s were to be avoided in future by a world currency and payments system in which gold reserves would be replaced by the US dollar as the basis of the value of national currencies. Unlike gold, the supply of the US dollar would expand in step with the size of the American economy and consequently of the world economy of which it formed so large a part. This system was agreed at the Bretton Woods conference in New Hampshire in 1944. Bretton Woods, being based on the idea of an equalisation of economic activity between countries, implied American aid, and receipt of the aid implied, sooner or later, participation in the Bretton Woods system. The conference led to the establishment in 1945 of the International Monetary Fund (IMF), a US-funded structure for international payments. The IMF, which was designed to help countries with serious balance of payments deficits to achieve parity, was intended to function for a short time only, until member countries had stabilised their accounts. More lasting was intended to be the work of the World Bank (officially titled International Bank for Reconstruction and Development [IBRD]), which was set up by the conference to make development loans to backward countries.

This and other conferences affecting the post-war world were attended by representatives of a number of European countries, including governments in exile, so there was no *fait accompli*. On the contrary, the foreign representatives generally welcomed the American initiatives, which seemed logical, practical, and in the interests of all. The Bretton Woods agreement, for instance, was signed by the representatives of forty-five countries. World trade was closely linked to the currency question. Obstacles to free trade were likely to produce imbalances and to reduce the volume of trade overall. Payments imbalances would undermine the Bretton Woods currency system and restrain output, in some countries more than others. So, in 1943, the USA launched a series of negotiations which led to the interim agreement reached at Geneva in October 1947 where a first round of tariff reductions was agreed, affecting half of world trade. The General Agreement on Tariffs and Trade (GATT), a long-term programme of trade liberalisation agreed by twenty-three countries at Geneva in 1947, came into force on 1 January 1948.

Implementation took much longer than the initial agreements. The International Trade Organisation (ITO), planned during the war to create a structure for world trade, was the subject of a conference at Havana in 1947–48. The undeveloped countries objected on a number of counts and only one country ratified the resulting Havana Charter. This meant that ITO had to be dropped, which put the main onus on GATT.

The main problem for western Europe was that the sum of its imports from the dollar area, and debt payments to it, were much greater than its exports to the dollar area after the war. It was therefore unable to enact the full currency convertibility envisaged at Bretton Woods. To do so would create a big flight of funds into US dollars and a disastrous fall in reserves, as Britain found in 1947 when it carried out an experiment in convertibility at the urging of the USA. In fact, in 1947 the USA had to accept that the Bretton Woods system could not be established (and not only because of the misgivings of the European countries). Full convertibility between the major industrial nations would not be achieved until 1959, by which time the dollar deficits had been reduced or eradicated.

The European overseas empires

Western Europe's most tangible world interests before 1939 were the great overseas empires which the powerful industrial nations had built up, mainly during the nineteenth century. The British and French empires played a big part in the war against the Axis, sending military forces to Europe and defending their territories and waters, but they did not play a large part in the development of western Europe after 1945. The big white dominions of the British empire continued to develop as independent nations, while the 'colonies d'exploitation' (as the French candidly call colonies with only a small white population) had no independent contribution to make.

Parts of these empires had been occupied by Japan between 1941 and 1945, but Japan's unconditional surrender in August 1945 had restored them to their original masters. After 1945 the European countries moved, some more slowly than others, towards conceding colonial independence and/or the granting of citizenship to the colonial populations. However, the economic significance of these extra-European territories for western Europe lived on through trade, investment and cultural ties.

Reconstruction

As the Allies advanced through Europe, liberating great areas which had been under Axis control since 1940 or 1941, the local populations began to consider their future in a more optimistic light. From as early as 1940, BBC broadcasts had held out the hope of European reforms after the war. Increasingly, specific changes were discussed, with leaders of the governments in exile speaking on the radio. The British wartime reform debate provided many attractive ideas, and the radio broadcast a vision of democracy and a generous Welfare State available for Europe after the war.

From 1942 this radio propaganda was reinforced by the statements made jointly by the Allies, such as the Atlantic Charter. German defeats at El Alamein and Stalingrad were greeted throughout Europe as a sign that Germany would lose the war, but it soon became clear that German resistance would be long-lived. The people of the occupied countries had to be buoyed up to discourage collaboration and the Allied promises became even more attractive. With the Communists prominent in the resistance movements, especially reassuring things had to be said about cooperation with the Soviet Union. Full employment was often promised, and a move away from the attitudes and policies of the 1930s was held out.

In 1944 and 1945, the Allies had a growing opportunity to show what they could do in western Europe as the Nazi defences were rolled back. In the early post-war years western Europe was in any case afflicted by short-term problems, many of which needed direct military intervention. The biggest problem was Germany,

where production and distribution had been reduced to a fraction
of pre-war levels. Italy faced similar difficulties, though they were
not as acute, and the persistence of Fascism was not a serious
threat there. The Allies, led by the USA, had to organise and
finance the delivery of supplies to the areas they occupied, food
and fuel being the most important. However, almost the whole of
western Europe was dependent on American credit at this time,
because its ability to earn foreign currency, and especially US
dollars, had been sharply reduced by the collapse of its export
trade during the war.

In the American occupation zone in southern Germany, and in
Italy, the USA could pursue stabilisation, and eventually, reconstruction, policies largely according to its own sense of what was
required. Elsewhere in Germany they had to work with the Allied
control commission, though they were the dominant influence
here. As for the neutral and liberated countries, the USA found
itself working with governments many of which faced problems
similar in nature if not in degree to those of the Allied-occupied
countries, but which expected to make their own decisions on how
to resolve them. Reconstruction in some of these countries will be
discussed below, in Chapters 2 and 3.

Towards the Marshall plan

Meanwhile, the USA continued to pursue continental objectives,
often at great financial cost to itself. As soon as Japan capitulated
in August 1945, the USA had terminated its Lend-Lease
arrangements with its European allies, mainly to reassure the
Congress that wartime burdens would not be extended into the
peace. Lend-Lease had provided the bulk of US support for the war
effort of Britain and France, and its cancellation was a big
problem, especially for Britain, even though the USA cancelled the
whole of Britain's existing Lend-Lease deficit in December 1945
(Foreman-Peck, 1983, 263). At the end of the war, however, the
USA became involved in a number of funding programmes in
western Europe. These were directed mainly at food supply and
emergency reconstruction. By early 1948 some $25 billion had
been disbursed in Europe, including the big loan to Britain of
1945, and grants to eastern Europe. The biggest single effort was
the GARIOA (Government and Relief in Occupied Areas) programme. Between 1946 and 1950 GARIOA supplied $1.6 billion

worth of food, goods and services to Germany (Schildt and Sywottek, 1993, 83). Britain and France could not contribute on this scale, and even found it a strain to supply their zones of occupation in Germany. In any case their shipments of supplies to their own zones had to be largely financed by American loans. These payments and loans were intended to be short-term and there was a lack of coordination between them. They did not, on the whole, provide a basis for long-term reconstruction, and the USA gradually moved towards forms of assistance which provided a political return. For this reason, the UNRRA was wound down in 1947, and other programmes were reduced.

By 1947, therefore, the Americans were looking for ways of limiting or ending their financial commitment. The most obvious solution was to liberate the potentially huge German economy so that Germany could at least pay for its own food imports, and to stimulate production and trade in western Europe. At the most basic level, this development was necessary to allow the rest of Europe to pay for imports from the USA and Germany. The Americans encouraged Germany to concentrate on exporting producer goods, which were needed for the revival of the rest of Europe. This solution began to produce results in 1946 and early 1947, as output revived in western Europe. However, basic problems remained, and they would lead to one final US aid effort on a continental scale, the Marshall plan.

By the first half of 1947 the western European economy had begun to recover well and the various US programmes were in decline. However, the recovery was creating balance of payments problems for most countries, because their import bill increased faster than their income from exports, as they paid for expanding imports such as raw materials, machinery, and coal and oil. The total trade deficits of the western European countries averaged more than $5 billion per annum over the three years after the war, compared to $2 billion in the late 1930s. The total overseas deficit was $7.4 billion in 1947, whereas the account had been roughly in balance in 1938 (Aldcroft, 1993, 124). This situation was not merely the result of exceptional wartime conditions; countries expanding output quickly tend to generate a balance of payments deficit, as Italy, Spain and Britain would find well after the war. What was distinctive about the post-war situation, however, was that the west European countries found it very hard to earn US dollars, as their relatively backward industrial economies produced little that could find purchasers across the Atlantic, while their failure to improve productivity during the war, together with their over-valued currencies, made potential exports uncompetitive. Primary product exports to the dollar area were not the answer either as America produced almost everything it needed (Eichengreen, 1993, 13).

Meanwhile, the producer goods that they needed to expand their industrial output still came mainly from the USA rather than from Germany. In fact, because of the big expansion of the US economy during the war, nearly *half* the world's manufactured goods were produced in the USA (Foreman-Peck, 1983, 270). They could, of course, restrict their imports of consumer goods to limit their deficit, but this created other problems, notably in terms of the political reaction of their populations to continuing austerity when most people looked forward to some remission. The general prospect in early 1947, as perceived by the USA, was of a depression in Europe within the next two years as individual countries took action to contain their deficits, or of an American depression as Europe was increasingly unable to pay for US goods (Carew, 1987, 9). Indeed, Italy was already beginning to take restrictive action (Harper, 1986, 192, fn 1). Meanwhile, efforts to promote trade within Europe by multilateral arrangements were making no progress in 1947 (Eichengreen, 1993, 17–20).

As Alan Milward has pointed out, in economic terms the problem was not disastrous and there were various ways of tackling it (Milward, 1984, 90–2). However, there was a political dimension (Milward, 1989). By early 1947 Communism was mounting a strong challenge to western Europe in the shape of an increasingly coordinated bloc of Communist countries to the east, and the national Communist parties in the west. Stalin had sent back a clutch of Communist leaders to western Europe after the war, telling them to take part positively in national reconstruction in order to take advantage of the goodwill accumulated by Communism during the war. By 1947 they were gaining support and also encouraging direct trade union action (Girault, 1993, 5). Most west European countries were afraid to restrict public expenditure by reining back their post-war social reform programmes, because the electorate would have resented the loss of their biggest wartime dream. A number of countries, such as France, which were trying to modernise their economies, found that they could not finance modernisation investment and pay for imports at the same time. France had hoped for a big US loan in 1946, in the wake of the huge British loan of 1945, but despite strenuous efforts it had been unable to obtain one (Bossuat, I, 1992, 99). The USA had been prepared to tolerate restrictions on trade and payments by some European countries in order to avoid a political reaction, but these contributed to a series of difficulties in 1947 which severely retarded progress towards general currency convertibility and tariff reductions (Milward, 1984, 466). Something was needed to win back the initiative for the American concept of reconstruction, whereas a depression would have the opposite effect.

The Marshall plan

These considerations were thoroughly weighed up by the US Secretary of State, George C. Marshall, and his staff, in early 1947. Like many US office holders after the war, he was a former military man who, as Army Chief of Staff, had been the senior American military administrator throughout the war. His direct experience of the liberation and occupation of western Europe helped him to build up a clear view of the problems there when he went on a long tour in early 1947. From his foreign policy perspective, Marshall was sensitive to the growing estrangement with the Soviet Union and eastern Europe, and the danger that the Communists might take advantage of popular discontent in the West if the various national post-war political compromises ever seemed to be wanting. At the same time, he knew that Congress might warm to a programme which could resist Communism, especially after President Truman's big Congress speech on 12 March 1947 calling for funds to support Greece and Turkey, the launch of the 'Truman doctrine' (De Jouvenel, 1948, 14).

On the economic front, Marshall was worried that the post-war revival of western Europe would soon falter as countries had to switch from their efforts to boost production, and especially their exports *to* the dollar area, to funding their growing imports *from* the dollar area. These imports would include a high food component, as the revival of European agriculture was lagging badly behind industry. A growing dollar deficit would undermine such growth as Europe was now achieving, draw the United States into further aid payments over an uncertain period, and weaken the American capacity to contribute through trade to the general world economic revival. Over all this loomed the vague but disconcerting threat that Stalin could present himself as the world's great provider and example. After all, as everyone could agree, from then until 1991, 'there was no unemployment in the Soviet Union!'. Marshall was particularly struck by the failure of the Moscow conference of March–April 1947 to reach a four-power agreement on a German settlement, including a basis for economic stabilisation. On his return from Moscow he stopped in Berlin to see the American and British military governors, and on 28 April he said on American radio that the economic revival of Germany and Austria was essential to European reconstruction (Hardach, 1994, 29–31).

Marshall was convinced by now that a single, high-profile programme with a clear aim, and a definite funding period, was needed. At the end of the programme, no further US aid would be required or provided, a feature which would make the programme more acceptable politically in the USA. Marshall's approach had much in common with the D-Day invasion in 1944, and owed a great deal to the military concept of the 'operation'. As the commander of a series of dusty camps in the American mid-West between the wars, Marshall had been noted for resharpening his pencils down to the shortest stub. If he had his way, Europe would get what it needed to become the equal trading partner of the United States, but it would receive no more than it needed and the resources would be used solely according to the operational plan.

After further work by his staff in Washington, Marshall put his name to a plan for massive aid to help the west European countries eradicate their dollar deficits, combined with American inspired or directed planning designed to make the countries work more closely together, and the diffusion of American methods and mentalities. He announced the plan in a speech at Harvard University on 5 June 1947, where he had gone to receive an honorary doctorate. His choice of platform associated the intelligentsia and wealthy elite of the USA with his proposal, and allowed him to stress the profound reasoning which underlay the programme.

Behind his idea was an American vision of a united and effective Europe which had been in circulation towards the end of the war. Both Marshall and Truman, in key speeches at this time, stressed that the United States was the product of Europe (D'Hérouville, 1949, 73–5). In the background was the idea that western Europe would acquire American values and would play an even more productive role in the world economy as envisaged by the USA (Milward, 1984, 123). A prosperous structure of exchange between the countries of western Europe would reduce the importance of transatlantic trade and resolve the problem of western Europe's dollar shortage (Girault and Lévy-Leboyer, 1993, 17). High productivity using American production methods would win over the workers from socialism to the American way (Girault, 1993, 19–20).

The Marshall plan sought to integrate western Europe into a single economic area, mainly on the basis of free trade, but also accepting the principle of democracy. Later, the continent could be integrated politically on US-approved lines (Milward, 1984, 466). The emphasis on democracy was not mere talk, and Franco's Spain was excluded mainly on this ground. Officially titled the European Recovery Program (ERP), the Marshall plan was launched in the spring of 1948 after Congress had approved the enabling legislation on 2 April. It involved the provision of some $13 billion over a period of four years. Nine-tenths of the total was in the form of outright gifts and the remainder was in the form of loans at low interest (2.5 per cent repayable over 35 years from 1956). Funds arrived in Europe in large quantities from the summer of 1948. The ERP was directed by an American administration in Washington, the Economic Cooperation Administration (ECA), with a European office in each country.

Central to the integrationist aspects of the programme, however, was the Organisation (initially, Committee) for European Economic Cooperation (OEEC), which first met in Paris in July 1947. This was a panel representing all the countries receiving Marshall aid (originally fourteen, to which western Germany was added in March 1948). As early as June 1947, the USA had called participating countries to London to ask what their needs were, and what plans they had in mind. The countries had to sign agreements committing themselves to a strong production effort, expansion of their foreign trade, the maintenance of financial stability, and the development of European economic cooperation (Carew, 1987, 6). It was here that a European priority programme was agreed. This meant, for instance, that Germany's big share of Marshall aid was understood and approved by countries like France which had suffered from German attack and occupation during the war (Brinkley and Hackett, 1991, 99). Meanwhile, Stalin refused to allow any Soviet satellite to accept Marshall aid, claiming that the conditions were not appropriate.

American funds were provided in the form of dollar credits (a

total of $12,817 million between August 1948 and June 1952)
which were used by participating countries to offset the cost of
imports, principally from the dollar area. The main recipients
were:

Britain	$3,176 million
France	$2,706 million
Italy	$1,474 million
West Germany	$1,389 million
Netherlands	$1,079 million
Greece	$ 700 million
Austria	$ 700 million

Source: Foreman-Peck, 1983, 273.

The European governments functioned as the purchasers of the
imported products, which they resold to consumers in their
countries. Consumers paid for these products in their national
currencies and the governments thus acquired large non-dollar
balances. These were known as 'counterpart funds' and were used
for a variety of purposes, subject to the agreement of the ECA.
Their main use was to help set up new forms of production which
would either substitute domestic goods for those previously
imported from the dollar area, or create dollar-earning exports.
However, some countries were allowed to use part or all of their
counterpart funds for infrastructural projects or to reduce non-
dollar trading deficits, budget deficits, or even the national debt.
The use of counterpart funds had to have the approval of the
Marshall Plan Mission in each country. The US intention that the
OEEC should allocate funds in detail within each member country
caused difficulties, and a more flexible system was adopted in
1949. This produced national variations of some magnitude,
especially in the use of counterpart funds. For instance, the
Americans wanted France to spend more on public housing as a
bulwark against Communism. The French wanted their counterpart funds to go mainly into productive investment. Not until
1951, when they were good and ready, did they invest enough in
housing to satisfy the USA (Wall, 1991, 182–3). Whatever the use
of the counterpart funds, their designation for approved purposes
countered the inflationary effect of the dollar aid. Overall, the
Marshall plan was not inflationary, as it led to the production or
the import of sufficient goods to meet the extra demand created
by the dollar aid.

The ERP incorporated a large advisory and educational programme, designed to disseminate American methods and institutions in Europe. The Labor Division sought to educate workers on the importance of increasing productivity. Paul Hoffman, Administrator of the ERP, once said rather crudely that it was a contest between the American assembly line and the Communist party line (Carew, 1987, 8). In the more backward countries, big campaigns were organised by the Americans to encourage and foster capitalist attitudes. One of the biggest was in the main American bugbear country, Italy. Leaflets, films, meetings and competitions all figured in this raucous campaign (Ellwood, 1993, 84). As so often in Italy, the techniques used recalled earlier days, now out of fashion, with operatic voices amplified through loudspeakers and the big Fascist propaganda tool in remote villages, the mobile Fiat cinema van, again in action.

The more advanced countries received much less direction. Britain was affected least of all. As a fully developed and largely undamaged industrial economy, Britain was allowed to spend nearly all of her counterpart funds on the repayment of short-term government debt. France was an intermediate case. The majority of her counterpart funds were invested in the nationalised industries, most of which had been taken over since the Liberation, or in the steel industry, already powerful but scheduled for further modernisation in the context of developing relations with Germany. Italy came in for special direction, though here the Americans were partly frustrated by domestic politics. In the long term, the ECA wanted to achieve fiscal stability and a consumer economy, with higher productivity based on American techniques and the American mentality (Wall, 1991, 159–61).

The issues raised by the Marshall plan were extensively taken up by the Europeans. The French Commissariat du Plan, Jean Monnet's creation in 1946, set up a working group which sent a total of 450 missions to the USA. There was an Anglo-American Council on Productivity. These and other initiatives were especially interested, not in technical backwardness, but in the European lag in industrial relations and attitudes (Maier, 1987, 65). The strong ERP interest in the reduction of tariffs and other barriers to trade led to a significant liberalisation of trade by the OEEC members from 1949, though the European countries were allowed to maintain their barriers to US imports until 1956, by which time it was assumed that their economies would be fully reconstructed. Repayment of the loan element of Marshall aid also began in that year.

Between 1948 and 1951, Marshall aid amounted to some \$13 billion. This was equal to about 3 per cent of US GDP for the four years 1948–51 (Maddison, 1989, 66). This equalled 2.1 per cent of the GNP of the sixteen countries receiving it (Giersch et al., 1992, 98). There was direct US intervention in the affairs of countries receiving aid, separately from the work of the programme administration. Staunch allies like Britain, and countries where there was no serious Communist presence, were spared this high-level influence, but Italy and Greece, for instance, came under strong pressure. One US aim was to isolate the Communist trade unions and to involve only the non-Communist unions in the recovery programme (Girault and Lévy-Leboyer, 1993, 20–1).

The contribution of Marshall aid to the economic recovery of western Europe in the late 1940s and early 1950s cannot be determined precisely. During the three and a half years of Marshall funding, the GNP of the countries assisted increased by about one-quarter, industrial production went up by 64 per cent, and agricultural production rose by 24 per cent (Galbraith, 1994, 159–60). Some recovery of output would probably have taken place in western Europe without Marshall aid, as even a complete collapse of international trade would have led to a surge in domestic production and import substitution. It is impossible to conceive, however, that such a spectacular growth in output could have been achieved without the Marshall plan. Moreover, the rise in national aggregates was only part of the picture. The fall in Europe's current account deficit with the USA from \$5.6 billion in 1947 to \$3.2 billion in 1949 was a significant achievement (Eichengreen, 1993, 11). The impressive revival of German production and exports during these years played a big part. So did the devaluation of the majority of European currencies in 1949 in the later stages of Marshall aid, following Britain's inconsiderate example (Postan, 1967, 14). By the end of the Marshall aid period in 1951, the problem of the big dollar deficits had largely disappeared, which meant that projects for the multilateral liberalisation of trade in western Europe could again be put on the agenda. Indeed, the most important of these, the European Coal and Steel Community, was already at treaty stage. Without the confidence engendered by the Marshall plan, this important next step might not have taken place so soon. And with the end of the Marshall plan, European reconstruction can be said to have been complete. However, the OEEC remained in existence as a coordinating body at the wish of its members. In 1960 it was succeeded by a similar body, the OECD (Organisation for Economic Cooperation and Development). Meanwhile, George C. Marshall had received the Nobel Peace Prize in 1953. This rare award to a military man by a foundation based in neutral Sweden paid a fitting tribute to all that America had done for Europe in both war and peace since 1941.

Nationalisation

Also complete was the wave of nationalisation which had followed the end of the war. Much advocated, especially in the main industrial countries, towards the end of the war and immediately thereafter, it was never a general phenomenon in Europe, and it did not represent the creation of an effective control over the national economies. Even more, it was not used as a means of sharing income and wealth, or of providing the basis for a fundamentally socialist economy or society. Closest to a nationalised economy was Italy, but much of the nationalised sector was inherited from pre-war days and therefore from a doctrinaire Fascist economy. The Labour Government's nationalisations in post-war Britain were mainly intended to direct fresh capital into the main producer industries and transport, and to secure efficient national operation. There was no desire to use them to plan the economy as a whole. In France, the objective was much the same, though some firms, such as Renault, were in effect confiscated, to punish them for working for the Germans. In France and in Italy, about 40 per cent of the banking sector was nationalised, but in each case public banks had existed before the war as a means of marshalling capital for productive purposes in relatively backward economies.

This limited result was partly due to American influence. In Germany and Italy, the Americans had been generally unhappy about the idea of post-war nationalisations, and the effect of their attitude may have spread elsewhere. Extensive nationalisation, whether in the occupied countries or outside, would have implied the growth of socialism or even Communism, and strengthened the trade unions and the parties of the Left.

Recovery progress

One criterion of the success of reconstruction in western Europe is
the time it took for economic activity to return to its pre-war level.
If we exclude Germany and Italy, which faced special problems,
nearly all of western Europe was back to its 1938 level by 1947/48,
insofar as industrial production was concerned. Agriculture took
longer, with 1950 being the year in which production was again at
the 1938 level. Germany and Italy were once again at the pre-war
level in manufacturing *and* agriculture in 1950/51.

FIGURE 1.1 *Manufacturing production, 1947–50.*

	1947	1948	1949	1950
UK	115	129	137	151
France	95	108	118	121
Germany	33	50	75	95
Italy	93	96	101	115
Belgium	105	121	122	125
Netherlands	104	113	126	139

Total manufacturing output by value, in the form of an index. The base year (100)
is 1938, the last full year of peacetime production in western Europe.

Source: Piquet Marchal, 1985, 7.

This was a successful recovery, especially as it was achieved
under conditions of stability, in contrast to the recovery from the
First World War which had generated a huge 'restocking' boom in
1919–20, followed by a sharp recession. Each annual increase in
output was a step forward from a firm base. By 1950 western
Europe could look forward to further progress, taking it forward to
achievements outmatching its pre-war standard. In this sense,
reconstruction was over, a new age had begun.

Reconstruction of war damage

Ironically, however, there was one area in which reconstruction
was far from complete in 1950/51. Indeed, it had hardly begun,
even though the object of the reconstruction was a direct result of
military action.

The accepted meaning of the term 'reconstruction' tended to obscure its sense of rebuilding damaged towns and cities. This task was most acute in Germany, but it was also necessary in Britain and France where large areas had been destroyed in certain towns and cities. In Italy, damage was more scattered and repair could be postponed without difficulty. Ironically, this type of reconstruction was often delayed so that capital could be devoted to the recreation of productive capacity. The problem of foreign payments which prompted Marshall aid could not be resolved by urban reconstruction; on the contrary, it would have made the problem worse.

In Britain, the volume of housing destroyed in German air raids was small enough to allow those affected to relocate into the surviving built stock. This was also the case in France except in a number of devastated small towns, and big targets such as Le Havre and Caen, where some temporary accommodation was provided in hutments. In Germany, the occupying forces provided some hutments but the main solution was to jam two or more families into the surviving flats. In most of the larger cities, half the residential stock was out of action, so this 'doubling up' solved the problem for the time being, together with families living in cellars, their pathetic stove pipes poking through the ruins. The rubble was cleared, beginning in 1945, by grim-faced gangs of old women and war widows, and used for levelling and the terraces of future sports stadia, but rebuilding was out of the question. In Hamburg, the British authorities allowed the cavernous ground floor spaces of one of the giant flak-towers to be used as a cinema from 1945, and this was typical of the flexible adaptation of such structures as remained.

New building was, however, replaced by planning. Reconstruction plans were produced for all the damaged cities across Europe. In Britain, planning began as early as 1941 thanks to the absence of occupation, the government's desire to maintain morale, and the growing sense that Britain would be on the winning side in the war. By 1945 all the bombed cities had one or more advisory plans. Town planning legislation in 1943 and 1944 enacted special powers that would be needed after the war. The radical Town and Country Planning Act, 1947, established comprehensive controls over all new building and a system of betterment taxation which would prevent private interests delaying reconstruction. Most impressive of all, the New Towns Act of 1946 created a programme for the building of a number of completely new towns to accommodate excess population from the redeveloped cities outside the revolutionary 'green belts', fore-shadowed before the war but made general after it, which would stop the further outward growth of the large cities. The new town concept was a development of the Garden City idea launched by the social reformer, Ebenezer Howard, in 1898. Thus revived, it secured great influence elsewhere in Europe, though not entirely in its pure form.

In Germany, planning legislation was voted mainly by the individual states and was not greatly different from what had been available before the war. In France, the Vichy planning law of 1943 remained in force and a general planning law was not voted until 1955. Formal green belts on the British model were not generally adopted elsewhere in western Europe, though the crowded Netherlands protected the central agricultural area which formed the core of the Randstad, a ring of large cities in the south of the country.

The reconstruction of bombed cities began almost everywhere in the early 1950s (Durth and Gutschow, 1993, 393ff). Some of the most impressive schemes were in France, where much was rebuilt on the old lines, to foster a sense of continuity, as at Saint-Malo. Le Havre was a striking modern scheme in reinforced concrete. In Britain the damage was generally too limited and scattered to permit extensive replanning, but at Coventry the city centre was rebuilt on the most advanced lines in Europe, with extensive pedestrian precincts, adjacent parking, and new traffic routes. A comparable scheme was built in central Rotterdam, victim of concentrated *Luftwaffe* bombing in 1940. German rebuilding was generally hasty, and to a low standard. The priority was to get the city centres operating again as soon as possible. With notable exceptions, such as Kassel, the existing street system was largely retained, though with widening and new parking in anticipation of the growing number of motor vehicles. Some streets and buildings were restored to something like their pre-war state, but Münster's example in rebuilding the old frontages along its main central streets was not widely followed (Petsch, 1983, 66). In the 1950s and 1960s, the failure of the bombed cities throughout western Europe to replan radically by expropriating private sites and creating a completely new structure was generally regretted, but after about 1970 the renewed respect for the urban past generated a rather different view, that the old streets and building scale were of great value, even where they had been hastily rebuilt.

The reconstruction of the cities thus took place on the basis of a prior economic reconstruction. The result was a combination of old and new, which looked a little crude, a little skimped. And it looked more so as time went on, an obvious utility exercise. Could the same be said of the economic reconstruction? To see, we shall have to turn to the individual countries of the post-war years.

CHAPTER TWO

The Northern Industrial Core: Britain, France and Germany, 1945–c.1960

Chapter 1 stressed the crucial role of the United States in the economic revival of western Europe after 1945. The strength of that revival depended largely on the big industrial countries of the northern core: Britain, France and Germany. These three countries were linked by a great band of coal deposits which ran across northern Europe from Ireland to Slovakia and had provided the basis for industrialisation since the nineteenth century. Since the turn of the century, electrification and the growth of services had produced a diffusion of urban employment away from the coalfields, with cities such as London, Stuttgart and Munich emerging as centres of advanced industry. Coal, however, remained the main power source for industrial Europe in 1945.

Britain

At the end of the war, Britain's international prestige was back at its 1919 level. She was an honoured member of the new international organisations, the accolade being her appointment as a permanent member of the Security Council of the United Nations Organisation in 1945. She also held on to her world strategic role as the main ally of the United States and head of the British Empire. The pound sterling was the leading *international* currency, with more than half the world's trade conducted in sterling (Graham, 1990, 31). It was on this basis that the pound sterling accepted the role of reserve currency to the US dollar in 1944. Britain's living standards, the highest in Europe after Switzerland, her temporary post-war position as Europe's biggest economy, and her energetic approach to economic and social policy after 1945, made her a respected exemplar in European reconstruction. However, her aspirations in the field of national welfare, and particularly the creation of the National Health Service, were, like her world strategic role, very expensive and required a highly productive economy to finance them. The British economy recovered very rapidly in the second half of the 1940s but then encountered serious problems centred mainly on international payments and the pound sterling. In the 1950s, the British performance would begin to contrast with the striking economic progress of most of the Continent after the war.

Discussion of reconstruction policies for post-war Britain was launched by the government as early as 1941. Victory was by no means certain at this stage and the reconstruction debate was partly used as a means of sustaining the war effort by drumming up popular support and participation. In 1942 an impressive-sounding Ministry of Reconstruction was set up to coordinate government efforts. Much of this planning dealt with economic concerns, but the public was more excited by plans for a series of welfare policies which were to be introduced in the context of full employment and an ordered economy. The Conservatives, as the dominant force in Churchill's coalition government, were largely persuaded that generous welfare policies could be introduced in a victorious Britain without causing too much inflation or undermining the will to work. The Labour Party, for its part, wanted to take advantage of this unprecedented opportunity for social reform in order to raise the living standards and morale of the poorest, while creating a more equal and possibly more just Britain.

The concept of the ordered economy achieving full employ-ment was largely the work of John Maynard Keynes, the academic economist who became an adviser to the Treasury during the war. The vision of the 'Welfare State' was based on the report on employment and related services by Sir William Beveridge, an academic economist and former civil servant, published in November 1942 (Beveridge, 1942). Departmental proposals for health services, education, and town planning soon followed. Public optimism about the plans was boosted by the increasing success of the British war effort, which suggested that national planning, backed by massive public expenditure, could achieve goals from which all would benefit. This confidence, which contrasted with the orthodox budgetary views and non-interventionist policies prevailing before the war, contributed to a growing electoral support for the Labour Party, which was able to present itself not only as the party of the masses, but also as the party of modernity and national progress. London's role as the temporary home of governments-in-exile and political refugees helped the developing vision of post-war Britain to influence discussions on post-war Europe. The vision was linked to thinking in the USA via the Atlantic Charter of 1941–42 and later statements which associated it, however remotely, with the Roosevelt New Deal of the 1930s. This sense of a general progress towards a better post-war world strengthened British confidence in the possibility of social reform at home.

The force of this vision was not fully sustained, however, by the strength of the British economy nor by the world economic climate. Britain's war debts were immense, while one-quarter of her overseas investments of pre-war days had been liquidated to secure foreign currency to pay for the war. Britain faced a heavy balance of payments deficit after the war, with an acute shortage of US dollars, yet exports faced heavy domestic competition in the American market, where the survival of barriers to trade belied US interest in world trade liberalisation. The initial disruption of parts of the European market were a further problem.

Britain's only realistic solution was nevertheless to boost its exports, particularly into the dollar area, and to minimise its imports, together with reducing its borrowing. Labour, which came into power with a big majority at the general election of 1945, had the task of implementing these policies even though they looked likely to delay or weaken the more expensive social reforms. In essence, Labour maintained wartime levels of taxation, the system of production quotas, and rationing. These policies had the additional advantage of preventing the high level of domestic liquidity accumulated by the end of the war from flooding onto the market and generating high inflation, as it did in France and Italy.

As a result, British public revenue (including that of local authorities and the insurance funds), which amounted to 37.7 per cent of GNP in 1946, was still as high as 34.9 per cent in 1951, compared to a mere 19.0 per cent in 1938 (Pollard, 1983, 243). High taxation financed the new welfare facilities without heavy borrowing. The Bank Rate (central lending rate) was held at the pre-war level of 2 per cent and the government sought to reduce other interest rates, partly on ideological grounds. Home consumption was kept firmly in check and rationing became even less generous than in wartime. For instance, the bread and potato rationing imposed after the severe winter of 1947 was unprecedented, though it had its equivalents in France. 'Utility' products continued to circulate, and shoppers were constantly on the look-out for seconds and export rejects returned to the home market. The wartime black market lived on, with the spiv, shrouded in his gabardine raincoat and droopy-brimmed homburg joining the less sinister back-room boy as one of the suspicious characters of the era. Women worried about getting caught wearing their black-market nylons. For car drivers the big fear was being stopped for a traffic violation with a tank of 'red petrol' (commercial vehicle fuel).

The export drive, however, took time to implement and to produce the desired results. Sterling's chronic weakness was clear as soon as the USA abruptly ended its Lend-Lease arrangements in August 1945. By December 1945, Britain had found a solution to the expected shortfall of dollars over the next three years by negotiating the American Loan Agreement which included a huge loan of US $5,650 million from the USA and Canada. However, Britain had to agree to make the pound convertible within two years in pursuit of US plans to create a single world trading and monetary system, which had made little progress since the end of the war. When Britain did so, beginning in late 1946 and culminating in full convertibility in July 1947, sterling holders rushed to buy dollars and the resulting drain on British reserves led to a return to the *status quo ante* in just six weeks (Pressnell, 1986, 366–7). The pound continued to weaken until it was heavily devalued by 30.5 per cent in 1949 during a slump in the USA, leading to a chain-reaction of devaluations across western Europe, most of which were greatly resented by the countries involved even though the USA saw them as necessary.

Hereafter, however, the balance of payments stabilised. By 1950 the dollar shortage was less acute, the economy grew, exports increased, and domestic production partially replaced manufactured imports. The British economic performance under the two Labour governments of 1945–51 was creditable in relation to both the 1930s and the 1950s. British GDP increased by 16 per cent between 1946 and 1951, an annual average rate of nearly 3 per cent.

FIGURE 2.1 *British industrial output, 1936–50.*

Average	Total production	All industries	Manufacturing industry only
1936–38	86.0	97.5	95.6
1946	100	100	100
1947	97.8	105.4	105.8
1948	100.1	114.4	115.4
1949	103.9	121.0	122.7
1950	108.3	127.9	131.1

The index base year (100) is 1946. The growth of total production by 1950 is retarded by the slow development of agriculture and of services, which are restrained by the area of land under cultivation and the restricted home market. Manufacturing, the major participant in the export drive and a big supplier of producer goods to the home market, achieves considerable growth and sustains the output of industry as a whole.

Source: Pollard, 1983, 251.

Because of the emphasis on saving hard currency, and on the reconstruction of British industry, the government gave priority to the development of the capital goods and export industries, raw materials, and agriculture. The coal mining industry did not respond fully to the challenge, despite nationalisation in 1946. Iron and steel did rather better, but as an 'old' industry it was outshone by some of the newer industries in the engineering and chemicals area, especially those which had a chance to export. The motor industry, seen as a key exporter to the dollar area and with little competition from the rest of Europe until the end of the decade, resumed its 1930s position as Europe's biggest producer and exporter, with 903,000 cars, commercial vehicles and tractors rolling off the production lines in 1950, compared to 526,000 in the peak pre-war year of 1937. The aircraft industry, strongly backed by the government, was the technical and commercial leader of Europe into the mid-1950s, with the Comet, the world's first commercial jet airliner, making its first flight in 1949 and beginning passenger services in 1952. Britain's military commitments helped the civil aircraft industry to adopt the very latest technology in this case, but there were few such clear examples. In any case, when the Comet was grounded in 1954 after a series of accidents, Britain lost her five-year lead in commercial jet technology to the American firm of Boeing. The shipbuilding industry, which could sell anything it built during the world replacement boom of the later 1940s, failed to rationalise and modernise, allowing European and Oriental competition to undermine it from the 1950s (Pollard, 1983, 252–5). The export drive was nevertheless a big success overall, with an excellent start fully maintained after 1948 as Marshall aid began to flow into western Europe, though the dollar shortage remained a residual concern. In 1950, the value of Britain's exports equalled $125.59 per head of population, far outstripping France ($73.67) and Germany ($39.87) (Maddison, 1989, 44).

Some crude regional planning was carried out under the Distribution of Industry Acts of 1945 and 1950, and fourteen New Towns were designated under the Act of 1946. Potentially mobile firms were directed from the South-East and the West Midlands to the old industrial areas in the North and Scotland, and some were attracted to the New Towns. The government attempt to create new employment in the areas of the depressed inter-war staple industries, and away from the crowded slums of the big cities, went far beyond anything attempted elsewhere in western Europe. However, the British electorate was more aware of the rationing, controls, frustrating shortages, and power cuts which were a constant product of Labour's efforts to control the economy and build the world's most ambitious public welfare structure. These difficulties arose from a fundamental irony. Labour's solution to the problem of launching social reforms at a time of big economic challenges was, in effect, to continue and even extend wartime rationing and controls into the post-war years. By 1950, though, the public wanted more than social reform.

In one important respect, an ambitious Labour policy went well beyond wartime arrangements. This was nationalisation. Between 1946 and 1949, the Labour government passed legislation to nationalise power (gas, electricity), transport (docks, railways, canals, road transport, airlines), coal mines, and iron and steel. Also nationalised was the Bank of England, though this did little more than formalise its position since 1931. Although the Labour Party's constitution had called for the nationalisation of all the means of production since its approval in 1918, Labour's national-isations between 1946 and 1949 were directed more towards efficiency and high output than a socialist system of production (see Millward and Singleton, 1995). In this respect they resembled post-war nationalisations elsewhere in western Europe, for some of which they were the example. Their scope and number were, however, impressive enough to resemble a national strategy for the public ownership of key industries, and by 1950 they had become an item of dogma for the Labour Party and its supporting trade unions, whose membership and influence had been reinforced by the war (Pollard, 1983, 224–5).

The industries chosen for nationalisation were essential to production rather than consumption. All had suffered from lack of maintenance and investment during the war, yet were unlikely to attract private capital quickly enough in the crucial post-war years. Coal already enjoyed State support. Public control of basic industries also seemed likely to contribute to the strategic development of the economy in the absence of statutory planning powers. Altogether, a strong case could be made for their national-isation and political opposition from even the Conservatives was perfunctory, except in the case of the steel industry.

In the absence of comprehensive, long-term economic planning in Britain, which Labour did not attempt, the nationalised industries appeared capable of providing some structural coherence. However, the nationalised industries reinforced the trade unions, with the coal miners increasingly important as defenders of the post-war economic structure, as well as doughty fighters for improved pay and conditions. The main features of Labour's post-war nationalisation structure would survive into the 1980s, accompanied by a trade union alliance which was generally inflationary in its effect, and probably a discouragement to industrial innovation.

The more time passed, the less was Labour's combination of control and reform able to convince. The social reforms of 1944–48 were widely appreciated, and not just in the working class, but opposition grew to the system of controls and the resulting bureaucracy and shortages which arose from Labour's efforts to influence the economy, even though these efforts were generally successful and could have been replaced only by something like the indicative planning on the lines pioneered by the French from 1946, or the partially command economies being created in eastern Europe under Soviet guidance. The building of new houses, almost entirely limited to the public sector, was very disappointing and only 360,000 units had been provided by 1950, including 160,000 temporary dwellings ('prefabs'). Labour shortages, and the diversion of capital to dollar-earning activities, were partly to blame. Most of the building effort, until the end of the decade, was devoted to the repair of bomb-damaged houses but this tended to extend the life of inadequate terraced houses in crowded working-class areas, while the New Jerusalem of the wartime city plans remained hidden by advertising hoardings around bomb sites in the city centres. Weakened in the election of 1950 and defeated in 1951, Labour gave way to a Conservative party still led by an ageing Winston Churchill.

Honouring election promises to cut out red tape and 'waste', the Conservatives had eliminated all rationing by 1954. Meanwhile, they removed most of the controls on the workings of private industry. They returned steel and road transport to private ownership, but did not question Labour's concept of a large public sector of producer industries and strategic services. The revival of the world economy continued to encourage exports. Commonwealth preference and quotas allowed Britain to bring in cheap food while limiting manufactured imports from the Continent and the USA. The pound was more secure since the devaluation of 1949 and inflation was moderate at first.

At the same time, Britain largely lost its place as an example to the rest of western Europe. Under the Conservatives, Britain fell short of creating the growth- and export-oriented market economy as practised by western Germany, while progress towards social reform was halted. Government economic policy was largely inherited from Labour's day, but there was no further move towards national planning. On the contrary, the Conservative government relaxed controls on the location of industry without foreseeing the implications for housing and transport demand in the West Midlands and the South-East where most manufacturing expansion now occurred. The Conservatives were proud to restore Britain to 'free enterprise', as they termed it, but they were reluctant to threaten the high wages secured by the trade unions and their encouragement of home demand discouraged exports.

Britain enjoyed the highest per capita average income among the large industrial nations of western Europe until about 1960 and many manufacturers of consumer goods targeted the home market once the Labour export drives were a thing of the past, in the hope that their products would find ready export markets thereafter. In practice, these hopes were often disappointed, with expensive and idiosyncratic British products undersold and out-promoted abroad by continental exports designed *ab initio* for the world market, in conditions of relatively low demand and low costs at home.

As early as 1953 Cabinet papers were referring to British exporters' failure to adapt their products and their selling efforts to overseas requirements. The government recognised that improvements in product type and quality required investment, but the inclusion of investment allowances in the 1954 budget led to an investment and consumer boom which was so inflationary in its effects that the allowances had to be withdrawn in 1956. The alternative – the reduction of public expenditure – could not be achieved to an appropriate extent in the Cabinet's view. This episode summed up the weakness of the British economy as well as any other, especially when we note that the reduction in public expenditure sought by the Treasury, and denied by the Prime Minister, Sir Anthony Eden, was in food subsidies, with Eden's long-term objective being the control of inflation via the negotiation of trade union wage restraint. This preference reflected a broader recognition on the Cabinet's part that productive investment, though highly desirable, should not be allowed to threaten social investment (Di Nolfo, 1992, 143, 146–7).

FIGURE 2.2 *Britain's export performance, 1950–73, in comparison with more successful European countries.*

UK	3.9
France	8.2
Germany	12.4
Italy	11.7
Netherlands	10.3
Switzerland	8.1

This table shows the annual average growth rate (compound) in the total volume of exports in six countries over the years of rapid economic growth, 1950–73. The British figure is strikingly low, though it has to be said that Britain's big post-war surge in exports had occurred rather earlier than that of the other countries, in the late 1940s.

Source: data drawn from Maddison, 1989, 67.

That German producer goods outsold their British rivals in Europe after about 1950 reflected the revival of German production in a field in which it had enjoyed a comparative advantage since before 1914. The German surge in motor production was more worrying. The Volkswagen mass production car, a crude but rugged 1930s design, produced under the guidance of the British Army from 1945 to 1949, swept the world from the early 1950s. British equivalents, of which the Morris Minor, launched in 1949, was closest in size and price, were newer and more comfortable, yet they struggled to secure big export sales outside the Commonwealth in the 1950s. By the mid-1950s, French and Italian cars, though uncompetitive in Britain, were dominating export markets in southern Europe. The Mini, launched in 1959 and an elegant, versatile symbol of the 'Swinging Sixties', did very well on the Continent but the British Motor Corporation failed to develop a successful export range of larger cars. High consumption in Britain obscured these developments from the mass of the population and from most politicians and other opinion-formers, but the seeds of the gloomy 1960s had been sown.

The 1950s were seen at the time as something of a golden age as the gloom and dilapidation of post-war Britain were replaced by growing flows of consumer goods, cars, the television, foreign holidays, and smart new clothing. As the Conservatives, still respecting the wartime consensus, had retained the essentials of the Welfare State, Britain seemed to be enjoying the best of both worlds and the public became very demanding, a sentiment expressed in Prime Minister Macmillan's riposte to press criticism, which circulated universally in a distorted form as 'You've never had it so good', in July 1957.

In the 1950s the growth of British GDP per head progressed at an annual rate of something over 2 per cent, a little lower than in the later 1940s when British exports faced little European competition. After 1954 the final removal of controls and rationing allowed much personal income to be moved out of saving, and production could respond fully to effective demand on a scale not seen since 1939. As in the 1930s, residential building and motors were at the core of a wide range of growing consumer industries. After a big Conservative effort in public housing to overcome the post-war backlog had achieved its target in 1954, private building was allowed to expand to unprecedented levels. Motor car ownership expanded rapidly from the early 1950s as the British motor industry was allowed to turn more towards home demand. In the mid-1950s colour and chrome displaced the previous Fordian style and began an era of choice. The government launched a big programme of road improvement and construction in 1955 and the M1, Britain's first long limited-access motor road, from near London to near Birmingham, was opened in 1957. The next task was to bring high-speed roads into the city centres. The first step was the opening of the first section of the Birmingham Inner Ring Road in 1960, but with such projects multiplying, a virtually unending programme of high public expenditure was in view.

Equally important to the new climate was television which had resumed services in the London area in 1946, and which began a slow march across the country with additional transmitters from the late 1940s. In 1955 the Conservatives broke the public broadcasting monopoly when they set up 'commercial' television. As well as reflecting a growing move towards leisure among manual workers, its novel advertising ('commercials') extended consumption of a wide range of goods and services.

A recurring feature of this book is the country which, within a historical context of western European integration and the emergence of a European economy, under-performs in relation to the continental level. This effect is often explained by the theory of 'catching-up'. 'Catching-up' occurs when the methods, technology, capital and even markets of an advanced industrial country are taken over by less industrialised countries, producing a high rate of growth in the latter and a much lower one in the advanced country. After the war, the USA was the prime victim of the 'catching-up' process, though American efforts to create a world trading and monetary system based on the dollar produced considerable compensating benefits, at least until the late 1960s. Britain had a rate of growth similar to that of the USA but its much lower national product per capita, the weakness of sterling, and the gradual economic fragmentation of the British Empire meant that it did not secure comparable benefits.

From the early 1950s most of the countries apparently 'catching-up' the USA and Britain were on the continent of Europe and this process was fully in line with American plans for the post-war world economy, in which Britain had been implicated since 1941. In the context of a developing European economy, enterprise and capital were moving to areas where resources could still be exploited at low cost, using existing methods. As Europe's most completely industrialised country in 1945, Britain no longer had a large agricultural sector which could rapidly transfer labour into manufacturing and services on German and French lines. Moreover, Britain's low growth rates did not mean that she did not benefit from high growth rates on the Continent, which was an important market and a source of semi-finished and finished goods. Britain's growth rates were, however, very low in European terms and certainly offered no prospect of 'catching-up' US per capita output.

FIGURE 2.3 *Annual percentage growth in gross domestic product (GDP), 1950–64.*

	1950–55	1955–60	1960–64
UK	2.9	2.5	3.1
France	4.4	4.8	6.0
Germany	9.1	6.4	5.1

Source: based on Alford, 1988, 14.

Harold Macmillan, who became Prime Minister in 1957, was more aware of the problem of Britain's low growth rate than his predecessors, Churchill and Eden. Disturbed by the disastrous Anglo-French invasion of the Suez canal zone in 1956, he reassessed Britain's massive contribution to Western defence (between 7 and 8 per cent of national income) and big reductions were decided in 1957. His main initiative on the economic front was to apply for membership of the European Economic Community in 1961. Britain's trade was moving towards the EEC as growth accelerated there, and industrial methods were moving ahead of Britain's, especially in Germany. However, as in the field of world strategy, Britain was caught between two stools. Macmillan wanted to join a dynamic regional trading community to accelerate economic change in Britain, but Charles De Gaulle, the French president since 1958, saw Britain as still wedded to the USA, the Commonwealth, and its established trading partners (Porter, 1987, 124–6). He vetoed the British application in 1963. Not until 1973 would Macmillan's 'solution' be achieved.

This is not the place to pursue Britain's economic woes into the 1960s. Suffice it to say that the country that gave the world the concept of the Welfare State became trapped in an out-of-date productive system and over-ambitious military pretensions, combined with a demanding populace. Of course, this is an easy judgement for the historian to make over three decades later. During the later 1950s Britain's high living standards were not only recorded in official statistics, but were still visible to the growing numbers of British businessmen and holidaymakers who travelled on the Continent. This was the time when British tourists seeking a holiday in the Alps went automatically to a still affordable Switzerland, with the French Alps considered under-equipped and Austria scarcely a holiday destination at all, owing to poverty, poor facilities and dilapidation there.

FIGURE 2.4   *Gross domestic product (GDP) per capita,*
in terms of purchasing power, 1960.

Belgium	95.4
Denmark	118.3
Spain	60.3
France	105.8
Greece	38.6
Ireland	60.8
Italy	86.5
Luxembourg	158.5
Netherlands	118.6
Portugal	38.7
West Germany	117.9
United Kingdom	128.6

100 = average GDP in terms of purchasing power of the
Twelve EEC countries in 1960.

This table uses exchange rate adjustments to make the
national GDP figures comparable in real terms. Luxembourg
is too small to be comparable with Britain. Switzerland, not a
member of the EEC and therefore absent from this
comparison, would have ranked above Britain but British
living standards are still higher than those of expanding West
Germany and France.

Source: derived from Féron and Thoraval 1992, 177.

France

The basis of the French recovery from the war was complex.
Thanks to Allied recognition of Charles de Gaulle's government in
exile, France ended the war as a victorious Ally. It had, however,
been utterly defeated by Germany in 1940 and from 1942 the
whole country had been occupied. Pétain's 'Vichy regime' had
become associated with some of the worst aspects of National
Socialism, including the murder of the Jews, and De Gaulle swept
it away in 1944, putting Pétain on trial for high treason and seeing
that other collaborators were dealt with. Moreover, France had
been in the doldrums in the 1930s, with governmental orthodoxy
favouring drastic deflation provided that the franc were protected.
Industrial modernisation had been restricted, and productivity had
dropped. Thus there was much scope for a fresh start in 1944 and
1945.

The provisional government, under De Gaulle as head of state, was set up on 3 June 1944. The Resistance secured a number of socialistic reforms, including random nationalisations. In practice, however, continuity prevailed as French officials and politicians, together with writers, artists and other public figures, secured ready recognition as potential participants in post-Vichy society. The country had, after all, been forcibly subjected to Fascism and the German occupation, and no massive clear-out of tainted people took place. Several thousand summary executions occurred during the Liberation, but the official trials, which continued until 1951, resulted in only 767 executions, most of the death sentences, like Pétain's, being commuted. Uncertainty will always prevail, but it looks as though no more than 60,000 French people were brought to book, in one way or another, for collaboration or war crimes. Nearly 50,000 more were sentenced to 'national degradation' (demotion or dismissal from their wartime posts) but most were relieved within a few years and many took on their former jobs. As for the Vichy judges, who had meted out punishment under the twisted legislation of the day, most remained in place to punish the collaborators after the Liberation. Clerics fared well. The Pope eventually agreed to remove an archbishop and three bishops, but De Gaulle would have liked to see many more dismissed (Larkin, 1988, 124–6). In these circumstances, the fresh start was much more restrained than Germany's and radical changes were very hard to achieve. On the other hand, French national identity was very strong after the Liberation, especially thanks to De Gaulle. There was a strong contrast here with Germany, where national pride and consciousness were erased for some years.

De Gaulle wanted a new constitution to back powerful government and destroy the pre-war 'system of the parties'. He wanted, above all, 'renewal' and modernity (Shennan, 1989, 71, 76). However, the parties resisted and a frustrated De Gaulle resigned as provisional head of state in 1946. Later that year, the Constituent Assembly's much-revised text for the constitution of a new, Fourth Republic was approved by a referendum, but it was little different from that of the Third Republic. Among its many defects was its inability to generate strong governments. During the first five years of the new republic, eight governments were formed. De Gaulle, meanwhile, sought to rally mass support outside parliament. Popular sympathy for him was strong, but the parties kept him at arm's length and clung to their new constitution.

Neither the Americans nor the British had had great confidence in De Gaulle, who did not seem to be an effective politician and whose national aspirations for a new, powerful France did not chime well with their integrationist aspirations for continental Europe. However, they were also unhappy with the results of his departure. The Communists, whom De Gaulle would have kept well away from power, could now press for major changes in both parliament and industry. Having led the French Resistance, they were not strong enough to form a government but they could prevent the other socialist and centre parties from forming an effective coalition which might have taken France down the same road as Britain and other countries which elected socialistic governments after the war. Instead, the Communists paid heed to Stalin's wishes. After joining fully in the parliamentary process during the years 1944–46, like the Italian Communist Party over a similar period, they bent readily to the developing Soviet Cold War strategy and in 1947 they started to support industrial action by the Communist trade unions. In May 1947 they were expelled from the coalition government, for supporting a clutch of strikes in April, after which they declined to take part in any further coalition governments. The year 1947 saw the beginnings of a difficult period of strikes which made the numerous governments of the day think twice about pursuing non-inflationary economic policies. On the contrary, they and their permanent officials started to anticipate inflation as a means of assuaging popular demands. France's rapid inflationary trend was confirmed, while the strikes multiplied. By 1949, French prices had increased twenty times in comparison with 1945 (Mauro, 1971, 330).

It is too often assumed that the result of all this was chaos. However, the lack of major change after Vichy reflected the stability and continuity of French society which had survived the war intact and largely unsullied, just as Philippe Pétain, the Vichy head of state, to give him his due, had intended. Under Vichy the French policies of the 1930s had been reassessed, and a return to narrow economic conservatism had been ruled out long before the Liberation. France, it is true, was much less industrialised than Britain and Germany, and little changed in this respect during the early years after the war. The continuing influence of traditional society generated a fundamental stability. Only the brief socialist experiment during the Popular Front government in 1936–37 had seriously disturbed this harmony and its failure had made a repeat episode unlikely. Changes of government and strikes there might be, like the Communist-led wave in 1947, but French life went on stolidly enough. Admittedly, like some other European countries, France introduced a new system of social security after the war. It was based on two strikingly early enactments in 1944 and 1945, which announced the government's intention to provide insurance against illness and old age, first to all workers, and subsequently to the whole population (Piquet Marchal, 1985, 192). However, French reform legislation was a mere shadow of the British achievement.

This happy conservatism would eventually prove to have its defects, but they were not visible immediately after the war. There was a general feeling in France, which had not been present before the war, that economic strength had to be the foundation of French power in the world, rather than military or cultural prowess. As the war had brutally shown that France lacked power, the need for reforms was acknowledged (Shennan, 1989, 287–96). However, this climate resulted in the execution of reforms which implied continuity rather than radical change.

Frequent changes of government were, nevertheless, an obstacle to policy formulation. Some ministers moved on from one government to the next, especially within the Centre-Left party group which tended to dominate the assembly, but the group's growing need to attract support from the Right as the Communists moved away, was a complicating factor. One effect of this uncertainty was that senior civil servants acquired great influence, not only over administration but over policy itself. Thanks to the system of *grandes écoles* set up by Napoleon Bonaparte, France's top administrators went through a demanding education and training which produced an elite well able to use power, influence and skills to shape policy at the highest levels. The system was extended when the *Ecole nationale des administrateurs* was set up by De Gaulle in 1945 as the only significant higher education reform of the period. Above all, senior civil servants could often provide a continuity of policy on which ministers came to rely.

The leading civil servants, led by De Gaulle's close associate, Jean Monnet, were especially interested in economic planning, which they saw as a means of protecting long-run change from political tampering. They could not secure permanent control, but they developed clear and consistent aims which could not be swept aside completely by the politicians or other interests. European integration was also a big interest of theirs. It had been engendered by wartime discussions, partly in exile, and for Jean

Monnet and others it had been prompted by the frightening events of 1940 when even France and Britain, as allies facing Hitler's advance, had found it very hard to work together. Now, paradoxically, it seemed that a reconstructed Europe might help modernise traditional France. Indeed, post-war France was more interested in planning than any other European country, and it built up a big reputation in this area by the later 1940s, much as Britain did in the field of welfare reforms.

France's economic problems after the Liberation were less acute than in most European countries. She was virtually self-sufficient in food and many raw materials. She could meet most of her needs in finished goods, a strength which had been reinforced during her semi-autarkic 1930s and her Vichy subjection. German policy had been partially directed at making France specialise in the production of consumer goods for the Reich, and the resulting exports, combined with French armaments deliveries to Germany, had made France a bigger exporter of industrial products than ever before. There were, of course, major shortages. French railways, which had been nationalised (SNCF) just before the war, had lost huge quantities of equipment to the Germans in 1940 and 1941. In 1945, they had only 3,000 working locomotives, compared to 17,000 before the war. The USA provided a number of locomotives after the war, but much antique equipment remained in service into the 1960s.

Shortages of equipment and stocks arising from wartime attrition led many French firms to make big purchases after the war. At the same time, the personal savings accumulated during wartime rationing and shortages were to a large extent converted into purchasing power. With domestic production and imports restrained by post-war conditions, a strongly inflationary climate built up from 1944. In 1946, for instance, a law confirmed the principle of the forty-hour week, established by the Popular Front government in 1936, but suspended under Vichy. The law fixed proportional rates for overtime, and provided a firm basis for post-war employment, but it was highly inflationary in its effect. This return to a Popular Front policy which had once horrified Churchill and which was still unique in Europe implied that the French post-war revival would be based on conditions very different from those accepted in Germany. These conditions were not necessarily an obstacle to economic growth but they gave a special importance to the national supply-side planning of Jean Monnet and his colleagues from 1946.

As ever, France lacked adequate domestic coal supplies but as an Ally she soon secured some of what she needed from her occupation zone, which contained the Saar. Coal production in the British-controlled Ruhr, to which France looked as her main source of German supply, was restricted by serious labour problems until 1947 and there were constant problems in meeting delivery quotas to France (Roseman, 1992, 23–58). Allied bombing of targets in France, and fighting on the ground, had done much damage, but it was considerably less than destruction in Germany and liberated France was able to carry on at a level of production close to that of pre-war. Thanks to its belated rearmament, and its early defeat in 1940, its wartime debts were few. This happy condition reduced the need for radical reforms in France at the end of the war.

The French economy recovered quickly from the war and as early as 1947 industrial production had returned to the level of 1938. Exports, however, were hampered by limited demand for many of the luxury goods in which France had a comparative advantage, and the need for the development of technical and mass products was widely recognised. All the political parties agreed that national recovery required rapid industrialisation, an objective which reflected the Vichy consensus that France needed to modernise, and De Gaulle's wartime confidence in *machinisme* (Kuisel, 1981, 187). This objective was incorporated in the Monnet plan of 1946, France's first essay in indicative planning, which will be discussed in more detail below (Graham, 1990, 56). Implicit in the economic policies pursued by Monnet since the Liberation was the idea that France would replace Germany as the industrial hub of Europe after the partial deindustrialisation of Germany (though this result depended on the increasingly unlikely success of French efforts to establish control over the Ruhr) (Hogan, 1987, 33). The modernisation of agriculture was equally an agreed priority. The need for new institutions and attitudes was also recognised.

One post-war development was of even greater significance in the long term than in the short term. This was the post-war baby boom which, with immigration, increased the population of France by nearly one and a half million people between 1946 and 1950. France had been resistant to the standard stimuli to population growth since the later nineteenth century and a continuation of the trend after 1945 was entirely on the cards, once the predictable post-war baby boom had passed. This was, after all, why the Vichy regime had tried so hard to encourage

births, with some success from as early as 1942. The baby boom
peaked around 1950 but did not greatly slacken in the rest of the
decade. This transformation of France from a demographically
moribund society between the wars ('the land of the only child')
to a vast pushchair park was perhaps the biggest of the many
revolutions which France would experience between 1944 and
1995. As late as 1954 the occupied population of France, at
19,520,000 people, was still smaller than it had been in 1921
(Chardonnet, 1958, 76). By the later 1950s, however, it was
increasing gradually, though thanks partly to foreign immigration.
It would return to its 1931 level at the end of the 1960s (Caron,
1979, 190).

The idea of national planning was widely entertained in
political and administrative circles at the end of the war (see
Duchêne, 1994, 148–51), especially after the post-Liberation
nationalisations had failed to generate a clear strategy of State
control. In late 1945 Jean Monnet brought together a small team
of civil servants in two rooms at the Hôtel Bristol, having secured
De Gaulle's quiet approval in August for his planning work
(Rioux, 1980, 235). This intimate group, of the type favoured by
Jean Monnet, quickly drew up an outline Five Year Plan (the
'Monnet plan'). The establishment of a Commissariat du Plan was
approved by decree on 3 January 1946, with the task of producing
a detailed plan within six months. Monnet became the
Commissaire du Plan, chairing a council whose members he
selected from both the public and private sectors. Taking effect
from 1947, the plan was designed to create a climate for the
confident growth of industrial production in both the private and
public sectors. It emphasised investment in industries crucial to
the growth of production – energy, transport, steel, cement and
agricultural machinery (Graham, 1990, 56). Its basic feature was
the setting of growth targets for industrial groups over five-year
periods. Twenty-four 'modernisation commissions', set up in 1946
and 1947, fixed the details of the targets in each sector. Civil
servants, industrialists, and a few trade union people sat in each
commission. The overall plan recommendations had to be
approved by the Assembly. The plan produced a planning partner-
ship between the State and industry which never emerged in
Britain because of the retention of wartime State controls which
were an ineffective alternative to Monnet's creative planning
machinery. The workers were involved not only in the planning
but also in the execution, through the post-war system of factory

councils, set up by De Gaulle in February 1945 as an anti-class conflict measure. These had much in common with the British wartime system which, ironically, faded away after the war. Perhaps most important of all, however, was the plan's ability to gain the confidence of the smaller private companies, which in the past had been distrustful of government. From 1947 they began to cooperate and, with the broader perspective which the plan gave them, they started to invest and to aim for export sales (Ardagh, 1990, 35). Monnet's biggest achievement was to achieve cooperation and comprehension without heavy-handed State intervention (Rioux, 1980, 236).

The Monnet plan reflected the widespread interest in western Europe in achieving full resource utilisation. This led to an emphasis on supply-side direction and planning, which diverged somewhat from British demand-side fiscal Keynesianism and German monetary stabilisation. Its parentage is not especially important, but to some degree it resembles the Vichy approach and the continuation of Fascist planning traditions in Italy and Spain. Groping even more widely, one might detect some of Colbert's mercantilism. More practically, however, the Monnet plan can be seen as the appropriate response to the needs of an economy which, in some sectors, was fully developed, yet was very backward in others. It was also intended at first to support France's case for the internationalisation of the Ruhr, by showing clearly how much coal France needed (Lynch, 1984, 229). When France had to abandon these claims in 1948, the Monnet plan readily provided a basis for international planning.

The announcement of Marshall aid in 1947 was warmly welcomed by France, and at the Paris Conference of 1947 and later discussions France played a leading part in the detailed negotiations (see De Jouvenel, 1948; Young, 1990, 109–20). Through the counterpart funds mechanism, France secured the bulk of the capital and some of the technology and expertise that it needed to achieve industrial modernisation under the Monnet plan, which would have been impossible to finance otherwise. France even dropped its surviving Ruhr pretensions in order to ensure its participation. Modernisation schemes for the national railway (SNCF) and electricity (EDF) networks started in 1947. The rationalisation of existing industries by the creation of new conglomerates was typified by the establishment of Usinor, the steel combine, in 1949. US firms were allowed to invest in France under the Marshall plan, and most of this investment took the form of equipment for subsidiaries of US firms like Ford-France. The Monnet plan was approved, and indeed much admired, by the Marshall administrators, and its existence allowed US funds to be directed to the most effective ends. Of the counterpart funds allocated between 1948 and 1951, 37 per cent went to coal mining, electricity and gas, 5.5 per cent to the railways, and nearly 13 per cent to housing (Rioux, 1980, 242). This distribution reflected the abandonment of France's Ruhr pretensions, and Monnet's determination to provide the infrastructure on which later industrial development would be based.

The main controls were over prices and the distribution of credit. These latter were unusual in Europe but were needed to control inflation. They were gradually removed in the later 1940s as the franc became more stable and inflation began to cause less concern. Like most other European currencies, the franc was heavily devalued in 1949 in the wake of the British devaluation but this parity was maintained until 1957/58, when the franc was devalued twice, first to help French exports on entry into the EEC, and second, to reinforce the new Fifth Republic. Rationing was removed in 1949, and prices were fully decontrolled by November of that year. Marshall aid was largely responsible for this achievement and after a budgetary stabilisation in 1948, economic conditions were very harmonious in 1949 and 1950 (Rioux, 1980, 255–6).

Meanwhile, the progress of modernisation helped France to proceed with confidence into the European Coal and Steel Community in 1952, and on into the European Economic Community in 1957. Seen largely as a technical issue thanks to civil servant involvement, the main objections to these two steps towards economic integration came from interested industries. Party politics and the interests of national strategy were strongly represented in the national debate but they played a smaller role than they would in Britain from 1961. The government, for its part, used ECSC membership to open up French firms to foreign competition (Graham, 1990, 66). By the time France entered the EEC in 1958, a number of major industries, including steel, had been so fully modernised that European competitiveness was not in doubt overall, especially as the franc was devalued in 1957 and 1958.

In the 1950s French economic growth proceeded at the respectable rate, by European standards, of just over 4 per cent per annum on average, but France's huge legacy of small-scale agriculture and artisanal industry proved very persistent. Having been under-industrialised by north European standards before the war, France's growth rate of 4 per cent could not produce a quick transformation, and inflation continued at a high rate. Antoine Pinay's price stabilisation programme in 1952–53 had restrained inflation but the economic upturn of the mid-1950s, initiated by Edgar Faure's policies in 1954 and 1955, produced a new surge of inflation. Fortunately, Jean Monnet was allowed to draw up and apply a Second Plan (1954–57) which, at a time of much higher growth rates, provided a structure for investment which favoured the more productive areas of the economy while ensuring new social provision in areas such as housing and education. Quality, rather than quantity alone, was the watchword (Rioux, 1983, 168). This uncertain phase came to an end, however, in 1957 and 1958 when the government brought inflation under control, partly to prepare the economy for EEC membership.

French modernisation was visible to all by the later 1950s, the product of a national rate of investment which had risen from 17 per cent of GNP in 1952 to 21 per cent in 1958 (Rioux, 1983, 187). Since 1948 the government had established a number of investment funds and these, together with existing public sources of capital like the Crédit Foncier, had greatly eased the flow of credit, with banks and the stock market providing an increasing volume of capital. Total productivity increased by 5 per cent a year in the 1950s (Rioux, 1983, 190). The French motor industry launched a series of new cars which were much admired for their cheap, simple construction, or for their technical brilliance. In 1954, 437,098 motor vehicles were produced in France, compared to 182,400 in 1938 (Calvet, 1956, 356). The Renault 4CV, launched in 1946 and the popular car of the later 1940s, was out-shone by the extraordinarily versatile Citroën 2CV after its introduction in 1949. Essentially farmers' cars, able to ride the ruts, they gained a large part of the urban market at prices which excluded the cheapest British cars and even the Volkswagen Beetle. The Citroën DS19, launched in 1957 as Europe's most advanced luxury car ('If it breaks down, take it to a watchmaker; he at least will frankly admit that he knows nothing about it' – German joke of the period), carried French presidents for more than a generation while achieving mass sales among all the *arrivistes* in France and challenging the Mercedes even in Germany. Even Renault, provider of basic transport for decades, took advantage of the onset of the EEC to launch a zippy four-seater onto the European market in 1956. The Renault Dauphine, an elegant upgrade of the 4CV, achieved big sales throughout Europe, including Britain. In 1958, 589,000 private cars were produced in France (Rioux, 1983, 174). However, the main stimulus to growth in France in the 1950s was – in contrast to Germany – home demand, and the achievement of the decade thus reflected a change in consumption patterns among French people (Rioux, 1983, 190–1). In this sense, French modernisation in the 1950s was a modernisation of people's attitudes. A social revolution was already under way, far more than in Britain or in Germany. This would be the source of the dynamism visible everywhere in France in the 1960s.

New aircraft made a similar point. After the technical failure of the British Comet airliner in the early 1950s, the success of Sud-Aviation in launching a cheap, medium-range, jet airliner, the Caravelle, in 1959, was a striking triumph for French industry. The Caravelle dominated world markets in its category by the early 1960s, and in 1963 it accounted for 77 per cent of all jet traffic in Europe (Ardagh, 1968, 62).

Retailing changed less rapidly. Town centres altered very slowly in the later 1950s. Small shops were still protected by taxation policy and multiple stores were largely limited to the low-price Prisunic. The concept of ready-to-wear clothing did not appear until 1949, and the first ready-to-wear fashion salon did not take place until 1957 (Borne, 1992, 30). However, the big furniture stores which grew up along the main roads just outside the towns, with their rows of flags and gaudy hoardings, announced a big change from as early as the 1960s. The first Carrefour, a huge, out-of-town chain hypermarket sited at a big road junction, opened in 1963. The ubiquitous Courtepaille restaurant chain, whose circular, thatched restaurants spread everywhere in the late 1960s and the 1970s, served steaks to businessmen along the main roads. The prefabricated, boxy buildings of the Novotel and Sofitel hotel chains showed from the 1960s that the linguistic spirit of the Benelux was not yet dead. The comedian and film director, Jacques Tati, satirised these changes in a way which charmed the French, who still felt a little guilty about the loss of 'grandpa's' France. His bitter-sweet *Mon Oncle* (1958), showed how France had moved 'forward' from the fussy but humane world of his *Jour de Fête* (1948) and *Les vacances de Monsieur Hulot* (1953) to the pretentious modernism of the obese *nouveaux riches*.

By 1960 France was well on the path towards becoming a fully industrialised country, and many of the weaknesses of the 1930s had been removed. In that year, 37.6 per cent of the French workforce was employed in industry, compared to 47.7 per cent in Britain and 47.0 per cent in Germany, and to 33.9 per cent in Italy (OECD, *Hist.Stat.*, 1991, 40). With so much new industrial enterprise, productivity was high, and the parallel expansion of domestic and export sales generated a high growth rate. In 1960, for instance, the economy expanded by 7.1 per cent. Carré et al. emphasise the importance of 'potential demand' to this impressive acceleration; low growth in the 1930s, the war, and the late 1940s had left France obsolescent or under-equipped in household durables, housing, industrial equipment, and other areas. The release of effective demand from the 1950s allowed this shortfall to be met very quickly, producing a high growth rate (Carré et al., 1976, 501).

FIGURE 2.5 *French economic development, 1938–58.*

	1938	1945	1950	1952	1954	1956	1958
Agricultural production	100	61	102	103	117	112	116
Industrial production	100	50	128	145	159	188	213
Volume of imports	100	34	104	116	126	166	174
Volume of exports	100	10	161	161	196	202	233
GNP	100	54	118	129	140	156	167

Output is shown increasing from a base of 100 in 1938.

Source: derived from Rioux, 1983, 169.

Allowing for the very different post-war circumstances of the two countries, the French rates of development are not much lower than Germany's, and are ahead of Britain's. Between 1950 and 1958, French industrial output increased by 50 per cent, compared to 51 per cent in Germany (Rioux, 1983, 192). The annual level of investment in France, having increased by 22 per cent between 1949 and 1954, went on to increase by 54 per cent between 1954 and 1960 (Carré et al., 1975, 109). Nevertheless, France, with its much larger agricultural sector, areas of backward industry, and small-scale commercial sector, still lagged well behind Germany in aggregate productivity terms.

This state of affairs would not last, however. The year 1958 marked the beginning of an even more dynamic phase which would build up France into a country which could stand with West

Germany as joint leader of western Europe in both economic and political terms. This phase was launched by two critical events: the establishment of the EEC on 1 January 1958, with France as a leading member, and the return of Charles De Gaulle to the leadership of France later in the year. These developments will dominate Chapter 8.

West Germany

Between 1933 and 1945 an aggressive Germany had struggled in vain to shape Europe's destiny. After 1945, an industrious West Germany did more to shape western Europe's destiny than any other European country. This sober, creative role sprang from the remaking of western Germany after the war by its Allied victors. This is an epic story, the backbone of western Europe's post-war history.

Before the war, Germany had been the largest economy in western Europe. By 1960, she was so again. That pre-war eminence had been based in part on Germany's great geographical area and the size of her population – 66,030,000 in 1933, compared to Britain's population of 39,952,000 in 1931. In 1960, with a much smaller area, and a population reduced to 56 million, West Germany's economic strength was based much more on her productivity, the highest in Europe. Between 1950 and 1973, German productivity (GDP per man hour) increased at an annual compound average rate of 6 per cent. In the OECD, only Japan (7.6 per cent) did better. Britain registered 3.2 per cent. Even fast-growing France (5.0 per cent) and Italy (5.5 per cent) could not emulate the German level (Maddison, 1989, 88).

In Germany and outside, this impressive result was known to journalists and some politicians as Germany's 'economic miracle' (*Wirtschaftswunder*). From a viewpoint in the 1990s, that 'miracle' appears less clear-cut because, in the longer term, most of western Europe would experience a similar 'miracle', while from the 1960s western Germany's economic performance would decline, on many indicators, relative to the achievements of the 1950s. Ludwig Erhard, the financial genius of the new Germany, always disliked the term, which implied divine intervention rather than the common sense and hard work which he had helped inspire (Erhard, 1958, 116). Miracle-worker or not, Germany was the key to the success of post-war western Europe. Most interesting of all, the economic and social structure created there after 1945 sprang from the unique circumstances of utter national defeat, and were influenced or imposed by occupying countries, and especially by the United States. The way in which a new Germany emerged, 'stronger and more beautiful than ever before', from the biggest national humiliation the world had ever seen, is of considerable importance to the history of post-war Europe, and it is worth looking at in detail.

Western Germany, the most badly damaged and dislocated country in western Europe in 1945, was also still the biggest in terms of population (46,560,000 inhabitants in 1946) and normal economic capacity, despite its serious losses of territory in 1945. Until 1948, however, this potential was outweighed by the reality of Germany's acute post-war difficulties. Britain and France faced serious problems at the end of the war, but their position as nation states, threatened only a few years earlier by National Socialism, was confirmed by their victory over the Axis. Germany was no longer a nation state at all, as a result of the total capitulation forced on it by the Allies. Denazification required the abolition or suspension of many national institutions, and the occupying Allies ruled Germany directly from the summer of 1945 onwards. These responsibilities put a big strain on supplies of German-speaking administrators, especially in Britain.

The Allies had to assume a directive role in the economy, especially as market mechanisms worked only in a fragmentary and distorted way. In 1945 they fixed prices at the level of 1936, using the Nazi price control mechanism. This resulted in an active black market, barter, and the use of cigarettes as a means of exchange to supplement the devalued wartime Reichsmark. Firms soon found that Allied allocations of production materials were unreliable, so they started to hoard, and to produce their own inputs. They also started to barter, and paid workers in kind. Investment fell to a very low level, there being little chance of profits. On the contrary, there was some risk of confiscation by the Allies, even as late as 1948.

Germany was divided into four occupation zones, under the control of the USA, Britain, France and the Soviet Union. An Allied council was set up to coordinate the administration of the four zones, but there was some divergence from the start. Disagreements with the Soviet authorities culminated in the 'Berlin blockade' of 1948, by which time the Soviet zone lay firmly behind the 'Iron Curtain' as part of eastern Europe.

The three western zones were in a state of near-paralysis in 1945. The Allied forces found it hard enough to make arrangements for emergency food supplies. In the British zone, the army housed many homeless families in Nissen huts, and similar expedients were used in the other zones. Military engineers made temporary repairs to the railways, and the authorities arranged early on for some of the mines to continue working so that the power stations could be kept going. Food supply arrangements improved in 1946 but adult rations were well below normal requirements. Not until 1948 did the quantity and variety of the German diet begin to return to their pre-war levels.

The general revival of production and distribution was complicated by the uncertainties and contradictions of Allied policy on the future of Germany as an industrial nation, and then by its application in each of the three Western zones. In the middle years of the war there had been much talk among the Allies of reducing Germany to a non-industrial state which could never start another war. This strategy was associated most closely with Henry Morgenthau, the US Secretary of the Treasury, whose 'Morgenthau Plan' won the support of Roosevelt and Churchill, in general terms, in 1944. From 1944, however, the American vision of world economic revival shifted much Allied thinking towards the idea of a potent German economy operating peacefully within a framework of strong European institutions. Gradually, the Morgenthau approach would fade away, but not until 1948 did it disappear entirely, with the advent of Marshall aid.

Occupation issues and problems were much too complex at first to allow a clear strategy to emerge. As early as May and June 1945, General Lucius D Clay, the Deputy Military Governor (from March 1947, Military Governor) of the American zone, came to the conclusion that punitive measures designed to reduce the German economy further would be disastrous. In October, however, a tough policy on Germany was laid down in a high-level document, JCS (Joint Chiefs of Staff) 1067, which confirmed earlier US positions (Gimbel, 1968, 9–15). JCS 1067 coincided with a long article in the *New York Times* on the Calvin Hoover Report, a government-commissioned survey on the post-war German economy, which pointed to the damaging effects of the loss of territory in the East, and predicted that post-war living standards would be the same as in 1932. In November, the Byron Price Report, personally commissioned by Truman, was submitted to the President. Byron Price stressed the urgent need for Germany to develop exports to pay for food imports which were likely to be necessary for some time. Other studies and reports, generated by the American pluralistic system of government, prompted a lot of rethinking in both Washington and Germany in late 1945 (Gimbel, 1968, 20–3).

By the end of the year, Clay had called together the Minister-Presidents of the German states and revived the *Länderrat* (assembly of the states) to deal with a number of pressing problems, including the refugees from the East (Gimbel, 1968, 36–9). By early 1946, Clay was pressing ahead with economic, administrative and political reorganisation, partially ignoring the Allied level-of-industry plan of March 1946 which would have reduced German manufacturing production on Morgenthau lines (Gimbel, 1968, 32–3). Finally, in 1947, JCS 1069 was discarded after the Moscow conference of March–April 1947 had failed to reach a four-power agreement on a German settlement, including an economic stabilisation (Gimbel, 1968, 3–5).

Although German industry was virtually paralysed by internal chaos at the end of the war, its potential capacity overall was greater than before the war. War damage between 1943 and 1945 was the equivalent of 12 per cent of the production level of 1943 (Piquet Marchal, 1985, 153). Of course, production in 1943 had already been boosted by the industrial programme of the Armaments Minister, Albert Speer, since 1942, some of it using foreign and concentration camp labour. On the other hand, production in 1943 was heavily distorted by the mass production of simple weapons favoured by Speer, and not all the associated capacity, much of which (like the suicidal *Panzerfaust* anti-tank grenade) used a low level of technology, could find a use in peacetime. Germany remained a well-equipped, industrial nation nonetheless. Its losses of young men in the Forces, though greater than in the First World War, were not a major problem, with millions of German refugees flooding in from the eastern territories. If the German potential could be released by constructive Allied policies in Germany and Germany's full participation in a freely functioning international trading system, output could soon return at least to pre-war levels.

Such a recovery was delayed for some time, however. The French disturbed the British and the Americans by pursuing a purely national strategy, directing industrial production in their zone towards products needed by France, such as coal and chemicals, at the same time as confiscating machinery for the direct use of French industry. Sometimes excluded from the highest levels of Allied discussions, France claimed the right to get production moving in its zone in the interests of the French economy. The other Allies were suspicious that the French aimed to keep Germany permanently divided, while securing access to its iron and coal. A covert effort to prepare the French zone for incorporation into France was also feared. Such manoeuvres were bound to encourage the Soviet Union to establish permanent control of its own zone. French policies even recalled Napoleon Bonaparte's plans for western Germany (Woolf, 1991, 83–132). The German population nevertheless experienced an early return to near-normality which was much longer delayed in the American zone and especially in the British zone. In the Saar and the other regions of the French zone, no attempt was made to shun the Germans to make them realise their sins. Instead, people were encouraged to believe that there might be a bright future before them in a reorganised south-western Germany. The French even set up an integrative French language radio station, Europe 1, as a commercial enterprise (Paulu, 1967, 86–7). This was intended to serve both eastern France and the French zone, especially the Saar. Using a powerful long-wave transmitter, it also functioned as a French national programme and it survived long after its original purpose had been surpassed and was still going strong in 1995. 'If they had had the radio in Napoleon's day, that is where they would have done it.'

Reparations and occupation costs, which all the Allies exacted in one form or another, could be partly extracted in the form of machinery and patented industrial processes, and these exactions could easily be confused by both Germans and occupiers with a broader deindustrialisation programme. In 1947, with elements of the Morgenthau approach still surviving, especially in the American zone, German industrial output was still a mere 34 per cent of the 1938 level, and agricultural output, dogged by fertiliser and equipment shortages, was lower than before the war. In the absence of an effective market economy in western Germany, the Allies continued to control production and consumption through a system of price controls, rationing, and production and raw materials quotas, most of which they had inherited from the Third Reich. It was difficult to develop a clear industrial strategy, even in the individual zones.

Reparations, however, were not an excessive burden on western Germany. Between 1945 and 1947, when reparations dwindled almost to nothing with the creation of the Bizone (common direction of the American and British zones) in January 1947, and greater Allied encouragement of German production began, western Germany paid reparations and other charges equivalent to a total of about $1 billion. Dismantling represented some 3 per cent of German production in 1943 (Piquet Marchal, 1985, 153). Eastern Germany, heavily pressed by the Soviet Union and with a much smaller economy than the west, paid at least $7 billion in reparations. Moreover, while eastern Germany received almost no Allied aid after the war, the west received about $4 million (excluding Marshall aid), most of it to cover food imports.

The Allies agreed, at the Potsdam conference in 1945, that the German populations should be expelled from the areas ceded by the Reich to Poland, Czechoslovakia, and other eastern countries, partly to prevent a new round of German territorial claims on ethnic lines. A mass exodus of German refugees took place between 1945 and 1947. Most of them made their way to the German territories occupied by the Allies. Some settled, if only for a while, in the Soviet zone, but the great majority – 8 million of them – came to western Germany. They created an additional demand for food and basic supplies. Many settled on farms in the north of Germany and in Bavaria, but their labours, provided in lieu of rent, did not add greatly to the food supply, owing to a serious lack of fertilizers and machinery.

So, far from moving towards Morgenthau's 'pastoral' ideal, Germany encountered serious agricultural deficiencies. With many German people living in conditions of near-starvation throughout 1945 and 1946, the Allies began to recognise, following Byron Price, that without a revival of German industry, especially in the export sector, the cost of German food imports would continue to fall on them. This lesson struck the USA, in particular, as Britain and France could not in any case finance large food imports without increasing their own dollar deficits. This realisation gradually moved the complex American view from one influenced by Morgenthau to the vision of a big German contribution to a strong Europe within a liberal world economy. This had been under discussion among the Allies since 1944. With the creation of the Bizone ('Bizonia') in 1947, the Americans began to plan seriously for German economic revival, and at this point German politicians, industrialists and civil servants were drawn into both the discussions and day-to-day administration. These pioneers of the new Germany found that they were very much in sympathy with the American economic concepts which, leavened by New Deal ideas, had been brought to Germany by a team of young administrators led by Clay. This was the melting pot which shaped the German 'economic miracle'.

In March 1946 the Allies, working with German representatives, had issued a Level-of-Industry Plan which set targets for industrial production which would have limited German industry to the level of output of 1932, the worst year of the slump. After the creation of the Bizone, with Stalin increasingly perceived as a threat to western Europe, and the Marshall plan in the offing, a second Level-of-Industry Plan was issued, for the Bizone only, in August 1947. This was influenced by the Bizonal Economic Council, with its German members, which had been set up in June 1947. It allowed German industrial production to rise to a level between 75 per cent and 100 per cent of output in 1936 (Hardach, 1994, 73).

The first three years of Occupation were nevertheless a sad time of malnutrition, cold, disease, black marketeering, fiddling and widespread inactivity for the German people. Their only gain was a determination to prevent Germany falling again into such misery. This meant that they wanted political stability above all, and an absence of extremism. For a while, the country was full of illegal guns and ammunition, but no resistance movements emerged.

The Allies gradually restored German local government, and set up a new system of regional representation in the form of the *Länder*, which were a modified form of the state system of 1871. Encouraged by the Allies, the Germans developed a system of strong, stable parties similar to the British pattern, with influence divided between a moderate socialist (SPD) and a moderate conservative (CDU/CSU) party, and a smaller, centre party (FPD). Replacing the chaotic, pre-1933 party system, the new arrangement allowed the Roman Catholic Church and the trade unions to influence politics through the parties. All this foreshadowed political stability without creating the kind of strong central state which could be taken over by a new Hitler.

This party system was applied to the representative and administrative system set up in the Bizone in 1947. In July 1947 the Allies set up the *Wirtschaftsrat* (economic council) there to complement the *Landrat* (state council), an assembly representing the Bizone *Länder*, created in June. This allowed German representatives to take part in economic planning in the Bizone, with growth increasingly the goal of all parties. Increasing freedom was offered to these German bodies and their successful operation formed the basis for the new German state in 1949.

Where Hitler had abolished pre-1933 institutions, there were serious gaps. The biggest of them was the trade unions, replaced by Robert Ley's puppet German Labour Front in 1934. The trade unions were seen by the Americans as essential in a democratic society, but, partly thanks to British advice, they decided to create new unions on an industry basis, rather than on a craft basis or in the form of general unions. The industrial unions included salaried staff as well as manual workers, and were seen by the Allies as an important democratising force.

Sixteen large unions had been set up by 1949, when a national confederation of trade unions was created. Involved in the achievement of industrial revival after 1945 under American supervision, when works councils could often achieve more than the management, they were happy to cooperate with the employers in order to create employment as quickly as possible after three years of stagnation and high unemployment. The implication – low wages, long hours, and poor conditions in some cases – was understood but in post-war Germany the alternative of continuing semi-paralysis was out of the question. Furthermore, the unions were allowed to play almost no part in the big national decisions which shaped the new Germany and its policy after 1948. The partially socialist programme which they agreed in 1949 never had much political impact. They contributed to the practical tasks of the time but they shaped neither structures nor ideologies. When rising living standards began to make themselves felt in the mid-1950s, the unions lost some of their socialist emphasis and became involved in the organisation of the increasingly productive economy which the Germans increasingly valued.

The more positive American attitude to the revival of the US zone, and American leadership of the post-war programme for an integrated and vital world economy, allowed the USA gradually to take over the administration of the whole of Germany. This process was complete in the Bizone by late 1947. The French zone remained independent at that time, but as the Americans pushed towards a new German currency and German institutions which could sustain an independent state, the French cooperated. Finally, in 1949, France joined with the other western Allies in the creation of the Trizone, which allowed the Americans to guide the economic revival of the whole of western Germany.

By 1948 it had become clear that the Soviet Union had no wish to take part in the inter-Allied creation of a new Germany. It was now possible to create institutions for the reduced, western Germany on the assumption that they would be permanent, national institutions. The situation recalled the creation of the Rhineland and other new states in west Germany in the early 1800s by Napoleon Bonaparte. The USA, with the help of the other two Allies, carried out a sweeping review of German institutions, some of which had completely disappeared in the defeat, while others were effectively in abeyance, or under military control.

The review extended to private firms, which were both denazified and called to account for their wartime activities, including the use of more or less forcibly imported foreign labour and concentration camp prisoners. Since the later nineteenth century Germany had seen the growth of huge, vertically integrated concerns (*Verbundwirtschaften*), on a scale unknown elsewhere in Europe, together with price-fixing cartels. The biggest of these structures were to be found in the coal-steel-engineering-armaments-chemicals sector and they generated efficiency rather than monopoly. However, most of these firms had been key war producers and they were ready targets for investigation.

Some of the largest concerns were now divided into a number of smaller firms. A giant steel firm, the Krupp concern of Essen, was taken out of the hands of the Krupp family and split into smaller units. IG Farbenindustrie, the largest industrial corporation in Germany, was divided into three firms of roughly equal size – Hoechst, Bayer, and BASF (Stokes, 1988, 202). Some of these arrangements did not work, like the division of the 'big three' banks, which soon produced a return to the initial structures. The successors of IG Farbenindustrie grew and prospered, but most of the other divisions of very large combines did not survive long. Many of the old combines came together again in the 1950s, and under their old names (Böhme, 1978, 129). The cartels, however, were resolutely broken up, because they offended American principles of free trade and competition. Most had been dispersed by 1948. However, nationalisation, which had been one of the measures discussed by the Allies, and especially by the British, was never put into effect. Most German workers wanted to see the big firms revive at all costs, with changes in organisation and ownership left till later. Their main priority was the creation of jobs, and they trusted the old firms to provide them. However, the USA retained a consistent interest in securing competition within the reconstructed German economy and as late as 1951 it joined with the other Allies in negotiating an agreement with the German government for deconcentration of the coal and steel industry as a prerequisite for Germany's participation in the European Coal and Steel Community (Diefendorf et al., 1993, 215). Ludwig Erhard worked hard from 1949 to achieve decartelisation in pursuit of his key goal of competition (Erhard, 1958, 117–40).

After a long and difficult period of study, a federal law on the restriction of competition was voted in 1957, replacing the Allies' own deconcentration legislation. However, it contained numerous exceptions, and mergers tended to increase in number into the 1960s and beyond. By this time, German concern with cartelisation had faded and the creation of bigger units by merger was seen as beneficial to the economy provided that competition were not threatened (Leaman, 1988, 58–74). As Volker Berghahn puts it, there was a move from cartel to oligopoly. Meanwhile, German management methods and attitudes were partly Americanised in anticipation, as Berghahn sees it, of a subsequent 'hegemonic' transformation of management elsewhere in Europe (Berghahn, 1986, 326–33).

One of the Allies' happiest discoveries during their occupation was that there was no sign of a National-Socialist resistance. Most German people were glad that a disastrous war was over and they had no wish to maintain a secret struggle against the 'invaders'. Dull acceptance was more visible than enthusiasm in the early years, but the disappearance of the National-Socialist movement simplified the denazification task, with much smaller numbers of former party members removed from their posts than in the Soviet zone. Nevertheless, in the revival of the economy from 1948 the national workforce showed a willingness to cooperate in a national economic programme which recalled something of the years from 1933 to 1945. National Socialism had gone, but German willingness to work hard in a common interest was still present.

By early 1948, Germans were moving into leading positions in economic administration. The Allies were aware by now that a German economic revival was not necessary merely to pay for food imports, but to boost European exports enough to overcome Europe's growing dollar shortage. The new German leadership welcomed the chance to show what Germany could do.

In April 1948, Ludwig Erhard, a university-educated Christian Democrat with a business background, became economic director of the Bizone, just as Germany was about to benefit from Marshall aid. Erhard pressed from the start for a free economy and a secure currency. German economists now began to make their voices heard, most of them bringing forward conventional, free-market views.

In 1948 it became possible to create a new national currency, the Deutschmark, to replace the temporary and local arrangements in effect since 1945. The Deutschmark's establishment had been postponed by fruitless efforts to create a pan-German currency in association with the Soviet Union, but by 1948 all hope of such cooperation had disappeared. The new currency, the new national bank (1948) (*Bank deutscher Länder*, becoming the *Deutscher Bundesbank* in 1957) which issued it, and the early revival of Germany's regional banking system after the Allies had set up a system of provincial banks in 1947, allowed Germany to take full advantage of Marshall aid and the combined boost to the economy from 1948 marked the beginning of an economic recovery which progressed directly towards the impressive growth rates of the early 1950s and beyond. The Deutschmark, initially undervalued in relation to the Reichsmark, and twice devalued in 1948 and 1949, would remain an asset to German exports until the 1970s.

The Allies' confidence in the reconstruction process was marked above all by the creation of a new German state, the German Federal Republic, in 1949. The enabling legislation was known as the *Grundgesetz* (Basic Law). It set up a national (federal) government, and eleven states. Here again, American preferences were crucial. The German federal structure which had lasted through a variety of regimes since 1871 was retained and reinforced, partly under the inspiration of the American example. The voting system for the national parliament was designed to foster large parties which would produce stable government from a moderate, centrist stance. There was no recurrence of the proliferation of small parties which had plagued the Weimar years, and the new republic quickly saw the emergence of conservative, socialist and liberal parties which echoed Britain and several other European countries after 1945. However, elections for the new *Bundesrat* in 1949 put the Social Democrats in a minority, with popular choice confirming the balance of power which had emerged in the Bizone institutions in 1948. The CDU, under Konrad Adenauer, secured a majority, and claimed popular backing for Erhard's 'social market economy' concept. Erhard himself became Minister of Economic Affairs. Meanwhile, the Social Democrats retained considerable influence over government policy and the new republic launched into its long era of social harmony which would still continue in 1995.

The economic and social policies of the new state were strongly influenced by the *Ordoliberalismus* movement of thought which had grown up, among other strands of German economic and political thought, in the early post-war years. Led by Walter Eucken, of Freiburg University, the Ordoliberals believed that a market economy based on completely free competition and strict control of the money supply would produce an ordered, stable and productive society ('a liberal order'). State intervention would be necessary, but its objectives should be limited to creating the conditions in which the liberal system could function freely. This could include expensive public services such as education, which allowed the individual to function to his fullest potential within the liberal system. They believed in personal freedom, which was linked in the eyes of some with Christian belief, but which also depended on a strong legal structure. The constitution of the State should include economic provisions directed principally to free competition within a system in which individual rights and property rights were protected. Their approach, which rested on the idea that scholarly discussion among experts would produce scientifically valid policies, had much in common with that of some of the German *Kathedersozialisten* of the later nineteenth century (Giersch et al., 1992, 26–7). At a further remove, it had much of John Stuart Mill and the British intellectual climate which had so influenced Germany in the beginnings of its own industrialisation process after 1840. It marked a return to an earlier German age of enterprise and freedom, but with a new awareness of the need for the social care and development of the population as a whole.

The Christian Democrats adopted much of this approach, which was also encouraged by the Americans. The British, with their interest in nationalisation and a generous welfare policy, were not happy with this result but their influence waned as the creation of the new German state approached. The completely free economy of the basic theoretical Ordoliberal position was never a possibility, however. The Ordoliberals themselves recognised the need for State intervention at certain points to sustain the free economy. The German Federal Republic quickly developed a modified approach known as the 'social market economy' (*Sozialmarktwirtschaft*). This was a concept generated among the Ordoliberals which came to be associated with Erhard and was widely used in political debate from 1949. It represented a minimum of controls over economic activity, competition, low taxation, only a limited degree of income redistribution, and the provision of social welfare for those who could not provide for themselves (see Erhard, 1958). In effect, this was an extension of Ordoliberalism into a practical world where political realities were accepted as modifying pure theory. The confirmation of the 'social market economy' in 1949 was surprising in view of widespread German interest in socialistic systems in the early post-war years when some European states, led by Britain, were moving in this direction, and when the SPD appeared to have majority support in Germany. American influence provides part of the explanation but an additional factor was the desire to break free of the controls established by the Nazis which, in practice, had been maintained by the Allies. Eucken and his group believed that the socialism of the 1920s had upset the balance of German society and allowed Hitler to come to power. The return to a free economy would ensure stability, with all interests acknowledged and protected. In consequence, economic freedom, social stability, and political conservatism would support one another. One of the main results of this would be a productive economy in which effort was rewarded.

The rapid recovery of the German economy, especially after the creation of the *Deutschmark* in 1948, quickly generated confidence in these free market concepts. On 24 June 1948, just three days after the creation of the new currency, the National Socialist price control structure of 1936 was abolished (though certain categories of product remained subject to control). By the last quarter of 1948, industrial production in the Bizone had reached 79 per cent of its level of 1936 (Abelshauser, 1983, 34). The wage freeze was abolished on 3 November 1948. Erhard's success in assuring the prosperity of the German economy without departing substantially from Ordoliberal principles meant that there was virtually no challenge to the 'social market economy', even from the socialists.

If the main obstacles to the revival of German production had been removed by 1948, the question of its market had not been fully resolved. Home demand would clearly fall short for many years to come, especially as so much of pre-war Germany had been lost to Poland, Czechoslovakia and other countries. By 1948, east Germany also appeared to be 'lost', its incorporation in an autarkic Soviet bloc cutting nearly all economic links with western Germany. The effect of these losses was that the area of western Germany was only 52.7 per cent of the area of the Reich in 1937. The only solution for a reviving industrial economy was to export, a conclusion which Ludwig Erhard soon reached.

Fortunately, western Germany was very strong in the manufacture of producer goods, which were especially in demand for the reconstruction or industrialisation of the rest of Europe. With dismantling at an end by 1948, and Marshall counterpart funds available, German firms could confidently acquire the latest equipment and tools, and apply advanced production methods, many of them acquired from the USA. Of course, Germany was also strong in coal, much of which was exported to France. The way forward was clear, but it meant that Germany needed a European and world trading system which allowed the free flow of goods and capital.

In the short term, however, the deflationary influence of the new currency and government credit restrictions pushed unemployment up to 10.4 per cent in 1950 (*Materialien*, 1974, 324). The government now turned to job-creating policies but the outbreak of the Korean War in June 1950 soon began to soak up some of the available labour, as international military requirements helped boost German production, though without creating the 'boom' which some historians have claimed to detect (Temin, 1995, 738). By 1951 the main problems still centred on foreign payments and the stability of the mark, but the government did not seriously compromise its liberal principles. By the end of the year, the German balance of payments account had moved into a long-term surplus which would last until the oil price increases of the 1970s. From 1952 the resolution of the international crisis allowed the German economy to move forward into the period of export-led growth and strength which soon generated the term, the 'economic miracle'.

The main phase of the German 'miracle' occurred in the 1950s, when GDP increased by an annual average of 8.2 per cent. The active labour force also grew fast, by 3.3 per cent per annum (Giersch et al., 1992, 5). Just as the refugees from the East were now attracted easily into the manufacturing workforce, so firms could quickly start to make use of unused machinery and buildings which had lain idle since 1945. This 'shadow' capacity made up 22 per cent of total actual and potential industrial capacity in 1950. By 1960 it represented only 10 per cent (Maddison, 1964, 82). Allied dismantling, even in the British zone, had clearly not been a serious obstacle to the German industrial recovery (Kramer, 1991). However, Germany had sunk a long way and recovery could not be immediate. It was not until 1953, for instance, that the Federal Republic's real net social product per capita regained the level of

1938 in the equivalent area of Germany (Schildt and Sywottek, 1993, 80).

Manufacturing was the main motor of growth in the 1950s, thanks to the prominent role of manufactured goods in German exports. Between 1952 and 1958, German exports as a proportion of GDP rose from 14 per cent to 21 per cent. In value, they increased from DM16.9 billion to DM37 billion. Commodity exports rose from 8.6 per cent of GNP in 1950 to 16.6 per cent in 1960, this being the biggest increase in Europe (Maddison, 1964, 66). Progress towards full use of the existing capital stock meant that there was heavy investment in replacement machinery and new machinery. Movement from less productive to more productive employment, like the refugees from the East who moved from their emergency farm employment to the cities, also created growth (Giersch et al., 1992, 69–70). Imports rose from 13 per cent to 17 per cent of GDP from 1952 to 1958, with the government pursuing a more liberal import policy in the mid-1950s, but the balance of trade moved in Germany's favour (Schildt and Sywottek, 1993, 97). Greater toleration of imports helped reduce the danger of foreign action against German exports, and indicated German support for the American objective of world trade liberalisation.

By the early 1950s manufacturing growth was beginning to stimulate the economy as a whole. In 1951, German industrial production at last reached pre-war levels, well after most of the rest of Europe, but this milestone marked the completion of a port-war recovery which had been carried out under very difficult conditions. Shorter hours, holidays, the development of services and the expansion of consumer goods production led to the development of all areas of the economy on lines which were no longer greatly influenced by Germany's deadly wartime inheritance. German GNP increased at an average annual rate of 9.5 per cent between 1950 and 1955, as much of the big accumulation of unused capacity was brought into action. Between 1955 and 1960 the rate of growth was 6.5 per cent, which was still at the top of the European league table. The total number of hours worked increased throughout the decade, as the growth in the numbers employed compensated for longer holidays and a shorter working week (Giersch, 1992, 5). The German economy thus moved very quickly from reconstruction to productivity-raising growth. From 1955, western Germany started to create an expensive welfare structure, increasing taxes, but drawing on the benefits of its big growth in productivity. The reconstruction of the bombed cities, well under way by 1955, was also expensive, but its multiplier effects contributed to economic growth. Unemployment had sunk to 4.2 per cent by 1956, and 1.3 per cent by 1960 (*Materialien*, 1974, 324). Meanwhile, the trade unions cooperated with the employers, happy to accept work and rising wages. Thanks to their restraint, and to Erhardian monetary and fiscal policies, inflation averaged less than 2 per cent per annum during the 1950s.

In 1953 a national system of works councils was introduced. These normally ensured that the workers could see the employers' point of view. This docile attitude would survive to imbue the official *Mitbestimmung* (participation) movement of the 1960s. By the later 1950s, with German living standards about to overtake Britain's, German material success compensated for the discipline and authority to which German workers were accustomed. Moreover, those groups which suffered from post-war changes, such as the agricultural workers, readily found satisfactory employment in the expanding sectors of the national economy. These adjustments contributed to the absence of fundamental political conflict (Borchardt, 1991, 108–9).

At first, rapid growth was largely due to a big increase in average working hours, the repair of damaged capital stock, and the moving of resources from less to more efficient uses (Giersch et al., 1992, 2–3). The biggest growth occurred in chemicals, motors, electronics, oil and plastics. The main priorities in production were price stability, and export competitiveness (Maddison, 1989, 69). A variety of incentives to firms encouraged investment and exports. Price stability was now secured readily and Germany built up substantial reserves of currency and gold thanks to her favourable trade balance.

The German refugees from territories now under Communist control began to make a big contribution to industrial production from around 1950. Some 9 million had entered western Germany by the early 1950s, and a further 3 million had entered by the time the Berlin Wall was built in 1961. Seven million of these people entered the labour force, and by 1951 they had been recognised as exceptionally productive and qualified (Kindleberger and Shenfield. 1967, 30–1).

The creation of the new German state gradually obscured the American role in the revival of Germany. Although the Americans had done much to instil the idea of freedom and personal enterprise into the German people and institutions, this was partially converted into a less virtuous American value, materialism. Materialism was associated with big business, which became a much stronger presence in the new Germany than before 1945. Socialism, as it was known in Britain or in France, was scarcely present. The name of the SPD helped keep the idea alive but improving material standards kept socialist principles well in the background.

With no effort at first to create a Welfare State on British lines, and no German military forces to support thanks to the Allied demilitarisation policy, taxes and interest rates were low, so demand and enterprise quickly expanded. From 1955, German rearmament and the expansion of welfare services created new burdens, but the foundation now existed to allow them to be taken up without undermining the economy or creating political contention. On the contrary, West Germany had no difficulty in 1958 in joining the general western European adoption of currency convertibility which marked the belated achievement of the Bretton Woods ideal. Moreover, it went on in 1959 to remove the remaining barriers to the exchange of the mark, showing that its fidelity to liberal principles could carry it beyond the position of most European states at the time. Liberal principles also underlay Erhard's anti-cartel law of 1957, and Germany's adhesion to the EEC in the same year.

Germany's massive housing needs had to be met mainly in the public sector, with rent controls in force until the later 1950s, but a growing proportion of new dwellings were built privately in the 1950s and the Housing Law of 1960 liberalised the housing market. Whereas 69.1 per cent of new dwellings were in the public sector in 1949, the proportion had sunk to 45.8 per cent in 1960 (Schulz, 1991b, 126, 135). The resulting housing output was massive, with 4 million dwellings built between 1949 and 1955 to absorb most of the huge post-war deficit, and building continuing at a rate of around half a million dwellings or more per annum between 1952 and the early 1970s to create the finest housing stock in Europe outside Scandinavia (Hallett, 1973, 122). Throughout, the government used tax adjustments and capital incentives to keep investment flowing into housebuilding, with employers' and trade union housing, more important in Germany than elsewhere, the subject of various encouragements which diverted the full cost away from the building agencies.

The resulting patchwork of urban housing meant that workers

were not relegated to one-class areas as they were, notoriously, on Britain's council estates. Even Germans were unable to distinguish the various housing tenures as they passed through their rebuilt cities. Of course, housing was not the only factor, but the convergence of the working and middle classes in prosperous post-war Germany, which was the deliberate product of the peaceful social policy of the Federal Republic, contrasted with the persistence of traditional class attitudes in Britain, as reflected in housing contrasts.

In 1949 Germany accepted an invitation to join the GATT negotiations at Torquay. It accepted the principle of free trade and went on to prepare a new customs system in the interim (Schildt and Sywottek, 1993, 85–6). The new German tariff rates were introduced in 1950–51. They replaced Germany's previous protectionism by fixing most tariffs at intermediate levels between the high tariffs of Italy, France and Britain, and the low tariffs of Denmark and the Benelux (Wurm, 1995, 43). With this indication of its longer-term intentions, West Germany signed GATT in 1951 and proceeded to benefit from the entire range of tariff reductions agreed under GATT, and to negotiate further agreements (Wurm, 1995, 44). This step established Germany's potential role as western Europe's biggest trader, and as the main agent in the very high western European growth rate which would mark the 1950s and the 1960s. By 1952, 63 per cent of German exports were going to the countries which would form the EEC in 1957, while 45 per cent of German imports came from those countries. Seen from another angle, Germany's large foreign payments surplus in the mid-1950s was obtained almost entirely from the area of the European Payments Union, in other words from western Europe. In 1956, Germany's dollar deficit on foreign trade was still *rising*. What converted it into a surplus was payments made to German suppliers by the US forces in Germany, and the fact that, under the rules of the European Payments Union, Germany could convert part of its export surplus into gold or hard currency (OEEC, *Germany*, 1956, 12). In 1956 and 1957 Germany was also able to make a series of unilateral tariff cuts, which had the effect of reducing her export surplus while increasing the volume of her trade (Schildt and Sywottek, 1993, 95). German industrial products played a big part in both her exports and her imports. Between 1960 and 1971, investment goods accounted for 28.5 per cent of total German exports. Meanwhile, the share of manufactures in total German imports rose from 12.6 per cent in

1950 to 32.2 per cent in 1960, and to 50 per cent in 1970 (Wurm, 1995, 48). Viewed in general terms, this meant that West Germany was exporting much of the machinery on which its manufactured imports were made. This was a firm basis for the growth of European trade.

From 1950 the European Payments Union helped Germany to export to other European countries (Eichengreen, 1993, 30–2). Investment in producer goods and services was encouraged by the Federal government to some extent at the expense of the consumer goods industries, as for instance in the Investment Aid Law of 1952. The Federal budget was kept almost permanently in surplus from 1952. The value of the Deutschmark was maintained, and the fact that it became relatively under-valued in the 1950s, having been fixed in relation to the weak German economy of 1948, helped exports and the balance of payments, with the latter moving into surplus from 1951. Exports were 11 per cent of German GNP in 1950, and they had risen to 20 per cent by 1960. In 1961, 70.04 per cent of German exports went to European countries, while 59.73 per cent of German imports came from else-where in Europe (Leaman, 1988, 104). This meant that German economic success was contributing extensively to the revival of western Europe as a whole, just as the Allies had foreseen. The German solution was unique, but so were the circumstances from which it sprang.

As the years pass, the creation of these new structures in post-war Germany seems more, rather that less admirable. Not only did they provide a basis for German success, but they influenced other European countries which sometimes attributed their own relative lack of economic success to their divergence from the German example. Hitler's disastrous attempt to dominate Europe might well have condemned Germany to obscurity and a toiling ignominy for decades. Instead, German cooperation with the Allies and a careful rethinking of its national economic and social principles allowed Germany to dominate an admiring western Europe to a greater extent than she had done since the time of Charlemagne. Marshall aid to Germany was less that to Britain and to France, partly because so much aid was received in other forms. However, the programme played a a big part in the recovery of Germany, and its principles were probably more influential there than anywhere else in Europe.

Germany quickly became a favoured European son, gradually replacing Britain as the key American partner in all but military terms. More than any other European country, Germany was a land of business which Americans could recognise and admire. From as early as 1950 the USA was pressing its NATO allies for support for German rearmament as a bastion against the Soviet Union. This rearmament, which would eventually be agreed (against strong opposition in Germany) in 1955, reflected the success of American planning in creating a powerful Germany in economic terms. Part of the American success lay in the absence of any inclination in Germany to use its economic strength to pursue military objectives or to use its economic power to suborn other countries. This result, however, was also due to European efforts to achieve integration after the war.

The causes of the British economic 'failure' continue to be a matter of controversy among British historians. The explanation of the German 'success' is not a cause of disagreement in Germany. Its causes are now so obvious that they are scarcely worth investigating any more. Certainty, so rare in economic history, is worth having and so, unusually in this book, we will provide a bare list of causative factors at this point. This list is based on the recent summary by Bührer and Schröder (Di Nolfo, 1992, 176–80), with slight adjustments drawing on comparable lists by other German historians. Germany enjoyed:

(i)   an industrial structure (engineering, motors, chemicals, and electricals) which could meet the pressing requirements of post-war Europe, and the post-war world

(ii) price stability linked to an under-valued Deutschmark and Germany's renewed international credit-worthiness (1952)

(iii) a qualified and flexible labour force, thanks partly to refugees from the East, a labour surplus lasting into the mid-1950s, and cooperative trade unions

(iv) a continuous and consistent economic policy

(v)   Germany's rapid incorporation into the international community after 1949.

These factors remained fully effective until the mid-1960s, and any erosion thereafter was slow.

German development after 1945 deserves such detailed treatment because any weakness in the biggest economy in Europe would have been a weakness for western Europe as a whole. The creation or re-creation of Europe's most productive economy meant the rapid revival and further progress of the western European economy. By 1960 the revival had taken place and

Germany was leading western Europe through a surge of economic advance the like of which it had never previously known. Britain was no longer the leader, and the most influential ideas came from Germany. Germany had become, however, an open economy, quite different from the selfish and aggressive Germany of the 1930s. This openness would benefit western Europe as a whole, at any rate until the 1970s.

CHAPTER THREE

Contrasts on the Fringe: the Nordic Countries and the Mediterranean South, 1945–c.1960

The western European fringe

The spatial diffusion of industrialisation in western Europe since the eighteenth century had produced a large core of advanced countries by 1945, three of which we examined closely in Chapter 2. To the north and the south there remained two groups of less developed countries. These were the Nordic countries of Denmark, Sweden, Norway and Finland, often known (rather loosely) as Scandinavia, and four countries adjacent to the northern shore of the Mediterranean, namely Spain, Portugal, Italy and Greece. An intermediate country, Ireland, was the sole member of a small western fringe, its Roman Catholicism linking it to the South, and its pastoral economy to the North. Ireland's closest ties, however, were with a United Kingdom which in 1950 was its biggest trading partner and the main destination of its teeming emigrants (see Kennedy et al., 1988, 193–4). The fifth Nordic country, Iceland, is too distant from continental Europe to be considered here.

In this chapter we shall consider both these groups as fringe zones, in touch with the core and already influenced by it, and potential candidates for industrialisation after 1945. In doing so, we shall encounter a considerable openness to industrialisation in the North, and a number of obstacles to it in the South.

A few lines to explain concepts and terminology are needed at this point. The terms 'core' and 'fringe' are fundamental to the explanation of European development since 1945 which this book puts forward. They have not been greatly influenced by the very specific, and very stimulating, 'core-periphery' model which

Immanuel Wallerstein has applied to world development (see e.g. Wallerstein, 1974). The interpretation in this book is based simply on a spatial diffusion model of the type commonly used by geographers and economic historians. Indeed, its direct inspiration is the European industrialisation model developed by Sidney Pollard in his *Peaceful Conquest* (Pollard, 1981, 39–41). In particular, Wallerstein's theories of the exploitative and dynamic relationships between the 'core' and the 'periphery' play no part in what follows.

Nordic Europe and its continental context

In 1945 Nordic Europe (Denmark, Sweden, Norway, Finland) was a northerly sub-continental region of mountains and sea (1,260,000 square kilometres), with limited areas of cultivable land except in southern Sweden and in Denmark. It had great mineral reserves, notably iron, lead and zinc ore in Sweden, and access to rich fishing grounds which lay mainly in the broad territorial waters of Norway. The Nordic countries specialised in primary production, with Denmark in particular concentrating on food products and exporting a high proportion of its dairy output. Finland and Sweden were big exporters of timber. Sweden was the most industrialised, having developed a cluster of textile, engineering and allied industries since the 1860s. Other parts of the Nordic countries had an industrial potential, with raw materials, hydro-electric sites, a labour force, and good communications, especially by water.

The economic success of the Nordic countries since the war, their social policies, and certain aspects of their social life, have attracted much international interest. Much less attention has been paid to the fact that the populations of all these countries are very small. In 1995 Sweden had a population of nearly 9 million. Denmark and Finland each had around 5 million. Norway had nearly 4.5 million people. Put another way, Sweden had much the same population as Portugal, and the populations of each of the other three countries were the same as Scotland's. An economic association on Benelux lines might have helped, but their trading interests were too diverse for them to achieve much before 1959, when Britain's EFTA initiative at last gave them the necessary impulse. Moreover, owing to the very complex wartime events involving Finland, the Soviet Union and Germany, Finland was so heavily under the influence of the Soviet Union between 1945 and 1991 that its economic and social functioning set it apart from the other Nordic countries. In 1992 Finland signed a new friendship treaty with Russia in replacement of the one-sided agreement of 1948. Having joined EFTA as an associate member in 1961 (full member in 1986), Finland had been able to make some progress towards integration with western Europe, but it was not until 1992 that she was able to apply for membership of the EEC. Finland eventually joined the EU in 1995, but its post-war economic and social history does not justify detailed treatment in this book.

Nordic Europe after 1945

Democratic values had survived the war in Nordic Europe and the Allies were happy to allow the four national governments to pursue their own paths after 1945. In the case of Finland, of course, they had no choice as Finland lost territory to the Soviet Union in 1944 and emerged from the war partially within the Soviet sphere of influence. Little damage had been suffered except in northern Norway and parts of Finland, and occupied Norway and Denmark had not been badly treated by German occupiers who felt culturally and racially at home.

The Nordic economies had generally done well out of the war, and they responded readily to pent-up post-war demand. Domestic shortages were less acute than elsewhere in Europe and exports expanded quickly, mainly in the direction of Britain and Germany. The general reopening of the German market in 1948 was a big encouragement to the Nordic economies. As German agriculture revived after 1948, however, they found it harder to export some of their primary products. Denmark, for instance, had signed a trade agreement with Britain in 1945 to open up the British market to its 'breakfast table products' (bacon, butter and eggs), but the prices paid were much lower than those paid by Germany during the war and farmers' protests culminated in a long export ban in 1947. Denmark's post-war trade agreements with Britain soon generated a huge trade deficit as British goods flooded onto the Danish market (Johansen, 1987, 92–3). From 1948, similar problems began to affect all the Nordic countries as they agreed to reduce their barriers to OEEC imports under the Marshall plan negotiations. From the later 1940s, therefore, the Nordic countries began to look to industrialisation as the way forward, acknowledging the example of Sweden since the 1920s, and taking full advantage of Marshall aid.

As the only Nordic country with significant industrial features before the war, Sweden had been badly affected by the slump and, at the general election of 1932, had elected a socialist government in the shape of the Social Democratic Labour Party (SAP). The SAP would remain in power (with brief breaks in 1936 and 1976–82) until 1991. This socialist continuity was unique in western Europe (though there were some parallels in the other Nordic countries). It was linked to the powerful trade unions which had grown up during Sweden's rapid industrialisation in the 1920s and her strong recovery from the slump in the 1930s. The trade unions remained powerful after 1945, pressing for high wages and a high standard of welfare while keeping the socialist government in power.

The British welfare plans were much admired in Sweden during and after the war, and the rudimentary institutions set up in the 1930s were greatly extended after 1945. The other Nordic countries were also won over to social democracy at this time and their interest in promoting post-war economic development was linked to the concept of a humane industrial society backed by generous welfare and educational provision (Graham, 1990, 157). Their common perception of human needs and values reinforced their national approaches to welfare, which by 1950 was widely perceived as a 'Scandinavian system' which surpassed even the British Welfare State. In Germany, Erhard rejected it as requiring too heavy a taxation of the creators of wealth (Braun, 1990, 178). It did not, however, prevent the achievement of a very high rate of economic growth in the late 1940s and 1950s as the Nordic countries progressed towards industrialisation and the more efficient trading of primary products.

Sweden was the most vulnerable to the effects of the industrial revival of Germany. A sharp depression in 1952–53, exacerbated by the Korean War, rooted out many firms which had flourished under conditions of protection in the 1930s and during the war (Dyker, 1992, 160). However, an investment boom in the later 1950s reequipped many industries and introduced new ones, using foreign technology for the most part. The trade unions, negotiating nationally, were able to secure significant wage increases, but these were outweighed by the big increases in productivity (Postan, 1967, 37). A sharp increase in demand for technically qualified personnel boosted wages and salaries and prompted the State to invest in educational improvements. House construction boomed in the public and private sectors. The continuing understanding between the trade unions and the socialist government on full employment and welfare policy prevented a surge of wage inflation. Immigration increased, notably from Finland.

FIGURE 3.1 *Per capita real GDP growth in the Nordic countries, 1913–87.*

	1913–50	1950–73	1973–87
Denmark	1.5	3.1	1.7
Finland	1.9	4.3	2.4
Norway	2.1	3.2	3.6
Sweden	2.1	3.3	1.6

Source: data drawn from Maddison, 1989, 35.

The Swedish growth rate, which averaged 3.3 per cent per annum between 1950 and 1973, was low in European terms but it was achieved in conditions of great stability while maintaining some of the highest living standards in western Europe. A shortage of labour was apparent immediately after the war but high wages attracted a good supply of immigrants. Between 1945 and 1965, net immigration averaged about 10,000 per annum. Employers applied the most advanced technologies and developed factory welfare on sensitive and generous lines in order to retain and make the best use of their workers. Real wages in Sweden rose by 87 per cent between 1946 and 1961, but employers were able to keep their production costs under control (Mathias and Postan, 1978, 621). Swedish exports were expensive but their high quality and advanced technology gave them an advantage, rather like many German exports. By 1973, Swedish GDP per capita was the highest in western Europe after Switzerland, and this meant that Swedish living standards were also among the highest in Europe.

The other Nordic countries successfully diversified out of primary production. Denmark, whose dependence on agricultural exports had distorted its economic policy between the wars, reduced these products to about one-quarter of its total exports by 1970. However, industrialisation was not an easy option as Denmark's virtual lack of raw materials and power sources implied heavy imports of coal, oil, and other producer goods. In the 1950s efforts to contain the balance of payments deficit produced 'stop-go' economic policies, a low rate of economic growth and high unemployment (up to 10 per cent) in Denmark (Johansen, 1987, 104–9). Only in the 1960s, when dollar convertibility made it easier to finance temporary deficits by foreign borrowing, did a switch occur to heavy capital investment and productivity increases which helped export earnings to offset the import bill (Cipolla, 1976 [2], 405). Engineering, electricals and shipbuilding were the outstanding export successes. However, as elsewhere in the Nordic countries, the trade unions were willing to cooperate in this transition.

Norway, with a small population in relation to its rich natural resources, was able to invest heavily in industrialisation on the strength of its existing involvement in commodity exports and shipping, without undermining its high living standards. *Wehrmacht* industrial enterprises, such as aluminium manufacture, were taken over in 1945, and some formed the basis of nationalisation initiatives after the war. The Labour government, looking forward to the development of a socialistic society, sought to direct the economy on the basis of cooperation between the main productive interests. An Economic Coordination Council, functioning between 1945 and 1950, associated State, employer and labour interests, and branch councils for each industry were set up from 1947. Firms were encouraged to set up production committees from 1945. Production was directed by government quotas, subsidies, and price controls (Hodne, 1983, 142). The urgent need to replace wartime destruction prompted the initial high rate of investment and it was maintained without great difficulty thereafter, with the help of heavy borrowing abroad. Beginning in 1949, the Labour Party drew back from its socialistic ambitions and by the early 1950s Norway was developing as a mixed economy following Keynesian principles (Hodne, 1983, 144–6). Very high levels of investment were achieved from as early as 1946 and the stock of real capital in Norway more than doubled between 1945 and 1960, the highest rate of increase among the Nordic countries (Mathias and Postan, 1978, 622).

Like Denmark, Norway ran a big balance-of-payments deficit in the early years after the war and it became an enthusiastic participant in the Marshall plan after initial hesitations deriving from neutrality concerns and the fear that the country would be diverted from the path of socialism. The strategy submitted to the

OEEC in 1948 stressed the development of dollar-earning industries, notably electro-metals, shipping, and shipbuilding (Hodne, 1983, 159). Norway received about $400 million under the Marshall scheme, and began to dismantle its tariffs under OEEC guidance in 1949. Price controls were gradually reduced between 1950 and 1953, when a Price Law provided a long-term basis for intervention.

The centralised wage bargaining developed in the Nordic countries, including Norway, by Socialist governments in the context of generous welfare arrangements was much admired abroad, especially in countries prone to inflation. Beginning in the mid-1950s, British governments sought to follow the Nordic example, but the unions valued the wages and conditions of their own workers above all and they did little to resist the onset of serious inflation in the 1960s. Meanwhile, the Nordic unions had gone on to take part in national discussions on the character and status of different employments, including the relationship between skilled and unskilled, the effects of the growth of the service sector, and women's employment. The environment both in and outside work, and security of employment, were also discussed. These concerns seemed to be a product of high living standards, education, and stable Socialist government. Trade union cooperation went hand in hand with a high rate of growth in productivity. In Sweden, for instance, technological inputs accounted for nearly 60 per cent of the increase in production by the 1960s (Mathias and Postan, 1978, 623). Combined with a high rate of investment, advanced technology offset the Nordic labour shortage while permitting good pay and conditions.

Finland faced big difficulties after the war because it had sided with Germany against the Soviet Union. It had to cede territory to the USSR in 1944, and 450,000 refugees from eastern Finland had to be resettled. The Russians exacted heavy reparations, including machinery and ships. They also negotiated long-term trade agreements with the Finns which required the latter to produce capital goods. The import of machinery to produce them led to a big payments deficit and the Finnish mark was devalued three times in 1945, twice in 1949, and once in 1956. However, Finland, like Norway, adapted to a high rate of investment, and retained a generous supply of labour despite a high rate of emigration, chiefly to Sweden. The government strictly regulated foreign trade throughout the 1950s to prevent excessive imports. Government agricultural policy was conservative, designed to keep people on the land. Forestry remained a key industry but manufacturing expanded, notably in metals and engineering. Hydro-electric power was greatly expanded. Rigid export contracts with the Soviet Union nevertheless prevented a general review of economic policy and no reconstruction of the Finnish economy had taken place by 1960 (Tipton and Aldrich, 1987, 61–2).

By 1960, more than half the population of Sweden was living in towns, and nearly as many did so in Denmark. In Finland the figure was 40 per cent, while Norway's low level of urbanisation (one-third) was partly due to the location of some industries in rural areas using the country's abundant hydro-electricity.

The Nordic countries reduced their mutual tariff barriers after the war. Following Denmark's lead, they looked to Britain as their main industrial trading partner. The Nordic Council was set up in 1952. It was concerned mainly with the movement of people and goods between the member countries. The Common Nordic Labour Market was set up in 1954, though the complete removal of restrictions on the free movement of labour was not achieved until the late 1960s. The idea of a Nordic customs union was discussed in the late 1940s and the early 1950s but the likely dominance of Danish agriculture, and political interests in each of the countries, prevented an agreement (Johansen, 1987, 127–8). The Nordic countries' interest in joining the ECSC was consequently slight and the creation of the EEC in 1957 merely encouraged them to join Britain's free trade association, EFTA, founded in 1959. The Nordic countries, with Britain, formed the strongest component of EFTA, though the high volume of trade between them, and their low mutual tariffs, were much more a reflection of established arrangements than of EFTA reforms. The distribution of Nordic trade nevertheless swung strongly towards EFTA in the 1960s, at the expense of trade with the EEC (Cipolla, 1976 [2], 407).

In the 1960s the Nordic countries were a noted example of economic progress in conditions of tranquillity and stability. Their lack of obvious problems, very high living standards, and generous welfare structures combined with trade union cooperation, made them the envy of western Europe. Not all Europe's fringe countries had the same experience, however.

Southern Europe at the end of the war

Europe's southern fringe was made up of three economically backward countries – Spain, Portugal and Greece – and a country which combined advanced and backward regions, Italy. A shortage of natural resources plus their remote location in relation to the heartlands of European industrialisation had left them with substantially unmodernised economies and societies in 1914. The inter-war years had pushed the politics of Italy, Portugal and Spain well to the Right but authoritarian government had done more to retard their economic development than to promote it, except possibly in the case of Italy. The Roman Catholic Church was a strong conservative influence, especially in rural areas, and the authoritarian regimes had drawn on its support. Greece had additional problems. It had to absorb 1.4 million refugees in 1923 after a devastating defeat by Turkey. The immigrants brought capital and enterprise with them but the lack of productive opportunities in Greece led many of them to invest in the building of modern apartment blocks in Athens (Marmaras, 1989, 45–50). The serious political dissensions between royalists and republicans, which had grown up before 1914, grew much worse in the 1920s and 1930s. This political climate was highly discouraging to economic growth. The only consolation was that the Greek Orthodox Church, more secular in outlook than the Roman Catholic Church to the west, did not ally with conservative political forces to the same extent.

The Second World War offered nothing but a further depression of the status of the southern fringe. Franco's Spain declined to take part in the war on the Axis side and was spared direct invasion. Greece was invaded by two Axis powers, first Italy and then Germany. Italy's incompetent Greek campaign ruled her out of further consideration as an important Axis power and from 1943 she became a mere battleground, fought over by the Allies and the retreating Germans. Such development in her infra-structure and strategic industries as Mussolini had been able to bring about – and there was not much of either – was effaced by the massive destruction which Italians were powerless to prevent.

For the Allies, liberated southern Europe presented a much greater danger of Right-wing extremism than did the north. Its retarded condition did not allow it to be offered an economic revival of any significance and the dual dangers of Communist or neo-Fascist insurgency could not be discounted. In Greece, the Communist resistance set out in 1944 to take over power by direct means, much as some of the Communist members of the French resistance had hoped to do in 1944. The result was a civil war lasting from 1945 to 1949, in which the Communists were defeated by the government and the non-Communist resistance groups, helped by the USA.

Greece

Towards the end of the war, it was agreed among the Allies that the potentially volatile Mediterranean theatre should receive special attention. The USA took responsibility for Italy, and Britain agreed to ensure order in Greece. Britain regretted this undertaking as soon as it became fully aware of the gravity of its post-war economic problems. By 1947 it had withdrawn from the task and had formally told the USA that it could no longer sustain a role in Greece. The USA was embarrassed, having enough on its plate elsewhere, but the Communist threat was more serious in Greece than anywhere else in western Europe. The Greek Resistance, largely Communist in allegiance, was in close touch with the Communist partisans in Yugoslavia. Yugoslavia lay within the Soviet sphere of influence. Although Marshal Tito's Communist republic of 1945 eschewed an expansionist external policy, disorder in Greece could well have led to an intervention.

In these circumstances, American involvement in Greece had to be rather more robust than elsewhere in Europe. In 1947 the Truman Doctrine, a statement of American objectives in Europe in the new context of the Cold War, proclaimed that Greece would be kept as a 'free' nation with US support, and this undertaking implied financial aid once the civil war was over. However, the serious damage and dislocation during the war, followed by the civil war, had set the country back and an early economic revival was out of the question. Greece qualified for Marshall aid but the European Recovery Programme did not try to foster industrialisation in Greece. Instead, it tried to encourage the primary sector in order to make Greece an exporter of primary products (Kofas, 1989, 121). This was an indication of how backward the Greek economy was, and how limited the country's resources were. Nevertheless, the Greek government was sufficiently encouraged by Marshall aid to draw up a number of long-term plans from

1948. These, together with the new currency of 1944 and subsequent stabilisation measures, provided a credible basis for the country's development after the civil war (Freris, 1986, 121–30). They also included industrialisation objectives. Unfortunately, the persistent civil war, the Korean war, and the early end of the Marshall scheme, forced Greece to withdraw its plan of 1948–53 from the OEEC and by the early 1950s it was clear that the modernisation programme would depend entirely on American finance.

The Greek devaluation of the drachma by 50 per cent in 1953 was a symptom of continuing economic weakness. The economy did not respond to the opportunities offered by the devaluation (Freris, 1986, 143). The now firmly established conservative government of Greece announced a long-term programme of State investment in 1953, with the USA supplying one-fifth of the funds. Domestic prices were frozen, and restrictions on imports were ended. The aim was to absorb unemployment and to increase the standard of living in rural areas, while eradicating the foreign payments deficit. The plan was a failure, however, as the necessary investment funds could not be raised. The share of manufacturing in Greek GNP was the same in 1967 as it had been in 1950. Industrial employment made up an astoundingly low 17.4 per cent of the total workforce in 1960. This figure was by far the lowest in western Europe, and was not much higher than Turkey's 10.7 per cent (OECD, *Hist.Stat.*, 1991, 40). The urban population nearly doubled between 1940 and 1971, but this seems to have been due more to the growth of the service workforce than to the smaller increase in the manufacturing workforce (Kofas, 1989, 170–1). This suggests that a series of government initiatives to encourage industrial growth since 1953 had had little effect. Some compensation was offered by a government programme to develop agriculture and communications, which was launched in 1955, but in an era of 'economic miracles', Greece and its stretcher were very much at the back of the multitude.

Italy

British reticence also allowed Italy to fall entirely under American influence. No attempt was made to divide it into a number of occupation zones and the Americans were able to pursue nationwide policies from the start, in contrast to the initially confusing situation in Germany. Although the USA was not always able to secure what it wanted in terms of economic policy, its direct political involvement was of great importance in securing stability in the crucial post-war years.

Italy's very low rate of economic growth – a mere 0.73 per cent per annum between 1913 and 1950 – has been attributed by Rossi and Toniolo mainly to the Fascist regime which moulded Italy between 1923 and 1943. To meet the special problems of the 1930s, the Government developed a neo-mercantilist strategy which further restrained growth (Rossi and Toniolo, 1992, 552).

Roosevelt gave out the broad lines of his Italian reconstruction policy in a 'fireside chat' in July 1943, no doubt aware that many Italian Americans were among his audience. His programme took the form of democracy combined with interim economic aid. A mainly rural country, with nearly half the labour force working in agriculture, Italy did not present the same food supply problem as Germany, and the industrial capacity of the northern cities had not been greatly reduced by the hostilities. The main problem in Italy was the transport network, which had been ruined during the slow Allied advance up the peninsula, but emergency repairs and reroutings soon provided a basic service in 1945.

Both Fascist and Communist insurgency were seen as serious dangers and the slow recovery of the Italian export industries, of which cotton textiles was the most important, prompted the USA to meet the Italian dollar shortage. It thus maintained the conditions of the masses and allowed them to become involved in the activities of the political parties, offering inducements for the adoption of moderate policies and, in some cases, for the neutralising or expulsion of extremists. American plans for economic revival were very limited and US aid did little more than keep the economy afloat (Miller, 1986, 154).

These measures secured political stability but a clear path towards economic development was hard to discern, in contrast to the position in most of northern Europe. Even emigration, Italy's traditional response to rural poverty, seemed unlikely to begin again in the near future (Harper, 1986, 9). Inflation was rapid, especially in the South where Allied forces had been spending freely since 1943.

The USA was worried by the prospect of a continuing political role and the provision of aid without the assurance of growth. It was also worried by Italian industry's traditional failure to foster a mass market, which had produced high costs and a low scale of production reinforced by protection in the 1930s and during the war. Further constraints were high interest rates and a national obsession with frugality which limited the market for consumer goods (Ellwood, 1993, 84).

Italy needed dollars above all, but the most likely export industry, cotton textiles, with all its pre-war capacity available, had great difficulty in competing against other reviving European textile industries. Without dollars, coal, raw cotton, and other raw materials were hard to secure. The only answer to this vicious circle was to look to the USA, and to tolerate the continuation of State intervention in industry which the Fascists had built up (Harper, 1986, 1, 8–9).

The broadly based, moderate coalition governments which ruled Italy in the early years after the war were, however, conducive to a strategy of economic development, following American advice. By 1947 an understanding had been reached, with the USA holding out the prospect of a dollar-backed material well-being (Harper, 1986, vii). There were certain political parallels here with France, the most striking being the expulsion of the Communists and Socialists from Alcide De Gasperi's long-running coalition in May 1947. The USA wanted to use Italy to support its new presence in the Mediterranean, made necessary by the Cold War and by the partial withdrawal of Britain. For this it needed a conservative government in Italy, but this in turn required economic success there. All the American departments were agreed on this by 1948, so US aid could now flow more freely (Harper, 1986, 159–60).

Between 1945 and 1948 decisions were made to move towards a trading economy, with industry producing high-quality goods for export to the rest of Europe and the United States. The Italian public sensed a new wind of change in all this and exciting ideas and energetic people seemed to abound. Even the Communists were generally in favour, believing that they had Soviet backing for their objective, the creation of an Italian road to socialism (Graham, 1990, 105). This move from autarky to exchange would take advantage of the new world trading system planned by the United States. State controls over the economy would be reduced, allowing market forces to generate specialisation. Even the problems of the South seemed amenable to treatment within this strategy. However, the announcement of Marshall aid in 1947 provoked strong opposition from the Communists and the Socialists. The former claimed that Italy would fall under US domination, and the latter that Italy's neutrality would be compromised. Nevertheless, the elections of April 1948, which were fought mainly over the Marshall plan issue, produced a Christian Democrat landslide and the government pressed on delightedly with its negotiations (Willis, 1971, 20).

Admittedly, the election of a Christian Democrat government in 1948 was seen by many as restraining Italy's new dynamism. De Gasperi proved slow in pursuing reforms favoured by the USA. Southern land reform, for instance, was not started until the early 1950s, and was in such trouble by 1953 that it nearly brought the government down (Harper, 1986, 164). However, there was no going back and Italy had been set firmly on the path of modernity (Harper, 1986, 3–4). Government from the centre persisted until the early 1960s, and even then the move to the centre-left did not challenge the post-war economic consensus.

Marshall aid had mixed results in Italy. The Marshall plan mission to Italy wanted to modernise the country's industrial plant and to begin rural land redistribution, as well as securing full employment. The ECA, for its part, wanted to encourage industry to make goods for domestic consumption, rather than for export. This meant that aid would be channelled into firms capable of expanding their employment quickly, to boost home demand and to move towards full employment. However, the Italian government, using a development plan prepared in 1947–48 by the Institute for Industrial Reconstruction (IRI), a creation of the Mussolini era, wanted to resolve the balance of payments problem by stimulating productive investment and increasing exports. In these circumstances, no clear strategy was defined for the use of the counterpart funds, though a large tranche went to help fund the Cassa per il Mezzogiorno, the main source of public funds for southern land reform. In addition, a number of IRI-owned industries, and the expanding steel industry, were major recipients (Willis, 1971, 24). Overall, the home market for durables and consumer goods was encouraged.

The Marshall plan years nevertheless inaugurated a long period of growth in the Italian economy. Indeed, Vera Zamagni identifies 'an uninterrupted boom' in Italy from 1948 to 1963, with an average annual rate of growth in GDP of at least 5.9 per cent, and in manufacturing of at least 9.1 per cent. GDP inputs are hard to measure or even estimate because of the country's notorious 'black economy', but Zamagni is confident that private consumption per capita doubled over the fifteen years, whereas over the previous eighty-seven years it had increased by only one-third (Di Nolfo, 1992, 197–8). Variously responsible for the boom were the shift of labour from agriculture into manufacturing, the decline of unemployment and underemployment, Marshall aid, and orthodox monetary policies including the stabilisation of the lira and increased hard currency reserves (Harper, 1986, 164–5). Home consumption played a big part, with the 'demonstration effect' of American lifestyles persuading Italians to buy home-produced 'catch-up' products. All this was partly sustained by another 'demonstration effect', hire-purchase. In 1954 the Ministry of Industry and Commerce estimated that hire-purchase credit made up 5 per cent of total private sales of consumer goods, and 3.5 per cent of GNP (Di Nolfo, 1992, 204–5).

The growth of home consumption did not hinder a big increase in Italian exports. Agricultural exports quickly dwindled to a tiny proportion, and the long-run growth in Italian steel production fostered the development of motors, electricals, and various types of mechanical engineering. Industrial exports went largely to other European countries – 68.4 per cent of total Italian exports went elsewhere in Europe by 1963. Italy was the classic example of a country providing cheap manufactured goods for Germany and other industrial countries in northern Europe. Engineering firms took full advantage of American expertise during the Marshall plan period. Prohibitive tariffs were retained well into the 1950s on certain key products such as cars, and in a sense Italy had the best of both worlds. Nevertheless, this cannot detract from the extraordinary rise of Italian manufacturing from the later 1940s. Given that the industrial base after the war was very weak, the Italian achievement deserves to be ranked alongside that of Germany. In that achievement, the role of a small number of very large, forward-looking firms such as Fiat was very important.

By the end of the plan period in 1952/53, most of the IRI targets had been achieved or surpassed. The 'Sinigaglia plan' for the steel industry, which was partly based on Fascist projects of the 1930s, caused a number of doubts, partly because it involved a big role for nationalised enterprises and looked likely to flood foreign markets with cheap steel. American approval was secured in part by Fiat's agreement to buy a large proportion of the steel produced by Finsider's impressive new plant at Cornigliano. Finsider, a government organisation set up in 1937 to control the steel companies, and the Cornigliano project itself, were both survivals of the Fascist era (Zamagni, 1993, 301, 329). However, the

resulting heavy investment in steel, mainly using scrap in small
electric furnaces (mini-mills), had made Italy a major exporter by
the early 1950s, and had allowed it to negotiate membership of
the ECSC despite its distinct lack of a tradition in steel production.
Similar reorganisation and expansion took place in engineering,
power, and oil-refining.

By 1949 the USA was very concerned about the persistently high
rate of unemployment in Italy and, with some success, put
pressure on the Italians to distribute Marshall funds more widely.
IRI and the Italian government partially conceded this point, and
financed more regional development and replacement of factory
equipment using American technology (Zamagni, 1993, 332–3).

Zamagni concludes that the Marshall plan incorporated Italy
into the integration of Europe which America desired. Her
governments knew that for the time being her economy was too
weak to compete on equal terms with the big industrial countries,
but they were confident that the weaknesses could be overcome
(Zamagni, 1993, 332–3). By the later 1950s their confidence would
be clearly justified.

Italian economic success obscured the US failure to transform
Italy, as it had so much wanted to do. Harper, for instance,
concludes that in the end the USA failed to alter the nature of
Italian politics, and failed to secure the adoption of US-inspired
economic and social schemes (Harper, 1986, 166). This result
contrasted with the extensive Americanisation of western Germany.
Some of the implications of this failure would emerge in the
violent Italian politics of the 1970s.

Inflation was attacked by a stabilisation of the lira in 1947–48
and the resulting deflationary policy weakened the post-1945
power of the trade unions and permitted the initiation of a low
wages policy in the later 1940s. The State Department played its
part, attacking the Communist trade unions from May 1948 in
response to a perceived slow take-up of Marshall aid in Italy
(Miller, 1986, 255–63). The big labour reserve in the South also
helped to keep wages down. This restraint on labour costs helped
promote the export strategy, while deflation favoured the larger
firms relative to the smaller ones. Italy eventually joined in the
gradual post-war dismantling of tariff barriers, and investment by
the successful, larger firms led to the spread of new working
methods.

This revival was confirmed by Italy's acceptance as a member of
NATO in 1949 and by her participation in the European Coal and

Steel Community, which began operations in 1952. NATO membership was the final step in the stabilisation of Italy under US influence (Miller, 1986, x–xi). In the ECSC, Italy got the best of both worlds – full participation in an association of the most powerful industrial countries on the European continent, and a recognition of its still developing condition. Italy secured a preferential supply of iron ore, subsidised coal imports, and tariffs and quotas designed to protect its growing but vulnerable steel industry.

Despite the early difficulties in the application of Marshall aid, Italian industrialisation was well and truly launched by the early 1950s. By the end of the decade a massive shift of labour away from agriculture had occurred. The number employed in agriculture fell from 8.3 million in 1951 to 5.6 million in 1961. This was a sharper fall than in either Germany or France over the same period (Tipton and Aldrich, 1987, 114). Meanwhile, manufacturing employment rose from 6.3 millions to 7.9 millions.

By the mid-1950s, with Italy playing a full part in the preparation of the EEC, one of the most striking economic transformations in the early history of post-war Europe was well under way. A big accolade came in 1955, when Italy was admitted to the United Nations, and both Churchill and John Foster Dulles hailed Italy as 'a great power' (Di Nolfo, 1992, 101). The Italian example suggested that industrialisation could at last spread to southern Europe, and the other Mediterranean countries started to take note. Italy, however, had special strengths, some of which dated far back into its history, as Zamagni has shown (Zamagni, 1993). It had a tradition of craft manufactures, often based on the extended family, and capable of achieving very high quality. Italy's success in leisure, precision engineering, and tools was the product of the human capital generated over many years. The government's pragmatic approach to the economy was based on a tradition dating back to the later nineteenth century. Its holding companies and its control over banking encouraged cartels and inefficiency, but it ensured an adequate supply of capital to large companies and allowed them to build up a strong position in the home market before venturing abroad. The emergence of Italian multinationals like Fiat, Olivetti and Pirelli was a product of this policy.

Spain

Spain's successfully maintained neutrality throughout the war left her outside immediate Allied concerns in southern Europe. This meant that there was no external challenge to the country's chronic backwardness which the Franco regime and its Roman Catholic allies were willing to defend as a means of reinforcing their political power. This attitude had also spread into neighbouring Portugal since the 1930s, and the resulting Iberian bloc seemed both impervious to American modernising aid, and subject to a remote threat of Communist revolution.

The civil war and other disruptions of the 1930s had set Spain's economy back so far that output in 1950 was 10 per cent below the level of 1930 (Boltho, 1982, 554). The corporatist trade union system set up in 1939, and the Mussolini-inspired National Institute for Industry (INI), founded in 1941, which controlled State enterprises, were outright Fascist institutions designed to promote autarky and control labour on Italian lines. INI promoted important developments in coal and electric power, and set up the national airline, Iberia, in 1943 (Payne, 1987, 385–6). After 1945 this Fascist structure was completely out of touch with developing trade-related policies elsewhere in western Europe. At home, agriculture stagnated at production levels far below pre-1936 norms. Franco's anti-democratic principles excluded Spain from US aid and ruled out any integration with more advanced European countries.

The American attitude to Spain was altered by the onset of the Cold War in 1947–48. Franco's grimly anti-Communist stance was valued by the USA, which welcomed the prospect of military bases in Spain. Spain was not invited to join the Marshall plan but in 1953 Spain signed a mutual defence agreement with the USA and began to receive American economic aid. The UN economic boycott was lifted at this time. Growing American imports and technical support now began the process of modernisation which Marshall aid had brought to most of the rest of western Europe. From this point onwards, all of southern Europe was roughly on the same path, though national divergences would outweigh the similarities until the end of the 1970s.

Spain, however, was at the start of a very long road. Agriculture was by far the biggest employer; in Andalucia, for instance, over half the workforce was engaged in it, and the national average figure was about 50 per cent in the late 1940s. Cereals, beans and chickpeas were staple crops. Productivity was too low to allow much of this to be exported, and Spain remained a big importer of foodstuffs. The arid Spanish climate did not help but there was virtually no irrigation and fertilisation was a crude affair. In desert-like Old Castile, the cultivated soil resembled a clay tennis court by high summer. The rural labour force did not begin to decline until after 1950, when State involvement in agriculture at last became significant.

Poor transport left most of Spain divided into a number of large regions, each of which was linked to a central city which was the main location of market demand. Most manufacturing met regional needs, many of which were related to agriculture. It was minuscule in scale and virtually unmechanised. Only the ubiquitous *tapas*, seafood snacks sold in city bars, suggested a national market, served as it was by trundling trains loaded with ice packs. Professional football teams, idols of the Spanish masses as in backward Italy (but, in Spain, backed by the State as an urban opiate), travelled to their more distant fixtures in sleeping cars, often spending thirty or more hours on the journey. Trains could accumulate extraordinary delays, recalling pre-Fascist Italy. Long-distance 'rapidos' (the term had a largely literary value and merely distinguished these bigger trains from the hit-and-miss 'correo' and the local 'tren mixto') were often the only service across a region and one 'rapido' delayed by up to ten hours could paralyse communication between adjacent cities such as Seville and Cordoba. 'Try again tomorrow' was the normal advice at the station. A shunting engine dated 1883 was in rheumy operation at Cordoba in 1963. Permanent queues snaked across the ticket halls of junction stations as passengers strove to satisfy the archaic RENFE requirement that tickets be stamped at the start of each leg of a journey. People often preferred to travel on long-distance coaches, where, in theory, they could reserve a seat, but these were even slower than the trains. Climbing in through the windows was a regular feature of both train and bus travel. The Madrid metro was the hottest in Europe, and the virtual absence of escalators and lifts added to the discomfort.

External markets were virtually nil, though the industrial regions of Catalonia, the Basque country, and the Asturias had links with southern France and/or northern Italy. Imports of producer goods virtually squeezed out consumer imports, and the low value of the peseta and import controls excluded these from the mass market. Both Church and government were united in defending an educational system which stressed traditional values, and technical qualifications took a back seat. Political repression, which was aimed mainly at Communists but also drove liberal intellectuals and technicians into exile, cut the country off from change elsewhere.

Government autarky and import substitution policies, which dated back to 1939, were pursued well into the 1960s (Payne, 1987, 384). Spanish import substitution products were inefficiently produced, expensive and rarely competitive on foreign markets. The government did not make much use of the chance to promote industrial rationalisation. The much trumpeted but rarely seen Pegaso trucks ('el camion *español*'), the product of an INI initiative, and the nationalised, Fiat-linked SEAT cars, made in Barcelona since 1949 and ubiquitous in Spain in the early 1960s, were to be found nowhere in the rest of Europe. A small contract with a department store chain in France for the supply of cheap men's shirts in the mid-1960s prompted an exultant television commercial ('¡Amigos! ¡Volveo de Francia!') showing a smug Spanish businessman displaying Spanish shirts which he had bought in France (presumably at a substantial premium). Such minor successes were not enough, however, to prevent the accumulation of balance of payments deficits and high inflation from the early 1950s.

Poverty, combined with a system of political repression unique in Europe, produced a high level of permanent and seasonal migration. The growth of demand for labour in northern Europe from the early 1950s attracted the bulk of this movement, which paralleled a similar exodus from Italy. Unlike Italy, though, where domestic growth was absorbing most of the labour surplus by the later 1950s, Spain continued to produce emigrants in large numbers into the early 1960s. However, the government Stabilisation Plan of 1959, a response to the increasingly unstable conditions caused by the economic growth of the 1950s, was about to create a more modern stance.

These weaknesses did not prevent the Spanish economy growing at an official rate of around 5 per cent per annum in the 1950s, but the absence of detailed statistics makes this figure highly unreliable (Boltho, 1982, 557–8). On the other hand, Spain's chronically low productivity and underemployment allowed virtually any investment to increase output in a striking fashion. Franco's early decision to cut wages encouraged investment. Saving was easily marshalled because high personal incomes and

profits were spared heavy taxation in Spain, and the lack of altern-
atives meant that capital could be directed readily enough into
activities favoured by the State. Depressed agricultural earnings
and an inflated rural population (38.7 per cent of the labour force
still worked on the land in 1960) held industrial wages down until
the 1960s. Finally, the growth of US aid from the early 1950s eased
Spain's balance of payments problem, which would have
deteriorated in conditions of industrial growth as little of the new
output was for export. The extra output for the home market
arising from the State's import substitution policies helped ease
the serious inflationary pressures of the late 1940s and early 1950s,
though not enough to avert the crisis of 1958, by which time
inflation had risen to over 15 per cent per annum (Salmon, 1992,
36). Nor did fairly obvious potential growth exports such as citrus
fruit secure enough encouragement to achieve their full potential
as foreign currency earners.

However, by the 1960s, almost imperceptibly, a quiet breeze of
modernisation was blowing through Spain. Investment had begun
to rise in 1948. Rationing was abolished in 1952 and the huge
black market collapsed, except for tobacco and other national
monopolies. Tax inducements and other incentives for favoured
firms encouraged industrial investment from the 1950s. Autarky
was still the basis of these policies but some of the INI efforts were
beginning to show impressive results by the end of the decade
(Payne, 1987, 464–5). In 1957, important changes in the membership of the cabinet gave influence to a group of young administrators and economists associated with *Opus Dei*, the national
Catholic reformist movement (Harrison, 1985, 138–9). In 1958
Spain joined the World Bank, and in the following year, the IMF.
OEEC membership soon followed.

In 1959, the National Economic Stabilisation Plan, following the
inflationary crisis of 1958, marked the beginning of the end of
the autarky policy. With foreign markets now growing, especially in
the EEC, Spain could start to develop its exports while controlling
inflation at home. Serious efforts to attract foreign tourists to
Spain could now begin, together with investment from abroad
(Salmon, 1992, 36–7).

Signs of this change were visible on the ground in the early
1960s. A huge irrigation scheme near Badajoz, approved in 1952,
was well under way by 1961 when the author passed through the
area. Harrison is not impressed by the success of this and other
irrigation schemes, but at the time the Badajoz project looked like

efficient, impressive modernisation, in the absence, one has to say, of very much else (Harrison, 1978, 159). In 1963 the main lines running into Madrid started to use commuter railcars bought from Germany (*ferrobuses*). Foreign firms were encouraged to build large factories near major cities where, inter alia, they set up training schemes in cooperation with the Spanish government. By 1963 a big German factory outside Cordoba was a magnet for the young men of the city, paying high wages and offering advanced training and periods of work in Germany itself. Television sales increased enough to allow the 'Festival de la canzión' a gruelling four-hour parade of distinctly un-Spanish cabaret songs, held in Madrid, to become a national event. In the crowded cities, the distinctive boom of the Spanish television set, amplified by open windows, and a lack of carpets and upholstered furniture, echoed around the alleys and courts until the early hours. Only the youngest children, often carried around by their mothers in slings until well into the night, could sleep through it.

Spain even produced its first kitchen-sink film, *Los golfos* (1960), a study of Madrid rowdies directed by a native New Wave director, C. Saura. This Spanish equivalent of *Saturday Night and Sunday Morning* lacked the finesse of Italian and northern productions, but it is still acknowledged in Spain as the big turning point between Fascist posturing and sentimentality, and the portrayal of the real world which, for most Spaniards, was one of poverty, boredom and pain. It also showed some of the crude housing which emerged from the 1960s in Madrid, Barcelona and other cities as migration from the countryside accelerated. By 1973, an estimated 128,000 people lived in this 'illegal' housing in Madrid.

We now know that the Spanish economy was on the way to modernisation by 1960. A high growth rate in the 1950s, combined with increased investment in industry, was beginning to generate competitive manufactures and more efficient production structures. To the average Spaniard, however – and especially if he worked on the land – no improvement would have been visible, especially in the context of poor sanitation, restricted diet (e.g. chickpea soup daily), and mediocre consumer goods.

Portugal

Portugal was one of the more fertile parts of the Iberian peninsula. It enjoyed a copious rainfall from the Atlantic and the big rivers from Castile swelled as they crossed Portugal. On the other hand, the country was very mountainous and the deep, narrow river valleys left little space for cultivation. There were no natural resources of any significance and, in the absence of significant industrial development, an overpopulated countryside hampered the growth of industrial productivity. The population was very small in consequence – 8 million people in 1945, though the density of population was nearly twice Spain's.

As one of the most backward countries in Europe, Portugal offered a very low living standard to its people. Its biggest asset was its colonial empire, accumulated since the fifteenth century, and located mainly in Africa. It was an important source of raw materials, and a market for Portugal's inefficiently produced and over-priced manufactured goods, notably textiles. It generated some emigration, and was used as a propaganda tool by the government, diverting attention from problems at home. However, Portugal's tight grip on its empire, combined with its Fascist regime, undermined its international standing and discouraged American aid, except for NATO military ends.

The anti-Communist stance of the Salazar dictatorship in Portugal, which had been set up in 1932 and which had much in common with Franco's Spain, helped secure it US and NATO support from around 1950. A radical liberalisation programme announced by Salazar in 1945 also helped him secure support (Payne, 1973, 671). Unlike Spain, Portugal was allowed to join the Marshall plan in 1947 and NATO in 1949, partly because its naval facilities and its efficient navy made it a useful participant. There was no question of Portugal giving up its colonies, but this could not be a big issue while France clung to its much greater foreign territories.

Economically, Portugal's prospects were gloomier than Spain's and it attracted less foreign investment, partly because of its political regime. There was some US military aid but a regime that was even more Fascist than Spain's could not expect much civil aid. Growing demand for labour from northern Europe from the early 1950s generated a big movement of emigration from rural areas. As late as 1960, however, agriculture employed 43.9 per cent of the national workforce, more than any other country in western Europe except Greece (57.1 per cent) (OECD, *Hist.Stat.*, 1991, 40). Much of it was subsistence agriculture but where there was estate agriculture, as in the south, the owners generally lived in the cities and employed managers. With the price of wheat kept up by government regulation, there was little incentive to adopt advanced methods. Cheap wine was a serious export, but its quality varied greatly from year to year (Piquet Marchal, 1985, 360–1). At 31.3 per cent, industrial employment was high in 1960 (the comparable figure in Spain being 30.3 per cent), but this partly reflected the flood of population into the cities from the overpopulated countryside. Much Portuguese manufacturing was artisanal, and the mechanised industries, such as cotton and wool textiles, relied on a cheap labour force regulated by the government. Value added in manufacturing as a proportion of Portuguese GDP was only 27.9 per cent in 1960, which again put the country on a par with Spain (26.7 per cent). Private final consumption expenditure in Portugal totalled 73.1 per cent, more than any other western European country except Greece and Ireland, indicating limited State expenditure and low investment (OECD, *Hist.Stat.*, 1991, *passim*). As elsewhere in southern Europe, the remittances sent back by workers to their families in Portugal were a big asset because they were in foreign currency, and Portugal's balance of payments surplus was an important advantage to the government. There were signs of accelerating growth by 1960 but Portugal remained one of the most backward countries in Europe on every count.

Summary

Apart from northern Italy, the southern fringe remained the most backward region of western Europe in 1960. On the other hand, a degree of change had been achieved almost everywhere since 1945. The biggest export of most of the South was still labour, but most of the emigrant workers returned after a while. Their 'secret expertise', learned in Germany or France, probably did more to modernise the South than any other single factor of change. In the early 1960s they stood out clearly in the southern cities, multi-lingual, mentally and physically sharp, on the qui-vive, much admired, and often a great success with the ladies. Those who had worked in Germany had the highest prestige. Historians still have to assess the exact influence of these people. Through them, however, the North penetrated the South. Change was still limited, but it had begun.

CHAPTER FOUR

Towards the European Union,
1945–1995

Anyone who has lived in western Europe since the last war will have passed through a series of changing perceptions of the European Union. British people especially will remember a time in the mid-1950s when the idea of the European Economic Community (or the Common Market, as it was then known) was a cranky affair promoted by curious foreigners. The 1960s are seen as a time when rather tougher foreigners seemed to be keeping Britain out of the Community for no good reason. Only since the approach to the Single Market in 1992 has the Englishman begun to feel the daily impact of the Community (or, 'Europe', as it is now known in popular parlance) on his life.

In some other parts of western Europe, such as Luxembourg or Belgium, memories of the early days will be more precise and positive. The Community will be remembered as something creative, which grew out of developments going back to the war, and which would prevent another war in Europe. Some of its creators will be remembered as compatriots, and honoured ones at that. In parts of Nordic Europe, on the other hand, the Community is seen by many even now as a confusing and even threatening force, likely to disturb traditional institutions and values. As for the man on the Paris RER, he will believe at one and the same time that his countrymen created the European Union, and that they struggled manfully against an institution which threatened the national identity of France.

This chapter will take the reader from the early 1940s when exiles discussed a variety of forms of cooperation in London, and the national Resistance movements began to confer on the structure of post-war Europe, to the great milestone of the Treaty of Rome in 1957, through to the creation of the Single Market in

97

Figure 4.1 *The expanding boundaries of the EEC*

Date of entry into EEC

1957 (founding members)

1973

1981

1986

In 1990 the former German
Democratic Republic was
incorporated as result of German
unification (3 October)

1995

EST. = ESTONIA

LAT. = LATVIA

LITH. = LITHUANIA

FINLAND

Helsinki

kholm

EST.

LAT.

LITH.

BELARUS

COMMONWEALTH
OF
INDEPENDENT STATES
(CIS)

KAZAKHSTAN

AND

UKRAINE

AKIA)

RY

MOLDOVA

RUMANIA

BIA
AVIA)

NEGRO

BULGARIA

MACEDONIA

GEORGIA

AZERBAIJAN

ARMENIA

TURKEY

NIA

EECE

Athens

TURKEY

1992, and up to the point where, in 1995, the European Union stood on the threshold of creating a single European currency. This continuity reflects the political dimension of European integration, with founders and enthusiasts pressing on year after year towards discerned goals, and institutional processes moving onwards under their own momentum. And if political aspects are emphasised in this account, it is because economic objectives alone could never have justified the complex and ambitious European structures which had been created by 1995.

The origins of an integrated Europe

Several forms of integration were discussed in western Europe in the later years of the war. One consideration above all, however, was always likely to be decisive. Since industrialisation spread across the continent in the nineteenth century, western European countries have tended to trade a higher proportion of their output than those of any comparable continental region. The main reasons for this are, firstly, that there are many such countries and some are very small, and, secondly, that western Europe has a limited supply of raw materials (Dyker, 1992 [2], 1). In western Europe, trade and economic development go hand in hand.

From the Middle Ages onwards, the authorities of Europe had seen trade as an important source of revenue. Exchange between countries was ideal for this purpose as duties and tolls could be levied easily on foreign merchants, and at frontiers. From the seventeenth century, following the experience of France, some of the larger countries adopted a more or less coherent programme of national development based on encouraging domestic output, and charging duties on competing imports. This strategy has come to be known as Mercantilism. Jean-Baptiste Colbert, chief financial minister of Louis XIV from 1661, was the architect of an ambitious programme which both increased revenue, and protected or encouraged certain French industries. Emulated elsewhere in Europe, it associated economic progress with Absolutism. While results in the favoured industries, and in transport facilities, were often spectacular, it hampered competition and innovation diffusion.

France's huge area and population helped make it the most powerful European nation in the seventeenth and eighteenth centuries. However, two smaller countries to the north never plunged into Mercantilism as France did. The United Provinces (the Netherlands) were never ruled on Absolutist lines, and were heavily dependent on foreign trade. Their near neighbour, England, was much influenced by the Netherlands in the seventeenth and early eighteenth centuries, and also developed a largely free, trading economy under a constitutional monarchy. In the eighteenth century, productivity growth in all sectors of the economy made Britain the richest country in Europe in per capita terms, with industrialisation beginning there in the 1760s.

In 1776 a Scottish philosopher, Adam Smith, published a treatise, *The Wealth of Nations,* which explained how national wealth could be maximised by the removal of most, or all, forms of State control or intervention in the economy. This included duties, or tariffs, charged on all forms of foreign trade, and various constraints such as the limitation of exports of raw materials and the control of the movements of skilled workers. Smith's views were much admired. Duties continued to be levied in Britain, though on a random basis and without the coherent Mercantilist objectives which still prevailed in France.

Meanwhile, the Age of the Enlightenment in the eighteenth century saw a number of proposals for the political unity of Europe, including plans for a continental parliament by the Abbé de Saint-Pierre and Jeremy Bentham (Lee, 1982, 293). These were theoretical proposals but they reflected the greater movement of individuals across Europe and the spread of political ideas based on individual rights and democracy.

The rapid growth of British trade and output from the later eighteenth century greatly reduced the significance of tariffs there, but other countries used them more vigorously. Among other things, they saw them as a means of protecting their manufactures against the cheap, high-quality competition spawned by British industrialisation. The significance of this differential was emphasised by the British economist and liberal politician, Richard Cobden (1804–65). He sat in the reformed House of Commons after 1841, where he was a constant advocate of free trade. His ideas had their first success in 1846 when parliament removed the duties charged on foreign corn imports. He went on to secure free trade agreements with other countries, beginning with France in 1863 (the Cobden-Chevalier treaty).

By the 1870s, much of Europe, the British Empire, and the United States, were engaged in a widening system of free trade or reduced tariffs based on the 'most favoured nation' principle, whereby a bilateral agreement was normally extended to the other countries with which earlier agreements had been reached. Some developing countries, such as the USA and Germany, used tariffs to protect infant industries, but the principle of free trade, backed by a Britain which by now levied virtually no tariffs at all, was recognised everywhere. It formed part of the stable trading and monetary system, including gold-based national currencies, which contributed to the growth of the world economy in conditions of peace which marked the later nineteenth century.

This world structure was shattered in 1914. In the 1920s the main trading nations tried to return to the pre-war arrangements for international payments (generally known as the 'gold standard'), but the extent of European indebtedness eventually made this impossible. In the early 1930s there was a big shift to protection, currencies were devalued, and the tariffs reappeared. Even Britain turned to tariffs from 1931 in order to protect her industries, which in any case no longer had as much export potential as in 1914. In 1932, at Ottawa, Britain negotiated a trading system with the countries of the British Empire (imperial preferences) which allowed their products to enter Britain without duty. Germany under Hitler pursued a policy of out-and-out autarky after 1933. As the biggest economy in Europe, Germany set the pace and tariffs multiplied across Europe in the later 1930s. France was especially affected, with an economy which had never been a major exporter, except in the 1920s, and a gold-related franc now making its exports seriously uncompetitive. Replying with increased tariffs of its own, France moved further towards self-sufficiency.

From 1938, nearly all of Europe was drawn into Germany's economic New Order, which made tariffs redundant for the bulk of traded output, but this was very far from a system of equal exchange. Instead, it was an extension of Germany's selfish policies of the 1930s. German contracts in the occupied countries generated considerable output, but they were related to short-term military needs and they bore little positive relation to the economic development of Europe (Milward, 1977).

Anglo-French union

Hitler's easy conquests between 1938 and 1942 prompted a number of ideas of international cooperation in the defence of traditional European values. In June 1940, the British government, eager to keep its stricken French ally in the war, offered to unite Britain and France as a single state. This unusual, not to say desperate, offer was the brainchild of a French diplomat, and former businessman, Jean Monnet, who had the thankless task of liaising between Paris and London after the German attack in May (Brinkley and Hackett, 1991, xvii–xviii). Monnet had worked for the League of Nations before the war, rising to Deputy Secretary-General at the age of thirty. He spoke excellent English, knew many leading Americans, and had strong internationalist leanings. All this made him a rare bird in 1940 and his ability to stay in contact with very disparate interests marked him out as a European integrationist of great potential.

The proposed union of France and Britain was overtaken by the rapid German advance and the French request for an armistice in June. In any case, Monnet's negotiations soon identified a desire on the British side to water down the proposal. Monnet never forgot his work on this project, however. Bold though the proposal was, he saw it as a precursor and later in his career he was often inspired by it. He learned, though, that to merge or associate the institutions of established nation states was bound to raise great difficulties. From now on, he would look instead to the creation of new institutions outside the state structures, and in particular to economic institutions which could draw on existing international flows.

The Second World War and European integration

Shortly before the outbreak of the First World War, in 1910, an English internationalist and pacifist, (Ralph) Norman Angell (1874–1967), published a book called *The Great Illusion*. In it he claimed that wars between the European states were no longer possible because their economies were now so closely integrated. When war broke out in 1914, Angell was proved disastrously wrong. Curiously, however, Angell and his ideas did not pass into oblivion. His vision of an integrated Europe based on trade and specialisation lived on in the corridors of the League of Nations in the 1920s. In the 1930s Europe's plunge towards deflation and autarky created a different vision of competition and struggle. This time, the outbreak of war in 1939 seemed to be the result of isolationist economic policies and Angell's reputation revived all over Europe, at least among internationalist circles.

Benelux

Monnet stayed in London after June 1940 and worked for the Free French government in exile under General Charles de Gaulle. He was often in touch with other governments in exile which established themselves in London in 1940. The most important were Belgium, the Netherlands and Luxembourg, whose territories had been quickly overrun in May 1940. These were adjacent countries which, far from having a great deal in common, were ill assorted both economically and socially. Proximity in London, combined with a realisation that all three countries were virtually defenceless in a modern war, led the three governments to the idea of an economic union. Belgian coal and Luxembourg steel would help the Netherlands to industrialise and regain the position of European economic leader which it had enjoyed in the seventeenth century.

With Monnet adding his personal support, the three governments reached an understanding in London before the end of the war, and in 1944 they signed an agreement to create a customs union. In the quirky newspeak of the time, this association was known as Benelux. In 1948 the three Benelux governments set up their customs union. They negotiated a common Benelux position for submission in the early Marshall plan negotiations. The reduction of trade restrictions began in 1949, and in 1953 the three countries formed a full economic union.

Britain

From 1942 Britain found itself involved in discussions with the USA over Lend-Lease. The US aim was to ensure that the post-war world would be productive enough to repay Lend-Lease and other loans from the USA. As repayments would have to be in dollars, debtor countries would need to trade with the USA, or with other countries, in hard currency, in order to repay the loans. The War Cabinet looked very carefully at the issue between late 1942 and 1943. It concluded that a world of freer trade was in the interests of Britain and the Empire, provided that adverse trade deficits could be protected by import restrictions. This led to a general agreement between British and US officials in 1943. However, the War Cabinet qualified its position in 1944, calling for protection for agriculture and for new industries (Hancock and Gowing, 1949, 544–5). Britain thus ended the war as a supporter of trade liberalisation in principle but without clearly developed positions in relation to European integration.

France

When De Gaulle returned to France as head of state in 1944, his administration took much interest in the idea of a European federation. This was linked to French hopes that the Ruhr coal and steel region could be placed under international control, allowing France to secure cheap industrial supplies in a liberated Europe. The French second-best plan of incorporating the Saar into France ('The Saar is the poor man's Ruhr!') also had some bearing on the federation idea. Monnet was involved in these discussions, usually on the personal basis which he found most productive. Before the end of the war, De Gaulle, Monnet, Georges Bidault, Hervé Alphand, and other Free French leaders had come to believe that a European economic union would be needed to tame Germany, and to support a French economy which in its absence would always be inferior to Germany's. This opinion remained a powerful one after the war (Hogan, 1987, 64).

At the end of the war, France recognised the need for close collaboration with the United States but Monnet's efforts to negotiate a big dollar loan came to nought despite a number of French concessions. The initial French reaction was to acknowledge the strength of the case for cooperation with Britain, whose huge American and Canadian loan in 1945 appeared to offer the French the chance of an indirect access to American funds. In November 1945 a loan of £40 million from Britain seemed to open up the prospect of further cooperation. However, the British imposed stiff conditions on a second loan in April 1946, with Keynes advising that French policy was profligate. We now know, of course, that France would tolerate a high level of domestic inflation into the late 1940s, so Keynes's judgement was a perceptive one, but it was sorely resented in French government circles.

From now onwards, France began to seek economic cooperation elsewhere (Bossuat, I, 1992, 42–3). Later in 1946, France at last secured an Export–Import Bank credit of $650,000 under the Blum–Byrnes agreement in return for the reduction of trade restrictions and tariffs (Graham, 1990, 60–1). This reinforced French confidence in the USA and paved the way towards enthusiastic French participation in the Marshall plan.

In 1944, De Gaulle's new government had already begun to show interest in Benelux. As early as 1943, Paul-Henri Spaak had envisaged a big economic agreement with France after the war (Bossuat, I, 1992, 45). The idea of a western Europe led by Britain and France, in the spirit of Churchill's 1940 offer of a union of the two countries, began to fade, leaving Britain oriented towards the USA (Bossuat, I, 1992, 74–7). It also left the way open, in the longer run, for the idea of a western Europe led, not by Britain and France, but by France and a new Germany.

De Gaulle's first main task, however, was to bring the French Resistance under his authority. The Resistance had hoped to take over the government of France after the Liberation, and its many Communist Party members, in particular, looked forward to revolutionary change. In Italy, many of the imprisoned opponents of Mussolini developed a case for a federal Europe after the war as the only way to prevent further conflicts. After the Italian surrender in 1943, some of the opposition went to Switzerland, from where they tried to coordinate the Resistance in the other occupied countries (Willis, 1971, 4–7). In 1944 the European Resistance movements, of which the French was much the largest and the most successful, met in Geneva where they drafted a declaration calling for a federal Europe after the war (Collins, 1975, 3). De Gaulle's neutralisation of the French Resistance deprived this declaration of practical consequences, but the idea joined an accumulation of similar proposals generated by the liberated countries. In Italy, the federalists tried to build their ideas into the reconstructed polity of the country in 1945, but by the end of the year they were admitting failure (Willis, 1971, 13).

Federalism

The idea of a formal political union flourished in the early years after the war. Its main advocate was the European Union of Federalists. This was a loose organisation which had originated in 1943, when it was closely related to the national Resistance movements and the governments in exile. It was formally constituted after the war in December 1946. The European Union of Federalists was reinforced by the European Movement, founded in 1947 to represent a number of national councils and independent organisations. In January 1947, the US Secretary of State, John Foster Dulles, made a striking speech under the title, 'Europe must federate or perish', to a meeting of the National Publishers Association in New York (Gimbel, 1968, 121). However, at a conference of the main European federalist organisations at The Hague in May 1948, a proposal for a European parliament was rejected in favour of the idea of the Council of Europe, with a Council of Ministers and a Consultative Assembly nominated by the national governments. This weak, consultative body, which was largely the result of British objections to the loss of sovereign power, was set up at Strasbourg in 1949. This modest result was a disappointment for the federalists, who never again reached the same degree of influence with European governments. From now onwards, the locus of European integration switched to the economic and military areas.

The creation of the North Atlantic Treaty Organisation (NATO) in 1949 was the outstanding post-war achievement of military cooperation in western Europe. Its rapid negotiation, which sprang from the Brussels Pact (Britain, France, Benelux) of March 1948, was accelerated by the growing Russian threat, and direct involvement by the USA and Canada. (Collins, 1975, 4). The negotiations put the Council of Europe idea completely in the background and led to the eventual weakening of its functions. This rapid progress allowed proposals for economic integration to be studied without distraction.

The Marshall plan

The idea of European integration surfaced early in the talks on the Marshall plan. The first European discussions on the plan in Paris in July 1947 had seen the French at loggerheads with the USA and several European countries over the expansion of the German economy. France still wanted to secure its own industrial position and to pursue its long-running claims over the Ruhr (Hogan, 1987, 60–4). Initially frustrated, France turned to a plan which leading figures in De Gaulle's government had developed towards the end of the war. This was for a European economic union which would keep Germany in its place. France therefore proposed a European customs union during the early days of the July discussions (Hogan, 1987, 65).

Several countries were prepared to support this plan only if Britain joined. British ministerial interests were on the whole opposed to the idea, though Ernest Bevin, the Foreign Secretary and a doughty opponent of the Soviet Union, was in favour. The Nordic countries, following Britain as usual, were opposed. Italy was strongly in favour. The proposal had lapsed by August, though. After this the Americans took a stronger lead and the idea of formal integration was replaced by the details of practical cooperation.

As the Marshall plan took shape, France had to give up all but the last glimmers of its scheme for an internationalisation of the Ruhr. From June 1948 this idea was effectively dead, and the operation of Marshall aid became the main force working towards western European integration. However, as one of the aims of Marshall aid was to promote trade between European countries, and therefore the specialisation of their output, some of the ideas discussed between 1945 and 1947 survived to emerge in a new form. In particular, as France at last gave up her Ruhr pretensions in 1948, she began to seek a broader economic association with Germany which would both secure her supplies and prevent the rise of a new military threat (Milward, 1984, 468).

By 1949, France had given up most of her other ambitious post-war aims such as an understanding with the Soviet Union, the creation of a coalition of small European powers with France at their head, and opposition to the emergence of a strong, independent Germany. With Marshall aid at last making up for the French failure to secure a big post-war loan from the USA, France was able to join fully in the Marshall concept of cooperation between sovereign European states. At the same time, she dropped what was left of the idea that France and Britain could cooperate sufficiently to direct the rebuilding of Europe. Also abortive was the Franco-Italian customs union, approved in outline in March 1948 as part of Italy's plans to secure full rehabilitation in western Europe, but rejected by the French Assembly in 1949 (Willis, 1971, 21–2). The idea that Germany might become France's main partner, however incredible it might seem, now began to emerge. These developments in Germany and France during the Marshall plan period opened the door to the European integration which culminated with the EEC in 1957. They also pushed Britain to the edge of the debate on European integration.

Meanwhile, the Economic Cooperation Administration (Marshall plan) continued to press for economic integration in Europe. In

1949 it adopted it as a central policy which it conveyed formally to the OEEC, where it secured a good response (Schildt and Sywottek 1993, 86). However, progress in this general area was soon eclipsed by a practical innovation deriving from the Marshall plan.

The European Payments Union

In 1950 the approaching end of Marshall aid led to two important proposals for replacement arrangements which would continue the benefits of the American initiative even when the flow of dollars had ceased. The European Payments Union (EPU), set up in 1950, was a very effective cooperative system for ironing out bilateral imbalances in trade between individual countries. It was based on the idea that OEEC member countries should agree to accept the currency of *any* other member in payment for their exports. All members contributed to a currency fund from which countries with trade deficits were provided with credits to allow them to cover these imbalances, provided that they took action to remedy the imbalances in the short or medium terms. This had the effect of replacing a complex system of bilateral payments, with many of them moving into or out of deficit at any time, with a total system which could tolerate bilateral imbalances as long as the total system were in balance. The Marshall plan had produced a similar effect, more crudely, by increasing the volume of dollars available to finance internal west European trade. The EPU had the additional advantage of promoting the removal of trade barriers, as member countries were advised, for instance, to allow greater imports in return for EPU credits. Moreover, it helped to stabilise exchange rates as bilateral trade flows moved into balance (Eichengreen, 1993, 1).

The EPU had a striking effect. By the late 1940s, western European trade with the rest of the world had exceeded pre-war levels, but the volume of trade between European countries was still less than before the war. Between 1950 and 1959, however, intra-European trade expanded from $10 billion to $23 billion. Western Europe's hard currency reserves doubled between 1949 and 1956 (Eichengreen, 1993, 27–32). The EPU was not the sole cause of this progress but it could scarcely have come about if the cautious payments arrangements of the 1940s had survived.

The European Payments Union was able to wind up in 1958 as the west European currencies joined in the world-wide move to full dollar convertibility which marked the final, if belated, achievement of the Bretton Woods system of 1944. This great achievement, often underrated in historical accounts, confirmed the value of the American approach to the European and world economies at the end of the war, for it was the creation of post-war European prosperity based on a liberalisation of trade which had made dollar convertibility possible at last.

The Schuman plan

In the later 1940s most European integrationists sought a political means of uniting Europe. As we have seen, in 1948 the first Congress of Europe was held, with representatives of European governments seeking to create permanent institutions. It led to the establishment of the Council of Europe in 1949, after no agreement had been reached on the idea of a European parliament. Members of the Council were appointed by the national parliaments. It met for the first time, in 1949, under the presidency of Paul-Henri Spaak, the Belgian Socialist leader.

The weakness of the Council of Europe was a disappointment to federalists, especially as Winston Churchill had been a warm supporter of the political approach to European integration. However, it encouraged Jean Monnet in his view that economic links, even if limited in their scope, could generate a broader cooperation in the long run. With Franco-German cooperation now high on the list of French diplomatic aims, he started on a new lobbying campaign designed to bring about that end in a modest but practical way. Among his many allies and associates, the most important was Robert Schuman, Prime Minister of France in 1947–48 and subsequently Foreign Minister (Duchêne, 1994, 199–200).

On 9 May 1950, Robert Schuman, the French Foreign Minister, announced a proposal for the integration of coal and steel production in Europe which came to be known as the Schuman plan. It had been drawn up in secret by Jean Monnet and his Commissariat du Plan, to avoid ministerial opposition in France (though Schuman was fully briefed and an enthusiastic supporter, while two other ministers had been let into the secret) (Willis, 1965, 83–4; Giles, 1991, 124–5). Monnet had become disappointed with the results of the Monnet Plan since 1946 and had turned to the idea of European cooperation as a way forward. He used his influential position as Director of the Plan to secure tacit French approval of the Schuman scheme before the Cabinet was involved (Werth, 1966, 481). This episode epitomised the policy-making role of the senior civil servant in post-war France. The essence of the Schuman plan, however, was Franco-German cooperation, with the coal and steel arrangements partially taking the place of the internationalisation of the Ruhr which the French had pursued until 1948 (see Milward, 1984, 395–6).

Monnet saw the coal and steel plan, as did Schuman, as a route towards European cooperation on a broad scale (Werth, 1966, 478–9). It proposed cooperation in the production and exchange of iron and steel products between Germany and France, and such other producer countries as might wish to join. This plan combined a number of post-war requirements in a convincing way, and looked more realistic than the Council of Europe proposals for political integration, which were making slow progress (Willis, 1965, 80). It provided an important new field of economic cooperation as the end of Marshall aid approached (Hardach, 1994, 181–2). It also struck a mighty blow for Norman Angell, with Schuman's press statement emphasising that it would make war between France and Germany impossible.

Six governments agreed to discuss the plan in detail: Germany, France, Italy, and the three Benelux countries. Germany and France had already agreed it in principle. It was a moderate scheme, shunning nationalisations, increased public investment, and government intervention outside the general area of quotas and prices. Its main support came from Christian Democrat governments and parties (Lindberg and Scheingold, 1970, 20–1). Its basic purpose, however, as understood by all the members, was to overcome the traditional hostility of Germany and France. As a technical proposal, it caused little political opposition outside France and national ratification followed quickly in 1951.

The idea of a coal and steel pool sprang from Allied post-war efforts to keep Ruhr and Saar production going. It was preceded by the International Steel Cartel, an association of private European steel companies set up in 1926, but this had been designed to control Europe's export trade rather than trade between European countries. John ('Jack') McCloy, the influential US High Commissioner in occupied Germany from 1949, and successor of Lucius Clay, had called for a coal–steel pool (and he would later describe the Schuman plan as like a Tennessee Valley Authority for Europe) (Brinkley and Hackett, 1991, 135, 139).

Monnet, for his part, was acutely aware of the French need to control, neutralise or otherwise direct the economic and military strength of Germany. His solution rested on the obvious complementarity between the coal of the Ruhr and the Saar, and the iron ore of Lorraine. His intention was to link regions which in the past had produced war materials. To integrate steel production on this basis would prevent Germany starting another war. However, additional factors were, firstly, that France still wanted to achieve economic parity with Germany, and had already started on this road with the Monnet plan, while, secondly, Germany wanted to achieve international rehabilitation and full independence through working links with other countries. Where possible, these links should have the approval of the United States. Konrad Adenauer was a firm supporter of this policy.

To integrate just one sector was economically highly controversial. Monnet, though, saw the pooling of coal and steel as just the first step towards a general integration, as coal and steel reforms would have broader implications (Brinkley and Hackett, 1991, xiii). Monnet was very impressed by the Tennessee Valley Authority (TVA), a river control and power authority linking several states, and set up in 1933 as an early New Deal initiative (Monnet, 1976, 327). The parallels with the ECSC were clear to all who knew the TVA. Furthermore, Monnet's high-level lobbying, which was always one of his greatest strengths, had produced some powerful supporters. In addition to Schuman, Monnet had the support of Konrad Adenauer, Paul-Henri Spaak, the Belgian Prime Minister, Count Carlo Sforza, the Foreign Minister of Italy, and the long-running Italian Prime Minister, Alcide de Gasperi (Urwin, 1989, 104). And there was always Monnet's wider circle of friends and contacts. Thanks, for instance, to a period working for his family firm in New York before the war, he already knew Jack McCloy before McCloy took up his post in Germany in 1949. The two became great friends in the later 1940s. He had also got to know John Foster Dulles, the US Secretary of State between 1953 and 1959, the key period of negotiations for the EEC (Brinkley and Hackett, 1991, xvii, 66).

Monnet's excellent links with Britain, which dated from the war, allowed him to pursue his lobbying there, but he was unable to obtain influential support. Benelux were prepared to join provided that the big German coal and steel companies were broken up into small units, as the Allies had been trying to secure with limited success since the war. If the big German firms continued to operate, they would out-perform the smaller Benelux enterprises and allow Germany to dominate the whole community. Italy, which was building up a steel industry with virtually no natural resources, saw unlimited advantages in gaining access to raw materials and semi-finished products from northern Europe.

The European Coal and Steel Community

A conference on the Schuman plan, attended by the six countries (henceforth known as 'the Six') opened in Paris in June 1950. There was already a large measure of agreement, thanks partly to Monnet's work, and discussions went well, especially as they had the support of the USA, which was pleased to see the creation of effective European institutions. The European Coal and Steel Community (ECSC) was established in July 1952 on the basis of the Treaty of Paris, which had been signed in April 1951. Five of the six Foreign Ministers involved in the final negotiations were Christian Democrats. Indeed, the ECSC implicitly represented the triumph of the Centre-Right approach to European reconstruction (Urwin, 1989, 4). In this respect, Britain's absence was significant, the ageing Labour Foreign Secretary, Ernest Bevin, having turned down the opportunity to join in the negotiations. Outstanding among the aims included in the treaty were rising living standards, increased and secure employment, and an equalisation of living standards and conditions for all workers (Collins, 1975a, 16).

The Monnet structure for the ECSC, which allowed administrators to direct its operations, limited the scope for party political and inter-governmental disputes. The business of the ECSC was purely economic and it was difficult for non-specialists to penetrate. This allowed progress towards further integration to be achieved readily and without controversy. This means of avoiding political issues of mass concern was applied later to the EEC (Lindberg and Scheingold, 1970, 21–2). However, the operation of the ECSC gradually moved towards a cartel. It encouraged the development of a 'balanced' steel industry with all the members developing a wide-ranging steel industry as far as possible, without individual countries specialising in particular branches (Shepherd et al., 1983, 59). The development of a single market for coal was complicated by widely varying production costs, with Belgian coal by far the most expensive (Collins, 1975a, 26). Its interest for European integration lies much more in the processes, which

Monnet had foreseen, by which the ECSC led on to fuller forms of integration.

The executive was the High Authority, with nine members including one from each country. Its decisions could not be countermanded by individual governments, and it was funded by its own tax, levied on coal and steel firms. It was shadowed by a Special Council of Ministers, proposed by Benelux to protect the smaller countries, and a Common Assembly which functioned as an international parliament, but the High Authority retained the initiative on policy. The first president of the High Authority was Jean Monnet, who welcomed the chance to ensure that the ECSC worked according to plan, and to promote further developments.

As the Treaty of Paris foreshadowed, the ECSC soon had to develop social policies. By the later 1950s, demand for coal was dropping and some of the members returned to subsidising their industries. ECSC steel also found it hard to compete with steel from underdeveloped countries and with plastics from the early 1960s (Collins, 1975a, 26–31). Nevertheless, the ECSC produced the growth in trade which it had sought. Aggregate trade in ECSC products across national boundaries increased much faster than production, and ECSC production increased faster than in the rest of Europe.

By the early 1980s, though, the fall in demand for coal which had begun around 1960 was accompanied by a long-term drop in demand for ECSC steel, caused by the European recession and competition from outside the region. The ECSC now concentrated on restructuring the two industries, with an emphasis on retraining and job creation. However, the incorporation of the ECSC in the administration of the EEC from 1958 had meant that its activities gradually became subsidiary. Indeed, already in the mid-1950s its main historical interest lies in its contribution to the creation of the EEC.

The Common Market

The outbreak of the Korean War in 1950 shifted American attention towards defence against the Communist bloc. The Americans were in favour of German rearmament and this idea caused much concern in Europe. Monnet now became involved in a counter-proposal for a European army, known as the European Defence Community (EDC), and an even more unlikely European

Political Community (EPC) which would control the army. By 1954 the EDC idea had lapsed, after the French Assembly had delivered a clear vote against it in that year, and Monnet and other integrationists could look elsewhere.

In 1954 Jean Monnet founded what he called the Action Committee for a United States of Europe. The idea was to bring integrationist party leaders and senior officials together to discuss European cooperation. Monnet played a leading role and his thatched house at Houjarray, near Versailles (now a French national monument), was frequently used for meetings (Lindberg and Scheingold, 1970, 33–4). Meanwhile, Monnet announced his intention to retire from the presidency of the High Authority of the ECSC, the scope of which had been surpassed by these new ideas, and which in any case was already showing worrying signs of developing into a cartel. Monnet handed over the presidency in June 1955.

In this confusing atmosphere of debates and proposals in various integrationist arenas, the idea of a European common market began to generate interest. It had originally been proposed in 1952 by the Netherlands during ECSC discussions, and it was the ECSC once again which took it up in 1955, together with a proposal for European cooperation in atomic power which Monnet had recently developèd (Urwin, 1995, 73–4). By this time a big reduction in tariffs in Europe had occurred thanks to the efforts of the OEEC and GATT, but many low-level tariffs remained. With the demise of the European Defence Community proposal, which had had strong American encouragement, the idea of economic cooperation secured wide support. The USA favoured it as a step towards European integration, and one which did not require strong British support as the EDC had done, and which it had not fully received. In fact, 1955 marked the beginnings of an American rejection of Britain as its preferred leader of European integration. This perception was strengthened in 1956 by the Anglo-French invasion of the Suez canal zone.

Thanks to the driving enthusiasm of the Benelux countries, which were represented by leaders who had drawn up the original Benelux agreement at the end of the war, a statement in principle to prepare a market that would be free of all restrictions on trade was adopted (Urwin, 1995, 74). A ministerial committee was set up under the chairmanship of Paul-Henri Spaak, and rapid progress was made on the two main proposals, the Common Market and the European Atomic Energy Authority (Euratom). After the announcement of the plans in the Spaak Report in March 1956, the Foreign Ministers of the Six approved them at a meeting in Venice in May. French reservations might have postponed an agreement but the failure of the Anglo-French intervention in Egypt in late 1956 strengthened the French determination to seek strength through European cooperation rather than by association with Britain or the USA (Wurm, 1995, 20). Germany was a strong supporter, seeing the Common Market as an international expression of its principles of integration and competition (Erhard, 1958, x–xi). The next step was to prepare the treaties and to resolve remaining difficulties at up to prime ministerial level. By March 1957 the Six were able to sign the treaties in Rome, referring them to their parliaments for ratification.

The European Economic Community

The Rome treaty displaced the term 'common market' by 'European Economic Community', as the title of the organisation. The older term remained common parlance in Europe into the 1960s, but the treaty embodied both more and less than a simple customs union. Paul-Henri Spaak was to say later that the creators of the Treaty of Rome were not primarily interested in an economic union. Instead, they saw it as a step towards political union (Urwin, 1995, 76). The very name of the new organisation echoed the abortive European Defence Community, which in Monnet's hands would have required a continental parliament. On the other hand, the economic success of the ECSC, which was in part a customs union, suggested that a broader customs union would be an ideal vehicle for ideas of European integration.

The EEC was based on the idea of competition as the main means of controlling the European market. Embodied in the Treaty of Rome, it was featured in the First Report on Competition in 1972. Monopolies, cartels, company cooperation and concerted conduct were alike shunned (Jacquemin and de Jong, 1977, 198–242). The process of tariff reduction was planned to be very slow, however. The intention here was to keep in step with the OEEC and GATT. The harmonisation of economic and social policies to promote free and fair competition was also intended to be slow. The Common Agricultural Policy, which was a separate aim, could be set up more quickly. Overall, the targets were to be achieved over a period of between twelve and fifteen years. This would allow economic growth to absorb the changes and make them almost imperceptible.

In the event, the steps towards the implementation of the EEC were indeed very difficult to discern for the average citizen of the Six, and even more so for people living elsewhere in western Europe. Decision-making processes were very complex, and the national right of veto, which France used frequently during the presidency of Charles De Gaulle, meant that moderate policies were emphasised.

The first stage of general tariff reductions, however, came into operation very quickly, in January 1959. Tariffs were reduced by 10 per cent, and import quotas were increased by 20 per cent. This reform was so successful that the timetable for further changes was accelerated in 1960, and by 1968 EEC trade in non-agricultural products had been completely freed of tariffs, while a common external tariff had been set up. By 1961 trade within the EEC was expanding at double the rate of that with non-members.

The European Investment Bank (EIB) was set up in 1958 to provide loans or guarantees for investment projects which contributed to the balanced development of the EEC. The work of the bank would later be extended by the European Investment Fund (EIF) which was set up in 1994 to extend loan guarantees. The European Investment Bank was soon making loans, especially to Italy. In about 1960 the Eurodollar market began to operate. In 1961 the EEC issued its first regulations concerning cartels (Urwin, 1995, 85).

The growth of trade within the ECSC and the EEC is epitomised by the experience of their two biggest member countries.

FIGURE 4.2 *Trade between Germany and France, 1950–63.*

	German exports to France (DM millions)	% of total German exports	French exports to Germany (DM millions)	% of total German imports
1950	613.9	7.34	691.2	6.08
1955	1,457.5	5.67	1,444.9	5.90
1957	2,252.8	6.26	1,546.5	4.88
1960	4,202.1	8.76	3,997.9	9.36
1963	6,432.0	11.03	5,495.0	10.51

The value of the annual trade of the two countries is expressed here in Deutschmarks.
Source: Willis, 1965, 235.

An almost forgotten cultural incident reflects the atmosphere of the time. In 1960 the jury at the Venice film festival gave the Lion d'Or to *Le passage du Rhin*, a French film in which Charles Aznavour plays a French prisoner of war who, like many such, worked on a farm in Germany between 1940 and 1945. Liberated, he returns home only to find that he prefers his life in Germany, where he had risen to the rank of mayor in a village denuded of men. His 'Rhine crossing' is his return to Germany to take up life there once again (Buache, 1988, 83). *Le passage du Rhin* was part of a great internationalist tradition in the cinema, going back to Jean Renoir's *La grande illusion* of 1937. However, whereas the internationalist films of the British cinema, like Michael Powell and Emeric Pressburger's *A Matter of Life and Death* (1946), emphasised links with the USA, the French and German cinemas were much more interested in European internationalism. Now neglected as a work of art, *Le passage du Rhin* was rewarded in 1960 mainly for its Franco-German internationalism. This was the spirit of the new Europe, with the prevention of war at least as important as the achievement of economic growth.

Agriculture

The first major act of the EEC was to agree a general reduction of tariffs in 1958, with implementation on 1 January 1959. This was the first of a series of reductions designed to encourage trade without damaging any of the member countries. The first major spending policy to be implemented by the EEC was the Common Agricultural Policy, which became operative in 1962. Its aim was to increase agricultural productivity, to ensure a fair standard of living for those working on the land and reasonable prices and supplies for consumers. These aims were to be achieved by rationalisation of markets, and the guarantee of supplies. A common financing system was assured by the European Agricultural Guidance and Guarantee Fund. Agricultural products would move freely within the EEC, but imports from outside would be tightly controlled, using a system of 'threshold prices'. An array of price-support mechanisms guaranteed a high level of production and high incomes for those working in agriculture.

The principle that western European agriculture should not be allowed to decline further in the face of competition from overseas could be justified on more than one ground. Since the later nineteenth century, cheap food imports to Europe had come mainly from North and South America, and to some extent from Australia and New Zealand, where production of cereal products and meat could be carried on on a scale impossible to achieve in Europe. European food imports, as the early post-war years had shown, had to be paid for mainly in dollars. European agriculture, with the exception of Britain, the Netherlands and Denmark, had not to any great extent responded to these imports by specialisation, and exports of food from Europe were low, especially to the dollar area. In terms of monetary exchange, therefore, food imports had to be paid for mainly by manufactured exports to the dollar area. In most of Europe, small-scale peasant production, or, as in the South, labour-intensive agriculture on large estates, encouraged the survival of regional or even local self-sufficiency and a low standard of living. Innovation and productivity increase were a painful process.

A further consideration was social. Although industrialisation since the nineteenth century would have drawn large numbers of people into the cities on the basis of the normal earnings differential between manufacturing and agriculture, the decline of agriculture which set in after about 1870 produced a rush to the cities which caused concern about social stability. Germany, with its small-scale agriculture and rapid industrialisation, saw a great deal of concern among social commentators about the decline of traditional social values and lifestyles in the cities. Britain, where the Garden City idea made great progress after it was launched by an obscure social reformer, Ebenezer Howard, in 1898, generated the concept of a combination of town and country through which agriculture would survive at a high level of efficiency. Similar formulae were developed in Germany and France, though with less success.

After 1918 the peasant was seen as a stabilising force in a world rent by economic shocks, and some of this thinking survived after 1945. By the early 1950s a new flood of rural people into the cities was under way and the idea of retaining at least a significant minority of country people was attractive to those thinking about the future of Europe. However, the remaining country people would need to be assured a living standard comparable to that of the cities. In the mid-1950s agricultural workers still made up about one in four of the western European workforce, but in the early stages of discussion of the Treaty of Rome, the inclusion of agriculture was by no means certain. It took a resolution of the

Council of Europe in 1956 to ensure that agriculture was included in the Treaty (Le Roy, 1994, 11).

The higher living standard would be assured in the long run by greater productivity, but if it had to be assured in the short run by guaranteed higher prices, the competitive principle on which the EEC was based would be undermined. Here, a potential conflict of interest arose between France and Italy, which had very large agrarian sectors, only partially modernised as yet, and Germany and the Benelux.

The agricultural ministers of the Six met at Stresa in July 1958 to start work on a common agricultural policy. This heavenly location on Lake Maggiore reflected the already established tendency to hold high-level EEC meetings in the most beautiful places, and the food, wine and excursions probably matched the views. From the very beginning, France pressed for the implementation of an agricultural policy which would assure high prices for French products. With the newly elected President, Charles de Gaulle, seeking to create a firm basis for his national modernisation programme, France made a strong case. On the day, France secured much sympathy, partly because De Gaulle represented a more stable and productive France which might fail if his imperialist opponents defeated him over the retention of Algeria.

Germany had mixed feelings, for it also still had an important agricultural sector, some of it quite backward. However, Germany had lost extensive agricultural areas to Poland at the end of the war, not to speak of those which now lay in the German Democratic Republic. The idea of associating, as Europe's biggest industrial country, with Europe's greatest producer of food, was not unattractive, especially as it echoed the basis of the Franco-German association in the ECSC. Such symmetries appealed to the French, while the Germans were always happier if the French were content, not least because they needed French approval to secure their ultimate rehabilitation as a respectable European nation. When De Gaulle went out of his way (on grounds which stretched far beyond agriculture) to build up a personal understanding with Adenauer, and a link with the German people, in the early 1960s, Germany finally conceded the essence of the French case and the other EEC members accepted it in their turn.

The CAP meant high food prices in the EEC. To secure rural living standards comparable to those in the towns required a system of guaranteed prices and, eventually, guaranteed purchases using EEC subsidies. The external barrier kept out cheaper foreign food. It also complicated the negotiation of Britain's applications to join the EEC, because British imports of food from the Commonwealth had been linked for nearly a century with an ethnic and cultural network which, though no longer an empire in the old sense, provided a fundamental sense of security. Even imports from non-Commonwealth countries such as Argentina were hard to sacrifice, as their world market prices were normally much lower than CAP prices. These were genuine problems for Britain, while none of the Six imported as much food. France, it is true, still had a big empire in the mid-1950s but only Algeria had a large population of French origin and, in any case, France used its position as a founder member to secure very favourable terms for EEC trade with its colonies.

The EEC's first detailed proposals for agriculture were not published until 1962. They were the work of Sicco Mansholt, the EEC commissioner for agriculture, who had begun his studies in 1958. Mansholt was almost over-qualified for his complex task. Notwithstanding his eclectic name, he was a senior Dutch statesman and distinguished agriculturalist who had taken part in the Benelux negotiations in 1946. After further work on the basis of Mansholt's plan of 1962, most of the main market organisations were set up between 1965 and 1970. Specific agricultural products were incorporated into the policy structure, beginning in 1967 with fruit and vegetables, eggs, olive oil, and others. The incorporation of silkworms in 1972 might suggest that the task was over by that time, but some products proved difficult and were not included until much later, including horsemeat and potatoes (Le Roy, 1994, 19).

While in Britain and certain other countries farmers produced at less than cost in order to compete with world imports, and received government subsidies in compensation, the EEC adopted the French system whereby the farmer was guaranteed a price capable of assuring him an adequate standard of living. However, the CAP guaranteed price system inevitably placed the burden of any shortfalls in agricultural productivity directly on the EEC consumer. It also took the responsibility of selling the product away from the producer, and this tended to generate overproduction. With the EEC responsible for buying the product, huge surpluses could be generated. With the media cackling on the sidelines, butter 'mountains' and wine 'lakes' had to be disposed of, usually at well below cost, sometimes in the Third World or the

Communist bloc. Some products, such as cheap EEC wine, were virtually given away for industrial use.

At the same time, with money pouring into agriculture, new equipment, new crops and new techniques proliferated. In southern Europe especially, where peasant agriculture had not responded much to post-war agrarian encouragement and reforms, the CAP transformed the rural scene. Even the British farmer, arguably the most productive in Europe, did well out of high prices and guaranteed purchase after 1973. Specialisation, already far advanced in Britain by the 1950s, pushed further ahead. There was even a move away from the ubiquitous rough pasture which had proliferated in Britain after the war, and a return to root crops. Wheat swayed for mile after mile in the Midlands and South in the 1980s, and rape fields dotted the slopes in the spring. As the smaller farms fell into ruin, the larger ones came to look increasingly like rural factories and warehouses, with pukka signs oozing agri-business success.

This rural paradise had to be paid for. By the mid-1980s agricultural payments made up two-thirds of EEC expenditure. Exports from the EEC were largely out of the question because the offer prices were much higher than the world level. In 1992, however, the CAP was at last reformed in anticipation of the single market and consequent upon the progress of the GATT negotiations. This followed the abolition of unlimited price guarantees in 1984. Cuts in intervention prices reduced production, and farmers received compensation if they agreed to take some of their land out of production. The effects of the new CAP were still unclear in 1995, but the reform of European agriculture since the early 1960s had put it in a stronger position to face the problems of a tougher world.

The enlargement of the EEC

During the EEC negotiations and the early years of the EEC, the Benelux countries had hoped that Britain would be attracted into the association. They were mainly concerned that the new understanding between France and Germany would become the main driving force of the EEC. To the north, the Nordic countries, big traders with Britain, were also prepared to contemplate a link between Britain and the EEC, which might allow them to join in their turn. Britain's approach to the question, going back as far as the 1940s, was to urge the creation of a European free trade area, with no internal tariffs but no external customs wall either. Historically this was a bona fide position, as it conformed to Britain's pathbreaking free trade policies between the 1840s and the early 1930s (see Dell, 1995). As much of the economic world had been made in Britain's image, the idea of a return to free trade in Europe, which could be combined with the British Commonwealth and the other empires or ex-empires, had its attractions, and not only in Britain. For instance, Ludwig Erhard, the German Minister of Economic Affairs, welcomed British proposals for a free trade area extending the EEC in 1957 (Erhard, 1958, x–xi).

Attractive or not, the British vision had failed to tempt the ECSC and it failed to tempt the Six as they approached the Treaty of Rome. One objection was that it left Europe open to the products of American industries still more advanced than Europe's. More substantial was the recognition that it would not contribute to the political integration of Europe. Certainly, it did not appeal to Germany and France on that score alone. The political integration of Europe, on the other hand, did not appeal to Britain for a number of reasons, but mainly because it still clung to the idea of an association, however tenuous, between the British Commonwealth and the United States, an English-speaking union of gargantuan proportions.

In 1958 Britain made one more attempt to propose a free trade area that would include the Six. It was again rejected by the Six, mainly on account of Britain's wish to continue favouring its trade with the Commonwealth, and Britain's close links with the USA. France, in particular, was worried about competition for its industries and agriculture (Foreman-Peck, 1983, 298). The European Commission also feared that the consolidation process of the Six would suffer (Abrams et al., 1990, 4–5). Britain now set up, in 1960, its own free trade area (European Free Trade Association – EFTA) with three Nordic countries (Finland became an associate member in 1961) and four other countries which can fairly be described as peripheral – Ireland, Portugal, Austria and Switzerland. EFTA's aim was to remove all barriers to trade between the member countries by 1969. Britain's motives were complex, but the main aim was to set up an operating free trade area which could join later on with the EEC to create a free trade area including all of Europe. However, the volume of EFTA trade was so small that no exciting growth effect like that of the EEC could be expected. After further consultations with its 'friends', Britain under Conservative Prime Minister Harold Macmillan applied to join the EEC in 1961.

Jean Monnet had foreseen a British application, which would follow a successful start to the EEC, as the British recognised a *fait accompli* even though it had shown no interest in the initial enterprise: '. . . if we go forward and show concrete results, they will join at the right time.' However, the British application was also due partly to the recognition that the USA was very interested in the new European institutions, which threatened the 'special relationship' (Brinkley and Hackett, 1991, xix–xx).

At first the negotiations went well, but Britain gradually built up a series of requests for concessions, mainly in the areas of Commonwealth trade, British agriculture, and EFTA. In 1962 the EEC agreed on its Common Agricultural Policy, which supported small (peasant) farmers, and this created a further problem in the negotiations. If granted, these concessions would strike mainly against the economic interests of France. However, in 1962 De Gaulle reached an extraordinary personal understanding with Adenauer which he followed by a tour of Germany during which he made a number of rousing speeches in very creditable German. The German people, recognising that the reconciliation with their former bitter enemy was now complete, received De Gaulle with an enthusiasm which no German politician had enjoyed since the war (or, to put it more bluntly, since Hitler). In the late 1940s France had looked to Britain as its ideal associate in the re-ordering of Europe, and had been constantly disappointed by a Britain that looked rather to the USA. After 1962, De Gaulle had no great need of Britain, and he did not want EEC concessions to weaken his understanding with Germany. Moreover, his growing distrust of the United States made him sensitive to Britain's transatlantic links.

In 1963 De Gaulle vetoed the British application, mainly on political grounds. Shortly after, he signed a bilateral treaty with Germany. This was designed to draw the two peoples closer together culturally as well as economically, with a view to avoiding further misunderstandings. When, in 1965, France withdrew from the Council of Ministers over an issue affecting the independence of the European Commission, it looked as though the EEC's capacity to generate a coherent policy was being undermined. In 1966 the Council agreed that majority decisions would not be taken in matters of 'important national interest' and this allowed

France to secure its own interests in the negotiation of the Common Agricultural Policy, which was pending at that time.

By the mid-1960s, De Gaulle's efforts to make France partially independent of the Western alliance was having a major impact on Europe. France's nuclear weapons became available in 1960, and France withdrew from the NATO command structure in 1966. More broadly, De Gaulle wanted to stem the flow of Americanisation in Europe, the USA having partially replaced Britain as his long-term bugbear. His views were beginning to be influential elsewhere in Europe, and particularly in the East where he seemed to offer a middle way for the smaller countries between domination by the Soviet Union or by the West.

Many of these ideas were summed up, independently of the French government, by a book called *Le défi américain (The American Challenge)* in 1967. This was the work of a French journalist, Jean-Jacques Servan-Schreiber. It argued that unless Europe could organise and overcome its remaining weaknesses, the American economy and the products of its industrial society, including ideology, would continue to take Europe over, as they had been doing since the war. Servan-Schreiber's book was so rapidly translated into most other European languages that French government backing can be suspected. It received wide coverage in the European press. Its influence is hard to gauge but it must have reinforced sympathy for De Gaulle's EEC policies by making them look less nationalistic and more in the interests of Europe as a whole.

In 1968 the Common Agricultural Policy, which was based on an agreement between France and Germany, was set up. In the same year, the elimination of customs duties and quantitative restrictions on trade among EEC countries was fully achieved (Balassa, 1975, ix). Meanwhile, Britain had applied again to join the EEC under Labour Prime Minister Harold Wilson in 1967. De Gaulle vetoed the application in the following year, in much the same terms as in 1963. De Gaulle's decisions were respected but the other EEC members, especially the Benelux, felt that a compromise could have been reached with Britain. When De Gaulle resigned the French presidency in 1969, the EEC ministerial meeting at The Hague agreed to open the way for more members. The new President of France, Georges Pompidou, launched a big initiative to place France once again at the head of EEC developments. This encouraged three EFTA members – Britain, Denmark and Ireland – to apply in 1971. They joined the EEC in 1973.

The oil crisis of 1973 somewhat tarnished the entry of the three new members. All three were severely affected by the OPEC action, and the downturn in EEC growth rates meant that they did not benefit from the rapid escalator effect enjoyed by the Six after 1957. However, the resolution of the long-running issue of the British entry allowed the EEC to entertain further applications. In 1974–75 it encouraged approaches from Spain, Portugal and Greece. These were backward countries which were likely to slow down EEC growth in the short term, but the EEC wanted to encourage their recent moves towards democracy. It was also willing now to take the difficult steps of raising the less developed parts of Europe up to the general level, without which full European integration could not be achieved. Meanwhile, the EEC pursued negotiations with the remnant of EFTA to reduce barriers to trade between the two. These efforts went well and by 1977 all tariffs on trade in manufactures between the two groups had been eliminated (Page, 1987, 39).

One EEC approach to this problem was to invest directly in backward regions. In 1975 it created a third 'structural fund', the European Regional Development Fund. The fund was intended to reduce regional economic disparities between the member states, and also within them. Its efforts to promote growth in backward regions concentrated on improving the infrastructure. In declining industrial regions it concentrated on job preservation and job creation. In backward rural areas its main aim was to create jobs outside agriculture.

When Greece (1981), Spain (1986), and Portugal (1986) joined the EEC in the 1980s, the ERDF became very active. It was supported by the two earlier structural funds, the European Social Fund which was activated in 1960 to improve employment opportunities for workers affected by structural changes by assisting training and the mobility of workers, and the European Agricultural Guidance and Guarantee Fund which was set up in 1962 to promote agricultural change and to fund the Common Agricultural Policy.

This growth in targeted investment, much of it intended to promote innovation, greater productivity, modernised infrastructure, and restructuring of employment, shifted the emphasis of the EEC partly away from the indiscriminate support of agricultural prices which had been the mark of the CAP. In most of the schemes supported by the structural funds, the participating country provided half of the finance.

The economic problems connected with the oil crisis slowed down the integration sought by the EEC. The EEC played only a small part in the resolution of these problems, which were rather the concern of the IMF and the OECD. The EEC took a number of measures of protection, much as its member countries did. The EEC steel cartel, which operated between 1977 and 1980, the Multi-Fibre Arrangement in textiles (1978), and the agreement whereby Japan limited its car exports to most of the major producing countries in the EEC (1981) were the main examples of these restrictions (Shepherd et al., 1983, 21). From 1980 the EEC increased its external tariffs to protect its own industries. By the early 1980s these were higher than those of the USA and similar to those of Japan (Seers and Vaitsos, 1982, 6). Member countries also had recourse to non-tariff restrictions on trade, and the growth of trade within the EEC slowed down (Jacquemin and Sapir, 1989, 1).

Further complications were caused by the efforts of Britain, under Prime Minister Margaret Thatcher, to reduce its contribution to the Community budget. These efforts, which she launched at the very beginning of her mandate, in 1979, were related to the very cooperative negotiation of Edward Heath in the early 1970s, when contributions based on Britain's status as a leading manufacturing nation had been agreed. Thatcher stressed the inequity of the original formula and certain medium-term changes in the structure of the British economy, including the steep decline of British manufacturing. Following De Gaulle's example in the 1960s, she was obdurate, and had most of her way in a series of agreements between 1980 and 1984 (Thatcher, 1993, 62–4, 83–6, 537–45).

Other EEC leaders were taking a broader view. The oil price increase of 1979, and the deflationary response of the industrial world, implied that the EEC would grow and develop much more slowly for a number of years. In 1981 West Germany and Italy put forward proposals for strengthening EEC central institutions. There was much interest within the Community and in 1984 the European Parliament added its support by adopting a Draft Treaty on European Union.

In 1985, Jacques Delors, a former Finance Minister of France, became President of the European Commission. By the following year, the EEC would contain 90 per cent of the population, and 88 per cent of the GDP, of western Europe (Williams, 1994, 7). Aware that the Community was not making much progress towards its stated goals, he proposed the integration of a single internal market, to replace the collection of national economies at various stages of integration which was all that twenty-seven years of European endeavour had produced. The single market would promote greater efficiency throughout the Community and reinforce the position of western Europe in its competition with the East (Brinkley and Hackett, 1991, xiv). By 1988, the Cecchini Report was able to estimate that the creation of the single market would save 200 billion ecus of unnecessary costs, some 4–5 per cent of the gross domestic product of the Twelve (Crespy, 1990, 3).

A strict timetable was drawn up, according to which the single market would be fully in place, with all the national legislation enacted, by 31 December 1992. The Council of Ministers signed the Single European Act in 1986, and the national parliaments ratified it in 1986–87. The Act replaced the unanimity requirement in the Council of Ministers in matters of important national interest, which had allowed De Gaulle persistently to use his veto, by a 'qualified majority'. Britain, for once, supported the Single European Act because it emphasised free trade principles rather than interventionism and political union. However, Margaret Thatcher remained unhappy about the Delors aim of monetary union (Thatcher, 1993, 554–9).

As 1992 approached, studies commissioned by the EEC suggested that the removal of national economic and legal barriers in the single market would increase the volume of trade, encourage specialisation, and lead to an increase in productivity. As a result, the prices of many products would fall across the Community, leading to a greater standardisation of prices. It was even suggested, principally by EEC-related optimists, that the single market could transform the poor macro-economic conditions which had depressed the European economies since 1979 (Emerson, et al., 1988, 10–11). This aspect attracted rather less attention towards the end of the 1980s, when reflationary measures taken to counteract the effects of the stock market crash of 1987 increased demand and output in quite a striking way, but interest in it revived with the new recession of the early 1990s.

The case for implementing the single market as quickly as possible now became persuasive. From 1993, rapid progress was made, though by 1995, depressed world conditions, exacerbated by the continuing problem of low demand and productivity in the ex-Communist countries, obscured any possible positive effects of the single market on European growth. It was also increasingly difficult to separate the impact of EEC reductions of trade restrictions and compliance with the progress of the GATT negotiations. In the 1980s the EEC fell readily into line with the new GATT tariff reductions. In 1992 it altered its Common Agricultural Policy in line with GATT 1993.

By 1995 the European Union, as it had been known since 1992, was especially concerned with creating jobs without undermining the basic policies of the Union. Its *Livre blanc* of 1994, building on the advantages of the single market, set out a broad range of policies designed to reduce unemployment and promote growth, all without releasing inflation. It stressed the need to keep the EU competitive in world markets. It was not unoptimistic about growth (Commission européenne, 1994).

From the early 1980s the EEC was working in a deflationary context and its emphasis switched partly to monetary stability. The eventual target was a European currency, first agreed as an objective in 1969, and the member countries set a variety of courses towards this goal. As this book went to press, the target date for monetary union (EMU) was 1 January 1999, though it was widely acknowledged that some EU members might not be able to join the new currency at first. The effect was a convergence of national financial policies in the 1990s which was reinforced when new members joined.

The French strike movement in late 1995 reflected a growing concern in western Europe about the economic and sovereignty implications of EMU, with even German public opinion turning against the idea. Britain, now a model of financial probity thanks to the reforms of the Thatcherite era, but an EMU sceptic, watched these developments with a degree of detachment.

The other main target of the Treaty of Rome, the removal of barriers to trade, could be pursued without major public expenditure, and so it did not threaten the anti-inflationary policies. This explains the publicity given to the creation of the single market which was, after all, the basic objective of the Treaty of Rome and one which had been substantially achieved by 1980. The single currency, of which Britain was notably suspicious, was kept in the background until the achievement of the single market in 1992 meant that it could no longer be obscured. In 1995, it looked fairly certain that the single currency, to be called the Euro, would be in place by the end of the century.

Special aspects

The work of the European Union was so complex that this account has inevitably neglected many aspects so far. Some of these are not directly relevant to economic and social history and can be ignored. However, the following topics merit closer attention.

THE COUNCIL OF MINISTERS

When the EEC came into being on the basis of the Six, the countries which had drawn bitter but positive conclusions from the Second World War, consultation at the highest level could be achieved on a personal basis. The Brussels bureaucracy played an essential role, and Jean Monnet and other officials had of course been influential in leading the politicians towards the ECSC and, later, the EEC. However, as the Community expanded from 1973, and its expenditure grew in relation to a growing number of policies and projects, the work of the European Commission grew, rather like the United Nations in the 1950s.

The meetings of the national leaders in the Council of Ministers became at the same time more formal and more chaotic. Overpopulated, round-table sessions with national teams headed by the prime minister or head of state were interspersed by informal mingling and haggling in very large drawing rooms or on the terrace of some historic palace which had been fitted out for the occasion. Formal meals around long tables often had a similar function, with the seating plan worked out by officials to group the right people. George Brown, it is said, spent much of his time in conversation with the waitresses during his EEC forays with Harold Wilson in the mid-1960s, but his was not a normal reaction.

These complex arrangements gave great influence to the EEC and national officials, who had to clarify and specify the decisions reached. However, it also created a hierarchy of influence among the senior ministers, with some being excluded from the crucial stages in the informal discussions. Others, like De Gaulle's heads of government and later Margaret Thatcher, used their power of veto to divert the Council of Ministers from its general course. In theory, of course, the ministers should have made fewer decisions as the EU moved towards a market-based, non-interventionist system, but in the 1990s this stage had not yet been reached.

Those who wanted the EU to take controversial action, such as maintaining order in the former Yugoslavia, found that the political leaders had difficulty in reaching agreement. Consequently, the role of the EU as a military power remained as hard to define as that of the abortive EDC in the 1950s. Patience and understanding above all were required, and much the same was true of all the economic activities of the EEC.

TRADE RESULTS

EEC membership produced a big increase in trade into the 1970s. In the twelve years after the Treaty of Rome, trade between the Six increased six times. Imports from non-member countries increased less than three times, so trade between members came to account for one-half of the total imports of the EEC in 1969, compared to one-third in 1957. Productivity improvements in EEC manufacturing made a big contribution to the expansion of trade within the EEC (Balassa, 1975, ix–x).

Between 1961 and 1970, the total exports of EEC countries grew in volume at an average rate of 10 per cent per annum. This compared to a rate for the whole world of 8 per cent, and an EFTA rate of 6.3 per cent (Ashworth, 1987, 284). By 1988 the EEC accounted for 21 per cent of world exports (though this included exports from one EEC country to another). The USA provided 15.4 per cent of world exports, and Japan, 12.7 per cent (Crespy, 1990, 2).

TRADE UNIONS

The post-war movement towards European integration generated parallel developments among the trade union organisations of the western European countries. The trade unions were generally internationalist in their inclination, reflecting the nineteenth-century idea that international labour would unite against competing national capitals. During the war, they or their members had joined the Resistance movements and looked forward to playing a part in reconstruction. The move towards Christian Democrat government and the division between communist and non-communist trade unions after the war limited their role, but the Americans insisted that they play a big part in the Marshall plan (Barnouin, 1986, 1–5).

They went on to play a direct part in the creation of the ECSC, the social policy of which was based in part on trade union advice. By the mid-1950s the European socialist and Christian trade union movements had come to favour a federal Europe and they were strong members of Jean Monnet's Action Committee for the United States of Europe (Barnouin, 1986, 6).

However, they were largely excluded from the preparation of the Rome treaties, and the big role of the Council of Ministers in the EEC from 1958 put the trade unions in the background, together with their ideal of integrated federal and national institutions in which organised labour would be a constituent interest (Barnouin, 1986, 7). The EEC's limited social policies, at any rate in its early years, also restricted the potential influence of the trade unions. The expansion of EEC policies from the later 1960s encouraged the unions to seek greater influence in Brussels.

The unions faced an additional problem. This was their continuing division over most of western Europe into Christian, communist and socialist groups. A complicated series of negotiations reached a peak in the early 1970s as it seemed likely that the EEC would be enlarged by the admission of three more countries (Barnouin, 1986, 12–46). One of these, Britain, was the most heavily unionised in Europe and perhaps the most remote from the political and religious divisions which marked organised labour on the Continent. By this time, even the British unions were aware of the importance of European association, and they played a big part in the discussions.

In 1973, the European Trade Union Confederation (ETUC) held its constituent assembly at Brussels as an all-Europe body which focused its efforts on the EEC. It was an impressive product of the negotiations and did much to narrow the differences between the three main groups of trade unions. However, the creation of a European structure led to a new generation of disagreements related to the issues of national autonomy, integration, federation, and democracy. ETUC was formed at a moment when western Europe passed definitively from a long-term expansionary period into the more cautious, deflationary phase which began around the early 1970s. Unable to defend labour interests by direct means, it became involved in economic and welfare policy, much as the national trade union organisations did. However, ETUC encountered a discouraging economic and policy climate and it was not able to exercise much influence on policies relating to employment, earnings, welfare, and job security (Barnouin, 1986, 144).

US INVESTMENT

Ever since the 1950s, advocates of the EEC had looked forward to the day when the creation of a large European market would generate a single economy comparable to that of the United States. Meanwhile, the US government and businesses were aware from 1957 onwards that, as a customs union, the EEC's external tariffs could hamper American exports to EEC countries. As the main driving force behind GATT, the USA did not wish to set up additional retaliatory tariffs on EEC imports, especially as the Americans had been pressing for greater European cooperation since the war and had encouraged the movement towards the Treaty of Rome after the plan for a European defence community had collapsed in 1954.

An important American response was investment in the EEC area. From the time of the Treaty of Rome, with European demand increasing rapidly, American firms increased their overall volume of investment in the EEC. This was to allow them to produce more *within* the EEC tariff barrier. The EEC placed no restrictions on the free movement of capital. American firms had been investing in manufacture, trade and services in Europe since the later nineteenth century, and their involvement in the EEC area had increased after 1945 in step with economic growth. The EEC and the USA were by now closely associated markets for both sales and investment, and this link was highly beneficial in terms of scale of activity, specialisation, and innovation diffusion, particularly as neither could do much business with the world's other big 'market', the Communist CMEA (Comecon). US investment in the EEC was very high, as American firms sought to evade the high EEC external tariff barrier. By the 1980s an additional factor was the problems faced by US investors in the Third World, which diverted investment towards Europe. US investment still went mainly to Britain and Germany at the time.

Meanwhile, as was to be expected in associated markets, EEC countries increased their investment in the USA. Britain was a big source of capital, continuing its long-established involvement in the USA, and Germany, as the biggest economy in Europe and a big exporter, also invested heavily. Here also, the wish to evade US tariff barriers played a big part. As late as 1987, Britain and Germany were the two main EEC countries involved in investment in the USA.

INDUSTRY

The EEC was a major exporter from the start, mainly because of the presence of the strongly export-oriented German economy. The continuing growth of manufacturing in some of the quickly developing EEC countries such as France and Italy produced an additional growth of exports after 1957. When Britain joined in 1973 another great exporting economy was added.

From the 1950s, national industrial specialisation began to develop in Europe and this encouraged a growth in productivity. The signing of the Treaty of Rome in 1957 led immediately to a large number of mergers involving industrial firms within the EEC. Many of these were American firms preparing to function in a continental market. In France and Italy, where the degree of industrial concentration was lowest, the national governments encouraged the concentration process in order to make their manufactures capable of competing with other countries, notably the big exporting force that was Germany.

However, there were few cross-frontier mergers within the EEC. Most international mergers took place between EEC companies and companies from countries outside the EEC, which were motivated mainly by the wish to avoid the effects of the EEC external tariff wall. A high proportion of these external companies were American firms which wanted to establish themselves in Europe (Balassa, 1975, 242–3). This meant that while US firms operating within the barrier-free USA could grow to a size appropriate to the huge US market, European firms would find it difficult to reach a size appropriate to the EEC market. As a result, they would find it hard to compete with the big US firms operating within the EEC (Balassa, 1975, 244). In 1970 the European Commission published *Industrial Policy in the Community*. Much discussed, the document included recommendations on the removal of barriers to cross-frontier mergers.

SOCIAL POLICY

The EEC, like the ECSC before it, did not have a clear mandate on social policy (Collins, 1975, 219). Its main interventions related to employment, including unemployment, training, equal pay for women, and migration of labour. The main aim was to equalise labour market conditions across the community to permit effective competition and to support a healthy and contented labour force.

In 1975, the EEC set up the European Foundation for the Improvement of Living and Working Conditions. Based in Dublin, it aimed to promote improvements in the quality of life and the working environment. Its main contribution was through the dissemination of research.

EUROPEAN CURRENCY

In 1972 the EEC countries established the 'snake', a system designed to stop the exchange value of their currencies diverging too far from their biggest currency, the Deutschmark. They also reaffirmed the principle of monetary union. In 1978 the EEC countries signed an agreement setting up the European Monetary System (EMS). It came into existence in March 1979. Britain, whose currency still faced unusual problems, was unable to join the EMS. In 1990 Britain at last joined the ERM (Exchange Rate Mechanism), the basic component of the EMS, but after membership placed strains on her fiscal and economic policy, Britain withdrew in 1992, returning to her previous position as an independently floating currency, though within the 'broad bands' of the ERM.

Some of the other weak EEC currencies were able to obtain agreement for an adjustment of their value within the EMS. The EMS, like the 'snake' before it, was intended by its advocates within the EEC to prepare the way for a European currency. The EMS worked well (Ungerer, 1986, 1). By 1995 some progress had been made towards the common currency within the Council of Ministers, and there was some expectation that the common currency would be set up by the year 2000. One result of the currency was seen to be the integration of the economic policies of the member countries, creating conditions of fuller competition between producers and suppliers across the European Union.

CHAPTER FIVE

The Society of Success: Consumerism, Youth Culture and Protest, 1945–1970

Social history – especially that of our own time – has an immediate appeal. It is, however, far more difficult than economic history. It is complex, diffuse, partially subjective, and shaped by our own memories. Non-controversial quantitative data are available, such as birth and death rates, ownership of consumer goods, and distribution of population into occupational groups. Other quantitative data are normally used only with qualifications, and even then generate either controversy or indifference among many historians and social scientists. Among these are the structure of social class, the distribution of religious belief, and crime rates.

Recent years have seen the publication of two excellent social histories of western Europe based on statistical series and stressing structural change (Kaelble, 1989; Ambrosius and Hubbard, 1989). The use of such statistics does not, however, on its own, create a picture of society as a complete and lively experience. Moreover, in dealing with western Europe since 1945, the confrontation of the numerous national bodies of statistical evidence, and continental features and trends, produces scope for complex quantitative exercises, but it does not necessarily generate readable history. So in what follows, and in Chapter 11, the treatment will be more discursive and even impressionistic. There will be many omissions, and many arguable generalisations no doubt, but the reader can be the judge of these, for much of it will be dealing with the recent past – his (or her) own history.

Western European society and the Second World War

Historians recognise war as a major factor in twentieth-century social change. Arthur Marwick, above all, has emphasised the dominant impact of the two world wars on Europe and no social history beginning in 1945 can now ignore the Second World War (see Marwick, 1974; Marwick, 1982).

The Second World War had a much bigger impact on people in western Europe than did the First. Germany bore the main losses of military personnel; two-and-a-half million killed, with many more missing or held in captivity in Siberia until as late as 1955 – though most did not survive this long. Most of the fatalities were very young men, between the ages of 18 and 23, so they left few widows and children – though some got married at the time of enlistment or while on leave, responding to the heightened emotional atmosphere of approaching pain and death described by Erich Maria Remarque in *A Time to Love and a Time to Die.* This 'lost generation' left behind millions of girls and young women who would have great difficulty in finding husbands after the war. Indeed, many of them would never do so.

This unprecedented post-war generation of spinsters was more a feature of German society than anywhere else in western Europe. In western Germany in 1946, there were only 79 men for every 100 women (Piquet Marchal, 1985, 153). In Germany and Austria in 1995 these spinsters and widows can still be seen shaking dusty rugs from the windows of their tiny flats. Some married the young German refugees and immigrants from the eastern territories who flooded into western Germany after 1944, but young women came in equal numbers and so the overall imbalance remained.

In the other belligerent countries this effect was less acute. Britain, with only 450,000 military deaths, was scarcely aware of the problem. France lost 2 million men to German prisoner-of-war camps but most returned in 1945. Italy's intermittent involvement in the war produced only a small number of fatalities. The main burden of the war was borne by the Soviet Union in its eastern struggle with Germany and its allies, but the social implications of these horrors lie outside the scope of this account.

The First World War had been fought mainly in Belgium and northern France. In the Second World War, most of western Europe was directly affected by hostilities and/or military occupation. Only Sweden, Switzerland and Spain were spared (and Spain was still recovering from the effects of its own civil war [1936–39]). The Second World War also required a greater economic effort than the First, and this implied a greater social mobilisation of the masses. In the Axis countries this took the form of intrusive propaganda and a frightening limitation of the freedom of the individual, especially in Germany in the later stages of the war. Variants of this control were applied in the occupied countries. In Britain, and among the continental Resistance movements which Britain encouraged, the emphasis was on a mass defence of freedom by enthusiastic democrats.

The popular response

The people of the belligerent countries responded vigorously to these demands, whether they lived in the Axis countries or in Britain. As Arthur Marwick has explained, they had a sense of greater self-worth, certainly greater than in the depression years in the 1930s (Marwick, 1974). Life seemed more exciting, especially for young people. In Italy popular enthusiasm for the war had largely disappeared by 1943 owing mainly to government incompetence, but in Germany and Austria most people were persuaded to grin and bear it (*ausharren!*) until early 1945. Not that there was much choice – even minor backsliders and casual critics increasingly risked a death sentence as the end of the war approached. In the occupied countries wartime conditions were endured rather than welcomed, but they were seen as a common experience which brought people together.

When the war ended, Britain had developed a very strong popular demand for social reform. In Germany, conditions were so bad that, in the absence of a national State until 1949, political awareness was very restricted, with the Allied re-education programme arousing dull acceptance rather than enthusiasm. In the German-occupied countries, such as France, a polarisation was to be found between the Communist-led Resistance and opponents of Left-wing extremism, with new or reformed political parties of Christian-Democrat tendency providing stability. Everywhere, however, the discussion of new policies led to a general expectation that conditions could be improved after the war in comparison with those experienced in 1944 and 1945, and even in the 1930s.

Although Britain's new Labour government, elected in 1945, enacted a spectacular package of social reforms – popularly known as the Welfare State – and Sweden's almost contemporary welfare enactments were known and admired throughout western Europe, post-war economic difficulties discouraged such ambitious reforms elsewhere (though improvements in the social security system, as in France, were common). At the elections of 1950 and 1951 the Conservative Party displaced the Labour government and Britain ceased to set an example as a social reformer, though Labour's 'Welfare State' legislation was retained. In the 1950s and 1960s the main changes occurred on the Continent as big increases in GDP permitted greater public expenditure on education and welfare provision.

The years between 1945 and the early 1950s did not therefore engender social sentiments or social movements which marked a clear change of climate from the war years. In Britain, rationing, controls, and the emphasis on a major effort by the workforce, prolonged the wartime atmosphere. The construction of public housing to meet the post-war backlog was very slow until around 1950. Almost no private housing was built, and with repair and maintenance work accounting for about half building output, the older areas of British cities, already battered or degraded in the war, looked dowdy and even sinister, their tangled chimney pots puttering the grey remnants of 'nutty slack' and home-made 'brickettes', both make-believe variants of coal dust. Not until the early 1950s did the Conservative government launch a big programme of public housing and relax controls on private building, allowing total production to top 300,000 units in 1953. From then onwards, in Britain and on the Continent, a new wave of social change would begin to occur, but it would be based more on rising living standards than on developing demands for social reform.

'Americanisation'

The concept of 'Americanisation' is introduced a little hesitantly here. Many historians would question its precise meaning, or dismiss it as a vacuous concept generated by the media and lazy social scientists. What it is meant to convey in this book is the adoption by western European people of a lifestyle and values similar to those common in the USA, where per capita living standards at the end of the war were much higher than those of any European country, ranging between 1.6 times higher than Britain's and 3.15 times higher than Austria's (Maddison, 1989, 19). This process was always likely to follow from the European economic 'catching-up' process described above, particularly as much American involvement in western Europe after the war – for instance in occupied Germany or during the Marshall plan – was intended to disseminate American culture for economic and political reasons.

American reconstruction planning for Europe included a big cultural Americanisation strategy, now almost forgotten, partly because it was so successful. This was intended to create a pro-American sentiment across Europe which would reduce the danger of resistance movements in the former Axis countries and prevent Communist activists from persuading people that post-war poverty and dislocation were endemic to capitalism and could best be resolved under the guidance of Moscow. There was also a fear that dissidents of all types could drum up support from cultural minorities and remote enclaves.

Americanisation took many forms. It was at its most thorough in Germany, from radio programmes to the instructions issued to the humblest US soldiers for dealing with German people. American forces in Italy were briefed in a similar way, and Italo-Americans were sent there in large numbers because they could communicate. The US occupation of Germany, more generous on a personal level than the British one, helped generate a great enthusiasm for America and the American way of life after the war, once an initial distrust had been overcome (Willett, 1989, viii–ix). American soldiers, despite a variety of unpleasant incidents in the early years, were much liked, and clearly preferred by local people to the French and British occupiers. Black soldiers won high praise for their generosity to children, and their willingness to fraternise (Willett, 1989, 3). Many married German girls and some settled in Germany, fostering blues and jazz after the Nazis had largely destroyed American jazz in the 1930s. A huge cultural programme was developed, and at one point the American efforts in cultural relations and exchanges in Germany exceeded the total of all US efforts everywhere else (Zink, 1957, 3–4). German prisoners of war who had been held in the USA returned speaking good English. They had been well treated and had much admiration for the Americans. Many Germans secured jobs on the American bases. As early as November 1945, the US military employed 169,000 Germans, and by 1951 the total had risen to 248,000. Reverse influence also needs to be taken into account; by 1960 the total of US military personnel in Germany had risen to 409,590 as a result of the Cold War (Browder, 1993, 601–6). Elvis Presley, in Germany for a short stay as a GI and the brief squire of, so the papers said, a German girlfriend, symbolised the presence of an attractive, largely male group of young Americans. It was no surprise that most young Germans spoke English with an American accent by the 1950s, and launched into rock 'n' roll with more vigour than their French and southern European counterparts.

In France, the USA secured the purchase of a large quota of American films for showing in French cinemas between 1946 and 1948. It also tried to persuade the French government to admit large-scale Coca-Cola production into France from 1948. Both were seen by the Americans as symbols of the American way of life which could have a big modernising influence in France (Wall, 1991, 113). Inter alia, the Americans saw soft drinks, virtually unknown in France apart from lemonade, as a means of reducing alcohol consumption in a country with one of the highest rates of alcoholism in Europe.

Crude or brutal intervention was nevertheless avoided, with Americanisation deliberately presented as an improvement in standards in most cases – a claim which Europeans were usually only too ready to accept. At first, nothing came of the Coca-Cola initiative in France. In 1948 the Coca-Cola Export Corporation sought to invest $2 million in France and North Africa under the Marshall plan, but the ECA turned it down. In 1949 imported Coca-Cola went on sale in France, and the Coca-Cola Company was keen to go on to make France its bridgehead in Europe. Its plan was to manufacture the drink entirely in France, importing only the concentrate. The State Department supported the idea and in 1950 it was considered by the French Cabinet. Public reaction was mixed but the opposition included the Communists. The controversy continued until 1952, by which time the Coca-Cola Company had other plans for Europe (Wall, 1991, 121–6).

American sales of films to France were pressed more strongly. In the 1930s, France had resisted American pressure for quotas, but in 1946, when France was negotiating its big dollar import credit, the 'Blum-Byrnes agreement' committed France to accepting an annual quota of American films. From the American viewpoint, this was a political as well as a business deal. It allowed the screening of Hollywood films released between 1940 and 1944, as well as new releases. Better than any other art form, American films could disseminate a range of national values including achievement, perseverance, loyalty and honesty. The inclusion of wartime films in the quotas helped to remind French audiences of the efforts made at that time, the democratic meaning of those efforts, and the links between the wartime and post-war worlds.

In the early years after the war, American films made up a high proportion of the films screened in France. *Citizen Kane* launched the whole process when it was screened in Paris in 1946, five years after its American premiere. By 1948, every other film shown in France was American (Lovell, 1967, 129). Meanwhile, apart from a few neo-realist films prompted by the war, and a number of disturbing *films noirs*, the French cinema reverted to mainly conventional or pretentious entertainment films between 1945 and the mid-1950s. Some of these films strove after a defensive cultural nationalism recalling the French cinema of the 1930s, while others sought a large audience through themes and techniques which resembled American work.

In Germany, Coca-Cola faced no difficulties. The drink had been produced in Essen since 1929, but the interruption of American supplies (concentrate syrup) during the war meant that it had to be relaunched in Germany in 1949. This time, six factories were used, with the slogan 'Coca-Cola ist wieder da!'. Until then, only overflow supplies from PX shops had placed it, tantalisingly, before German young people. In charge of national outlets was the pro-American former heavyweight boxing champion, Max Schmeling, who had fought in a parachute brigade in Crete and who had once boldly told a German army magazine that his big ambition was to live in America after the war (he realised this ambition when he formed an after-dinner-speech duo with his erstwhile opponent, Joe Louis, after the war) (Willett, 1989, 104).

From 1955 the company used a new slogan, 'Mach mal Pause', which was so successful that it it lasted until 1965. It implied that even Stakhanovite German workers deserved a break and symbolised the German transition from constant effort to merited leisure. Ironically, Coca-Cola helped the soft drinks trade more widely after the war. The manager of the German Coca-Cola company, Max Keith, faced the wartime shortage of supplies by developing a lemonade-based drink for the German market. After the war, this was marketed across Europe under the brand name of Fanta, often from the same automatic machines as the American drink (Willett, 1989, 105).

Overall, the French reaction against American culture was greater than in the rest of Europe. Western Germany and Italy accepted it readily enough, Italy as a part of modernisation, and Germany as a replacement for a discredited Nazi culture. Britain, as the main American ally, was not made the object of big acculturation campaigns, being regarded as already culturally compatible and fully acquainted with people and things American by the build-up of American forces there between 1942 and 1945. Those high American living standards were persuasive enough; there was little chance that effective demand in Europe could generate innovations which were not already available, and more cheaply, in the USA.

Britain in the vanguard of social change

Throughout western Europe, the post-war economic revival, continuing industrialisation, and the widespread increases in living standards in the 1950s, quickly replaced the war and its aftermath as the prime mover of social change. However, Britain continued to be in the vanguard. During the early years after the war, Britain enjoyed the highest living standards among the major industrial countries in Europe. In the 1950s the gap started to narrow as Britain's economic growth rate lagged behind the west European average, but it was not until around 1960 that German living standards overtook Britain's, to be followed in the 1960s by other industrial countries.

The election of a Conservative government in 1951 heralded the liberation of the market. All rationing had been abolished by 1954, and controls over the use of materials had been removed even earlier. A big building effort in the public sector cleared the way for a switch to private house building and slum clearance from about 1954. Average working hours began to fall as wage rates rose, and plenty of overtime remained available. The middle classes began to enjoy the overseas holidays which had so far been the prerogative mainly of the rich. Private cars became generally available for purchase on the domestic market, and the middle classes were widely motorised from the later 1950s. Car ownership in Britain rose from 48 per thousand people in 1950 to 105 in 1960, and to 209 in 1970 (Ambrosius and Hubbard, 1989, 224).

Middle-class owners usually left servicing and repairs to the garages but cleaning and polishing became a weekly domestic ritual, especially when coloured finishes became available from around 1952. The shellac paints in use at the time could not retain a shine without a weekly waxing, and the new owners' pride dictated a Sunday hour of effort in the front garden. The beginning of a motorway programme was delayed until 1956, mainly because of government reluctance to commit massive public funds, but the volume of traffic caused even bigger problems in the clogged city centres. Parking meters, an American innovation, came to central London in 1958 and spread to provincial cities in the next few years.

Meanwhile, church attendance, long sustained by the English middle classes, started to decline. Observers blamed the Sunday outing in the new car, or television. Rising craftsmen's wage rates forced part of the lower-middle classes into domestic maintenance and improvement work, or Do-It-Yourself (DIY) as it came to be known in the 1950s. As for domestic servants, who had remained in generous supply in the 1930s thanks to unemployment, these retreated completely out of the reach of the middle classes, surviving only in the homes of the upper classes and the aristocracy. Women's magazines, led by *Woman's Own*, emphasised cooking and dressmaking. The private building boom, disseminator of the uniquely English form of the semi-detached villa above all, increased interest in gardening, with the professional gardener out of the reach of most owners, like the other servants. Golf and tennis became more popular among the middle classes, as did the social life of the clubs which organised the facilities. British suburbanism reached full maturity in the 1950s.

The children of the middle classes shared in most of these changes, but they also found themselves enjoying a fuller and more varied education than their parents. The Education Act of 1944, first major fruit of the wartime reform drive, increased the number of places in grammar schools, while working-class children saw very few of the new technical schools intended for bright children without an academic bent. Most found themselves in secondary modern schools, many of which offered them little more than shelter during their extra years at school.

Both the convergence of middle-class and working-class life styles which had accelerated during the war and the convergence of demographic behaviour, which had accelerated between the wars, continued after 1945 (Thompson, ed., 1990, 2, 66–7).

However, with the abolition of rationing by 1954, and the big public housing programme after 1951, the convergence had begun to slow down by the later 1950s. This made room, however, for the emergence of a new working-class culture which, for the first time, would secure national respect in the 1960s.

Social change on the Continent

Other countries in northern Europe developed along similar lines, within the limitations of their lower average earnings. In France, outlay on food, clothing and drink was at the very high level of 65.1 per cent of total personal consumption in 1950. By 1959, it made up 54.1 per cent, and in 1968, 44.5 per cent, leaving growing space for housing, transport, and leisure (Coffey, 1973, 38). The reconstruction of Germany in conditions of low wage rates produced very long working hours there once the economy began to revive after 1948. In 1950, the average working week for industrial workers was 48 hours, not much less than the 50 hours worked on average in 1941 (Hardach, 1990, 219). Unemployment remained high until the mid-1950s but in straitened German conditions no attractive culture of leisure could emerge. It was in the later 1950s that change began to occur. Average working hours dropped to 42 in 1960, and to 39 in 1970 (Hardach, 1990, 219). Real wages rose steadily from the mid-1950s, and the rate of growth increased in the 1960s. In manufacturing, for instance, hourly wage rates rose by 53.1 per cent between 1962 and 1969 (OECD, *Germany*, 1970, 67). German economic success could at last be expressed in living standards and in the 1960s Germany's society of consumption came on the scene. However, the economic historian, Werner Abelshauser, put it better than most when he said that the history of the Federal Republic was above all its *economic* history (Abelshauser, 1983, 8). German society, at all levels, seemed to have been deprived of its instinctive, traditional features by years of Nazi and Allied re-education, to be reshaped on materially determined lines. By the 1960s there was much talk in Germany about a new, classless society in which most people, including manual workers, enjoyed a standard middle-class life-style (*nivellierte Mittelstandslebenart*) (Abelshauser, 1983, 132–4).

Rising living standards, and the associated cultural changes, were most visibly expressed in motor car ownership. In 1950

Britain had had over four times as many private cars as West Germany, and over one-third more than France. By the late 1960s, however, the density of private car ownership in the northern industrial countries was almost equal. In 1970, West Germans owned nearly 14 million private cars, the French had nearly 13 million, and the British, 11.5 million. In the South, the variation was much greater owing to differential progress towards industrialisation. Italy had made rapid progress in the 1960s, and had over 10 million private cars by 1970 (Mitchell, 1978, 350–1). Spain, with 4,310,000 cars in 1974, Portugal, with 990,000, and Greece, with 380,000, lagged well behind Italy in per capita terms (*Economist*, 1976).

The new culture of the working class

The prosperous, fully industrialised Britain of the post-war years was the birthplace of a new phenomenon, at any rate in Europe. This was a confident, non-deferential working-class culture based on city life, full employment and high earnings. There was a precedent for it in the industrial cities of the eastern USA at the turn of the nineteenth century, when skilled workers enjoyed a living standard 50 per cent higher than that of their equivalents in Britain. In Britain it was based partly on improving material conditions from the 1950s, but also on the self-confident working-class attitudes which emerged from the war.

Full employment after the war, and rising wage rates, provided a secure basis for working-class life. Overtime was readily available into the 1960s. Female employment expanded as the service industries responded to growing demand. Married women were more inclined to take up employment after they had had their children. The number of hours worked annually per head fell from 1,958 in 1950 to 1,688 in 1973 (Maddison, 1989, 132). The number of hours spent in housework fell from the early 1960s (Bowden and Offer, 1994, 734). With immigrant workers (see Chapter 6) moving into unskilled jobs from the late 1940s, a growing proportion of the native working class found themselves in high-paid jobs.

FIGURE 5.1 *Average hours worked annually per person in selected western European countries, 1950–86.*

	1950	1973	1986
Austria	1,976	1,778	1,620
Belgium	2,283	1,872	1,411
Denmark	2,283	1,742	1,706
Finland	2,035	1,707	1,596
France	1,926	1,788	1,533
Germany	2,316	1,804	1,630
Italy	1,997	1,612	1,515
Netherlands	2,208	1,825	1,645
Norway	2,101	1,721	1,531
Sweden	1,951	1,571	1,457
Switzerland	2,144	1,930	1,807
UK	1,958	1,688	1,511

Source: data drawn from Maddison, 1989, 132.

However, adult workers and their wives were slow to develop new leisure patterns and life-styles. In the Midlands and North, an inter-war development of the working-men's club, based on drinking and entertainment, matured into the massive, raucous halls of the 1950s. Working men started to buy cheap, second-hand cars in the early 1960s and the terraced streets, and sometimes the front gardens of council estates, began to fill with cars, many of them in various states of repair by their owners.

The main change in leisure, however, came about through television, with the BBC reopening its pre-war London service (1936–39) in the South-East from 1946, in the Midlands from 1949, and spreading to the remaining regions by the early 1950s as extra transmitters were built. A rival service of 'commercial' television, financed by advertisements, was launched in 1955, in pursuit of the Conservative government's belief in competition. Until the 1960s these two programmes, broadcasting during a growing number of hours each day, gave Britain the fullest television service in Europe. Appealing more to the working class than to the middle class, television filled in most of the growing total of leisure hours for manual workers.

Meanwhile, television spread across continental Europe, with the basic national programmes launched in the late 1940s and early 1950s. In France, full weekday television began in 1947 (Smith, 1995, 67). There were only 24,000 television sets in France in 1952, not many more than in London in 1939, but by 1958 there were 988,000. During the same period, French production of wine *dropped* from 53.9 million hectolitres per annum to 47.7 million hectolitres (Rioux, 1983, 174). The direct connection between the two may have been very slight, but there was probably an indirect link resulting from increased migration into urban areas, where continuous inebriation was less common. Some aspects of *la France éternelle* could survive anywhere, however. Production of Gauloises cigarettes went *up* from 1,421,000 packets in 1952 to 1,491,000 in 1958 (Rioux, 1983, 174).

The rise of television might well have persuaded the British middle classes that working people were lazy and unimaginative. However, the post-war growth of sociology as the most fashionable social science disseminated a greater knowledge and respect for working-class life. In 1957, Richard Hoggart, a sociologist whose education had begun in the Victorian back-to-back streets of Leeds, published *The Uses of Literacy*, a much-admired study of working-class life which became one of the most cited books of the decade. Clearly influenced by the educational reforms since 1944, Hoggart's study secured much greater respect for the post-war working class, mainly because of the strength of their communities and their vibrant local culture.

A number of working-class novelists, successors of D H Lawrence, supported this interpretation. Some writers dealt, pre-dictably, with dogged working-class spiralism. In *Room at the Top* (1957), John Braine portrayed a working-class *arriviste*, Joe Lampton, succeeding not so much by charming the boss's daughter as the boss's wife. Alan Sillitoe, brought up in a series of Nottingham slums, within a few miles of Lawrence's natal Eastwood, stressed frustration. He based his most popular stories on the city he knew, portraying a bitter and nihilistic society of young workers who no longer aspired to social ascent, so stifling were the barriers and norms of British society. His *Saturday Night and Sunday Morning* (1959) was an outstanding success as a novel, with over a million paperback copies sold by the early 1960s, and his short story, 'The loneliness of the long-distance runner' (1959), made an even clearer connection between industrial poverty and the pointless existence of many working people.

The influence of this writing was extended by a wave of neo-realist films set in working-class environments. Many were based on literature or on West End plays, which also had turned to working-class themes in the later 1950s. Some of these films were hailed on the Continent and in the United States as a British 'new wave' based on a tough, working-class vitality. Stan Barstow's *A Kind of Loving* (1960), a mixture of grit and lyricism set in a declining textile town, was closest to the new French style. Karel Reisz, a specialist in this genre, directed *Saturday Night and Sunday Morning* in 1961. In the same year, Tony Richardson made *A Taste of Honey*, a story of young outcasts near Manchester, based on a neo-realist play by a teenage writer, Shelagh Delaney. First produced by the Theatre Workshop in the East End of London, the play had a long run in the West End in 1958. John Schlesinger's *Billy Liar* (1963), the story of a Walter Mittyesque youngster, was based on another popular novel and West End play by a *Daily Mirror* journalist, Keith Waterhouse. Later, the story was turned into a television series and a successful stage musical. Ironically, few of these films attracted many working-class film-goers, who remained faithful to Hollywood products.

Working-class culture acquired an even broader respect in the field of sport. Association football, the main British working-class spectator sport since the 1880s, product of industrial towns, railways and newspapers, flourished after the war. Attendances had reached their peak in the late 1940s, since when they had tended to decline, together with another mass working-class pursuit, the cinema. These trends seemed to reflect the growth of new leisure patterns, especially television. In the 1950s the quality of British football declined relative to later developers on the continent of Europe and in South America, and probably in absolute terms as well. England's dramatic home defeat by Hungary in 1953 did not produce an immediate revival and there was some talk in the press of a *weakening* of working-class communal traditions at this time as television made its mark in an increasingly 'classless' society.

However, when British teams entered the European Cup from 1955, standards improved and between 1959 and 1964 the elegant play of one side, London's Tottenham Hotspur, made the game fashionable in the West End for the first time since another London team, Arsenal, had had a long run of success in the 1930s. Led by the Cambridge philosopher, A J Ayer, whose vocal support for 'the Spurs' was warily respected among the intelligentsia, growing numbers of the middle classes began to see association football as the essential sport of a potentially classless Britain. It represented modernity, effort, efficiency and style. Rugby football, the game of the public schools and the officer class, clogged by game-stopping rules, lost some of its already limited popularity.

Meanwhile, the spread of municipal golf courses, in Birmingham and other cities, allowed the working class to penetrate an elite game.

In 1966 football excellence spread to the England team when it won the World Cup in a series of matches at London's Wembley Stadium. The entire English nation (and many Scots) backed the team, in a surge of enthusiasm unknown since VE day in 1945. Within a few years the climate of British football would become soured for a generation by juvenile crowd violence, but in 1966 a venerable working-class pastime became one of the symbols of a new British national culture.

The new culture of youth

Within this culture, youth stood out as the main agent of change. Full employment boosted the wages of young workers, especially in unskilled jobs. Traditional apprenticeships in the skilled trades continued to be valued, but the earnings of apprentices could easily be surpassed in semi-skilled jobs and these attracted many hard-working youngsters. Manual drudgery could be borne easily enough when money could buy an escape. During their most active social period, courtship, they poured money into clothes, public dancing and private music. Rock 'n' roll, which reached Europe in the shape of Bill Haley and his Comets in 1956, introduced the jive to the working classes. Britain's prosperous youth, always open to American innovations, took up rock 'n' roll with vigour. The later 1950s saw the spread of the 'teddy boy', who wore an expensive, narrow-trousered suit loosely inspired by Edwardian fashions. A great jiver and smoker, he originated in inner London but soon spread to the provinces. He was associated with informal fisticuffs outside pubs and in dance halls and cinemas, but some of the rougher of the breed bought 'flick-knives' which could be carried in the pocket and primed by a spring switch. Meanwhile, a more languid youth culture had grown up in Sweden, linked to long summers, high incomes, sex and alcohol. Tales of Swedish tolerance spread across Europe in the 1950s, making life a misery for any blonde girl on holiday in southern Europe.

The launch of long-play and 45 rpm records in the later 1950s made popular music a personal as well as a group experience and created a direct relationship between the lonely teenager in his or her bedroom and the musical star. The transistor radio, developed in the later 1950s, made music more mobile. In the later 1950s the big stars were Americans, led by Elvis Presley, reflecting the size of the American market for the music of youth. By the early 1960s, however, British demand was strong enough to generate a clutch of British stars. Most of these emerged from bedroom music-making in earlier years. The guitar had flourished in a million amateur hands in the later 1950s, with 'skiffle' emerging as the first teenage group music, one guitar being bolstered by a variety of home-made instruments, including the packing case 'double bass'. The more serious groups bought electric amplifiers and moved towards rock 'n' roll. For a while, they still played American music, but in the early 1960s there emerged a British alternative to rock 'n' roll, born in the dance halls and clubs of the big cities. The Beatles, who had played for peanuts in clubs in Liverpool and Hamburg, before going on the radio, came to the fore with their first big national hit, 'Love me do', in 1962. The 'Merseybeat' style created female stars including Cilla Black and Dusty Springfield. The Rolling Stones, founded shortly after The Beatles, created a rougher tradition of drugtakers and groupie-masters.

During the 1960s these British musicians not only reduced the Americans' share of the British market, they also became the out-standing European leaders of youth culture. The Beatles' US tour in 1964, together with two much-praised films, *A Hard Day's Night* (1964) and *Help!* (1965) even established their leadership on a world scale, and Europe's young people, their culture already partially Americanised, were happy to conform.

France had already developed its equivalent of the Teddy boys. The *blousons noirs*, who sprang up around 1960, wore black leather jackets and bushy moustaches which reflected artisanal traditions, but they followed their British mentors by breaking up theatres after rock concerts. The leading French clones of American pop, Johnny Hallyday and Sylvie Vartan, prospered in the early 1960s, but they were almost submerged by British music from 1963. Britain, however, had no equivalent of the philosophical folk singer, Georges Brassens, who wrote his own songs and built up a big following among educated young people in the late 1950s and early 1960s. Satirical in a thoughtful way, he reflected traditional values in a modernising France. The young Belgian star, Adamo, specialised in a sentimental style which won him invitations to the royal palace as well as a big jukebox following in France and Belgium.

A French pop culture nevertheless developed, a little after Britain's. The influential youth magazine dealing with pop music and the stars, *Salut les copains*, launched its first issue in 1962 when 50,000 copies were printed. It built on the success of a musical programme with the same title, launched on Europe 1 (the neo-Napoleonic station) in 1959. In 1963 the print run reached one million. At much the same time, the girl's magazine, stressing clothes, makeup, and boys, *Mademoiselle âge tendre*, was launched, quickly achieving 800,000 sales. Such magazines were important to French youth because so many readers still lived in the country or in small towns. Later, television could provide the link, and *Salut les copains* became a popular television programme by the mid-1960s. The youth culture in France was as powerful as in Britain, but it was more centred on the capital city than on the provinces, and on the middle class rather than on the working class. German youth, with the excellent English which Americanisation had given it since the war, plunged into British music. Spain generated a number of Beatle clones, their dark suits merging with daily respectable wear in that most conformist of countries.

Italy's youth culture did not develop so clearly. Close ties within extended families, the local culture of cities and city districts, a large rural population, and the backwardness of the South, resisted the mass movements of consumption which had swept northern Europe. Italy was influenced instead by another sub-culture which had originated in Britain. This sub-culture was football, which became a mass movement in Italy in the 1950s. The big industrial cities of the North were the main centres. Here, football was especially attractive to new immigrants, especially those from the South who lacked other connections with northern society. Ticket prices and travelling costs were much higher than in Britain but an additional incentive was the close link between the teams and the cities themselves. Many observers suggested that football revived medieval and Renaissance traditions of urban pride and rivalry. If this was so, Italy was able to transfer pre-industrial community traditions to the industrial world more successfully than Britain had done, though this was no doubt a function of Italy's rapid but partial industrialisation in the 1950s and 1960s.

Women

It is a commonplace of social history that total war tends to enhance the role of women outside the home and that their sense of self-worth and their self-confidence increase as a result. These effects were clearly visible in the Second World War and contemporaries expected women to play a bigger role in peacetime society than they had in the 1930s. In a number of countries, women's voting rights were extended at the end of the war in recognition of their new importance. In France, De Gaulle gave women the vote immediately after the Liberation in 1944. In Italy, they received it in June 1946, when the country became a republic. However, as armaments production declined, many women lost their jobs. Most, like 'Rosie the Riveter' of American reconstruction propaganda, were prepared to accept that it was their duty to make way for men returning from the war. In any case, the marriage and baby boom of the later 1940s produced a new move towards domesticity.

In southern Europe, even Italy had not seen a big movement of women into war production because a mass mobilisation of the economy had never occurred there. The survival of a huge peasant sector in the South, and in France, was a big obstacle to new attitudes among women. The expansion of the service sector in northern Europe in the 1950s created more women's jobs but most of these did not encourage a feeling of equality with men as much wartime factory work had done. The growth of the women's magazine, like the British weekly, *Women's Own*, suggested that rising personal outlay among women went into clothes and make-up, as well as the home. By the mid-1950s the wartime spirit had largely been forgotten. However, a new era in women's history was about to start.

From the mid-1950s the 'catching-up' process was extended from industrial production to domestic labour. Equipment widely used in North America before the war now became available in western Europe at the attractive prices made possible by American engineering and production methods. Washing machines, for instance, were displayed for the first time in France in 1948, at the *Salon des Arts ménagers*, having been virtually unknown in France before the war. Only 8,000 tons of washing powder were made in France in 1952, but by 1958 production had risen to 164,000 tons, an increase of 2,050 per cent (Rioux, 1983, 174). Supply and prices of electrical equipment were a problem at first, but from the mid-1950s the middle class and a large part of the working class acquired, at much the same time, a variety of consumer durables such as a television, a washing machine, and a refrigerator (Ambrosius and Hubbard, 1989, 77). In West Germany, the density of ownership of refrigerators reached near-saturation point – 92.9 per cent – as early as 1968 (Leaman, 1988, 204). In southern Europe, where new Italian firms like Zanussi were able to undercut the big multi-nationals like Hoover and Philips, many urban homes were equipped not much later than in the North. The life of the housewife now went through big changes.

The partial liberation of women from domestic labour allowed more married women to take up paid work in the late 1950s and early 1960s. Little of it was in manufacturing. Women were concerned about nursery and creche facilities and schooling, and equal wages. The more aware of them saw the need to obtain acceptance for women as a group with a distinct potential and distinct needs, rather than inferior versions of men. The result was a greater women's consciousness but one that was rather different from the spanner-wielding camaraderie of wartime. Instead, it stressed professional competence and potential, and freedom to think and behave independently, without subjection to convention.

The 1960s saw this new awareness develop into western Europe's first major social movement not to be based on class, nationalism or religion. This was the feminist movement, known popularly as Women's Liberation and its equivalent in the other languages. This movement had originated in North America, and it was most successful in northern Europe where a high proportion of women had jobs, and the Church and other conservative institutions were less influential than in the South.

The story of European feminism would fill a book on its own. In the present context, however, it is worth pointing out that feminism was another example of post-war Americanisation. Much of the initial feminist literature discussed in Europe was American, and the underlying assertiveness of the movement, and its emphasis on inalienable rights, was quintessentially American. Feminism nevertheless did more to help women achieve their potential in society and as individuals than any encouragement generated within western Europe. It also helped women to figure even more prominently in the arts and the professions. For instance, women writers proliferated in France after 1968, even more than in previous years. (Cook, 1993, 15).

The sexual revolution and the decline of traditional values

Historians are hesitant to identify social revolutions, as social change is essentially evolutionary. The sexual revolution of the 1960s nevertheless merits the title. It was connected with the rise of a youth culture, and its effects were already visible in advance of the arrival of feminism. It was connected with a decline in traditional values and beliefs which had begun during the war as the norms of civilised society were upset. The changing function of organised religion and the beliefs which it engendered were also central to this decline. The strength of Roman Catholicism in southern Europe and France was a uniquely European factor, and American influence played a very small part in it.

Political revolutions tend to occur in the most repressive environments. The French and Russian revolutions of 1789 and 1917 reflected extreme conditions. Britain, which generated Europe's biggest post-war sexual revolution, laboured under conditions of repression unparalleled in Europe outside Switzerland and Spain. State censorship was just one expression of it, but it was the most visible and the most vulnerable to embarrassing challenge. The British sexual revolution was launched in this area.

Government censorship kept tight control over the arts in Britain after the war. Political constraints were removed during the war to encourage social cohesion. Sex was now the main target. It was not until the mid-1950s that a serious challenge to censorship was mounted. It took place mainly in the theatre, a middle-class pursuit with a strong intellectual content. The main iconoclasts of the day were a group of writers known to the media as the Angry Young Men. Some of these productions encountered serious problems with the State censor, the Lord Chancellor, whose powers contrasted with the freedom of the Paris theatre.

A serious of censorship encounters, fanned by the London press, had already begun with the unsuccessful prosecution for obscenity of the novel, *The Philanderer*, in 1954. They continued with a number of theatrical *causes célèbres* followed by the gradual relaxation of theatre censorship by the Lord Chamberlain from 1958, and ended with the court case which arose in 1960 from the decision of Britain's biggest publisher of classic literature in paperback, Penguin Books, to publish D H Lawrence's last novel, *Lady Chatterley's Lover*, which had been banned in Britain, though available on the Continent, since 1928. When the State lost its case, literary and theatrical censorship came tumbling down.

In the 1960s the collapse of censorship in the theatre led to a big relaxation of cinema censorship, and of the control of minor publications of a titillating nature. Much more influential among students and the educated classes, however, was a revolutionary weekly television programme, *That Was the Week That Was*, which was first seen in 1962. This was an influential example of the 'satire' which became fashionable in the early 1960s. A combination of schoolboy sardonic humour and the repartee of the Paris *chansonniers*, 'satire' made fun of British institutions, politicians, and assorted members of the upper class, including their sexual activities. Traditional Britain had never been lampooned on this scale before and it was made to look very vulnerable. In 1962, the movement was extended to a 'satirical' magazine, *Private Eye*, which provided a rich diet of scandal based on news which had been gathered by more serious newspapers, but which Britain's strong libel laws prevented them from printing. Often compared with the Parisian *Le canard enchaîné*, *Private Eye* was in fact a cruder, less intellectual affair. Cumulatively funny at times with in-jokes and code names, the British publication derided almost everything visible in Britain.

Of course, most British institutions were strong enough to survive the onslaught. However, British values were not as strongly rooted, at any rate among the young, where cynicism now spread to a degree unknown in the 1950s. Moral conventions were a major victim of this trend, especially in the areas of sex, crime, and general fiddling. Transatlantic influence was now free to make itself felt, and experimental Broadway shows such as *Hair* and *Oh! Calcutta!* appeared on the London stage in the 1960s. Britain now became a convert to what was known as 'permissiveness', a frame of mind which lasted into the early 1970s until it was snuffed out by the new climate of the oil crisis era.

The fuller representation of sex on the stage and in the cinema was accompanied by rather more of the real thing. In the 1950s the main technical means of contraception had been the rubber sheath, as it had been since the later nineteenth century. However, experiments with contraceptive pills in the late 1950s were sufficiently reassuring for 'the pill' to be fully launched onto the American and European markets by the mid-1960s. Girls and young women, beginning in Britain and the Nordic countries, used the pill to avoid the need to control their own sexual activity, and the result was a growth of promiscuity. The British Abortion Act of 1967 gave a further encouragement to sexual freedom. Combined with new fashions spreading from London (Carnaby Street) and the new music of the Beatles and the Rolling Stones, London's mini-skirted excesses and international party scene, increasingly supported by soft drugs, produced the 'Swinging London' of the 1960s which for a while became the European youth nirvana in place of Paris or Munich. The result was a national youth movement which surpassed all class barriers.

By the mid-1960s this libertarian youth culture had spread all over Europe. A pacifistic and hedonistic variant, hippy culture, spread from the USA and established its main centre in the ultra-tolerant Netherlands, especially in Amsterdam (Urwin, 1989, 230). Drugs began to play a bigger part, and heroin, LSD and other hard drugs began to take their toll. Homosexuality became more visible after it had been legalised, between 'consenting adults', in Britain in 1967 (Sexual Offences Act, 1967), in the wake of the Wolfenden Report of 1958. Some of the innocent joy of the early 1960s was lost by the end of the decade, as 'flower people' switched to 'flower power' and a political dimension to the youth movement came to be seen. This emerged in serious fashion with the student revolts of the later 1960s. In the 1970s, high unemployment among the young would produce a new culture of resentment and inactivity among many.

Holidays

The modern holiday is the product of industrialisation. Even as late as 1950, most rural people in western Europe had no formal summer holiday, either in terms of time off or of a change of scene. Many industrial workers, outside France where national legislation had applied since 1936, did not yet enjoy paid holidays, but rare were those who did not, during extended public holidays or works weeks, take their families away. In southern Europe most workers could afford no more than days out to the seaside or to a shrine or public park. In northern Europe, seaside resorts had been growing up since the nineteenth century and workers could afford to travel further to them and stay longer.

The virtual completion of western Europe's industrialisation and urbanisation in the half-century after the Second World War maximised the holiday clientele, with even many of the reduced

number of agricultural workers prosperous enough, and sufficiently part of national culture, to go away for a while by the
1970s. The spread of the private car encouraged holidays away
from home even when household budgets could scarcely sustain
them.

Holiday entitlement and potential varied greatly across western
Europe. France was in the vanguard. The reforms of the Popular
Front in 1936 had established the right to two weeks' paid holiday
for all employees. Revived after the Liberation, the measure
continued to give French workers a holiday culture which, in the
later 1940s, was unparalleled in Europe. In 1956, the statutory paid
holiday entitlement was increased to three weeks.

Paid holidays, of course, did not mean that manual worker
recipients could go very far. As late as 1963, only 44.3 per cent of
French workers went away on holiday, and by 1976 this proportion
had risen to no more than 48.8 per cent (Fourastié, 1979, 127).
The middle classes of Paris and the north went mainly to the
Atlantic resorts such as Deauville and the much-promoted 'Paris-
Plage' of Le Touquet, two hours from the Gare du Nord. The
French and international rich favoured Nice, Cannes and the rest
of the Côte d'Azur, which had attracted the leisured classes since
the turn of the century. This coastal strip became more popular
from the 1950s as Brigitte Bardot made sun worship fashionable
and the Cannes film festival became associated with starlets and
beach bums.

Jacques Tati's satirical film, *Les vacances de Monsieur Hulot*, a
huge success in 1953, portrayed the mass holiday rush to the coast
at the beginning of August, the timing of the national paid holiday
still reflecting the rhythms of the harvest. In a country still only
semi-urbanised, many manual workers went to stay with parents on
their farms, but rapid urbanisation from the early 1950s reduced
the scope for such cheap holidays and camping emerged as the
classic holiday for the lower middle and working classes.
Economies of scale became significant in the early 1950s, with
large private and municipal campsites spreading behind the
beaches, and Trigano, the mass producer of cheap but stylish
camping equipment, dominating the market ('Le camping, c'est
Trigano!).

The open air style of seaside holiday was extended to the
younger members of the lower middle classes when the Club
Méditerranée was founded by a young entrepreneur, Gérard Blitz,
in 1950. In 1954 Gilbert Trigano, owner of the camping company,

joined Blitz and in 1956 it was decided to expand the Club's holiday village network and to increase the degree of comfort above the original spartan level (*Le Capital*, **35**, 1994, 85). This was a great success and the Club had become the epitome of the fun-loving, sociable holiday for young office workers by the 1960s, as John Ardagh portrayed it in a memorable vignette (Ardagh, 1968, 283–91). No other country developed a similar phenomenon; perhaps the French traditions of beach monitors, and of the *colonies de vacances*, communal residential holidays for schoolchildren, were an influence.

The French were always Europe's main campers. The Italians, though enjoying seaside and lake holidays, preferred hotels and boarding houses. However, the heavy migration from the South to the industrial cities of the North meant that, from the 1950s, holidays took the form of a return to their old villages in the South for a growing number of industrial workers. The world's first seaside holidaymakers, the British, continued to flock to their great nineteenth-century holiday resorts. Blackpool returned to its pre-war glory in 1949, when the decorative lights along the front shone once more and all Lancashire flocked to see them. Until the easing of currency controls in the early 1950s, foreign holidays were difficult even for the middle classes. Most people's period of paid holiday, one or two weeks, was much shorter than in France, and many working people booked very short periods in rooms at the nearest seaside. Some industrial cities had their 'own' resorts, like Nottingham's Skegness ('Skeggy'), and Sheffield's Bridlington ('Brid'). Belgians had a similar holiday culture, with industrial towns lying in the immediate hinterland of an almost continuous string of seaside resorts, the biggest, Ostend, also being a seaport. Germany's geography did not favour big seaside resorts, though Hamburg's Travemünde was an important exception. Lake holidays were very popular, despite the cold water.

The North Sea climate discouraged camping and even the health-conscious Germans shunned tents. In the early post-war years, however, most German workers were so poor that a distant holiday was out of the question. Instead, they stayed at home and attended the huge park-cum-sports centres which had been built outside German cities in the 1920s to cater for the physical and mental needs of a previous generation of impoverished workers. (These were the 'swimming baths' that the profligate Germans had built instead of meekly paying their war reparations.) The water was very cold here as well.

By the later 1950s most Germans could afford to go away for their holidays. They proved to be Europe's greatest travellers, their humble VW Beetles probing to the very limits of Europe in Portugal and Greece. More than any other nationality, German touring motorists used to wave or hoot (usually both) when passing each other on some dusty foreign road. By the later 1960s, with German motorists pullulating everywhere, they had tired of this camaraderie.

Culture

Ever since the eighteenth century, France had been Europe's most advanced country in the arts and letters. Industrialisation had not undermined this feature of national life. On the contrary, Paris had emerged in the later nineteenth century as the cultural capital of the new Europe. Liberated in 1944, wartime Paris proved to have harboured a multitude of cultural movements and initiatives which began to exercise an influence both inside and outside France just as soon as the Germans had left. As soon as tourism became possible once more in the later 1940s, Paris was once again the main European, and American, traveller target.

In France, culture developed on national lines, and even quite ignorant people took pride in French superiority in the humanities. France retained, more than any other country in Europe, a respect for the intellectual and the man of letters. When the scholarly poet, Saint-John Perse, won the Nobel prize for literature in 1960, his photograph filled the front cover of *Paris-Match*, the mass circulation weekly of popular reportage, under the headline, 'Monsieur! Vous avez le Nobel!'.

In the early post-war years the intellectual society of Paris produced the first clearly war-influenced doctrine. Quickly noted throughout Europe, this was known as Existentialism, which flourished in the fashionable intellectual district of Saint-Germain-des-Près. Existentialism was a complex body of ideas, which maintained that man was essentially what he made of himself, that the world was not intelligible on its own, and that ideas were the product of action.

Its best-known expression was in the work of the writer, novelist and philosopher, Jean-Paul Sartre, who had joined the Resistance towards the end of the war after a period of imprisonment in Germany, and his friend Albert Camus. They jointly launched a daily newspaper, *Combat*, after the Liberation, and published a variety of novels, polemics and theoretical works during and after the war. Both promoted the idea that writers had a duty to be *engagé*, meaning that they had to be active in fundamental political struggles, from a Left-wing perspective. Socialism and even anarchism were encouraged by this approach. Their philosophy also called traditional morality into question and advocated the pursuit of individual satisfaction. Sexual morality and marriage disappeared altogether. They parted company after a quarrel in 1952, and Camus' early death in 1960 left Sartre as the sole leading representative of this challenging tendency. Until his death in 1968, his unremitting Left-wing views and his unchallenged reputation as a writer sustained a politico-cultural amalgam which was respected throughout most of western Europe by the intellectual Left. His message above all was that bourgeois writers and artists had a duty to serve humanity rather than the book-reading minority drawn from the middle class. Humanity did not always, however, understand the work of the bourgeois intellectual, though French pride in Sartre extended well down the social scale.

Perhaps the biggest cultural revolution in France in the immediate post-war years was the launch in 1953 of the Livre de Poche series, equivalent of the British Penguin Books. Nearly all the titles were reprints of the classics and were cheap enough to be bought in large numbers by young people. To call the Livre de Poche a paperback series could mislead, as most French books were sold in drab paper covers with the pages uncut (if you wanted to read on the beach, you took your paperknife with you). The Livre de Poche offered a solidly bound volume with the signatures machine-cut, and, above all, a striking colour illustration on the cover. When these books first appeared in bookshops and newsagents, they were a sensation. To say, though, that they transformed French publishing would be excessive, as most houses carried on with the slovenly style of book production which they could now, more than ever, claim to represent serious art and scholarship. However, other popular publishers started to follow the Livre de Poche example. Above all, in a country with no tradition of public libraries, the new style extended serious reading to sections of the population which previously had had no access to it. Knowledge of the French classics was the main result.

The post-war association between culture and politics in France reinforced the hegemony of French culture in western Europe as a whole. This unique association of culture and national identity was strongly expressed in 1959 when Charles de Gaulle, once more at the Elysée and embarked upon a modernising and stabilising programme for France, set up a new ministry, the Ministry of Culture, and put his old wartime colleague, André Malraux, at its head. Malraux launched a conservation programme for historic towns, and set up a number of provincial *Maisons de la Culture* (Cook, 1993, 63).

Britain was not very open to Left Bank influence in the later 1940s, or indeed from anywhere else in Europe. Its interest in practical problems and in pragmatic solutions, all perceived within a British social tradition linked closely to social class, tended to exclude overseas theories, though images were more acceptable. Nevertheless, it produced its own group of writers who, from the early 1950s, questioned tradition without creating a clear alternative. Known by their media name of the Angry Young Men, their first influential product was Kingsley Amis' novel, *Lucky Jim*, in 1954. However, John Osborne's even more socially critical play, *Look Back in Anger*, produced in 1956, made a clear statement, suggesting that Britain's post-war 'social revolution' had been false, and that the departure of the Labour government in 1951 had left a series of frustrated ambitions for equality and freedom.

West Germany had no such pride or self-confidence after the war. Its cinema produced little of note. It had no clear message, for specifically German values were no longer fashionable, and few German films were shown abroad. Meanwhile, American films flooded into Germany. The practice now began of dubbing English-language films for a mass audience, rather than using sub-titles.

German literature revived fitfully after the war in discouraging conditions. For a couple of years all reading matter, including newspapers and magazines, was in short supply, and long queues could often be seen at the street kiosks. Most new writing related to the current condition of Germany or to the political events and war which had brought it about. In 1947 a group of writers known as Group 47 came together under the leadership of Hans Werner Richter. The group sprang from the initiative of some young German prisoners of war who had founded a cultural review for circulation among the camps in the USA in 1945. Known as *Der Ruf*, this publication continued to appear in Germany after the prisoners returned home in 1946. Its realism proved too outspoken for the US military authorities, who banned it in 1947. In their frustration, the writers came together as a discussion group. Group 47 would remain in existence until 1974 (McClelland and Scher, 1974, 153). The writings of Heinrich Böll and Günter Grass exemplified the work of Group 47. Strongly realistic, sometimes pessimistic, sometimes transcendental, Group 47 writers used mainly the format of the novel and the short story to portray Germany's experience under National Socialism and its effect on post-war mental reconstruction. Most were serious, critical works which expressed a continuing tension between the individual and German society. Böll, older than Grass, stressed the plight of the individual as inhuman forces threatened to overwhelm him. Grass put forth a more overtly political message, leading to struggle. His novel, *Die Blechtrommel* (The Tin Drum), published in 1959, exemplified the plight of the powerless individual in National Socialist Germany. It quickly won him a world reputation and secured international respect for the continuing struggle faced by the arts in Germany.

Group 47 was the major influence on German writing until well into the 1960s. Among other things, it helped to bring twentieth-century foreign literature into Germany after it had been banned by Hitler. Translations were organised, with Ernest Hemingway, for instance, being opened up to German readers. In fact, Hemingway proved very popular with Group 47. The timing of these influences in Germany meant that much German writing combined a tough, independent expression so typical of German creativity between 1890 and 1933, and the results of an avid consumption of overseas writing stretching from almost historic authors such as Jack London, and the contemporary avant-garde such as Camus and Sartre.

Distorted links with East Germany generated political influences which were unique to Germany, and the country's growing material success, conservation and complacency had driven many writers to the extreme Left by the 1960s. Engaged politico-philosophical movements like the Frankfurt School were admired by many writers, and this blurred the line between creative literature and revolutionary tracts. These tensions would become only too visible in the 1970s.

German art also had to reestablish its position after its atavistic phase of Nazi national romanticism. Some of the expressionistic, critical tradition of the 1920s was revived in the work of older painters such as Richard Oelze, but many younger artists chose the path of abstract art, partly because realist interpretations were hard to formulate in a Germany where older traditions had been called into question. The painting of town scenes continued from the 1920s in the work of Werner Heldt and others, with bomb destruction often implicit. Joseph Beuys, the structural sculptor, used iron, stone and other simple materials on a large scale to express the rigid immobility of industrial society. At the same time, his use of large quantities of scrap recalled scenes of wartime destruction in the cities.

Little known or appreciated outside Germany, German art seemed to be in a constant struggle with itself and the German past after 1945. The great Royal Academy exhibition of twentieth-century German art in 1985 suggested a continuing agony and provided a clue to the German psyche which the ordered life of western Germany could not reveal (Joachimides et al., 1985).

Cinema

Across western Europe, the main trend in the cinema after the war was the movement to realism (Manvell, 1966, 7). The main source of influence here was the Italian cinema, which had been making historic epics and other Fascist films since the 1920s. Roberto Rossellini shot *Rome Open City* (1945) in German-occupied Rome in difficult and dangerous conditions. The result could scarcely fail to be neo-realist and the film was quickly shown in Paris where it was much admired. Vittorio De Sica went on to make *Bicycle Thieves* (1948), while a younger director, Federico Fellini, made *La strada* (1954).

Realism was only part of British cinema production, but it continued a wartime tradition of films stressing popular support for the war effort. Robert Hamer's *It Always Rains on Sunday* (1947) was closest to Carné and the Italians, though its crime and chase aspects made it end as an adventure story. Britain's war victory and tolerable post-war conditions probably meant that it had no market for the cinema of desperation. The lower middle class had been portrayed as the stuff of England in David Lean's *This Happy Breed* (1944). The upper class, subject of pre-war plays by Lean's elegant mentor, Noel Coward, faded somewhat from the screens, just as his French equivalent, Sacha Guitry, 'the last boulevardier', could no longer make his intricate and wordy farces.

In the early years after the war, French studios joined in the European wave of realism which seemed to emerge from war-time experiences, with audiences now willing to face hard realities in the cinema just as they had stood up to the acute challenges of wartime. René Clément's *La bataille du rail* (1945), the story of Resistance sabotage on the railways, was an essay in dramatised reportage which stimulated other realist films. In the early 1950s, however, when a big effort was made to infiltrate the American, British and German mass markets, the French industry began to produce films which dealt in either a serious or popular fashion with sexual themes. In 1956 Roger Vadim released *Et Dieu créa la femme*, his first film with the teenage star, Brigitte Bardot. This and later French films dealing with the lives of young people and semi-degenerates were heavily censored in Britain, to the growing derision of the public. The *Le Monde* film critic, however, saw something representative of a new generation and a new lifestyle in the Vadim–Bardot films (Coppolani and Gardair, 1976, 141). They had much in common with the novels (1954–) of the young Françoise Sagan, who became a symbol of the life of rich, young, neurotic Parisian layabouts in the 1950s and the early 1960s.

A group of young directors, led by Jean-Luc Godard, started in 1959 to make films in a completely new style. Known as the New Wave (*nouvelle vague*), these directors rejected the fantasy and irrealism of the majority of French directors of the 1950s, many of whom had aped Hollywood styles, and tried to capture the reality of the street, the cafe and the apartment.

They benefited from a government scheme, launched in 1959, whereby directors and small companies could borrow on the security of the film's future earnings (*avance sur recettes*). Films such as Godard's *A bout de souffle* (1959) portrayed a youth culture among students and fairly leisured lovers of life (and opponents of work). The general climate was not so much nihilistic as puzzled and selfish. It would be reflected in 1968 in the Paris student protests.

New Wave films may have done good business in the tiny art cinemas of the Left Bank where elbows, and often more than elbows, touched throughout the auditorium, but in the grander cinemas of suburban and provincial France less pretentious fare remained on offer. Here, the rise of the lower middle class was visible. Claude Chabrol's *Les bonnes femmes* (1960), one of the few New Wave films with a mass appeal, dealt with a day in the life of a group of young shop girls, emphasising their unattainable dreams of love and riches in a mundane Paris district near the Bastille. Then, in 1966, Claude Lelouch released *Un homme et une femme*, a love story about two thirtyish people living fashionable lives in

sport and the media. Rightly identified as a women's magazine
story by the Paris critics, this film was the success of the decade in
France. Though a real 'histoire de concierge', it appealed to far
more than France's declining breed of irascible and indifferent
doorkeepers. It expressed a popular desire for a stylish life without
the loss of personal values. In this it reflected the prospering
France of the day.

The New Wave and the resurgence of realism around 1960 at
last opened up the German cinema to European influence. A
number of young film-makers joined in 1962 in the Oberhausen
Manifesto, which called for the production of truthful and critical
films on contemporary Germany (Pflaum, 1990, 9–10). With State
funding, several young directors of shorts were able to complete
their first feature films in the mid-1960s. Alexander Kluge's
Abschied von Gestern (1965) hit harder than most, suggesting that
traditional values could not survive in the new Germany.

Theatre

By now, the reader will not be surprised to learn that France – and
not just Paris – was Europe's most important home of the theatre.
Paris had forty or more theatres and each of the main provincial
cities had a clutch of them. Serious theatre-going was a purely
middle-class activity, however, and it rarely functioned as anything
more than elite entertainment.

When the Paris theatre returned to normal in 1945, neither
playwrights nor producers used the opportunity to portray
ordinary life either under the Occupation or after the Liberation.
Jean-Paul Sartre's disturbing play, *Huis Clos*, was the great success
of 1945 but its portrayal of Hell as an endless conversation in a
Parisian drawing-room suggested an intellectual incarceration
which looked back to pre-war society (and was pretty true to life as
well). In the 1950s the plays of Ionesco and Beckett created
grotesque situations and caricatured figures which contained little
obvious meaning. Towards the end of the decade the Theatre of
the Absurd enhanced this effect. The theatre seemed to be an
arcane entertainment for a leisured and cultured elite. The diet of
new plays was complemented by numerous revivals of the (mainly
French) classics, linking the theatre with French national pride.

In 1968 the French theatrical companies joined in the mass
protests engendered by the students and dozens of committed

performances were put on in Paris and the provinces. Jean-Louis Barrault's Odéon theatre in Paris was the scene of a permanent, plebeian debate which encapsulated the whirlwind of ideas which raged during that unique summer (Cook, 1993, 65). For the first time since the French Revolution, the theatre was a major form of mass political expression. Within a year or two, however, the theatre had returned to its elite role. The theatre festivals extended drama to modest towns in the provinces. Jean Vilar's Festival d'Avignon, founded in 1947, was one of the most successful (Cook, 1993, 56). By the 1990s there were thirty-nine annual theatre festivals in France. The diffusion of high-quality theatre to the provinces militated against Parisian elitism, though the cultural dominance of Paris was not seriously threatened by 1970.

In Germany, a rudimentary revival of the theatre in the later 1940s was linked to the re-education process. In some cases the Allies determined the choice of plays, while in others the theatre managements consciously selected productions which bore on both the depressing conditions of post-war Germany, and on the hope for the future which might arise from the ashes if German attitudes could be changed. All productions, though, required the approval of the military authorities until 1949. The French, entirely predictably, encouraged Molière and other classics. The Americans, on the other hand, promoted plays which portrayed the reality and the ideals of contemporary US society. About fifty American plays were specially translated and over 8,000 performances were given in the four occupied zones between 1946 and 1950. Over half were light, escapist productions, however, and politically engaged theatre of the Left or the Right was not permitted (Willett, 1989, 61). Thornton Wilder's *Our Town* was a great success as a portrayal of 'the American way of life' in numerous productions between 1945 and 1948. It echoed the German concept of *Heimat*, which would link traditional Germany to the modern Germany of Edgar Reisz's television epic, *Heimat*, in the 1980s. Of the early German productions, Carl Zuckmayer's *The Devil's General*, first performed at Frankfurt in 1947, was a huge success. Set in the Third Reich, with uniformed officers on stage, it allowed audiences to accept the past and to look forward to a national revival which would be based on some of the human strengths which had always been a feature of Germany (Willett, 1989, 63).

As before the war, the British theatre was heavily centred on

London, with provincial cities entertained mainly by touring productions. Theatre-going was largely a middle- and upper-class pastime which did not provoke much thought. However, in 1956 John Osborne's *Look Back in Anger* transformed the British theatre. Together with Colin Wilson's novel, *The Outsider*, published a few days after the opening of the play, it launched a new phenomenon into British society, the alienated intellectual as both subject and creator. It stressed the defects of British society in the era of the Welfare State, with frustration, hypocrisy, ignorance and poverty still preventing personal achievement. Osborne was hailed by the cultural arbiters of British life, the Sunday newspapers, as the leader of the new group of 'Angry Young Men', drawn from lower-middle and working-class origins, whose plays and novels created a new age of realism and criticism (Hewison, 1981, 130–1). This led on to a series of plays and novels by Angry Young Men such as John Braine and Kingsley Amis. All dealt realistically with everyday life, but most attacked the complacency of life in a country which the Welfare State had altered but not transformed. The year 1956 also saw the West End success of Theatre Workshop, a low-cost, cooperative company set up by the socialist producer, Joan Littlewood, in 1945. Based since 1952 at an old music hall in Stratford, East London, Theatre Workshop encouraged experimental plays which also focused on ordinary life among workers, prisoners and patients (Hewison, 1981, 143–4). By the later 1950s, there was much talk of a theatre of the 'kitchen sink', which soon began to affect television.

Student protest

Post-war educational reforms gave British teenagers the right to attend university if they were qualified, together with the necessary public funds to maintain them. Throughout most of the Continent, youngsters with standard secondary qualifications could attend university as of right, but there was almost no public funding for them. Rising living standards allowed growing numbers of European students to study at university by the later 1950s. In France, the total number of university students rose from 136,000 in 1949–50 to 615,000 in 1969–70 (Berstein, 1989, 183). Nearly all were middle class. Most obtained part-time work to finance their studies, and their degree courses could last for seven years or more, especially as, in the Netherlands and Germany, the degree programme demanded at least five years full time, compared to three years in England and (for many students) four years in Scotland. With many students studying into their later twenties, and some into their early thirties, political doctrines flourished at the continental universities and Marxism secured many adepts, particularly in France, Germany and Italy. In Britain, Labourist reformism was the norm among a younger, more contented student body.

Student revolts began in Italy in 1966, when rioting occurred. These early protests were mainly the result of the especially bad conditions in the Italian universities. However, the politically aware can always place local grievances in a broader context and a bigger wave took place in 1967 in sympathy with the worker's militancy which built up in Italy during the decade. Also influential was the Left-wing campaign against the American war in Vietnam, which had spread from the USA after Presidents Lyndon Johnson and then Richard Nixon had increased the American effort there from 1964. This issue allowed the protesters to express the anti-American feeling which lay just under the surface in Europe and which could no longer be smothered and controlled by a strong American presence like that of the early years after the war. Leftist and anarchist violence surged up among the students but as yet the phenomenon was limited to Italy and the idea of a universal student cause was not yet in view.

In 1968 the Paris students launched a bigger campaign, linking university deficiencies to national and also international issues. The war in Vietnam, which had been giving concern on humanitarian grounds, became the target for Leftist attacks on American imperialism and capitalism, which were presented as dominating Europe. Riots spread to Germany, and were resumed in Italy. A more restrained version of the protest spread to Britain in 1969, when 'sit-ins' occurred at almost all British universities, mainly about issues of university education and government.

The Paris student protests of 1968 were the most violent and influential that Europe has ever known. The Sorbonne attracted large numbers of students from the French provinces because of the renown of its teaching and the student culture of the Left Bank. A halo of large and distinguished national professional and technical schools, such as aeronautical engineering, surrounded the University of Paris to form a giant Academy of higher education institutions. More foreign students studied in Paris than in any other city in Europe, and they included large numbers of

Germans. Only the British, cosseted at home by public grants and small classes, and lacking in language ability, were scarcely to be seen.

The French government had launched university reform proposals in 1967. Their leading opponents were the sociology students and professors of Paris, a new and expanding group engaged in a fashionable and inchoate subject, who had been relegated to the Sorbonne's first suburban outpost, the Nanterre campus in north-western Paris. A strike of students and professors at Nanterre in November 1967 was led by Daniel Cohn-Bendit, the son of Jewish refugees from Germany, who had strong links with student revolutionary groups in Germany. It seemed at first to be based on local complaints about poor facilities, but it attracted media interest.

In February 1968 a student strike took place in Paris itself. In May, the Nanterre campus was closed by the Rector of the Academy of Paris. Many of the Nanterre militants now moved to the Latin Quarter. A series of demonstrations in Paris in early May were heavily repressed by the police and the student leaders took the chance to draft a critique of the university and of society as a whole. With much popular support in Paris, the students now began to talk about a revolution against De Gaulle's declining regime. They tried to make contact with the Communist trade unions (CGT – Confédération Générale du Travail), which had launched a series of strikes and occupations to take advantage of the pressure created by the students. Meanwhile, the socialist trade unions (CFDT – Confédération Française Démocratique du Travail) had declared their support for the students. When the French students' union, UNEF (Union nationale des étudiants de France) called for a general strike on 13 May, the trade unions declared their support. This was the high point of student-worker collaboration in 1968.

However, the Communist unions, and the Communist Party, saw no point in being dragged into massive civil disobedience or even a revolution by a group of middle-class students fired by Trotskyist or anarchist ideas. In fact, their national position, and that of the socialist unions, was secured by compromises obtained from the State, and they feared that they might emerge weaker from a free-for-all in which the unpredictable forces of mass democracy were unleashed (Larkin, 1988, 319-23). The CGT and the Communist Party remained fundamentally distrustful of 'petit-bourgeois revolutions'. This was, of course, unfair on the 'petits étudiants' who had their skulls cracked by mega-truncheons in the Rue Gay-Lussac and on the many bourgeois intellectuals who had shaped Communism and socialism down through the years. However, one thing that the students now learned was that fairness was not to be expected of the heirs of Stalin. One effect was that student thinking moved further to the Left, opening up fantastic, anarchic perspectives which would generate even more violence in the 1970s in Germany and Italy.

With the CGT using the chaotic situation in the second half of May to secure material gains for its members and to outmanoeuvre the non-Communist unions, and the Socialist and Centre parties trying to secure a presidential election, the danger of revolutionary change had passed. By early June the government was again in command, and in a general election hurriedly called at the end of the month, the Gaullists won 74.3 per cent of the seats in the Assembly (Larkin, 1988, 324–7). Meanwhile, the student protest movement had spread to West Germany, where it at first took a milder form demanding *Mitbestimmung* (participation), which was an official concept in Germany at the time, rather than a revolutionary slogan. However, the worryingly dogmatic students of Germany soon developed far-reaching theories of new societies. Their leader, Rudi Dutschke, himself had come to symbolise violent change after he was shot and wounded in Berlin by a deranged youth on 11 April 1968. It was already only too easy to establish parallels with the anarchic Germany of the early 1920s. In the early 1970s these parallels would acquire an even clearer form.

The university protest movement was a middle class phenomenon and in the long run the protesters went on to build well-paid careers in government, management, the media, and higher education. What most of them never lost, however, was the powerful and rather rigid Marxist outlook which they had taken from the Frankfurt School, Louis Althusser, and other leading intellects of the university world of France, Germany and Italy. Later, of course, when some of the protesters joined violent groups in Germany, it became clear that the message had never been one of liberty. Instead, it was about what an educated elite could tell everyone else to think. The French voters used to complain that De Gaulle told them what to think, but, given the choice, they preferred him to the intensity of youth, as they showed in the emergency general election of 1968.

Outbreaks of student protest occurred over most of western Europe in 1968 and 1969. The Italian demonstrations became more serious, and the phenomenon spread in a limited form to Spain and even to eastern Europe. In Britain, the main effort came in 1969 and 1970, when students used the weapon of the 'sit-in', occupying the administrative offices of most of the country's universities. In the absence of a widely disseminated Marxist ideology in British education, the students based their campaign on their demands for a higher quality of education based on greater choice and democracy. At the University of Warwick, enough university files were opened in a sit-in in early 1970 to allow an alliance of students and radical staff to claim that they had exposed a plot between local industry and the university to subvert education there (Thompson, 1970, 31–41). At the London School of Economics, a similar campaign stressed racism, imperialism, and capitalism as hidden foundations of university education. However, this politico-intellectual critique was as close as the British students got to the Parisian assault on society. The protesters did not go outside the campuses and there was no violence.

Crime and 'impropriety'

The climate of greater personal freedom in the 1960s generated a greater tolerance of individual behaviour. A series of 'scandals', though their content was not new, excited the public. In Britain, the resignation of John Profumo, the Defence Secretary, in June 1963, after a liaison with Christine Keeler, a courtesan who had links with Soviet intelligence, exposed a call-girl system run by an ex-public schoolboy and society osteopath, Stephen Ward. It served rich London businessmen, politicians, and aristocrats. The media exploited this story to the full, pursuing the people involved, and their friends and relatives, to see how far the networks extended (they extended a long way, of course, both upwards and downwards). The general public enjoyed this episode more than any other scandal in Britain since the war. It did nothing at all to sustain conventional ideas of morality among the younger members of the middle and working classes.

The main moral prophet of the affair was Keeler's close friend and darling of the media, Mandy Rice-Davies (a former fifteen-year-old 'Miss Austin' and star of the Motor Show in 1960), who on being told while under oath in court that her 'benefactor', Lord Astor, denied any 'impropriety' (Westminster lingo for sexual relations) with her, replied: 'He would, wouldn't he?' (Young, 1963, 74; Thurlow, 1992, 173). This tart riposte, which made headlines across the land, marked the end of any surviving British belief in traditional upper-class morality, not to say honesty. As Wayland Young put it at the time, 'lays, leaks, and lies' (Young, 1963, 7). In 1995, this 'Rice-Davies Principle' would still be widely acknowledged as the whole country, from rich to poor, honoured the demanding maxim, 'above all, don't admit it!'.

In the world of the Astors, sex cost money, and only the rich and famous could indulge. In the world of the poor, illegality could make a lot of money. In the 1960s, the two worlds could meet, usually with dangerous results for both. The main meeting-ground was gambling. Gambling had been regarded as a social problem since the nineteenth century but by the later 1950s it had come to be seen as socially discriminatory, with the rich able to gamble on horses by telephone while the poor had to go to the track. The Betting and Gaming Act, 1960, a typical liberalising measure of the time, removed this class discrimination. The Act established a wide official tolerance of public betting by allowing casinos and gambling clubs on the lines long established in French resorts, and local bookmakers' establishments for horse racing (betting shops). By June 1962, over 13,000 betting shops were in operation. This expansion of betting helped create an atmos-phere of pleasure-seeking in the early 1960s which sometimes combined with the greater sexual freedom of the time. Income from gambling in the luxurious West End clubs could employ attendants and subsidise food and drink. Hugh Hefner, whose Playboy Clubs had been a big success in the USA in the 1950s, opened a London Playboy Club, followed by several more across Britain, in the early 1960s. The young female attendants with bunny tails and ears were said to be purely decorative, but nothing in the 1960s was ever that simple.

Clubs holding a lot of cash and open all night were vulnerable to protection rackets and by the early 1960s several unpleasant gangs from inner London were 'protecting' a number of West End clubs. The Bethnal Green 'firm' run by the violent Kray twins was so successful in its protection work that the Krays found them-selves in complete occupation of two West End gambling clubs. Taking advantage of the new respect for working people, they bought dinner jackets and started to hob-nob with their rich and influential clients, including MPs and peers. Media interest sprang up, and soon some of the celebrities were lionising *them*. One former Conservative MP, Lord Boothby, ended by being supplied with teenage boys by Ronnie Kray, himself a pederast and developing psychotic. Boothby had also maintained a long affair with Lady Macmillan and so he was, at the very least, a potential blackmail target of giant proportions. His reputation was very lucky to survive his links with the Krays. The exact nature of the connections with the other celebrities remains unclear, but this is probably because their power and influence helped them to cover their tracks. The much-loved, 'bubbly' film star and actress in the mass-produced 'Carry On films' which typified British working-class humour, Barbara Windsor, was a close friend of the Krays, and especially of the slightly more intelligent Reggie Kray, but she was an East End girl who never lost her links with the Bethnal Green milieu. Other celebrities appear with the Krays on photographs taken at their West End clubs, but all this probably meant was that the Krays liked to employ an in-house photographer. However, with media interest and their growing personal contacts with informal blackmail potential, the Krays were in a better position by 1965 to pervert the course of justice in the pursuit of their more sordid crimes in the East End, and despite a number of gangland murders they were not arrested and successfully charged until 1969.

Like the Profumo affair, the adventures of the Krays reflected an erosion of traditional morality, and a blurring of the truth, based on the decay of the traditional boundaries between the social classes, easy money, and a media-linked assumption that 'scandal' was interesting rather than disturbing. 'He would, wouldn't he?' became 'he will get away with it, won't he?'. In Britain, European leader of the 'Swinging Sixties', the great State lies of Hitler, Mussolini and Stalin became the lies of the promiscuous politician and well-connected businessman. The great golden freeway which in the 1980s and 1990s would carry the shining white limousines of Bernard Tapie, Robert Maxwell and their ilk was already being built in the sky between Maidenhead and Stratford, via Westminster and Holborn, in the 1960s.

Perhaps these excesses were the product of the collapse of traditional structures and values in a Britain moving from affluence towards decay. Comparison with a rich but sober Germany might suggest an answer. German society was very restrained in the post-war years. Wages and salaries remained low into the later 1950s. Workers could earn good incomes by working long hours of overtime but this left them with little time or energy for other things. German schools and universities stressed hard work and discipline, perhaps even more than before 1945. This society did not generate much scandal and corruption. However the motives and machinery of the State were brought into question in 1962 when the publisher of the news magazine, *Der Spiegel*, and several other people were charged with publishing defence secrets as part of a campaign questioning the competence of the government (Turner, 1987, 84–5). Adenauer's government survived the challenge but he resigned in the following year, at much the same time as Harold Macmillan. From this point onwards, doubts began to emerge within the German political system and German society as a whole. The SPD began to gain popular support while confidence in the CDU economic philosophy was undermined. When, in 1966, the SPD entered into a coalition government for the first time in the history of the Federal Republic, the way was open for a government controlled by the SPD, with a SPD Prime Minister. Such a government came to power in 1969. The SPD handled their position as leaders of a social–liberal coalition very well, but more disturbing was the gradual erosion of the common political ground of which Germany was confident in the 1950s. The way was now open to the extremism of the early 1970s.

Ironically, just as the 1920s ended with the depression of 1929–32, so the 1960s were ending with an oncoming economic crisis which would culminate in the oil crisis of 1973. The fears of the day were not solely economic; western Europe had moved within a few years from the youthful, careless joy of the mini-skirt and the rock band to the danger of a new anarchy or a new totalitarianism. Youth culture would never be the same again.

CHAPTER SIX

The New Europeans:
Immigration, Immigrants and their
Descendants

Western Europe experienced an unprecedented influx of immigrants after 1945. Some came for social or political reasons, but most arrived in response to a massive demand for labour in the expanding economy of the 1950s and 1960s. With economic growth faster than it had ever been before in western Europe, natural increase and the movement of the existing population into employment could not fill all the potential new jobs.

It was especially hard to find people to do unskilled work, much of which was in the growing service sector. By 1945 western Europe had built up an educated population of high expectations. Even emigrants from the land were reluctant to move into unpleasant, low-status employment in the cities. This meant that rapid growth required an inward movement of cheap, pliable labour. In the view of Charles P Kindleberger, who attached particular importance to the presence of a copious labour supply in economic development, labour force flexibility was the main factor permitting the very high growth rates of the 1950s and 1960s. Immigration from outside Europe was by no means the only contributor to the growth and adaptability of the labour force, but it was an important component. It also had important social implications.

Most of the immigration into western Europe came from outside Europe altogether. This was a completely new experience for western Europe. In the second half of the nineteenth-century immigrants from eastern Europe had flowed into the West, settling mainly in western Germany and other industrial countries. Some were Jews, who came mainly from Poland, and many others were Germans, who came mainly from east Prussia and the other eastern provinces of the Reich. Numbers of ethnic Poles and Slavs also moved west, settling mainly in western Germany. All these immigrants, including most of the Jews, were readily assimilated and the process of migration has attracted little historical attention, at any rate outside Germany (see Berend and Ranki, 1974, 19–21).

The arrival of people from the Caribbean, from Africa, and from the Near, Middle, and Far East after 1945 was more revolutionary in its implications. They did not pose serious economic problems, as they arrived voluntarily to meet a visible demand for labour. Many of them became unemployed after the early 1970s but immigration now slowed and a reverse migration occurred. The social aspects of this immigration were much more significant. By 1995 they had transformed most of the cities of northern Europe into a multi-racial and multi-cultural society which had much in common with the large cities of the USA. The way in which this transformation was achieved over less than fifty years merits careful examination. Together with the changing role and consciousness of women, it is arguably the most important social change in Europe since the war.

The European territory and race

Europe covers 8 per cent of the world's land surface and is home to a quarter of the world's population. However, in terms of area it is small; only Australia is smaller among the continents. This thriving, densely populated territory had experienced very little immigration from outside its boundaries since Roman times and their immediate aftermath in the barbarian invasions, when the Huns and other Mongol peoples had settled in Europe. Its population was almost exclusively fair skinned; in other words, 'white', or 'Caucasian', as the European racial group was some-times known. Its culture had been based on a number of variants of Christianity for nearly two thousand years. The greater labour force needed for industrialisation from the late eighteenth century was supplied mainly by natural increase and migration from the land. That post-war western Europe should experience a wave of non-Caucasian immigration from outside the continent that would represent some 5 per cent of its total population by 1970, and many more, if descendants of first-generation immigrants are included, by 1995, was one of the biggest discontinuities in European history. The situation which brought it about is

interesting in itself, but its implications for European society are
even more important.

Migration and the post-war world

The Allied vision of the post-war world required free mobility of
the factors of production, including labour. Migration, it was
envisaged, would move from countries of labour surplus to
countries of labour shortage. This would equalise resources and
increase the range of opportunities for the individual, producing
greater personal contentment and reinforcing democracy. With
non-European military personnel serving with distinction in the
British, Italian and French forces, few Europeans would have
argued in 1945 that they could rightly be excluded from their
'mother country'.

In the early post-war years, however, labour shortages in the
industrial countries were met mainly by movements within Europe.
In 1945, the rapid economic revival planned for Britain prompted
official thoughts of offering stateless persons and other uprooted
people the chance to come to work in Britain, at the same time
acquiring British citizenship. Most of these workers, under the
European Volunteer Worker (EVW) and other schemes, came
from eastern Europe. As Europeans, most of these people were
very quickly assimilated, though the Poles and the Yugoslavs, in
particular, tended to retain a very strong accent. In France, the
departure of 40,000 Polish miners and most of the German
prisoners of war in 1946–47 caused problems for the Monnet plan,
but by 1950 some 190,000 foreign workers had arrived, together
with 103,000 from North Africa (Mauro, 1971, 333).

By 1948, however, it was clear that eastern Europe could no
longer be a significant source of labour, because Stalin wanted to
use all the manpower he had for his own industrialisation
programme. The populations of the new satellite states such as the
German Democratic Republic (East Germany) and Czechoslovakia
were generally better qualified and more motivated than those of
the Soviet Union and Stalin, in his rather crude way, saw the
satellites specialising in particular industries and exporting to the
Soviet Union. These arrangements, most of which were based on
barter and quotas at arbitrarily fixed prices, were made slightly
more tolerable by the Council for Mutual Economic Assistance
(Comecon), set up in 1949.

Soviet tutelage, despite its rhetoric, was never able to secure living standards in eastern Europe comparable to those of the West. A big outflow of population would have taken place had it not been for Communist controls and the physical barrier of the Iron Curtain defences. Berlin was a big loophole in the early 1950s but by dint of military efforts, culminating with the building of the Berlin Wall in 1961, the flow was stemmed even from East Germany. In the 1960s some of the Iron Curtain countries, notably Hungary and Yugoslavia, started to supply labour on a contract basis, principally to Germany. Ironically, when the Iron Curtain finally collapsed in 1991, people from eastern Europe found it hard to secure jobs in the West because of high unemployment there. A big influx to take advantage of high wages in western Europe did not occur and, without residence or work permits, the people of eastern Europe were almost as immobile as before.

The European empires

All the European imperial powers had drawn on the resources of their empires during the war. The French and the British, in particular, had used colonial troops. Many West Indians had served in the British ranks and in the merchant navy. The Indian Army had served in Europe as well as Asia. Many of these men wanted to remain in, or to come to, Europe after the war and governments recognised them as an important source of labour as eastern Europe was closed off. The possibility of social tensions was not seriously considered at this time. However, the context of migration was already changing as the future of the empires began to be reviewed.

A price that western Europe had to pay for US support against the Axis was American pressure for the democratisation or dissolution of the European colonial empires. This was part of the Atlantic Charter ideal of freedom, and of the concept of a world economy (Röpke, 1959, 79–113). In certain cases (France, Portugal) the USA was prepared to support colonial rule for strategic reasons but in general they tried to ease the imperial powers towards withdrawal or accommodation with local interests. There was no precise timetable for decolonisation but without it there could be no complete development of the world trading economy, as the USA saw it. Nor could the old strategic tensions and indigenous hatred of the West be removed.

The Dutch, demoralised by Japanese occupation in South-East Asia, made their colonies independent within a few years and concentrated on catching up on their big backlog in industrialisation within their new Benelux association. Indonesia, the most important Dutch colony, became independent in 1949 after two years of American pressure, expressed in part through the United Nations. Italy lost nearly all its colonies by virtue of its defeat, just as Germany had done at the end of the First World War. Belgium, with a huge, difficult territory, the Belgian Congo (later, Zaire) to administer, was unable to take action immediately. Britain, which had already been making noises about freeing its colonies in the 1930s, gave independence to India in 1948, with other colonies following from 1960, the year in which Ghana became the first colony in black Africa to achieve independence.

The only important recalcitrant was France, whose defeat in 1940 had revealed a variety of weaknesses which encouraged it to hold onto its 'jewels'. This mentality had something in common with its efforts to secure the Ruhr between 1945 and 1948, and the Saar until as late as 1955, and its failure in these respects strengthened its desire to keep its earlier gains overseas. Its main problem, however, was the colony of Algeria, acquired in 1830 purely for reasons of national aggrandisement, and now inhabited by a mixed European and Arab population. France claimed that Algeria had already been democratised, with the Algerian Muslims being given French citizenship in 1947, and that no further action was needed. For their part, however, the Algerian Muslims complained that European discrimination against them continued in a number of forms. The other problem was Indochina (Vietnam), already under Communist guerrilla attack by 1946 and strategically so important to the USA that it was prepared to support the French defence of the territory. In 1954 France had to grant independence to Indochina after a bitter war; in the same year there began an Arab revolt in Algeria which would cause even greater suffering until the French capitulation in 1962.

Where colonies were retained, their populations normally enjoyed the right to travel freely to and from Europe. However, and whenever, the colonies became independent, there was a general understanding that their people would have citizenship rights, or rights of abode, in the European mother countries. This meant that they could come to live or work in Europe without excessive formalities, and that they would probably know the language of the mother country. Wages were considerably higher than in their own countries, so they could send money home to their families or pay to bring them to Europe. Some countries made specific entry agreements, like that between France and Algeria in 1947.

The following flows had built up by the late 1950s:

1. To Britain from the West Indies, India/Pakistan, Hong Kong, Cyprus, and other British colonies
2. To France from Algeria, Tunisia, Morocco, colonies in central Africa, the Caribbean, and Indochina
3. To the Netherlands from Indonesia and other Dutch colonies in South-East Asia
4. To Italy from Libya
5. To Belgium from the Belgian Congo (Zaire).

Britain

Britain was the first country to attract large numbers of immigrants from its empire. The successful transition to peacetime production generated labour shortages from as early as 1946. At first, certain categories of skilled labour – such as building labour – were the most in demand. Official training schemes were set up in some of these areas and many young English people were able to move quickly into skilled and semi-skilled jobs in the later 1940s. Many returning servicemen took advantage of special educational and training schemes which allowed them to improve their economic and social status. By the late 1940s, employers and the Government were becoming aware of a secondary shortage of unskilled labour. There were special problems in low-pay areas such as hospitals and public transport.

In 1948 a group of travel agents in Kingston, Jamaica, chartered an old troopship, the *Empire Windrush*, to bring several hundred Jamaican jobseekers and their families to London. The event was fully covered in the British press and newsreels, which stressed the warm welcome and rich job opportunities which awaited the newcomers. The British Nationality Act of 1948 gave them citizenship and helped them in their search for employment. Most of these early immigrants were not disappointed, and many more followed.

Immigrants from India and Pakistan started to arrive in numbers rather later, from the early 1950s. By now, employers were actively recruiting both there and in the West Indies. Public

sector employers like London Transport and the National Health
Service were very successful in the Caribbean while northern
textile firms attracted labour mainly from India and Pakistan.
Some of these workers had textile experience in Bombay and
elsewhere, but most came from villages where overpopulation prevented their securing a good plot of land.

The rate of Commonwealth immigration tended to increase
during the 1950s. In 1961, 336,600 non-European people were
living in Britain, compared to only 74,500 ten years earlier
(Walvin, 1984, 111). By the later 1950s, however, signs of popular
and political opposition started to appear. These would lead to
Britain, having been the first to attract large numbers of
non-European immigrants, becoming the first to try to slow down
the influx. Britain's problem lay partly in the fact that its slow
economic growth was no longer creating jobs quickly enough to
employ an ingress which may have been attracted in part by the
high level of Britain's social services and other social comforts.

The occasional violent incident suggested a gradual accumulation of popular opposition to the presence of the immigrants.
Some incidents had occurred at the very end of the war. Later
incidents in Liverpool and Birmingham, respectively involving
black seamen and Indian immigrants in 1948, suggested an
increase of scale but they appear to have remained isolated and
unemulated (Panayi, 1993, 16). In the 1950s, letters to local
newspapers and the spread of 'no coloured' signs on boarding
house doors suggested a growth of white antipathy in the older
districts of the industrial cities. Then, riots in two big districts of
West Indian settlement, Hyson Green in Nottingham and Notting
Hill in London in August and September 1958, suggested a
worrying transition from sullen confrontations in the back streets
to a potentially political confrontation.

The riots prompted a big effort by the authorities, the press,
and academics to detect the causes of the problem. Employment
and wages were not an issue, partly because the British trade
unions had incorporated the immigrants as soon as they took up
work, in order to prevent an erosion of unskilled wages. Housing,
however, was a constant worry not only to the immigrants themselves but to the civic authorities, which feared a decline of
environmental standards in the immigrant areas.

Since the early 1950s, the national and local authorities, backed
by the Church and the other main institutions of civil society, had
insisted that all the coloured immigrants should by treated exactly

the same as white British citizens. The Conservative MP, Enoch Powell, broke this consensus when he started to campaign in 1958 for a ban on immigration, and progressive repatriation. Powell's activities were widely repudiated, but they contributed to the political climate which generated the Commonwealth Immigration Act of 1962, which was later reinforced by the Commonwealth Immigration Act of 1968. This legislation set up a voucher system to limit the number of new immigrants to the amount of employment available, generally on the lines of US immigration procedures.

Although its advocates claimed that it would reduce racial tensions, the legislation focused attention on the problem without greatly reducing the flow. This was because established immigrants, most of whom had come alone, now brought their families to Britain, including dependent parents in many cases. This put more pressure on the health services and accelerated the development of urban districts dominated by non-European populations. The idea that all would mix, in houses and in schools, which had been the ideal of central and local government in the 1950s, was abandoned in the 1960s. In 1981 Britain redefined British citizenship in order to exclude those not born in the British Isles, or descendants thereof. Meanwhile, however, the birth of children widened and deepened the non-European areas.

As elsewhere in Europe, the economic deceleration of the 1970s further increased tensions in the immigrant areas. For the most part, however, violence was not the result of European resentment of the immigrants but of a sense of grievance among the immigrants themselves at unemployment and police harassment, as they saw it. There were serious riots in Brixton, south London, in April, 1981. West Indians were the main instigators here. During the summer there were further riots, again mainly involving West Indians, in Birmingham, Bristol, Liverpool, and other towns. In many cases buildings were burned down and there were attacks on police and firemen. In 1985 there was a serious riot on a West Indian housing estate in London (Broadwater Farm, Tottenham), during which a policeman was murdered. All these riots were brought under control by the civil police and the army was not called in. Sensitive treatment by the authorities and the influence of the leaders of the immigrant communities prevented a recurrence of incidents like Broadwater Farm, but occasional ethnic disturbances continued into the 1990s. By this time, rioting by mainly white youths on suburban council estates was attracting much greater media interest, and the problem of unemployment, poverty and general boredom had become a national problem shared by all.

In later 1980s and 1990s, some efforts were made to gather population statistics based on racial origins or skin colour, but this remained a very difficult area of inquiry, especially because of the political implications. Britain's huge stock of municipal housing – much the largest in western Europe and amounting to one dwelling in three in the early 1980s – helped to permit the dispersal of non-white immigrants and their descendants from the inner-city 'ghettos', beginning in the 1970s. Nevertheless, the older areas of immigrant settlement were still consolidating and spreading in 1995.

In a sense, this was much more of a multi-racial society than the one dreamed of by British liberals in the 1950s. Integration into white society on a piecemeal basis was replaced by the emergence of racial and cultural communities with their own shops, schools, temples and churches. With similar trends visible all over western Europe, only a small minority seemed to be acquiring middle-class status and moving out to the suburbs (and many of these, such as the Indians expelled from East Africa in the 1960s, were business people of long standing). The way seemed to be open to the racial and ethnic mosaic visible in so many US cities. Whether this would enrich or complicate European urban life remained to be seen, but it was likely that the higher the rate of growth in living standards, the greater the enrichment would be.

France

France set up a National Office of Immigration in 1946. Intended to prevent labour shortages, it was more a product of the post-war planning drive than a response to pressing needs. However, the low pre-war birth rate continued to reduce the working population after 1945, the total dropping by 2 million people (10 per cent) between 1931 and 1954. The government thought that between 1 and 1.5 million foreign workers would be needed between 1946 and 1951, but this proved quite unrealistic (Graham, 1990, 60). There was some immigration, mainly from southern Europe, after 1945, but there was no big growth in the numbers of immigrants until around 1955, when the economy was at last expanding fast, the average working week was very close to the legal maximum, and national service still absorbed a significant part of the potential labour force. This meant that while French conscripts were sent to fight in Algeria between 1954 and 1962, Algerian men came to France to work in factories and public services. This exchange accelerated from 1956 when the Algerian war entered a worrying new phase.

In 1963, similar access agreements were signed with Tunisia and Morocco, which had secured independence from France in 1956, and with Portugal. The former colonies in Black Africa, made independent by De Gaulle in 1960, became a big source of immigrants thereafter. These agreements strengthened France's influence in Africa, but they would not have been feasible had not the rapid growth of the French economy in the early 1960s created a big labour shortage. In the 1960s the annual average number of immigrants into France was 164,000 (Graham, 1990, 60). By 1969, nearly 4 million immigrants were living in France, 1.3 million of whom were naturalised (Berstein, 1989, 180–1).

Housing was a big problem for these immigrants, most of whom came from north or west Africa. The building of public housing could scarcely keep up with migrants from the French countryside at this time. Many immigrants found rooms in the overcrowded inner districts, as they did in Britain, but in France the overall housing shortage was much worse and expedients were necessary. The main result was the *bidonville*, or shanty town. These grew up from the 1950s outside Paris and other large towns on derelict land. There was some precedent for them in the 1920s, when the notorious *lotissements* had grown up around Paris, and they were tolerated by both the police and the planning authorities. There were over 200 such shanty towns by the 1970s. Poor housing and other deprivations were linked to poor health. In 1964, between 70 and 80 per cent of people being treated for tuberculosis in French hospitals were foreign workers (Kindleberger, 1967, 175).

North Africans started to bring their families into France in growing numbers from the mid-1970s, when barriers to further immigration were under serious discussion. Immigrant communities now became much more visible in the cities, and their residents began to influence urban life as a whole (Hargreaves, 1987, 3). By 1986, France contained about 4 million foreigners. The biggest national group was that of the Portuguese (765,000), but the combined North African groups, known as the Maghrébiens (people from the populated coastal strip north of the Sahara) made up a considerably larger population which was much more visible to the native French. These main Arab groups were the Moroccans (494,000), Tunisians (201,000), and Algerians (535,000) (Clout, 1994, 90). As in Britain, there were political implications, but they would emerge rather later, and in a European context of Right-wing revival.

Switzerland

The biggest recruiter of foreign labour in relative terms was Switzerland. Its neutral status had helped it pass through the war without damage to its capital stock and its living standards, and after 1945 it was able to expand its manufacturing production, especially in the precision and high technology areas. With educational standards improving above their high pre-war level, skilled and highly qualified employment was easily filled by the native Swiss, but manual and low-paid service jobs were much harder to fill.

In the 1950s the government and leading firms combined to attract foreign workers. A rotation system for foreign labour was adopted by many employers along German lines. By the 1960s foreign workers made up nearly one-third of the labour force, with the year of peak influx occurring in 1972, when 179,500 foreign workers entered Switzerland (Milward et al., 1993, 56). Though they remained cheap labour, their social needs involved the State in heavy investment and outlay, and in the end they began to undermine the competitiveness of the Swiss economy (Kindleberger, 1967, 41–2).

Beginning in the 1960s, the large number of foreign workers attracted to Switzerland produced serious problems of assimilation. The irony here was that most of the newcomers were Europeans, recruited from nearby Italy, but there seemed to be a difference between Swiss Italians and Italian Italians, perhaps because many of the latter came from the Mezzogiorno. The native Swiss general public started to complain against 'overforeignisation', and in 1964 the government took action to restrict the further recruitment of foreign labour. Investment from abroad was also restricted at the same time. A parallel measure allowing foreign workers already in Switzerland to bring in their wives more easily, and to apply sooner for rights of permanent residence, was rejected by the legislature. In 1965 the government imposed a reduction on the number of foreign workers living in Switzerland (Kindleberger, 1967, 46).

The Swiss response to foreign immigration was unique in western Europe and suggested that there was something special in both cultural and ethnic terms about a country which had taken pride in its successful isolation for many hundreds of years. As in other countries where a demand grew up for a reduction in the numbers of 'foreigners', so many had acquired residence rights, and were raising families, that the critics were unable to detect much improvement. As elsewhere, 'foreign' districts developed in the towns, unnerving the native Swiss even more. By 1995, Switzerland had become a culturally divided country with much of its traditionally valued character lost, at any rate in the cities.

Germany

The arrival of 9 million German refugees between 1945 and the early 1950s meant that western Germany did not begin to import foreign workers in significant numbers until the mid-1950s. A high level of unemployment persisted until the middle of the decade. Large numbers of immigrants (311,000 in 1955 alone) were still entering West Germany, mainly from East Germany. Most of these were ethnic Germans, and their easy assimilation into the labour force made them preferable to foreigners in most jobs. As late as 1955, only 80,000 foreign workers were employed in Germany. The Federal government nevertheless planned at this time to increase the flow of foreign workers (OEEC, *Germany*, 1956, 7). The authorities and the importing firms now combined to negotiate batches of labour with a number of exporting countries. By the mid-1950s the German authorities were providing housing for foreign workers, and from 1957 they and the employers went abroad to recruit. First, western Germany turned to southern Europe, with agricultural labour largely in mind. Recruiting of Italian workers began in 1956 at the request of the Italian government, which saw it as a means of reducing the country's unemployment problem (Kindleberger, 1967, 185). Recruitment of Spanish and Greek workers began in 1960, as Italy became a less prolific source owing to industrialisation there (Kindleberger, 1967, 185). The construction of the Berlin Wall in 1961 merely accelerated the official search for new sources of labour, with a recruitment agreement signed with Portugal in 1964, for instance (Kindleberger, 1967, 185).

In the 1960s the emphasis of recruitment switched from the

industrialised countries of southern Europe to more distant, more backward countries which already had links with western Germany. Without an empire since 1919, western Germany would normally have expected to attract labour from the eastern lands which had been in its sphere of economic and political influence in the 1930s – countries such as Hungary, Rumania and Bulgaria. However, all Germany's eastern friends and allies from the war were now under Communist control. Western Germany solved the problem by attracting immigrants from a more distant zone of south-eastern Europe and nearby Asia, which had also been under German influence before the war. The main countries involved were Greece, Turkey and Iran. Later, two Communist countries, Hungary and Yugoslavia, joined the list because by the later 1950s they were prepared to export their labour surplus. Moscow and the national governments tolerated this loss of labour because it took the form of departures by individual workers on a contract basis, and remittances to families brought in hard currency.

The number of foreign workers in Germany surged from 72,906 in 1954 to 279,390 in 1960. By 1965 there were over 1 million, and the total rose to 2 million by the end of the decade (*Materialien*, 1974, 326).

FIGURE 6.1   *Total foreign workers in the German Federal Republic, and percentage of the total workforce, 1954–71.*

Year	Total	Percentage
July 1954	72,906	0.4
July 1960	279,390	1.3
June 1965	1,164,364	5.5
June 1970	1,838,859	8.5
June 1971	2,163,766	10.0

Source: data derived from *Materialien*, 1974, 326.

With hindsight, this extraordinary rate of increase looks like asking for trouble, especially as the German authorities worked much more closely with the employers than in either Britain or France.

Much of this recruitment recalled some of the more legitimate aspects of Germany's efforts to bring labour to the Reich during the Second World War. This slightly sinister similarity was, however, entirely understandable as the two big surges of demand for labour in German industry (1942–44, and 1965–70) were bound to be met in the same way, by the organised recruitment of single foreigners. Aware of the potential analogy, the German govern- ment and the employing firms did their best to secure fair and generous treatment for the recruits, and to prevent any hostility or jealousy on the part of the native population. While full employment persisted, what danger could there be? And if it ended, they would go home, wouldn't they?

The German authorities were well aware of possible problems in the assimilation of non-European workers. Like the Swiss, who were already bringing in more migrant workers than Germany in proportionate terms, the Germans assumed that the non-Europeans would return home sooner or later. Most were supplied with barrack accommodation by their employers and did not come into contact with the German population very much. The authorities and the firms issued publicity about happy workers who felt honoured to be in Germany, and fulsome interest was shown in the folk culture of the guests. In 1964, the arrival of the millionth 'guest worker' in Germany was celebrated by a highly publicised ceremony of welcome at Cologne railway station. The obsequious official term, *Gastarbeiter* (guest worker), reflected both the publicity problem and its solution.

All this care and publicity fitted in well with West Germany's caring, generous, outward-looking diplomatico-economic policy, which owed much to American post-war international strategy. However, to import non-European labour on such a large scale was risky in a country which had no great imperial tradition and which, under Hitler, had been encouraged to value its ethnic-national identity above all other strengths. All the labour imported into Germany during the war had been European, but the Slav elements had been singled out for special denigration, and even the French had been rated racially somewhat below the Dutch, who qualified as near-Aryans. National Socialist rhetoric, humbug, spite, and general nonsense were of course not taken seriously any more, but the question remained whether workers from Turkey, Iran, and even Greece, Yugoslavia and Italy would secure real respect in Germany.

The numbers of guest workers increased rapidly after about 1960. Only a minority went home after 1973. In 1982, Germany still contained 624,000 Italians but they had now been overtaken by the largest East European group, the Yugoslavs, of whom there were 637,000. The biggest national group by far, however, was the

Turks, of whom there were 1.5 million in Germany (Clout et al., 1994, 40). By 1986 the four largest national groups of foreigners came from Turkey (1,481,400), Yugoslavia (597,600), Italy (544,400), and Greece (279,000) (Cheles et al., 1991, 76). From the 1960s growing numbers brought their families to Germany, or founded families there. The German authorities estimated that, in 1964, only 10 per cent of the foreign workers in Germany wanted to bring their families to live with them (Kindleberger, 1967, 183–4). This preference was, however, transformed by the crisis of the early 1970s and the German government moves towards the restriction of the flow of foreign labour into the country. The growth of unemployment from 1974 and the suspension of recruitment from non-EEC countries reduced the number of foreigners in the labour force from 2.5 million in 1973 to 2 million in 1980 (Braun, 1990, 211).

It was in the 1960s, when the guest workers started to bring in their families and moved to the older districts of the towns, that the first serious social problems arose. The Turks, in particular, did not integrate easily and the Germans found them hard to like or respect. They were the equivalents of the Algerians in France, as the least-liked immigrants. The fact that both groups were Moslems may have had some bearing on the matter, at least in respect of cultural norms. These problems became more serious in the 1980s. The increase of unemployment, especially among the young, coincided with the continuing arrival of 'foreigners' of various categories, together with ethnic Germans from East Germany and other eastern countries, both before and after the collapse of the Communist regimes in 1989. In 1982, when unemployment reached a total of 2 million, the government offered big cash payments to foreign workers who would agree to return home permanently. However, only small numbers did so.

With nearly 8 per cent unemployed in West Germany in early 1989, the country's official total of nearly 5 million 'foreigners' seemed to some to threaten Germany's generous post-war role as the recipient of people seeking political asylum from all over the world. Between 1980 and 1987, 480,508 people secured political asylum in western Germany. This number included large Turkish, Iranian, Sri Lankan, and Polish groups. As for the ethnic Germans, 813,176 of these arrived between 1968 and 1987 (Cheles et al., 1991, 75–6). With so many of the refugees coming from the big sources of normal immigration, suspicions were aroused in Germany, especially among the Right-wing groups. With many foreigners housed in camps or other temporary accommodation, there was much scope for political exploitation and violent protest. A number of arson attacks in the early 1990s recalled *Kristallnacht* and other violent anti-Jewish episodes under the Third Reich. In 1995 the trend of German opinion remained unclear, but the parallels with wartime Germany were disturbing.

Nordic Europe

In the nineteenth century Nordic Europe had been a big source of emigrants to north America and also to Germany. By the twentieth century, however, the beginnings of industrialisation absorbed much of the excess population from the land. After 1945 its expanding industries, combined with its high living standards and welfare services, discouraged movement, even to Germany. The Nordic countries, and especially Sweden, became net importers of labour from the 1950s. Their sources were similar to Germany's and a big Turkish population built up in Sweden. Popular reaction was not dissimilar to the German one, but the authorities were able to prevent the emergence of strong political opposition. Sweden's very high living standards and sense of civic responsibility helped in this.

The South

The economic expansion of the Mediterranean countries, which had exported so much labour to the North, drew in immigrants from North Africa. Many of these were illegal immigrants. Their numbers were much less than in northern Europe, but in 1988, 0.4 per cent of the population of Italy, and 0.2 per cent of the population of Spain, were 'foreign' residents (Féron and Thoraval, 1992, 41). These low numbers reflect the delayed industrialisation of the South, and the persistence of a rural labour surplus there.

The politics of immigration

Beginning in Britain in the early 1950s, signs emerged of popular opposition to the growing number of immigrants from the Commonwealth. As most of the immigrants lived in extremely poor and even rough neighbourhoods, incidents of violence and vandalism, with slogans painted on walls, were not surprising. However, it was not long before rabble rousers and minor politicians became involved. Everywhere in western Europe, the authorities did their best to restrain these conflicts.

In Germany there was a danger that the foreign presence could be used to whip up feeling by the residual Right or, to put it bluntly, neo-Nazis. The old target, the Jews, could no longer be singled out. The German constitution (Basic Law) of 1949 went to great trouble to prevent a recrudescence of National Socialism and anti-semitism. Some of its measures looked like a denial of democratic rights but the justification was that any revival of National Socialism would itself destroy democratic rights. In Germany, therefore, Right-wing critics of immigration had to be very careful about how they expressed their views.

In the 1940s and 1950s, Right-wing views of all sorts were scarcely ever heard apart from the odd after-dinner speech at a veterans' association reunion. In the 1960s, though, they began to revive in ways which attracted a small number of young people as well as the veterans. In Germany, the National Democratic Party (NPD) was founded in 1964. Its ideology and rhetoric recalled the Nazi party. It took advantage of an economic recession in 1966 to campaign successfully in the state elections. One of its biggest targets was the million or so 'guest workers'. The government could have banned the new party as anti-democratic under the Basic Law, but it decided to tolerate it as a minor irritant. This decision was sound, but more disturbing was the gradual erosion of the common political ground of liberal values of which Germany had been confident in the 1950s.

When unemployment rose in the 1980s the Right began to gain votes in earnest. The NPD was still the most prominent anti-immigrant party but by now a fringe of even more extreme Right-wing and neo-Nazi political parties had come into being. They enjoyed some election successes in the late 1980s, but more worrying was the fact that their supporters also started to break the law more frequently in the 1980s. Most of these offences took the form of slogan-painting and other propaganda activities but there were a number of incidents of personal violence (Cheles et al., 1991, 81–2).

In January 1989, a neo-Nazi party known as Die Republikaner (REP) gained 7.5 per cent of the votes, and eleven seats, in the election for the West Berlin House of Deputies. In June, it won six seats in the election for European Parliament, where it sat with the French Right-wing party, Jean-Marie Le Pen's National Front (Cheles et al., 1991, 86). The success of this almost unknown party, campaigning almost exclusively on the immigrant issue, suggested a new stage in anti-immigrant feeling in Germany. In the early 1990s, with unemployment reaching unprecedented levels, a surge of attacks on foreign workers and their families led to some fatal arson incidents. Even the neo-Nazi political groups dissociated themselves from these murders, but daubed slogans and associated minor demonstrations by hooligans suggested a political link, usually to tiny Nazi groups linked remotely to the established neo-Nazi parties. Unification in 1991 made matters worse, as neo-Nazi hooligans soon multiplied in East Germany, where non-European workers had previously been unknown. These events suggested that German national identity, and sense of ethnic homogeneity, remained very strong in the 1990s. The authorities took immense care to avoid ethnic and racial incidents, and in 1995 the prospects looked much better as the German economy revived.

Europe's biggest anti-immigrant movement grew up in France. It was not just a function of the number of immigrants but of the Algerian War. In 1947, France had allowed Arab Algerians to move freely between North Africa and France, and during the 1950s Algerians became the largest immigrant group. Many gave moral support to the independence fighters and Algerian residents were roundly distrusted and disliked in France. Most were ill-educated country people and they lived on the edge of urban society in relative poverty. When the war ended in 1962, the continuation of free access to France was secured and the initial difficulties of the new Algerian republic boosted the northward flow.

The disappointed supporters of French control of Algeria were greatly increased in number by a huge influx of 700,000 French people from independent Algeria in 1962. They continued to associate in Right-wing groups and parties, and many broadened their opposition to all the coloured immigrant groups. The National Front was set up in 1972 as an alliance of a number of parties of the extreme Right. Its title echoed that of a much smaller extremist party in Britain which fell apart after a few years. The French National Front was led by a former conservative (Poujadist) deputy, Jean-Marie Le Pen. The original alliance split up almost immediately but the core survived, and by 1983 it was attracting up to 10 per cent of the votes in local elections (Cheles et al., 1991, 217). In the early 1990s the National Front could secure between 10 and 20 per cent of the votes in elections at any level all over France. Le Pen's strongest support was in the Paris area, where the immigrants were so visibly concentrated, and in the Mediterranean south, where many of the French refugees from Algeria had settled in the mid-1960s. By the later 1980s, Jean-Marie Le Pen, now a neo-Fascist, had emerged as the leader of the European anti-immigrant movement, with seats in the European parliament.

For a while, the Assembly was elected by proportional representation. This gave Le Pen about thirty seats and the chance to use tactics in the chamber which recalled those of Mussolini in 1922. Le Pen's reputation increased during this period as he acted as broker between the other parties and occasionally appeared to show statesmanlike qualities. Worried, the Assembly abandoned proportional representation and at the next elections Le Pen lost all his seats. In the presidential elections of 1995 he obtained about 15 per cent of the vote in the first round. This level of support was, however, the highest in Europe for a Right-wing party. Even in Italy, where a Right-wing movement with Fascist roots, the MSI, drew on a certain amount of affection for Mussolini, support was not quite as strong. This was probably because the presence of immigrants was not as pronounced in Italy.

Anti-immigrant pressure in France did not come solely from extremists, however. For instance, a long article in the conservative *Le Figaro* on 13 April 1994, by Jean Mottin, a member of the Conseil d'Etat, explicitly linked immigration and unemployment, and called for immigration controls or repatriation to allow young French people to find jobs. This broader, non-extremist debate was paralleled by the free contribution to the discussion by articulate, younger immigrants. In the 1980s France had generated a critical, second-generation response by its immigrants which was arguably the strongest in Europe. It centred on the French-born descendants of Algerian immigrants who, owing to the special features of the Algerian War and its aftermath, were ready to challenge the values and assumptions of the host society in a more coordinated way than other European immigrant groups. Resistance was encapsulated by the colloquial term, 'Beur', which young Algerians used of themselves but which became common currency in 1981 when it was used by North African participants in media debates. In 1983 North Africans joined in a national 'Marche des Beurs' which was organised in opposition to Le Pen's anti-immigrant National Front programme and its success in the elections of that year (Cook, 1993, 42). By the 1990s the French public increasingly associated the 'Beur' phenomenon with the high-rise suburbs of public housing. In linking the immigrant situation with an environmental disaster, they developed exaggerated fears. The headline in *Le Figaro* on 7 September 1995, during a disturbing period of terrorist bomb attacks linked to Algerian religious extremists, summed up this perception: 'Terrorisme: la piste des banlieues' (terrorism: the suburban trail).

Social implications

Political reactions varied from country to country, but the social aspects associated with immigration from outside Europe were generally consistent across the sub-continent. Perhaps the most striking was the 'myth of return' which most immigrants entertained on arrival. This was the assumption that after a number of high-earning years in Europe, they would return home to buy land or set up a business. This myth did not coincide fully with reality. Although many foreign workers returned to their home countries, often sufficiently enriched to buy their economic independence, the number residing in western Europe on a more or less permanent basis increased from the late 1940s onwards. The increase came to a virtual halt in the early 1970s when the European recession led to the ending of recruitment and efforts to secure the return of some short-term and contract workers to their countries of origin. The granting of permanent rights of residence was virtually discontinued at this time, except to family members of established permanent residents. By this time, about 11 million immigrants from outside Europe were living in western Europe. This represented about 4 per cent of the total population of western Europe, which was about 276 million at that time. In western Germany, immigrants accounted for 20 per cent of the manual workforce in 1974, and 4 per cent of the total population.

Immigrants, and especially non-European immigrants, encountered cultural difficulties when they moved to Europe to take up jobs. Most of the available employment was in towns and cities, but almost all the immigrants came from rural areas. They found it hard to adapt to city life, as well as to European life. The non-Europeans and their families tended to live in very dense districts in the city centres which were increasingly abandoned by the Europeans and whose culture gradually became visibly non-European. In Sparkbrook, a decaying district of inner Birmingham, this process was under way in the later 1950s. The progressive conversion of large, older houses into lodging houses for single men, or into multi-occupied accommodation for families, created a social situation which by the early 1960s was generating hostility to the newcomers among the European population. Many of the latter wanted to leave the area and the prospect of an immigrant 'ghetto' was already in sight (Rex and Moore, 1967, 3, 73).

This result, which began to emerge in Britain and France in the later 1950s, and in Germany in the 1960s, had not been foreseen by the authorities and at first quite serious efforts were made to disperse the non-European population. In Birmingham in the 1960s, the city council tried to control the creation of new lodging houses in order to prevent the emergence of non-European enclaves. A few years later they had to reverse the policy as more non-Europeans flooded in, making the enclaves inevitable (Sutcliffe and Smith, 1974, 243–4, 378–80).

France and Germany did not generate permanent residence to the same degree, at least in the early years. Their 'rotation' or 'guest worker' systems, often operated by individual firms, recruited a group of workers who were employed for a fixed period before being taken home and replaced by a new group. Many firms specialised in employing particular nationalities, who could be given special treatment in housing, food and facilities, and trained for special tasks on the job without requiring advanced language training. In Germany, for instance, Ford-Werke specialised in Italians and Turks. If a national group became scarce, as the Italians did from the 1960s, firms could switch en bloc to another nationality, with minimal disturbance. Many firms developed preferences; Spanish workers, for instance, were often identified as harder workers than the Italians, and firms tried to secure them as replacements when the Italians started to leave. Employers often favoured workers who came from a great distance, as they were less likely to travel home for short periods of leave as the Italians notoriously did (Kindleberger, 1968, 187–8). As employers became accustomed to employing these more distant workers, they could dispense with the Italians. From 1958, however, the Italians could continue to live and work in Germany under EEC regulations, which explains why the number of Italians living in Germany did not fall as the Turks and Iranians began to arrive. In the long run, therefore, German cities developed immigrant enclaves in the same way as elsewhere.

As the Europeans left the enclaves the non-Europeans recreated their native cultures and religions, while their children demanded non-European teachers and subjects in their schools. In some cases, proximity strengthened non-European resentment, which generated political extremism and illegal acts. In Germany male immigrants congregated in the main railway stations, partly because of the varied services provided therein, either free or at low cost (including the cinema showing pornographic films), partly because as mainly single men they had nothing to keep them at their lodgings, but partly also because this social centre reflected the role of German railways in the movements of the Turks and other influential immigrant groups. This presence was a powerful symbol of transience and non-assimilation in German society.

Immigrants as a solid European presence

After the early 1970s the number of immigrants from outside Europe becomes less significant than the total number of immigrants and their European-born descendants. With the unemployment rate rising in the 1970s, most European countries strengthened the barriers against immigration from outside Europe. An OECD study of 1977 completely reversed the standard arguments in favour of labour migration by maintaining that economic efficiency was best served if workers from backward countries stayed at home (Bourguignon and Gallais-Hamonno, 1977, 225–30). By 1980, very few new immigrants were arriving to take up jobs, though families of people already established in western Europe were often allowed to enter. By 1990, the number of 'foreign' residents in the EEC was estimated at 10 million, including illegal immigrants (Féron and Thoraval, 1992, 41).

Eurostat figures for non-EEC foreigners resident in European countries give the following results for 1988:

FIGURE 6.2 *Non-EEC resident foreigners as a percentage
of the national population in 1988.*

Germany	4.2
Belgium	3.3
Denmark	2.1
France	3.8
Netherlands	2.9
United Kingdom	1.8
EEC	2.4

Source: figures derived from Féron and Thoraval, *passim.*

At the same time, immigrants generated increasing numbers of
children. Statistics for these new Europeans are hard to obtain, as
they were nationals of European countries rather than of the
countries from which their parents had come. Raised in western
Europe, these children often clashed with the host society which
did not give them what they required, and the instructions and
values of their parents. The first generation of immigrants had
been a social problem, but the second was a political problem.
However, by the 1980s and 1990s, the initial poverty of the
immigrants had been replaced in many cases, either in the first or
the second generation, by an entrepreneurial spirit which made
them less vulnerable to recessions and to domestic reaction.
Immigrants and temporary workers were generally ambitious and
dynamic, at any rate in relation to those who stayed behind. By the
1980s many had moved from employment to running their own
businesses. Taxi-driving was a classic immigrant activity, with
longer hours worked than native drivers would tolerate. With the
spread of immigrant business people into the towns and cities of
western Europe, and the education of the second and third
generations within a European culture, many of the initial
problems were likely to fade away. The question remained,
however, whether large numbers of immigrants would ever be
allowed into Europe again. As the end of the millennium
approached, this looked highly unlikely on economic grounds
alone.

CHAPTER SEVEN

The New Climate of External Events: (1) The Oil Crisis, 1973, and (2) The Collapse of European Communism, 1989–91

The return of the external event

This book has been an almost unqualified 'success story' so far. Once the first few post-war years had been weathered, western Europe launched into a long period of economic growth which seemed largely immune to the effects of the trade cycle. Cyclical fluctuations were registered but they were pale shadows of those of the inter-war years and even of those of the later nineteenth century. The French observer, Jean Fourastié, coined the phrase, 'the thirty glorious years' (*les trente glorieuses*), to describe the post-war experience of his country, but the expression can justly be applied to western Europe as a whole. It was also a time of social and political stability, in which living standards rose almost without interruption throughout western Europe and levels of consumption and leisure advanced for almost everyone.

Contemporaries attributed the stability and growth of this period to liberal world trading conditions and to government policies which were often loosely described as 'Keynesian'. As growth and full employment continued through the 1950s into the 1960s, the military and strategic threats of the Cold War seemed more likely to undermine the prosperity of western Europe than did internal or international economic pressures in the West. However, hostilities did not break out and western Europe was spared the impact of external events comparable to those of 1914 and 1939.

This 'glorious' period came to an end between the late 1960s and the mid-1970s, both in western Europe and in the western world as a whole. These years saw a return to sharp economic fluctuations, inflation, and slow growth. By 1980 governments were adapting to the new conditions but only at the cost of deflationary policies which forced them to tolerate high unemployment and the persistence of slow growth. This cautious stability would carry on into the 1990s, and these words are being written within this new climate. By 1995, more encouraging signs could be detected, at any rate by the OECD, on the basis of a slow upturn since 1992, but it was too early to identify a movement into a new phase of growth.

Although the new, deflationary period from the later 1970s had similarities to the 1930s, many observers were struck by its prolonged character, which suggested that the long-run growth period from c.1945 to c.1975 had been followed by a long period of very slow growth, within both of which the standard trade cycle fluctuations were attenuated. This observation encouraged interest in the 1970s in the long cycle interpretations of economic history developed by Kondratiev, Kuznets, Schumpeter and others (Maddison, 1991, 89–111). These theories stressed cultural, psychological, political and technological influences, rather than trends in exchange and investment which were central to the trade cycle.

Long waves remain highly controversial and we do not intend to promote them here. Suffice it to say, however, that the economic history of post-war western Europe can be divided effectively into two long periods: the thirty 'glorious' post-war years, and an as yet incomplete period of difficulties and slow growth beginning in the early 1970s. This second period has lasted for around twenty-five years and this temporal symmetry has influenced the interpretation and structure adopted in this book.

This second period of slow growth, in contrast to its expansionist predecessor, was affected by two almost unpredictable external events. The first was the 'oil crisis' of 1973 and the continuing impact of artificially high oil prices until the early 1980s. Initiated by Arab oil producers in the Middle East, it was the first serious blow struck by the Third World against the economic domination of the capitalist world. Although, with hindsight, it can be seen as part of a growing economic crisis in the West, it was a historical event of massive proportions and one which will loom as a grey eminence during most of the rest of this book.

The second external event was the collapse of the Communist system in Europe between 1989 and 1991. Here again, the West may have contributed to the collapse, notably by sustaining its expensive military effort through the relatively impoverished years after 1973, and by promoting an economic orthodoxy based on the market which presented an increasingly convincing alternative to the modified command economy which still survived in the East. However, the forces unleashed after 1989 were mainly internal to the Communist system, and were indeed largely impenetrable to Western observers. Though the effects of the collapse were still unclear in 1995, they had not yet called forth the productive boom which had been expected at first when there was much talk of the 'peace dividend'. Although largely an independent economic system, and therefore incapable of having a depressive effect on the Western economies, the East's immature market institutions and disastrously low productivity, at any rate in the former Soviet Union, restricted its potential as a market for Western goods and as a supplier of both cheap and high-quality exports. It was also an unattractive creditor. Meanwhile, the gradual reduction in Western military expenditure increased unemployment more quickly than it boosted domestic demand.

The end of the post-war boom

During the later 1960s the US dollar, which had sustained the great monetary liberalisation of the post-war years, began to lose international confidence. Low growth, a serious foreign payments deficit, and inflation in the USA weakened the dollar while the strength of the Deutschmark and the yen prompted speculative currency dealings. Big international capital flows, linked to the integration of financial markets since the end of the 1950s and changes in interest rates, put pressure on national exchange rates. At first, the weaker currencies such as the pound sterling and the Italian lira came under threat, because their big foreign payments deficits and high interest rates made them likely candidates for devaluation. But, when the pound sterling, a reserve currency, was devalued in 1967, speculative pressure increased on the dollar itself. As the second of the key currencies in the Bretton Woods system, the pound had shared the task of maintaining world liquidity with the US dollar and its devaluation put an extra burden on the USA. The American balance of payments deficit now increased and gold losses became serious by the end of the decade.

The strong currencies, led by the German mark, were reluctant to revalue in case they attracted speculative pressures to them. Germany had suffered a sharp recession in 1966–67 which, though mild in relation to what was to come in the 1970s, ended fifteen years of continuous growth and caused general concern. To reduce German competitiveness by a voluntary revaluation was out of the question. Such currencies were, however, prepared to 'float', meaning that their market value could oscillate according to short-term market conditions. Germany was the first country to 'float' its currency in this way, in 1970. Other countries followed this example in the early 1970s. Many OECD members began to adopt, or to experiment with, more ambitious monetary policies as a means of managing domestic demand or adjusting their balance of payments.

With speculative flows continuing, especially after the OPEC oil price increase in 1973, the Bretton Woods system became even harder to protect. In 1971 the USA suspended the convertibility of the dollar into gold and used a brief 10 per cent import surcharge to force a general revaluation of currencies. Exchange rate instability continued, however, and in 1972 the EEC Six created the monetary 'snake' whereby they undertook to maintain their exchange rates within 2.25 per cent of one another. Britain briefly joined the 'snake' but found the effort too much, and the pound sterling began to float in 1972. Meanwhile, the main industrial countries could not agree on a common system and so the central banks acted together to keep the value of certain major currencies between broad 'bands', though they were unclear about what the new 'equilibrium rates' should be. Uncertainty continued and, in 1973, fourteen countries signed the Paris Agreement which had the effect of ending the Bretton Woods exchange system. The US dollar was now floated. The early stages of the new system were a success, however, and the underlying weakness in the western trading and monetary system did not give serious concern until the extraordinary series of events in 1973 which are generally known as the 'oil crisis'.

The oil crisis

In 1973 a powerful cartel of primary producers used their near-monopoly power to multiply the price, and reduce the supply, of a product essential to the industrialised world. The product was crude oil. The cartel was the Organisation of Petroleum Exporting Countries. The occasion was the Yom Kippur (Ramadan) War between Israel and an alliance of Arab countries, in October 1973. OPEC had been set up in 1960 by five oil-producing countries, four of them in the Middle East. In its early years it had struggled in vain against the big international oil companies of the United States, Britain and the Netherlands, while its membership increased to thirteen. It had little success in negotiating price increases, and production soared as the West used more and more oil as its price relatively declined. So attractive did oil become in the 1960s that it increasingly replaced traditional energy sources such as coal. In Britain, for instance, a big programme of oil-fired power stations was announced even though the country still had huge coal reserves and a large mining workforce, together with expertise. France set up its own oil company, ELF, to exploit oil reserves in Algeria. Germany, too, was moving away from coal and the planned landscaping of the Ruhr was already under way.

The decline in world economic growth in the late 1960s and early 1970s was noted by OPEC, as it implied a fall in the price of oil. In 1972 and 1973 the industrial countries tried to reflate, with Britain outstanding in its efforts to 'go for growth' in order to make up for two decades of industrial complacency. The growth rate of OECD countries in Europe, which had been as low as 3.1 per cent in 1970, reached 5.5 per cent in 1972 and 6.3 per cent in 1973. OPEC now sought to ensure that a revival of the world economy would produce a higher price for oil while slowing down the rate of consumption. The Yom Kippur War found it well prepared. An immediate ban on oil exports was designed to force the West to put pressure on Israel, but the war was so short that OPEC chose to extend the ban and increase the price, in its long-term interests. An initial price increase of 70 per cent at the time of the war was followed, in late 1973, by a further increase of 130 per cent. As a result, the price of crude oil was four times as high in 1974 than the average for 1972.

These measures had an immediate impact on the West. Most industrial countries suffered an immediate decline in output, and this was general by 1975. This absolute decline in output was the first since 1929–32, though the earlier decline had been relatively greater (Aldcroft, 1993, 195–6). Notwithstanding the declining power of the dollar, the industrial countries turned to the United States for advice and example. The IMF concluded that increased Arab oil income should be 'recycled' with the Arabs lending to the

West. This would cover balance of payments deficits in the West and stimulate employment. However, it also encouraged inflation. Consumer prices in the European OECD countries rose by an annual average of 3.8 per cent in the 1960s; between 1970 and 1978 they rose by 9.8 per cent. In Britain, the rate of increase peaked at 24.2 per cent in 1975. In Germany, the peak came in 1974, with an increase of 7 per cent. In the same year, Italy experienced 19.1 per cent inflation. In 1979, inflation still ran at 16.5 per cent in Britain, at 15.8 per cent in Italy, and at 11 per cent in France. In Germany, the inflation rate was 5.3 per cent.

Higher unemployment also pushed up the level of social security payments. As a share of national income in western Europe, these had been rising since before the oil crisis, for instance from 9.4 per cent in 1950 to 13.4 per cent in 1965. By 1977 they had risen to 22.4 per cent. Sweden spent most, by this time, at nearly one-third of its national income (Ambrosius and Hubbard, 1989, 131).

At the same time, the industrial nations began a search for new oil supplies. These efforts would be successful, but they would not produce results until the end of the decade. Countries like Britain which could reasonably anticipate a big flow of oil were able to borrow on the security of future oil revenues, though this had inflationary implications. Alternative energy supplies were also developed. The most convenient was coal, and British and German mines were exploited to the full. This also had an inflationary effect as the miners' unions obtained big wage increases, especially in Britain. Nuclear power was a policy adopted particularly by France, which could not secure a big increase in coal production because of its limited reserves. To procure additional supplies through the ECSC was not an option as ECSC output was already falling short of the requirements of the member countries.

Meanwhile, high inflation and low growth meant that unemployment was worryingly high in Europe between 1974 and the end of the decade. In the later 1970s the OECD average unemployment rate was over 5 per cent (Aldcroft, 1993, 199). However, in another irony of the time, organised labour became more active in campaigning for the defence of its real earnings. This was possible because many governments were prepared to incur large budgetary deficits to maintain employment at as high a level as possible, and to sustain unemployment and retirement benefits. The governments of the big EEC economies increased their intervention in manufacturing in the later 1970s, trying to preserve a balanced range of indigenous industries, rather than acknowledging that industrial specialisation within the EEC would in the long run serve their interests even more effectively (Shepherd et al., 1983, 22). This allowed the trade unions to join in a period of militancy on behalf of their members who still had jobs. This effect was especially visible in Britain, with its very high inflation rate. Experiments with incomes policies, like Britain's between 1974 and 1976, and Italy's *scala mobile*, were either hard to enforce or they generated social tensions.

By the later 1970s inflation throughout western Europe was running at rates considerably higher than those normal in the 1960s. With low economic growth persisting, the English-language media and some economists liked to use the term 'stagflation' to describe these contradictory results (see Rostow, 1978, 358–62). A further result was that governments across western Europe were discredited by their failure to tackle the problem and the way was open for alternative ideas put forward by opposition parties.

The West's new response

In 1978 the Shah of Iran was deposed in a national revolution. The new government unilaterally raised the country's oil prices, and OPEC raised its own prices in line with Iran in 1979. World oil prices were now ten times higher than before the OPEC intervention in 1973. This second price rise was received more calmly and resolutely in the West. It now appeared that OPEC was prepared progressively to raise its prices in line with, or ahead of, Western inflation. The industrial countries therefore decided in 1980 to control their inflation in the hope that oil prices would fall, thus breaking the OPEC monopoly. The price which they agreed to pay was the risk of a world depression, more serious and prolonged than that of 1973–76. Their 'Keynesian' strategies, which had partly survived 1973, were abandoned and 'monetarism' and supply side planning took over. A big increase in unemployment was anticipated and tolerated. France's new, Socialist President, François Mitterrand, made a brief attempt to solve the problem by generating growth in 1981–82, but this ghost of the Popular Front in 1936 soon led to massive balance of payments and fiscal problems. The government had to abandon this strategy even sooner than Léon Blum had done, and France's return to conservatism strengthened other countries in their resolve.

By 1982 the world oil price began to fall owing to increasing supply at a time of recession. OPEC were unable to impose their price on the producer countries and the OPEC monopoly was at an end. But by this time the world had entered a period of low growth which, with the new anti-inflation policies and related mentalities, could not be readily brought to an end. Another price was paid by the Third World, which found itself unable to pay its debts by the early 1980s (Graham, 1990, 21). In fact, western Europe still, in 1995, languishes in a long-term period of low growth which dates back, allowing for various fluctuations, to 1973.

The west European countries thus experienced lower decadal growth rates in the 1980s than they had in the 1970s, though overall performance in the 1970s was influenced by high growth until 1973. The subsequent trend gives a fuller picture. The twelve countries which made up the EEC at the end of the decade recorded an annual average increase in real GDP of 2.2 per cent between 1973 and 1980. Between 1980 and 1985 growth dropped to 1.5 per cent under the influence of the oil price increase of 1979 and the associated deflationary policies. Between 1985 and 1990, however, GDP increased at the rate of 3.1 per cent per annum. Over the 1980s the Twelve had a growth rate of 2.3 per cent (Aldcroft, 1993, 221–2). Fluctuations in output after 1979 were much less abrupt than those experienced after 1973, suggesting that government policies were more in control. Moreover, living standards in the Twelve tended to improve throughout by about 2 per cent per annum as a result of their very low rate of population growth, especially in northern Europe, and even though unemployment continued to rise until the middle of the decade. The rate of inflation declined to the levels of the 1960s by the end of the decade. Industrial action was brought under control and investment increased in the second half of the decade.

With stabilisation in sight in the later 1980s, it looked as though western Europe might at last be able to look forward to a new period of growth with rates similar, if not to the 1950s, then at least to the 1960s. It was now, however, that a second external factor came into effect.

The collapse of Communist Europe

In the early 1990s the collapse of Communism in eastern Europe and the Soviet Union, initiated by the opening of the Berlin Wall by the East German government in 1989, created new conditions for the west European economy. Circumstances became so unusual between 1990 and 1995 that they will be discussed, in a different context, in Chapter 11. The end of European Communism was, however, an indication that western European capitalism, whatever its problems in the 1970s and 1980s, had proved more durable than the rival system set up in eastern Europe by Stalin. The world of the Atlantic Charter had prevailed over that of the Warsaw Pact. This was a greater tribute to the economy and society of western Europe after 1945 than a million statistics could provide.

Western Europe's economic difficulties in the 1970s and 1980s were paralleled by a certain relief in pressure from the East. The Soviet Union was influenced mainly by its relations with the United States, but there was a European contribution in the form of what became known as the *Ostpolitik* of the West German Federal Chancellor, the Socialist Willy Brandt. Brandt was Chancellor between 1969 and 1974. An enthusiast for international cooperation, Brandt used West Germany's traditional position as a link with eastern Europe, together with its great economic strength, to pursue a policy of greater cooperation with the Communist world.

Leonid Brezhnev, General Secretary of the Soviet Communist Party between 1964 and 1982, was already developing a new attitude towards the West. He followed Nikita Khruschev, whose de-Stalinisation programme had already introduced a certain liberalisation into the Soviet Union since 1956 and had made its foreign policy less threatening. Brezhnev continued this policy. In foreign policy, Brezhnev was influenced by the Cuban missiles crisis of 1963 which had been a disaster for the ambitious military strategy of the Soviet Union and had contributed to the removal of Khruschev in the following year. Brezhnev improved relations with the West but he maintained the strong defences of the Soviet Union, at damaging cost.

Finally, Mikhail Gorbachev, who took control in the Soviet Union in 1985, introduced new liberalisation policies there. *Glasnost* and *perestroika* were linked with new approaches to the West and a relaxation of Russian control over eastern European satellites led to the collapse of Soviet control there between 1989 and 1991, and the eventual dissolution of Communism across most of eastern Europe and the Soviet Union by 1991.

Throughout these years the Soviet leaders had been more or

less aware that the low productivity of the Soviet bloc, and the concentration on heavy industry, when combined with the heavy military expenditure which confrontation with the world's most powerful economies required, depressed living standards to a level far below that of the West. Beginning with Khruschev, the Soviet Union brought in economic reforms designed to achieve greater efficiency, in some cases through the introduction of various market mechanisms. These changes did not resolve the basic problem, but they weakened Communist orthodoxy.

The problems of the western economies from the later 1960s did not impinge greatly on the Soviet Union, which was nearly self-sufficient in oil and in other respects largely isolated from the western economies. However, the drop in the Soviet Union's rate of economic growth from the early 1970s was sharper than that experienced within the OECD. As it could not be blamed on external factors, it has to be explained in terms of structural weaknesses. High military expenditure was partly to blame, with Soviet military spending rising from 13 per cent of GDP in the early 1970s to 16 per cent in the mid-1980s, compared to 6.6 per cent in the USA at that time. The wasteful use of capital, natural resources and labour was not new, but it became worse after 1970, producing negative capital and labour productivity. There was a tendency towards the depletion of national resources, especially in agriculture, and the adoption of foreign technology remained difficult. Moreover, the perception of these weaknesses within the Soviet Union became more acute (Maddison, 1989, 100–1; Matthews, 1993).

Meanwhile, the material success of western Europe weakened the national Communist parties there and allowed its NATO members to contribute easily enough to defence costs. The society which Khruschev had once looked forward to burying showed no signs of cooperating in the funeral. There seemed no chance that capitalism would collapse in western Europe of its own accord. With the Soviet bloc facing its own difficulties after the oil crisis, there was no point in wasting resources to put pressure on the West. Once the USA withdrew its troops from Vietnam in 1973, East and West entered a period of greater calm. This eased the pressure on western Europe and allowed it to deal more easily with its economic problems. The problems of the East, however, were permanent; the system simply awaited a Gorbachev to realise it and to take action.

The response of the West

Several of the Communist satellites, such as Poland, had already been borrowing from the West and the initial assumption of the collapsing Communist world was that its governments and industrial concerns would be able to negotiate further loans. In practice, western lenders were hesitant because the economic weaknesses of the Communist system were so acute that security and return would alike be in question.

In 1989, during the initial stages of the collapse, President Mitterrand of France proposed the creation of an inter-governmental bank to assist in the economic reconstruction of eastern Europe and the Soviet Union. The resulting European Bank for Reconstruction and Development (EBRD) was founded in 1990 and began operations in 1991. All the major European companies were members of the bank, as were the major institutions of the EU. The EU countries held a controlling share, but the USA and other non-European states were also members. The secretariat was based in London, where its lavish expenditure on buildings and entertainment attracted the critical attention of the British media.

By 1995 the EBRD had developed a loan programme but its turnover remained very low. By this time, western European contributions to the CIS and the former satellite countries had been greatly overtaken by some very expensive transfer operations arising from the incorporation of the former German Democratic Republic into the German Federal Republic in 1991, the most spectacular product of the fall of the Iron Curtain. This episode will be discussed in Chapter 8. Suffice it to say here that Germany's borrowings in western Europe to finance its effort largely absorbed western Europe's perceived capacity to lend to the ex-Communist system as a whole. The USA provided some credit but in 1995 the East was still complaining about the lack of support from the West now that it had embraced capitalism. Of course, the West still wondered whether the East really *had* embraced capitalism, or whether political changes might not restore the *status quo ante* or create something worse. This uncertainty did not affect the West directly, as most of the East was still a self-contained economy, but it prevented the emergence of clear investment and business plans in the West. In this way, it probably contributed to the low growth rate in the West in the 1990s.

These two external factors greatly complicated the workings of the western European economy after the early 1970s. Ironically, the crude confrontation of the Cold War had been a simplifying and sustaining factor in the 1950s and 1960s. The atmosphere of uncertainty at the end of the century was more difficult to comprehend, and the constant fear of further external events always lay at the back of the mind. The story will be very different from now on.

CHAPTER EIGHT

National Problems and Progress: Germany, France and Britain since the 1960s

The new era of slower growth

Western Europe's success story since 1945 has no dramatic turning points, no disasters. From the later 1960s, however, a worrying transition occurred from the phase of rapid reconstruction and modernisation which followed the war to a period of higher inflation, lower growth rates, greater economic fluctuations, and more visible social problems. This phase has lasted into the 1990s. It was not a sharp break or reversal, for living standards continued to rise, western European integration progressed, and the continent's progress towards a fully urbanised society was virtually completed. Political extremism, allowing for a few surges, continued its post-war decline and Christian Democracy or its equivalents remained the dominant influence in 1995, just as they had been after 1945. Few questioned, though, that western Europe had entered a new era of relative difficulty which partially recalled the years between the World Wars.

The world context of the new phase has already been discussed in Chapter 7, with special reference to the 'oil crisis' of 1973. However, we have seen that signs of deceleration affecting the major industrialised countries were visible from the later 1960s. At that time, the problems of the United States were the most obvious, but western Europe was already affected as well.

Deceleration and progress: basic views

Economic historians often express the deceleration in terms of declining growth rates. This perspective is a gloomy one.

211

FIGURE 8.1 *Real percentage growth in GDP per capita, 1950–87.*

	1950–73	1973–87
Austria	4.9	2.3
Belgium	3.5	1.7
Denmark	3.1	1.7
Finland	4.3	2.4
France	3.8	1.7
Germany	4.9	2.0
Italy	4.8	2.0
Netherlands	3.5	1.2
Norway	3.2	3.6
Sweden	3.3	1.6
Switzerland	3.1	0.9
UK	2.5	1.5
USA	2.2	1.5

Source: data from Maddison, 1989, 35.

Nevertheless, the aggregate figures for national income stress continuing progress and a cumulative enrichment of spectacular proportions over the post-war years. The rate of improvement is slower after 1973 but changes in the level of GDP per capita indicate that most countries enjoyed a standard of living that was around three times higher in 1987 than it had been after the war.

FIGURE 8.2 *GDP per capita in international dollars (1980 prices).*

	1950	1973	1987
Austria	2,123	6,434	8,792
Belgium	3,114	6,937	8,769
Denmark	3,895	7,845	9,949
Finland	2,610	6,804	9,500
France	2,941	7,462	9,475
Germany	2,508	7,595	9,964
Italy	2,323	6,824	9,023
Netherlands	3,554	7,754	9,197
Norway	3,436	7,071	11,653
Sweden	3,898	8,288	10,328
Switzerland	5,256	10,556	11,907
UK	4,171	7,413	9,178
USA	6,697	10,977	13,550

Source: Maddison, 1989, 19.

By 1970, the integration of western Europe was more advanced on every level than in 1945. National experiences had converged in economic terms, and as a result of European institutions. National levels of industrialisation had converged everywhere. However, western Europe remained divided into countries of varying character and significance. How did they fare in a more difficult era? In this chapter we shall consider, as in Chapter 2, the three most powerful industrial economies, Germany, France and Britain.

Germany

With the largest population in western Europe (81 million in 1994), rich natural resources, and a productive industry, Germany remained the biggest and strongest economy in Europe and consequently the leading influence in the EEC. Germany's high export ratio – more than one-quarter of its GDP in 1970–73 – was an unrivalled basis for prosperity and stability (Borchardt, 1991, 110). The value of German exports per capita (at current prices) had risen from $39.87 in 1950 to $1,090 in 1973. This was twice the British figure in 1973, and much the highest of the large European industrial countries. By 1986 the German figure had risen to $3,984, which was still over twice the British level (Maddison, 1989, 44). With a strong Deutschmark, and a high rate of investment overseas, Germany could enjoy one of the highest living standards in Europe combined with one of the lowest rates of inflation. In 1981, West German direct investments overseas totalled DM101 billion, compared to just DM421 million in 1955 (Leaman, 1988, 236). In 1972, 64 per cent of West German households had a car, 90 per cent had a washing machine, 95 per cent had a television, and 98 per cent had a refrigerator (Materialien, 1974, 253).

Germany nevertheless failed to maintain its position as western Europe's leading economy in growth terms. This relative decline began in the later 1960s. This result bore some resemblance to the earlier experience of Britain. By the later 1950s German industry had applied much of the new American technology to which it had extensive access from 1948. The German labour surplus had been soaked up by 1956 and the growing influx of non-German workers brought few skills with it. Wages were now rising fast and the leisure preference of German workers was growing. Above all,

FIGURE 8.3 *Annual average growth rate (%) of*
GNP, German Federal Republic,
1950–79.

1950–55	9.5
1955–60	6.5
1960–65	5.0
1965–70	4.5
1970–75	1.9
1975–79	3.9

Source: data drawn from Piquet Marchal, 1985, 165.

Germany's export-led growth as supplier to a reviving Europe after the war was vulnerable to competition from the countries which Germany had helped to revive. This competition was mainly in the form of consumer goods, which western Germany had not encouraged in the 1950s owing to initial low home demand, and the Federal-encouraged concentration on exports of producer goods.

In terms of the Anglo-American post-war vision, this result was predictable and even desirable, as economic growth spread across western Europe and the initial leaders were overhauled. In some respects it was also the conscious product of government and Bundesbank policy. Germany took a number of further steps to reinforce its position as an open economy after 1960, willingly accepting implications which Japan tried to ignore. Beginning in 1961, the mark was revalued on several occasions, reflecting the growth of the German economy and its very favourable trade balance. Revaluation increased imports into Germany, but until the 1970s the increasing price of German exports did not reduce demand for them. This was because the structure of exports created by Germany's industries since 1948 was heavily weighted in favour of producer goods, and, within that category, in favour of equipment. Germany's willingness to open up its economy to world flows reflected its foreign-policy wish to be seen as a fair and generous contributor to world development, emulating the post-war United States which had done so much to help Germany.

Taking the period from 1950 to 1979 as a whole, consumer goods made up only 10 per cent of German exports, and primary products, including coal, another 10 per cent. Manufactured producer goods totalled 80 per cent. Eighty per cent of total exports went to industrialised countries (Piquet Marchal, 1985,

163). This meant that Germany was happy to buy a large part of its consumer goods and primary products from abroad with its increasingly valuable marks, while its manufactures continued to find a ready market abroad because their specialised character, quality, and firm delivery dates outweighed the effect of their rising prices. German exports thus won growing amounts of foreign currency for Germany, which created pressure for further revaluations of the mark. By the 1960s talk was less of a 'miracle' (for the miracle seemed to have become a natural state of affairs), than of a 'virtuous circle' with Germany (in contrast to a curiously embattled Japan) the new hero of the economic world.

However, German growth slowed in the 1960s in relation to western Europe as a whole. The average growth rate per annum was 5 per cent, lower than in France. Germany grew at very near full capacity, with unemployment at less than 1 per cent. The long-term labour shortage was expressed most clearly in the import of foreign labour. Foreign workers made up only 1 per cent of the labour force in 1950 but by 1960 they amounted to 4 per cent and, by 1971, to 9.5 per cent (OECD, *Monetary Policy in Germany*, 1973, 9) The deceleration was a predictable result of the relative cheapening of imports into Germany and it reflected the rapid industrialisation of France and parts of southern Europe which was part of the logic of the EEC. It continued a trend already visible in the later 1950s and was not overall a major problem, though the government had to take action on a number of occasions to stabilise the economy now that the huge, trading Germany was increasingly open to international pressures.

The government and the Bundesbank responded to the deceleration by maintaining fiscal and monetary stability. Moderate concessions were made to the Keynesian orthodoxy of the day after the Social Democrats became coalition partners in 1966. The government reacted to the mild recession of 1967 with limited deficit spending and the same methods were used in moderation in 1974 when the industrial world was looking to Germany and Japan to maintain demand (Lipschitz and McDonald, 1990, 167). However, monetary policy was used to restrain demand during the periods of expansion. Unemployment and redundancy pay was generous and Germany's growth rate remained respectable by European standards until the oil crisis of 1973 created unfavourable conditions for industrial exports.

Certain industries and regions of Germany were already in difficulties in the 1960s. The Ruhr, producer of what were now

relatively expensive coal, iron and steel, went into a slow decline.
Coal mining was in continual difficulties there from 1957. The
older pits began to close and unemployment increased. A 'Ruhr
crisis' was detected even by the cautious German media. In 1967
the Federal parliament passed a law on the adaptation of industry
and mining regions. The authorities began to plan for a land-
scaped Ruhr with the slag heaps and the sides of the motorways
converted into greenery.

Germany's problems increased, moreover, when its growth rate
declined further in the early 1970s. The Social Democratic Party,
in the shadow of the Christian Democrats and their social market
philosophy since the later 1940s, became the party of government
in 1969. Their dominance, though moderated by their coalition
partners, lasted until 1982. The oil crisis of 1973 was a big
challenge to the SDP. Faithful to the economic policies which had
built up Germany since 1948, they refused to adopt inflationary
solutions and Germany passed through several years of low growth
and high unemployment.

Like France, Germany chose to develop nuclear power and this
generated a political backlash at the end of the decade. A variety
of interests took part in the anti-nuclear protests, which led to the
formation of local Green parties which formed an alliance in 1979
with a view to winning seats in the state parliaments. By the early
1980s the Greens were a political force which outshone the
nationalist parties. Ostensibly democratic and socialistic, they
harboured some right-wing elements and their effect on German
politics was often destabilising.

Distributional conflicts now developed, and the balance of
payments caused concern, especially between 1975 and the early
1980s (Borchardt, 1991, 111). Germany, which had imported only
5 per cent of its energy in 1950, was nearly two-thirds dependent
on foreign energy in 1975 (Borchardt, 1991, 124). The strong
mark continued to encourage investment overseas, while foreign
investment in Germany declined. The rate of inflation began to
increase from 1972, before the oil crisis. The annual growth rate
averaged only 2.2 per cent between 1973 and 1980, and only 2.1
per cent between 1980 and 1990.

Hans-Joachim Braun attributes the deceleration of economic
growth in western Germany mainly to a labour shortage (Braun,
1990, 168). Immigration from East Germany fell almost to nothing
after the Berlin Wall was put up in 1961. Guest workers flooded in,
their numbers rising from 250,000 in 1960 to 1.8 million in 1970,

but most were little used to working in an advanced economy. The majority were given menial tasks, with employers reluctant to give lengthy training to potentially transient employees. However, labour can only have been a subsidiary factor, for German investment was increasingly directed towards productivity gains rather than the creation of new capacity. Already in the 1960s, half German manufacturing investment was devoted to increasing productivity, and by the late 1970s this proportion had risen to 75 per cent (Piquet Marchal, 1985, 163).

West Germany withstood the first oil crisis better than most European countries. The caution of the founders of the Bundesbank and of the Christian Democrat creators of German economic policy was now justified more fully than ever before. German inflation, which had tended to rise in the 1960s owing mainly to the huge overseas payments surplus, remained much lower than the European average. Exports and income from overseas investments stood up well to the higher cost of imports, and the German foreign payments account remained in surplus despite a sharp drop in 1975. The policies of the government and the Bundesbank made sure that the successful, post-war German formula of price stability and export competitiveness was not undermined by the oil crisis. Unemployment increased to over 1 million by 1975 but Germany's generous welfare payments and worker confidence in the future avoided serious discontent. Output recovered rapidly from mid-1975.

However, the second oil price increase in 1979 hit Germany hard. German manufacturing had become less competitive towards the end of the decade and the recovery slowed from 1977. Fiscal policy was again used to support demand (OECD, *Germany*, 1978, 5). The resolve of the industrial countries at this time not to borrow to maintain demand meant that German exports were hard hit. The decline in the terms of trade now became damaging. By 1980 Germany had the largest external current account deficit in its post-war history (Lipschitz and McDonald, 1990, 168). Measures to expand domestic demand would have been inflationary and were not open to the German government on any but a small scale, especially as the other industrial countries had agreed to follow the German example of 1974 and eschew short-term palliatives. The Bundesbank kept tight control over the money supply and the increase in public expenditure and the Federal debt restricted the supply of credit to the private sector. Growth slowed further, dropping to nil in 1981, and unemployment became a serious problem, reaching 2 million at the end of 1982.

In any case, public opinion had now swung against demand management after fifteen years of tinkering with it by the Federal government. Social Democrat chancellor Helmut Schmidt split his party when he advocated the reduction of fiscal deficits in 1981. In 1982 the Christian Democrats were back in power under Helmut Kohl. Sustained by a general election victory in 1983, they took Germany back to Erhardian principles (Lipschitz and McDonald, 1990, 168). The parallel with Erhard's day was all the more striking in that the revival of the German economy from 1984 was led by export growth. This soon generated a large external surplus and by 1987 Germany was agreeing, at the request of its partner economies, to expand domestic demand in order to increase international trade. The growth of home demand increased the rate of German economic growth in the late 1980s. This return to government influence on the level of demand was inevitable given Germany's big influence on the world economy and its generally cooperative stance in international discussions. Unemployment remained high, at around 8 per cent, but this was in line with the experience of other industrial countries in Europe. Overall, the big recovery, combined with low inflation, contributed to the optimistic atmosphere in Germany at the end of the decade, out of which sprang the confidence that eastern Germany could be absorbed with little difficulty.

Other countries, including even the United States, had looked to Germany to help inject demand into the world economy. In 1978, at the economic summit in Bonn, Germany agreed to engage in deficit spending even though this went against its established practice and mentality. By 1980 this policy had greatly undermined the German currency. A number of weaknesses were now visible, including labour-market rigidity, excessive budget deficits, too expensive a welfare structure, and a diminishing willingness to work as people chose to enjoy some of the benefits of hard work by their forebears.

In the later 1970s the German government acted to improve the climate for business in response to the oil crisis. The government did not, however, intervene directly to support ailing firms (Shepherd et al., 1983, 22). In the 1980s wages were held down and this improved the export position of German industry. Chancellor Kohl's Conservative sympathies helped him to build up a close understanding with Margaret Thatcher, the British Prime

Minister since 1979, whose bold anti-inflationary stance and developing rapport with the American President Reagan on strategic issues were already well on the way to making her Europe's most influential leader.

In the early 1980s concern grew in Germany about a possible industrial retardation which, to the alarmists, even recalled Britain's experiences in the 1950s and 1960s. Britain had become heavily committed to a small number of staple export industries which had ceased to be competitive after 1918. German manufacturing had retained its post-war emphasis on producer goods, dominated by the three great industrial sectors of engineering, motors and chemicals. It had failed to match the Far East in growth. The investment goods industries had increased their share of total industrial employment in Germany from 25.3 per cent in 1950 to 47.2 per cent in 1989 (Giersch et al., 1992, 2–3). Now, it was often suggested that Germany was losing ground in high-technology areas such as the electrical, electronics, and computing industries, while the Far East moved into a world lead. In particular, a slow adjustment to the demands and opportunities of micro-electronics was detected (Turner, 1987, 196). This diagnosis was entirely predictable, given that it was being applied to other western industrial countries, including the United States, but Germany's move into doubt and uncertainty marked a new phase in its post-war economic history.

In the late 1980s West Germany found itself face to face with a unique problem. The Communist regime in the German Democratic Republic was facing growing internal difficulties arising from Gorbachev's striking reforms in the Soviet Union and the short-term and long-term economic problems of the Communist system. As popular confidence waned in the State, East Germany's low living standards began to cause annoyance. In 1989 East German refugees began to cross into West Germany via East European countries which had already opened their frontiers to the West as part of the growing liberalisation. In 1989 the East German government, in response to popular pressure, allowed free movement across the Berlin Wall. This relaxation created further problems and in 1990 the Communists threw in the towel and allowed a popular vote on the future of their country. There was an overwhelming vote in favour of union with the Federal Republic and a formal reunification took place in 1991.

This joyful reunion of the two German states came at a difficult time. Ever since the war, West Germans had found it much harder to visit East Germany than citizens of most other countries. It was widely thought in the German Federal Republic that East Germany was an advanced industrial state, as Communist propaganda had claimed. However, as West German officials and industrial experts began to examine their new inheritance, they encountered a rickety, rusting structure of waste, inefficiency, outdated technology, brown coal, and 'bits of string'. Even allowing for exchange rate difficulties and the supposedly higher quality of public facilities in East Germany, the fact that average monthly gross earnings in East Germany in 1988 were *one-third* of those in West Germany implied a massive investment and retraining effort, for most of which the West German taxpayer would have to pay. In West Germany only 2 per cent of households did not have a telephone. In East Germany, only 7 per cent *had* a telephone (Lipschitz and McDonald, 1990, xv). What would it cost to give East Germany a completely new telephone system, without which it could not compete in a united Germany? Meanwhile, unemployment in East Germany quickly rose to around 30 per cent as enterprises collapsed in the face of western competition.

At first, East German personal 'restocking' with long-desired external consumer goods, paid for by various forms of credit extended by the West German government and banks, created a lively boom in West Germany. The East Germans were allowed to convert their Reichsmarks into Deutschmarks at par, an amazingly generous rate which contrasted with the confiscatory Reichsmark conversion of 1948. This easy transition was seen in West Germany as part of a package to reward the East Germans for giving up the idea of a new German federalism in which the East would retain some of its socialist institutions, at any rate for a while. Many East Germans went straight to the bank and drew the maximum personal loan that they were allowed under the transition arrangements, buying a large West German car with the money. As most of these people already had cars, albeit the Ulbricht-issue two-stroke Trabant or the Comecon export-quality three-cylinder Wartburg with the paper-thin body, a massive net flow of capital into West Germany occurred, while the market value of the Trabant dropped almost to nothing. And so did the value of most East German industry, in that external firms showed no wish to buy it, realising that they would be saddled with idiosyncratic products, outdated Comecon mongrel equipment with local bits bolted on, and an inflated labour force accustomed to going home during the day to deal with family problems. East German products proved hopelessly uncompetitive at home and, with the loss of Comecon export markets, East German aggregate output fell by at least 45 per cent in the first year after unification. Meanwhile, East German workers secured multi-annual wage agreements designed to raise wage rates to West German levels by the mid-1990s. These were not related to productivity and, by 1993, unit labour costs in the East German economy were 60 per cent higher than in the West (OECD, *Germany*, 1993, 12, 102).

The post-unification boom collapsed in late 1992, bringing economic expansion in western Germany to a sudden halt. With inflationary pressures consequent upon unification still effective, and West German workers pressing successfully for gains similar to those secured so easily by the East Germans, the government had to keep a tight rein on fiscal policy. High interest rates and growing excess capacity decelerated investment, while an appreciating Deutschmark and big wage increases in 1991 and 1992 reduced the competitiveness of German exports. Exports were in any case held down by the world recession and the overseas payments account dropped into deficit from 1991 (OECD, *Germany*, 1993, 101, 140). By 1993 the foreign payments deficit on current account was DM35.2 billion. Home demand was restrained by high taxation and rising domestic production costs. Unemployment increased, reaching 10 per cent in 1994 and 1995, with the usual unpleasant political effects as far as the foreign workers were concerned.

The initial belief that an injection of capital into East German industry would revive it enough to compete within the EEC was replaced by the glum recognition that West German firms and any foreign internationals who were so tempted would have to set up from scratch in the East. Until they did so East Germany would be unable to pay for its welfare and unemployment benefits, and for the modernisation of its housing. Far from being an increased source of demand for the West, East Germany was a major drain on the West Germany economy. A revival began in 1994 but in 1995 West Germany was still saddled with high taxation, high interest rates and a low growth rate, and its problems had a depressive effect on the European economy as a whole. The OECD predicted a growth rate of 2.7 per cent for 1996 (OECD *Economic Outlook*, **57**, 55). Meanwhile, many of the 15 per cent of East Germans who remained unemployed drove to collect their unemployment pay in their BMWs.

In 1995 Germany still awaited the revival in world trade that would, as in the past, relaunch the country's prosperity. Nevertheless, it was recognised that increased costs and low investment had eroded Germany's export position to the extent that it would not achieve its traditional share in world export trade. Wage inflation in East Germany was so firmly entrenched and protected by legal and political agreements that to control it seemed likely to be a slow process. Unification had, however, created western Europe's largest country in terms of population. With nearly 80 million people, the new Germany was 40 per cent larger than its three closest followers, France, Italy and the United Kingdom, each of which had between 56 and 57 million people. Before unification, Germany's population, at 62 millions, had not been greatly out of line with the others and there had been much talk of a balanced EEC with four countries of equal importance preventing Germany, or an alliance of Germany and France, imposing its view on the rest. By 1995, Germany's acute financial problems and dependence on foreign lending meant that it was in no position to be assertive. There was no telling, though, what would happen when eastern Germany was fully reorganised and reequipped, say around the year 2001. Perhaps there would be a new *Ostpolitik*. Perhaps this would coincide with the new 'Marshall plan' for the East, discussed at the end of this book.

France

France, Germany's main partner in the EEC after the De Gaulle–Adenauer initiatives in the early 1960s, grew more rapidly than Germany, maintaining its growth rate of the late 1950s while Germany's declined. In this respect it could claim to be the most successful EEC country.

In 1958 Charles de Gaulle returned as Prime Minister, and later President, to deal with the chaos of the war in Algeria, which was the most disastrous product of France's post-war determination to retain its colonies. This time, he insisted on a free hand and in late 1958 he secured a constitution for a new republic, the Fifth, which met his requirements for strong government, large parties, and stability. He immediately devalued the franc for the second time in two years, producing an undervalued currency, and took strong fiscal action to combat inflation. Then, in 1959, he created the 'new franc', a consolidated currency of mainly psychological value, designed to foster low inflation even in conditions of rapid

growth, and to accompany the return of the franc to full convertibility on the basis of a government decision of 27 December 1958,
in line with the Bretton Woods agreement. He set up a stronger
system of national planning, and strengthened agriculture by
reforms to reduce the number of small peasant farmers, and to
encourage younger farmers willing to create larger units.

These changes had only just begun to take effect by 1960, and
in some ways they merely continued many of the policies pursued
by the civil servants under the Fourth Republic. The cautious
Finance Minister, Antoine Pinay, brought back by De Gaulle in
1958 and in post until January 1960, was the main influence
behind the presidential economic strategy, reenacting much of his
legendary stabilisation programme of 1952, raising taxes, reducing
the budget deficit, cutting public investment, reducing social
security benefits, and abolishing the war veterans' pension.
Subsidies to nationalised industries were abolished, together with
indexed wages and agricultural prices (Ambrosi, 1981, 288–9).

In this new climate, economic planning by technocratic civil
servants came even more to the fore. The Third Plan, published in
1959 and adopted by the new government, aimed for rapid
economic growth. The foundation was laid for an acceleration in
the French growth rate in the 1960s and the belated completion of
the French industrialisation process by 1970. The plan also
included, for the first time, welfare, housing and social development. Rapid growth soon produced some inflationary effects, and
a further stabilisation programme, under a new Finance Minister,
Valéry Giscard d'Estaing, became necessary in 1963 but it was
achieving success by 1965.

By the mid-1960s the French growth rate had overtaken
Germany's and France had acquired a reputation for innovation
and quality in industries such as motors and aeronautics, and, as
ever, in luxury goods. The big growth of French exports since the
mid-1950s and major foreign investment contributed to a very
large balance of payments surplus by the early 1960s. With the
Algerian War resolved in 1962, France was able to negotiate with
the new Algerian government for rights to exploit Sahara oil. New
French companies were set up for this purpose, the biggest being
ELF.

Legal and fiscal reforms discouraged small-scale, inefficient
enterprise in agriculture and commerce. The principle of the
mixed-economy enterprise was developed to a degree unknown
elsewhere in Europe. In the country, a government programme of

land redistribution began in the late 1950s, producing larger plots and migration of labour to the towns. De Gaulle's administration followed this up with two agricultural orientation laws in 1960 and 1962. These were based on the principle that French agricultural produce would be sold at a price high enough to assure an adequate income to the farmer, and were linked to the concessions won by France in the formulation of the CAP. Agriculture's drive to greater efficiency became spectacular from the early 1960s, with bigger production units and a surge of mechanical equipment. The lone horse and ploughman, and the dungheaps in front of the village doors, which were still the mark of the French countryside in the mid-1950s, were scarcely to be found ten years later.

The excess rural population flooded into the towns. The urban population rose from 56 per cent of the national total in 1954 to 61.6 per cent in 1962, and to 66.2 per cent in 1968 (Berstein, 1989, 186). A big housing programme was under way by the early 1960s, with a national urban planning strategy to accommodate it in a host of rapidly developed 'projets' including planned suburbs (ZUP), renewal areas (ZAD), and new towns. Because most of the people housed were manual workers, the whole of France's rich array of public building and financial agencies was brought into play. In 1964, for instance, private capital financed only 57 per cent of residential building in France (Mathieu, 1965, 54).

This surge of growth, which averaged nearly 6 per cent per annum in the 1960s, was among the highest in Europe. For most of the decade, spare capacity was almost nil and unemployment was negligible, though a slight deterioration set in from 1970. Inflation, at 3 per cent or more, was higher than in most other European countries but it was kept under close supervision and the contrast with the 1940s, and even the 1950s, was reassuring. The volume of exports rose steadily, at a rate of about 13 per cent per annum on average. It became a time of quick profits and *nouveaux riches*, with cheap labour flooding in from Algeria and other former colonies on the lines seen in Britain a decade before.

The robust economy helped De Gaulle to restrict American influence and pursue a foreign policy which was independent of the USA and of the European members of NATO. The origins of this aspiration dated back to the Second World War and were linked to De Gaulle's grudge against Britain. As *Le Monde* put it on 11 November 1970, after his death: 'Few men have wanted to embody France as much as he did, from his birth to his death'.

(Coppolani and Gardair, 1976, 47). In economic and social terms, however, De Gaulle was prepared to participate in European integration, and for reasons of strategic security he was willing to work closely with Germany.

This integrationist stance was linked to De Gaulle's decision to give up French control of Algeria in 1962 and most of the other colonies from 1958 onwards. Although De Gaulle roundly rejected the idea that he was conforming to America's post-war policy on decolonisation, his withdrawal from imperialism did much to open him up to the potential of a wide range of cooperative policies within Europe, and especially with West Germany. For instance, Algerian independence in 1962 led to a big exodus of Europeans, 700,000 of whom returned to mainland France, where they increased the national population by 2 per cent. When combined with demobilised servicemen, no longer needed in Algeria, this influx produced an addition of 450,000 to the French labour force. With demand boosted as well by big transfers of funds, the French GDP increased by 6.3 per cent in 1962, compared to 4.5 per cent in 1961 and the annual average growth rate of 5.5 per cent in the Fourth Plan (1962–65) (OECD, *France*, 1963, 5–6). Cooperation with Germany was encouraged by his economic and related reforms, which quickly put France on a par with Germany as a dynamic economy and in the 1960s the Franco-German understanding dominated Europe, at the expense of British and American interests.

The new constitution for the Fifth Republic, approved in 1958, was of great importance. Although unclear on certain points because of the contribution of a supervising parliamentary committee, the constitution proved capable of securing strong and stable government, with a seven-year President choosing his own Prime Minister. This deprived the assembly of power to overturn a government and made it hard for the assembly and the Senate to refuse legislation desired by the president.

De Gaulle and his Prime Ministers were strongly committed to the modernisation of France. De Gaulle often used to say that France should 'marry her century' (metaphors based on relations between men and women are commonly used by French politicians) (Ardagh, 1990, 13). A productive economy and an energetic, qualified workforce were required. There was a tacit link between popular enthusiasm for French nationality, especially among the young, and economic efficiency. At the same time, pride and confidence in France's empire, which had helped sustain national morale between the wars, were increasingly replaced by a sense of achievement in Europe. The idea that France's great strength lay in its balance between agriculture and industry, learned by every French child at primary school, was at last left behind, together with the similar primary school myth that 'France's roads are the best roads in Europe' (Bossuat, I, 1992, 16). High-technology industries had to be promoted and a high rate of investment, together with public direction of funds, were needed.

De Gaulle's presidency ended with his abrupt resignation in 1969. The student and worker protests of 1968 had undermined his confidence in his ability to secure the support of the French people. The Grenelle agreement with the trade unions in 1968 had greatly increased wage costs at a time when expanding credit was accelerating inflation and drawing in imports. By 1969 France faced a big foreign payments deficit, rising unemployment, and declining exports. The government returned to two classic French post-war measures, a devaluation of the franc and a temporary price freeze. Bank credit was restrained (OECD, *France*, 1970, 6–13). These measures won the support of an electorate which had been frightened by the near-anarchy of the summer of 1968. The devaluation was a success, like its immediate predecessor in 1958, restoring French competitiveness and correcting the balance of payments, avoiding the need for a period of deflation. Thus launched by a painless devaluation, De Gaulle's successor, Georges Pompidou, was able to retain the essence of De Gaulle's policies and by 1970 stability and continuity had been restored.

By 1970 France enjoyed the second-highest standard of living in Europe, after Germany. Expenditure on food dropped from 37.7 per cent of the average household budget in 1959 to 24.9 per cent in 1975 (Berstein, 1989, 212). This was the reward for rapid growth since the mid-1950s under conditions of general monetary and fiscal stability (Graham, 1990, 64). The concept of a French 'economic miracle' never caught on in France, however, no doubt because it devalued the planned character of the French economic success. Nevertheless, when the French economic commentator, Jean Fourastié, coined the phrase, 'thirty glorious years', in a book which he published in 1979, the whole of the media and intelligentsia took up the idea (Fourastié, 1979). 'Les trente glorieuses' remained in frequent use in the 1990s to describe a French economic and social 'catching-up' between 1946 and 1976 which allowed the country to achieve the highest European standards in every sphere.

The oil crisis of 1973 produced a distinctive response on the part of the French government. The increase in the OPEC oil price was a serious matter owing to the heavy French dependence on oil imports. It was the equivalent of a fall of 3 per cent in French GDP (Piquet Marchal, 1985, 204). West Germany tackled a similar problem largely by a reduction of consumption, but France drew on its inflationary tradition and its recent record of a high growth rate to justify a continuation of expansion. The French government provided help or guidance for individual firms (Shepherd et al., 1983, 22). The nuclear power programme was accelerated, so that by 1991, some 75 per cent of French electricity would be nuclear generated, the highest national proportion in the world.

After a brief deflationary episode in 1974, inflation accelerated, forcing the franc to leave the European monetary 'snake' in 1976, only two years after it had re-entered it. In August 1976, Finance Minister Raymond Barre launched a stabilising strategy which became notorious for its sound principles and determined application. Traditional budgetary and fiscal checks were complemented by the fashionable monetarism of the day. Barre even looked the part, with all the features of an overweight provincial bank manager. The title of the low comedy film *Tiens bon la barre, matelot!* (loosely translated, 'Hullo, sailor!') was recalled with many a chuckle in the early days, but Barre's success gradually won respect and later helped him to a stolid premiership, a little like Erhard's. Barre used the control of the money supply as one weapon, but he also tackled the budget deficit, reducing it to a level which could be financed by long-term borrowing. He controlled the growth of wages and salaries, and defended the value of the franc so that an increase in the price of imports did not generate further inflation (Piquet Marchal, 1985, 206). Energy imports, including oil, were now declining as a result of earlier policies and Barre supported the continuing development of nuclear energy which had seemed the best solution for a France with limited coal reserves. By 1979, however, the Barre policies were becoming less successful and the new OPEC price increase could not be met in the same way, partly for political reasons. A return to 'social' policies increased the inflation rate and generated a degree of instability which helped the new President Mitterrand to power in 1981.

The election of the new president was superficially similar to that of Léon Blum's Popular Front government in 1936, partly because the Communist Party formed part of a broad alliance of the Left and its supporters and the media sometimes made use of the term 'Popular Front'. Mitterrand's support rested partly on popular resentment against the financial orthodoxy pursued by his centrist predecessor, Valéry Giscard d'Estaing, one of whose many misfortunes was to come to power immediately after the oil crisis in 1973.

Mitterrand moved to a boldly expansionist policy to generate employment and develop a socialist answer to the world depression. Its inflationary potential recalled both Edward Heath's 'go for growth' strategy in the early 1970s and Blum's programme in 1936, but the circumstances were now even less propitious. He wanted to generate a radical review of the French economy and society so that 'weaknesses' surviving from the 1970s could be identified and dealt with, and ineffective policies abandoned, in the context of a more competitive economy and greater social equality (Commission du Bilan, *Forces et faiblesses*, 1982, 5). Even with time, such semi-utopian results would have been hard to achieve, but there was almost no time at all. Shoring up demand with welfare payments, wage increases for the lower-paid, and expansion of public employment did nothing to tackle the weaknesses of the economy. The reduction of the working week to 39 hours and the creation of a *fifth* week of paid holiday must have made Winston Churchill turn in his grave. Much as in 1936, high inflation and a growing balance of payments deficit quickly ensued and Mitterrand had to return to deflationary policies in 1982–83. In doing so he parted company with his Communist ministers and the 'Popular Front' myth vanished with the morning dew (Gueslin, 1992, 194–5).

Mitterrand now embarked on a conventional course which his seven-year term helped him to maintain until the world revival in the second half of the decade. His main alliance from now on was not with the outer reaches of the French Left but with his EEC partners. The anti-inflationary strategy which he embraced in 1982 would survive in France until 1995, marking the final renunciation of a traditional French recourse and allowing his country to join Germany and Britain as the key European pillars of financial orthodoxy. At the same time, he abandoned his cherished ambition to lead Europe towards a socialist solution to the unique problems of his day. With the Christian Democrats returning to power in Germany, and Thatcher winning an extraordinary naval war against Argentina, European socialism took some heavy blows in 1982. In fact, it has never recovered.

Even nationalisation, an established French solution to management and investment problems, was affected. In 1978, the French government had taken majority holdings in the big steel firms, which were seen as lacking in capital and managerial competence. In 1981, a wave of nationalisations, pushed forward by Mitterrand, moved to the almost complete control of two big steel groups, together with other large industrial firms, including the glassware firm, Saint-Gobain, the engineering group, Rhône-Poulenc, and the huge steel combine, Usinor. Also nationalised were thirty-nine banks and two financial companies. However, in 1982, the government changed tack. It gave up its ambition to secure direct control of production, and encouraged the nationalised enterprises in each industry to group or merge, often on the basis of an established dominant firm. In this way, Bull computers, at one time De Gaulle's answer to IBM, became once again the leader of the French computer industry. These new combines were then encouraged to function independently within the market, guided mainly by what was known as 'strategic control', and by formal national planning (ADA, 1986, 150–6). This strategy was reversed in 1993 when the government announced a big programme of privatisation, with twenty-one State-owned companies to be sold off over the next few years.

Mitterrand's bold policies had an immediate depressive effect on the growth rate. Not until 1986 did the per capita growth rate climb back to 2.0 per cent. In 1988 and 1989, it reached 3.1 per cent, but unemployment still hovered around 10 per cent. However, Mitterrand's orthodox policies were now recognised as successful by the bulk of the French electorate. In 1992 France produced 24.2 per cent of the total EEC output of motor vehicles, and was the fourth-largest producer of motor vehicles in the world. French aluminium production was 19.0 per cent of the EEC total. In 1990, France was the world's fourth-biggest exporter, with 13.6 per cent of the world's total exports of glass, 12.2 per cent of total exports of rubber products, and 11.3 per cent of total aircraft exports (Eck, 1994, 107–8).

From mid-1992 France began to suffer from the general turndown in demand caused partly by the reunification of Germany and partly by the world recession. Unemployment increased from 8.9 per cent in 1990 to 11.7 per cent in 1993. Government policy clung firmly to disinflationary measures and to its commitment to the creation of a single European currency and there was no hint of a return to earlier days when inflation and devaluation were seen as acceptable solutions to economic problems (OECD, *France,* 1994, 93). The deterioration of the budget deficit since 1991 was mainly a cyclical effect but the government was determined to consolidate public spending even at the expense of social policies. France's very expensive health service was right in line for reform, and a long-run reduction of pensions was planned. The economy began to revive in 1994 and the OECD predicted a growth rate of 3.2 per cent in 1996 (OECD, *Economic Outlook,* 57, 61).

There was a serious, but temporary, disturbance in late 1995 when Mitterrand's Gaullist successor, Jacques Chirac, who had been elected President in May, presided over a bold attempt to reform the French welfare structure, mainly with a view to cutting government expenditure and holding wages down. One of his aims was to help France meet the Maastricht requirements for participation in the single European currency, without which France could not hope to maintain parity with Germany in leadership of the European Union. With Germany, herself straining under her eastern burden, giving strong support to the French government, the French public service unions, the university students, and a variety of dissident groups ran a long campaign of strikes and demonstrations which reminded many of 1968, 1947, and even 1936. The OECD growth predictions, which always tended towards optimism, now looked highly improbable. With the western European economy still in the doldrums, no national economy could escape from its long-term problems.

For all this, from a vantage point in 1995, most French people had a clear impression of unbroken national economic success since the war. In August 1994, the French popular money magazine, *Le Capital,* had published an issue devoted to the French economic success story, 1944–94. Putting the 1970s in the background, the journal boldly referred to the 'cinquante glorieuses' (*Le Capital,* 35, August 1994, 69). This judgment was partly intended to encourage small investors, but it had much in its favour. Between 1944 and 1994 French per capita purchasing power rose by two and a half times. The population increased from 40 million to 57 million, putting it on a par with Britain. These figures represented a transition from one of the most demographically stagnant countries in northern Europe to the most dynamic. Of course, France had started from a low base, and Germany still had much the bigger economy in 1995, but, taken in the round, France qualified as the biggest success story in post-war northern Europe.

Britain

The 1960s were a paradoxical decade for Britain. In terms of consumption, this was the decade in which Britain became the world leader of youth fashion – 'England swings like a pendulum-*doo*' went a folksy American pop song of the time. 'Swinging London' and Carnaby Street exported the mini-skirt worldwide, together with a host of ephemeral gewgaws. The Beatles must have put barbers out of business across the world, but in terms of records and clothes their impact on the British economy was entirely positive. If no longer the 'workshop of the world', Britain had become the world's teenage couturier as well as the world's popular musician. The English victory in the World Cup in 1966 put Britain on top of the world in the eyes of most of its people. The years of wartime effort and post-war gloom seemed to have given way to an era of consumption and leisure in which even the 'free lunch' could be seen steaming on the East End table of Alf Garnett in the crudely demotic television comedy series, 'Till Death Us Do Part'.

However, the 1960s were also the first decade since the war in which the weaknesses of the British economy became clear to many ordinary people, and entered insistently into the realm of public debate. In the late 1950s and early 1960s politicians, mainly in the Liberal and Labour parties, began to draw on EEC, UN, and OECD statistics to emphasise Britain's low growth rate and relatively declining living standards. The progress of the EEC emphasised these divergences and there was some suggestion from within the Liberal and Conservative parties that joining the EEC would stimulate the British economy, mainly by expanding the market for British exports and driving British industry towards greater efficiency.

This perception partly replaced a general view which had been reinforced by Britain's brusque devaluation in 1949, to the effect that Britain did not need exclusive economic links with continental Europe (Young, 1993, 27). As for political integration, this would infringe British sovereignty. Rather, British ministers looked forward to a general internationalisation and expansion of world trade, led by the United States, which would generate an increase in British exports (Di Nolfo, 1992, 148). In 1951, half of Britain's exports went to the Commonwealth, compared to one-quarter to the future Six. In 1952, departmental reflections on the significance of the ECSC included the observation that Britain produced as much coal as the whole of the ECSC, while its steel production was about half the ECSC total. Even at the highest levels, casual remarks of the 'either we beat 'em or we liberated 'em' ilk could be heard off the record in the early 1950s and even later. Meanwhile, the British standard of living remained higher than that of any of the Six throughout the 1950s (Di Nolfo, 1992, 156). In the long term, what Britain wanted to secure was a liberalisation of trade with the USA, and involvement with a European customs union seemed unlikely to further that end.

British views began to change in response to visible trends in the second half of the decade. British exports to the Commonwealth had fallen to 43 per cent of total exports by 1957 (Di Nolfo, 1992, 156). Britain now had a notoriously low growth rate relative to the rest of western Europe and Japan. When the ECSC countries began to move towards fuller economic cooperation in 1955, Britain was represented at their discussions for a while but decided to make alternative proposals based on a free trade area which, inter alia, would make it easier for Britain to negotiate tariff reductions with the USA and would strengthen Britain's 'pivotal' world role. The Six rejected this approach and went ahead with the Treaty of Rome in 1957. In 1958 Britain made new proposals, for an industrial free trade area, but these too were rejected by the Six. In 1959 Britain organised a free trade association of a number of its trading partners, the European Free Trade Association (EFTA). However, this was partly intended as a bargaining counter and in 1961 Harold Macmillan applied for EEC membership.

Harold Macmillan's application to join the EEC, together with an incomes policy and rudimentary national planning, were partly intended to bring about a modernisation of the British economy, though the Cabinet also hoped to restore Britain's political influence in western Europe. Macmillan's main tactic was to establish an understanding with De Gaulle whereby both countries, with the support of the USA, would sustain each other's sovereignty and establish themselves as the joint leaders of Europe (Young, 1993, 70). Macmillan's big hope was that an offer of nuclear weapons cooperation to De Gaulle would prove decisive. Unfortunately, before the end of the negotiations Britain had agreed to accept an American offer of Polaris missiles. With De Gaulle trying to establish French, and ultimately European, strategic independence from the USA, the British offer was now worthless. The De Gaulle veto in 1963 reflected a French distrust of Britain's association with the USA and a suspicion of Britain's willingness to work as a cooperative European partner, owing partly to its commitment to the Commonwealth (De Gaulle, 1970, 66–71). It was also a product of De Gaulle's awareness that British membership would baulk his ambition to become the leader of Europe (Young, 1993, 83–84). De Gaulle would later recall of his crucial interview with Macmillan at Rambouillet in December 1962 that he felt sorry for this English gentleman to whom he could give nothing. In 1963, Macmillan needed all the gifts he could get. The De Gaulle veto was just one of a number of bitter blows to the Conservative government, including the Profumo affair, and in the following year a Labour government came to power under Harold Wilson.

De Gaulle's rebuff, though mainly the product of strategic and political considerations, ruled out an economic strategy based on a major enlargement of markets for British exports. This limitation became increasingly damaging in the 1960s. Britain's tertiary sector developed rapidly enough, but its limited exports could not resolve the endemic balance of payments deficit and the weak pound. Manufacturing industry tottered on with low investment, high wages, and semi-anarchic trade union activity, particularly in the motor industry. Successful innovations, like the British Motor Corporation's Mini Minor, which went on sale in 1959, were few. Significantly, the Mini's biggest market was among the gilded youth of the 1960s, and its omnipresence on the Continent by the later part of the decade contrasted with the gradual disappearance of other British cars there. Britain could still export distinctive products towards the upper end of the market, like the Range Rover, an impressive luxury jeep launched in 1970 by BLMC (British Leyland Motor Company, which had been created by a merger in 1968 to help make the British-owned motor industry more competitive with its American-owned rivals) (Church, 1994, 84ff), and the perennial Scotch whisky, which could sell to board-rooms and officers' clubs throughout the world at a premium price. Certain well organised, high technology industries, such as the ICI-dominated chemical industry, could export bulk products cheaply, but most of British mass production was dogged by high wage costs, inefficient working practices, and antiquated machinery.

Wilson's election campaign in 1964 had stressed Britain's economic retardation and his role as a would-be moderniser was welcomed by the electorate (Pimlott, 1992, 306–19). His promise that Britain would be exposed to the 'white heat' of modern technology would prove to be the first of many glib undertakings and assurances which in the end made him a tedious caricature. At first, though, Labour's policies were effective. In 1966 manufacturing output reached a peak which has never since been surpassed, a small balance of payments surplus was achieved, and unemployment was only 1.5 per cent (Pimlott, 1992, 466). In the longer term, however, Wilson encountered a clutch of fundamental contradictions. Efforts to modernise Britain on socialist lines required higher taxation or greater government borrowing, both of which tended to reduce private investment and erode electoral support. Britain's endemic balance of payments problem was a constant scourge. It was exacerbated from the moment Wilson came to power in 1964 by international anticipation of an increase in the rate of inflation in Britain. In July 1966 the Cabinet faced its first major sterling crisis. After much debate, it decided not to devalue the pound but the resulting deflationary package reduced demand and tended to depress investment further. Wilson's application to join the EEC in May 1967 made matters worse as membership was bound to bring about a deterioration in the British balance of payments, at least in the early years. Britain thus became even more a target for currency speculation and large-scale capital movements.

These pressures, which Harold Wilson's deputy, George Brown, once blamed on 'the gnomes of Zurich', were aggravated by the strength of the British labour movement which provided the main electoral and financial support for the Labour Party. In Britain, about half the workforce was unionised, compared to about 35 per cent in West Germany and 20 per cent in France (Graham, 1990, 57). Powerful trade unions, affiliated to the Labour Party, were able to defend their acquired wages and conditions, so a reduction of labour costs could not be hoped for. Official and unofficial strikes could do direct damage to the national economy, with Wilson especially disturbed by the dock strike of 1966 which appeared to have started the big run on the pound (Pimlott, 1992, 527). In 1968–69, Wilson launched a big effort to promote legislation designed to produce a more ordered industrial negotiating system and to reduce the number of strikes. This focused on a White Paper, *In Place of Strife*, published in January 1969 by the new Minister of Labour, Barbara Castle. The trade union movement quickly united in rejecting the whole idea, forcing Castle and Wilson into a series of frustrating and humiliating negotiations which undermined the government's prestige in Britain and abroad. In June, the Government had not only to drop the proposed legislation but even the idea of a binding agreement with the Trades Union Congress (TUC)(Pimlott, 1992, 527–44). This failure epitomised Labour's inability to secure the full cooperation of organised labour in a national programme of industrial modernisation. It contrasted with the experience of the Nordic countries after the war (though here also the trade unions became more demanding in the later 1960s).

Labour's failure to deal with these fundamental economic problems reduced the prospects of increased growth and undermined Labour's long-term modernisation plans. Concealed export subsidies, import substitution measures, and short-term discouragements to imports were no substitute for joining the EEC, and they probably did not help Britain's case (Beckerman, 1972, 11). The author remembers seeing Harold Wilson on television with Sir Abubakar Tafawa Balewa, the Prime Minister of Nigeria, in 1964. Basking in a glowing deference on the part of the African, Wilson gravely announced his plans to stop importing products which could easily be made in Britain. So far so good, one might say, but the example he gave to clinch his point was the *lead pencil*. So much for the 'white heat'!

Of course, balance of payments problems and the whole predictable collection of side-effects were not unique to Harold Wilson's first administration in 1964. They had been developing since 1945 and no government had been able to resolve them. Wilson's reaction to these problems was also a development of previous practice. He tried to reinforce the strategic association with the United States, a policy which required him to give fulsome support to the United States in its efforts to defend South Vietnam against Communist infiltration and attack from as early as 1964 (Pimlott, 1992, 385). Wilson refused a British military commitment in Vietnam, recalling Franco's relationship with Hitler, but by 1970 his words alone had destroyed his world socialist and internationalist credentials, and many of his other credentials as well. Secondly, he used Britain's international creditworthiness, which, as Britain was a big trader and investor on world markets, was a major asset, to borrow on a large scale. The United States was the key prop of this policy, but it was also linked to the growth of the economies of the EEC. This led to Wilson's application to join the EEC in 1966, which was encouraged by the USA as part of its European integration policy. Finally, Wilson introduced – or talked about introducing – economic reforms in Britain which were designed to increase productivity through making fuller use of national resources, and notably human resources. These reforms were presented as modernising and socialist at the same time.

The economic reforms were epitomised by Labour's espousal of national economic planning on French lines, which had a brilliant reputation in western Europe by the early 1960s. In 1965 the Labour government launched an indicative National Plan on the lines pioneered by France from 1946. It was based on the creation of targets for national output, and obtaining the cooperation of the economic sectors in meeting allocated targets while scheduling public investment. Unfortunately, Labour's austerity measures of 1966, designed to defend the pound, killed the plan because its target growth rate of 3.5–4 per cent could no longer be achieved.

Meanwhile, the adventurous social policies were abandoned. When Labour came to power in 1964, the French left-wing intellectual magazine, *Le Nouvel Observateur*, in search of a convincing example of practical socialism to present to Gaullist France, published a long article on the new Britain every week. After a couple of months these articles were completely dropped, no doubt because the editors realised that they had been taken in as much as the British electorate.

British living standards continued to slump in relation to the rest of western Europe. In 1960, British per capita GDP had been 128.6 per cent of the average GDP of the twelve countries which were to form the EEC in the 1980s. Only Luxembourg, with 158.5 per cent, was better off, but this tiny country with its huge concentration of heavy industry was not comparable to Britain. Western Germany, with 117.9 per cent, was one of a group of three countries bunched in second place behind Britain, including Denmark (118.3 per cent), and the Netherlands (118.6 per cent). France's per capita GDP was close to the average, at 105.8 per cent. By 1970, Britain had dropped much closer to the average, with 108.5 per cent. The tendency towards the equalisation of economic growth which was a strong feature of the trading Europe of the 1960s meant that all the bunched second group of 1960 recorded lower percentages in 1970, but Germany (113.2 per cent) and France (110.4 per cent) were now more productive than Britain (Féron, 1992, 177). Britain's relative GDP could scarcely have done other than decline as the western European economy expanded on a continental scale in the 1960s, but to drop to sixth place, even allowing for changes in exchange rates resulting from the devaluation of the pound sterling in 1967, was disturbing.

Like Harold Macmillan, Harold Wilson hoped in a rather vague way that British membership of the EEC would do much of his modernising for him. When his second British application to join the EEC was vetoed by De Gaulle in 1967, on very much the same grounds as the first, the Labour government had little new thinking to offer. A sterling devaluation of nearly 15 per cent in November 1967 was presented as a chance to improve British competitiveness. It was hoped that ambitious government schemes to encourage industrial productivity would now have a greater effect. However, the devaluation led to an increase in inflation while significant productivity increases did not occur until the end of the decade. Its impact on the balance of payments was slow, and in 1968 Britain introduced a system of import deposits to discourage imports and to create short-term balances of foreign currency. By 1969 the balance of trade had moved into surplus, but only after sharply deflationary policies at home had greatly increased unemployment.

Labour was defeated at the general election of 1970 and the Conservatives returned to power under another moderniser, Edward Heath. With wages now rising again, the new government moved away in 1971 from the old defence-of-the-pound/ devaluation strategy to the floating exchange rates presaged by the problems of the US dollar. Some progress was made on trade union legislation and Heath made joining the EEC a major plank of his policies. He had been the chief British negotiator in 1961–63 and he was much more committed to securing British membership than Wilson had been. He negotiated more flexibly, and had good integrationist credentials. Perhaps most important of all, De Gaulle had retired in 1969 and the Six were now generally well disposed towards Britain's membership. Britain applied in 1971 and was accepted in 1973.

Ironically, the year 1973 was significant for Britain in a much less propitious way. The OPEC oil boycott and price increase singled out Britain as one of the most vulnerable countries in western Europe to OPEC pressure and its consequences. Heath's government had launched a bold 'go-for-growth' policy in 1970 at a time of high OECD growth. This was partly intended to lift productivity closer to that of the EEC, but in the short term it had the effect of increasing home demand (the 'Barber Boom'). Although Heath's policy was in line with that pursued by some

other European countries, the long inheritance of low investment
and low labour productivity was seriously inflationary, and sucked
in imports. As early as 1971, the monthly rate of inflation rose to
over 10 per cent, and by 1974 the oil price increases had pushed it
to over 15 per cent. The value of the pound deteriorated and
government borrowing increased. The resulting deterioration of
the balance of payments coincided with an increase in world
prices. With unemployment falling, conditions looked good in
Britain in the short term, but any destabilisation of world markets
was bound to affect Britain more than most other industrial
countries (Wright, 1979, 163).

It would be some years before EEC membership would provide
Britain with tangible economic benefits. The oil crisis, however,
had an immediate impact. Britain was heavily dependent on oil
imports, and a reduction in volume resulted in cuts in output in
late 1973 and 1974. Production of cars was especially hard hit by
both EEC entry and the oil crisis. With few new models available,
imports from other EEC countries did very well. British Leyland
production dropped from a peak of 916,200 cars in 1972 to a low
point of 395,800 cars in 1980 (Church, 1994, 104). Recovery of the
British motor industry did not begin until the early 1980s, and
even by the early 1990s the production levels of the early 1970s
had not been regained.

The OPEC action was catastrophic for Heath. When the
government sought to increase coal production as an alternative
energy source, the National Union of Mineworkers under the
ranting Arthur Scargill took its cue from OPEC and went on strike
for a huge wage increase in line with the potential value of coal as
an oil substitute. Whereas the unions in the nationalised industries
had been able since the war to secure large wage increases from
tolerant governments, Heath had to defeat the miners not only to
retain a shadow of his expansionist policies, but to stay in power.
The miners won, using every loophole of the picketing law. Heath
called a general election in 1974 in the hope of securing support
for the reform of trade union law, but he was narrowly defeated by
Labour under Harold Wilson in March, and a second general
election later in the year gave Labour a clear majority.

Labour introduced a compulsory incomes policy in 1974 but it
lasted only until 1976, the year in which Britain obtained a
humiliating IMF loan to cover its huge balance of payments
deficit. Labour preferred to maintain employment and control
inflation through national understandings with the trade unions

and, though more remotely, the employers. The most precise version was the original 'Social Contract' of 1974 (soon diluted to 'Social Compact' in a typical Wilsonian sideways move). Inflation slowed for a while from mid-1977 to late 1978, but the succession of general wage increases which, since 1974, had anticipated future inflation, combined with lavish government support for increasingly uncompetitive industries, 'to save jobs', did nothing to tackle the problem of low British productivity. Moreover, the government was obliged to maintain social and welfare provision as part of the understanding with the trade unions, so public expenditure could not be reduced easily. Investment was discouraged and the survival of old equipment and methods allowed both workforce and management to slump into an apathetic acceptance of a relatively low standard of life. Some unions were able to secure increases above the agreed level and the Labour government went into more contorsions explaining to salaried workers and the self-employed why these exceptions were justified. There were many occasions when the first interview on television news in the evening was of Jack Jones or another senior trade union leader, rather than of a senior minister. Harold Wilson, the 'white heat' man of the early 1960s, now sank into obscurity within his own government and resigned the premiership in 1976.

Government support for ailing firms was more redolent of Italy than anywhere else. By the later 1970s, high interest rates and the fall in export demand were hitting hard at Britain's export industries. Of course, the least competitive firms were affected most severely, but certain industries, such as shipbuilding, were clearly moving towards total obliteration. The Heath administration of 1970–74 had supported a number of overstretched firms such as Rolls-Royce (1971), the aero engine builder, and the conglomerate motor manufacturer, British Leyland (1974), in order to maintain employment and the quality of the labour force. Labour continued this policy (e.g. Chrysler, 1976), though within its declining resources.

In 1976, however, the Labour government abandoned its commitment to full employment, partly in deference to the IMF (Lowe, 1994, 2). The new Conservative government of 1979 would abandon the idea of supporting declining firms ('lame ducks') and between 1977 and 1983 most of the leading private sector manufacturing firms lost a large part of their labour force. Even highly efficient firms such as Courtaulds, Tube Investments, Dunlop and Talbot lost over half their employees. The huge public sector steel manufacturer, British Steel, lost 61 per cent (Supple, 1994, 453).

At the end of this difficult decade, Britain's GDP per capita had sunk to the average of the EEC Twelve, at 101.1 per cent. Britain now lay in eighth position. Britain was in a leading group of industrial nations, well ahead of the trailing Spain, Greece, Ireland and Portugal, but its closest neighbour was Italy (102.5 per cent). Germany registered 113.2 per cent, and France, 111.6 per cent (Féron, 1992, 177).

As the 1960s progressed, the failure of manufacturing to contribute anything like its share to the British growth rate became an increasing cause of concern. The other sectors developed on satisfactory lines, with employment in the service sector rising to 41.4 per cent of the total workforce by 1970 (compared to 33.9 per cent in Germany in 1971) (Abelshauser, 1983, 125), but their low export capability prevented their doing much to reduce the balance of payments deficit. Low productivity and low investment were the main problems in manufacturing, as Sidney Pollard has shown in a host of publications.

FIGURE 8.4 *Annual growth rates (%) of the real domestic product (GDP).*

	1950–55	1955–60	1960–64	1964–69	1969–73	1970–80
UK	2.9	2.5	3.4	2.5	2.8	1.9
France	4.4	4.8	6.0	5.9	6.1	3.6
Germany	9.1	6.4	5.1	4.6	4.5	2.8
Italy	6.3*	5.4	5.5	5.6	4.1	3.0
Japan	7.1	9.0	11.7	10.9	9.3	4.9
USA	4.2	2.4	4.4	4.3	3.4	3.0

* 1952–55.
Source: Pollard, 1983, 346.

Some observers and historians blamed cultural factors, with the most able people declining to work in manufacturing, and trainee managers denied the training that they would have received in Germany (Dintenfass, 1992, 71). At the same time, it could be suggested that the more able young people of Britain, nearly ten generations down the line from Britain's first industrialists at the end of the eighteenth century, were understandably turning to more pleasant and rewarding pursuits in the tertiary sector. The

FIGURE 8.5 *Per capita exports in US dollars, 1986.*

Belgium	6,740
France	2,256
Germany	3,984
Italy	1,716
Netherlands	5,451
Sweden	4,452
Switzerland	5,701
UK	1,885

The table shows the value of each country's exports in US
dollars, divided by the size of each country's population.
Source: Maddison, 1989, 27.

American historian, Martin J Wiener, detected a general rejection
of the values of industrialism by British opinion-formers which
undermined all efforts to modernise the economy in the 1970s
(Wiener, 1985, 162–6) With manufacturing suffering from low
investment and an awkward workforce, could its antiquated
environment and established production methods attract clever
people? Had Britain perhaps, as the first country to industrialise,
become the first to move into the 'post-industrial era'?

The Thatcher revival

In 1979, a Conservative government was elected under a young
and not very experienced Prime Minister, Margaret Thatcher. A
product of the lower middle classes (her father kept a shop in the
quiet provincial town of Grantham), she was determined to apply
values of hard work and thrift to restoring Britain to the enterprising, hard-working condition which she associated with the
Victorian era. She was prepared to eject ministers who did not
share her views, even if these came from a wealthy, leisured and
aristocratic background (Thatcher, 1993, 15, 150–3). Derided and
reviled at first by most of the British public and by many members
of her own party, she applied a vigorous deflationary policy and
launched an attack on the trade unions which transformed the
British economy. Combined with an equally resolute foreign policy
in close association with the United States, she built up a
worldwide reputation as a statesman. Her success was not only due
to her resolution, however. It was due to Britain's happy position

in the early 1980s as a big net exporter of oil, thanks to the hurried explorations in the North Sea since 1974 by British and American oil companies.

From 1979 Thatcher allowed the decline of British manufacturing to continue. Indeed, she reinforced competition in 1979 by removing British exchange restrictions and permitting a free flow of capital into and out of the country. This was possible because Britain now had an oil-backed currency and a large proportion of OPEC funds seeking foreign investment moved into sterling as a safe haven. Britain's real interest rate fell in relation to other countries, but the relatively high value of the pound hampered British exports and accelerated the decline of British manufacturing. Unemployment continued to rise, reaching 12.6 per cent in June 1983, with the government using its growing oil revenues to finance unemployment benefits. In 1981, unemployment relief in Britain totalled £8 billion, the equivalent of the government's total income from North Sea oil revenues (Dahrendorf, 1982, 4). However, the cumulative balance of payments surplus over the years 1978–82 reached £12.5 billion.

The government rejected Keynesian demand management which had already come under academic suspicion in the 1970s as a cause of low productivity. Thatcher became very interested in the newly fashionable monetarist economics associated with the elderly American economist, Milton Friedman. She saw the careful control of the money supply as an ideal means of controlling inflation without unpopular fiscal measures. The inflation rate, which reached 18 per cent in 1980, fell sharply thereafter, reaching 5 per cent in 1983. Pure monetarism proved inflexible and had to be abandoned, in Britain and elsewhere, by the mid-1980s, but in general terms it had undoubtedly contributed to a reduction of inflation. It was replaced by supply-side economics, with a reduction of public sector expenditure, tax cuts to encourage savings and promote more investment, reduction of regulation to promote efficiency, and a more flexible control of the money supply. The objective was a higher growth rate under conditions of monetary stability, and issues of distribution were put in the background. Thatcher dropped the Wilsonian idea of an understanding between the trade unions, the government, and the employers on the level of wage increases and the defence of employment. A programme of denationalisation, or privatisation as it began to be known, was planned.

Thatcher, worried about the strength of the trade unions in the

1970s, and associating it with low British productivity – nearly the lowest in Europe – introduced special legislation to make it harder to hold strikes, and urged employers to resist wage claims. She rejected the idea of a pay policy because it would not increase productivity (Thatcher, 1993, 93). In 1980 an Employment Act began the long and painful task of reforming British labour legislation. In 1982, the down-to-earth Norman Tebbit, Secretary of State for Employment and a close friend of Margaret Thatcher, pushed through another Employment Act.

These efforts were aimed mainly at controlling mass picketing, abolishing the 'closed shop' (a practice requiring workers to join a specified union before taking up work in a particular factory or workshop) and requiring formal trade union ballots before strikes were launched. They were strongly contested, but in the long run they were successful, partly because the trade unions were weak at a time of high unemployment. The steel strike of 1980 was a big challenge from an industry which had been over-expanded by previous governments and was now losing jobs in large numbers, but which sought a big pay increase to meet Britain's high inflation. This strike was a big victory for the government, which was able to face later challenges from a position of strength.

However, the government's efforts to weaken the miners' union (National Union of Mineworkers [NUM]) could not prevent a movement towards a gigantic confrontation. The NUM, producer of most of the coal on which Britain now depended, was strong enough to lead the trade union movement against the new labour legislation. The government was trying to undermine it by importing cheap coal from all round the world and the miners, sensing the long-term decline of their industry, decided to challenge Thatcher head-on. In 1984–85 the miners launched a national strike against the threat of pit closures in the wake of the big drop in OPEC oil prices in the early 1980s. Thatcher refused to give in and after more than a year the miners returned to work, their union divided and facing much bigger coal imports than before the strike. Other unions now realised at last that the days of a strike-based strategy were over and they became more moderate in their political position. Some of the smaller unions merged and the more moderate leaders approached the government with a view to securing the best benefits they could from government strategies.

By the early 1980s Margaret Thatcher had been confirmed in her view that sections of the British people, especially young people living in poor urban areas, had become demoralised and alienated not so much by poverty and unemployment as by the easy life which post-war British social policies had allowed them. With direction and training, and a degree of discipline, they would be able to lead full and productive lives again. To this end, unemployed youth were directed into training schemes not only to increase their versatility but to give them new hope and positive attitudes. From 1983, the government pursued a number of policies in housing, education and social security which became known in government circles as 'Social Thatcherism' (Thatcher, 1993, 147). Greater discipline partly took the form of new equipment and tactics for the police. This was mainly prompted by the big riots in the immigrant areas from 1981, but it helped the police to tackle normal hooliganism as well.

Gradually the British people responded to these new policies, welcoming greater order and organisation in the running of the public services. Redundancies affected older workers for the most part and a younger staff on the railways and in the post office, for instance, gradually replaced the old *laisser-aller* with more purposeful services. Car production began to recover in the early 1980s, as a number of multinational firms decided to build for export in Britain. Efficiency was greatly improved, and the new British plants of Japanese firms such as Nissan (1984) and Toyota (1993) provided both an example and a growing output. By 1993, Japanese car output in Britain made up over 25 per cent of the British total. In 1994 Rover (formerly British Leyland), the last major British producer, was sold to BMW. The growing production of cars in Britain therefore came increasingly to be the result of multinationals producing more cars in Britain, mainly for export, rather than of growing production by the British-owned car industry. This trend reflected the American and Japanese need to produce cars within the EEC in order to sell in continental markets, low British wage costs, and the presence of an experienced workforce. Meanwhile, high US investment in Britain was maintained, as was British investment in the USA. (See Figure 8.6.)

By 1985, Thatcher was in a strong enough position to move ahead with more fundamental economic and social reforms based on the 'privatisation' of the public sector. With oil revenues now in decline, income from the sale of public companies, and economies in the public services, allowed the government to reduce direct taxation. Although indirect taxation was increased, much of the electorate welcomed this policy.

FIGURE 8.6 *US investments in western European countries as a percentage of total US investments in Europe in 1986.*

	UK	Germany	France	Netherlands	Italy
Industry	26.7	24.9	11.7	8.6	9.3
Services	32.0	–	4.2	21.1	3.8

Source: data drawn from Crespy, 1990, 54.

The privatisation programme began with the sale of British Airways in 1986. The result was a great success. The labour force was cut while productivity increased. The least effective employees, many of whom were known within the business as 'the public schoolboys', were made redundant. Timekeeping and courtesy were transformed, and a new publicity campaign and livery suggested a highly efficient but caring airline. By the later 1980s British Airways were using the slogan, 'The world's favourite airline'. Based on the number of international passengers carried, this claim was sufficiently close to reality to suggest a big success since privatisation. Paradoxically, British Airways was a stronger symbol of British business as a private company than it had been as a state airline.

Thatcher did more than secure foreign admiration for her economic policies. In the early 1980s Britain's economic growth rate began to increase and over the decade as a whole the country recorded the highest growth rate in Europe. Britain's growth of some 27 per cent over the decade outshone both western Germany and France, with around 20 per cent each. Big oil exports in the early 1980s played their part, permitting low interest rates. However, the attraction of foreign firms such as the big Japanese car and electrical equipment manufacturers would not have been possible without the government's success in either securing the cooperation of, or 'smashing', the trade unions (as some union hotheads saw it). With the government clearly unwilling to reduce unemployment by inflationary means, both the trade unions and their individual members, together with non-unionised workers including women, accepted low wages and, in many cases, long hours.

Thanks partly to oil exports, Britain survived the 1970s and the 1980s without suffering a big fall in the rate of growth of its exports. With Europe's other big exporters badly hit, Britain's performance became normal once again. Between 1973 and 1986,

Britain's annual average compound growth rate in export volume was 3.7 per cent, compared to 3.9 per cent between 1950 and 1973. Germany's rate fell from 12.4 per cent in the earlier period to 4.4 per cent. Italy's fell from 11.7 to 4.9 (Maddison, 1989, 67).

The high value of the pound sterling resulting from the oil exports began to decline by the middle of the 1980s as world oil prices dropped and British oil exports declined. The government's refusal to join the European Exchange Rate Mechanism (apart from a brief and controversial period between 1989 and 1992) reflected a recognition of the problem of Britain's competiveness in international markets, and the continuing threat of speculative capital flows. It also showed that the government was prepared to sacrifice living standards in the interests of exports. This policy was partly justified when unemployment began to fall towards the end of the decade. By the end of the 1980s manufactures again formed the main part of British exports, with foreign multinationals accounting for a growing share thanks to the success of government efforts to attract overseas capital to Britain. The virtual absence of strikes in Britain by the end of the 1980s, and the growing willingness of the trade unions to cooperate with management in cases where jobs could be created or secured, was a major attraction to foreign employers.

The 1980s were the decade when Italian politicians and journalists, citing aggregate GDP figures, claimed that Italy had at last 'overtaken' Britain. The comparison was, and is, controversial, but its context is more important, in that Britain and Italy were Europe's prime examples of successful, fast-growing economies in the 1980s. Britain's biggest achievement was in manufacturing productivity, which had been its most striking failure since the 1950s. Feinstein has shown that during the complete business cycle of 1979–88, British manufacturing productivity increased at an annual rate of 4.2 per cent per annum. This was the highest-ever rate of increase in Britain, and one that was considerably higher than the other major European industrial nations. It was due mainly to the big fall in the manufacturing labour force: for every four manufacturing workers in 1979 there were only three in 1988 (Feinstein, 1990, 20). Britain's per capita GDP in relation to the average of the Twelve rose from 101.1 per cent in 1980 to 105.1 per cent in 1990. Germany, Europe's most productive country (apart from Luxembourg) registered no more than 112.8 per cent in 1990 (Féron and Thoraval, 1992, 177). There might even have been some ground for a 'British miracle' tag here, given that 'miracle' had been bandied about so freely in Italy. However, the British media probably concluded that their circulations and viewing figures would have suffered from too much good news. Thatcher's dogged pursuit of national efficiency had led her into the reform of redistributive and welfarist structures to which the majority of the population had become accustomed. To move towards the privatisation of the National Health Service was asking for trouble politically, but to reform local taxation overnight by shifting the basis of the assessment from the value of real property to a flat rate tax on individuals was courting disaster. Thatcher seemed to think that her role as a world statesman would sustain her, but while she gave free advice to Gorbachev's Soviet Union on democratisation and liberalisation, her 'Poll Tax' led to that traditional barometer reading, riots in Trafalgar Square. A huge demonstration in March 1990, including a woman protester knocked down by a galloping horse, called up hallucinatory images drawn from the London fogs of the 1880s and Edwardian Royal Ascot (Thatcher, 1993, 661). By this time, Thatcher was seriously worried about a situation in which the local authorities, complex financial mechanisms, and public opinion were escaping her control and even her influence. The reform of local taxation went into effect the day after the riots, but non-collection now compounded the continuing opposition of most of the public.

With many Conservative backbenchers now seriously worried about the Conservative Party's ability to win the next election, her position in economic policy and foreign policy began to be undermined. In 1989 she had carried through a big reorganisation of her Cabinet with the approaching election in mind. Unhappy with the enthusiasm of her stalwart Foreign Secretary, Sir Geoffrey Howe, for the ERM, she relegated him to a minor position. Shortly after, her slightly less stalwart Chancellor of the Exchequer, Nigel Lawson, resigned in a cloud of uncertainty which Thatcher did nothing to dispel. What disturbed both Howe and Lawson, among other concerns, was that as senior ministers they felt that they were being undermined by an increasingly autocratic Prime Minister. In 1990 Howe's speech in the House of Commons about his resignation from his new post as Deputy Prime Minister sealed Thatcher's fate and her poor performance in the leadership election later in the year led to her resignation (Thatcher, 1993, 832–58).

In 1990 Thatcher was replaced by a moderate, John Major.

Major nevertheless maintained the essence of Thatcher's policies until 1995. The departure from the ERM in 1992 was not inflationary in its effect, with new domestic regulators quickly brought into being to strengthen monetary policy (OECD, *United Kingdom*, 1994, 103). The reform of the National Health Service was launched in 1991, though with damaging effects on the government's popularity. Although Major seemed more interested in European integration than Thatcher had been, Britain used its new economic strength to negotiate from a position of independence, notwithstanding Major's understanding with Kohl.

The recession of 1991–92 affected Britain like all other EEC countries, but the peak level of unemployment was lower than it had been in the previous recession, whereas theirs was higher. Unemployment rose from 5.8 per cent in 1990 to 10.3 per cent in 1993, but it dropped below 10 per cent in 1994 and 1995. In 1994, the average unemployment rate of the EU had been 11.5 per cent. The foreign payments account remained in deficit and the value of the pound depreciated slowly. Inflation remained low (OECD, *United Kingdom*, 1994, 101–2). There was no question of Britain rejoining the ERM after 1992, but good fiscal and monetary management kept the pound within the 'outer bands' of the ERM and Britain was much admired for its good housekeeping. In fact, by 1995 Britain was one of a handful of EEC members which met the Maastricht conditions for participation in a single European currency.

With Germany facing special difficulties, Britain was now benefiting from fiscal, wage and employment developments occurring since the 1980s, which were generating significant gains in productivity and flexibility. Britain regained its 1990 peak level of output as early as spring 1994, but with 1.8 million fewer jobs and a bigger use of female and part-time workers. With the pound worth less than at any time since 1967, growing output, low inflation, and declining unemployment, Britain's short-term prospects in 1995 looked better than those of any other country in western Europe. In the longer term, the persistent balance of payments deficits seemed likely to restrain the rate of growth, however.

By 1995 Britain had an economic growth rate of 3.4 per cent, which was higher than that of any other major European country. Growth was export led, with home demand controlled by high taxation and inflation down to around 2 per cent per annum (OECD, *Economic Outlook*, **57**, 71). On these and many other indicators, Britain was the most successful economy in Europe in the mid-1990s. Germany, still bearing its eastern burdens, recorded only 2.6 per cent growth, together with Italy. France, with a growth rate of 2.9 per cent, did better (OECD, *Economic Outlook*, **55,** June 1944, A59). Admittedly, the size of the British economy, and average living standards, were still depressed by the many years of slow growth since the 1950s. However, in terms of living standards, Britain had never been detached from the other northern industrial countries. We find from OECD, *Basic Statistics* that in 1991, private consumption per head in Britain was $9,912. This compared to $10,672 in Germany and $10,928 in France. These differentials were a product of the higher growth rates recorded in France and Germany since the 1950s (together with the depressed value of the British pound caused by structural features of the economy), but the long period of Britain's 'decline' had not driven it down utterly into a lower class. On the contrary, with the EU based on the assumption that all members would have comparable living standards, thus maximising trade and growth, it was clear that all the big manufacturing countries were offering broadly similar conditions to their people. In these circumstances the British performance was respectable, particularly in view of the loss of so much of its older industry in the 1970s and 1980s.

Britain would never again be the 'workshop of the world', and still less the 'workshop of Europe'. However, by 1995 it had completed its painful transition to becoming an efficient, highly successful component of the European Union. Britain's rich inheritance of nineteenth-century triumphs had clouded its vision, understandably perhaps, for many a year, but as the end of the century approached, the imperial husk had fallen away, and a leading European nation of the future stood for all to admire.

CHAPTER NINE

The Benelux Countries: Modernisation through Association, 1945–1995

Our treatment of the northern industrial core has concentrated on the larger countries – Germany, Britain and France. By 1995, all three were closely associated in the European Union. We have had little to say of the three countries whose customs union, set up in 1948, was a forerunner of the ECSC and the EEC. Belgium, the Netherlands, and Luxembourg – the 'Benelux countries' – not only paved the way towards European integration, they also pursued a distinctive path of economic and social development which would make them one of the most successful economic regions in western Europe by the 1960s and one of the richest in 1995. In terms of GDP per head, Luxembourg was one of the most prosperous countries in Europe throughout the period (though this was partly due to the economic distortions produced by its very small population). Belgium and the Netherlands both developed, in terms of GDP per head, on much the same track as their close neighbour, Britain. With Belgium, and to a lesser extent the Netherlands, following Britain's example in their economic and welfare policies, a potential area of support for Britain's free trade aspirations will emerge as this chapter unfolds. That the three countries pursued a very different course via the ECSC and the EEC is partly due to the Benelux agreements, but also to the growing economic importance of Germany.

Belgium was, after Britain, the oldest industrialised economy in Europe. It had a population of nearly 8.5 millions in 1938. Its large coal reserves, maritime location, proximity to Britain, and urban workforce, helped it to industrialise from as early as the 1820s. Like Britain, it specialised in coal mining, textiles, metals, and engineering. After 1945, its economic evolution and government policies would shadow Britain's at many points. However, its post-1830 composition as two linguistic territories, French-speaking Wallonia and Flemish-speaking Flanders, would create growing problems in the formulation of national policy. These divisions were far more serious than those affecting England and Scotland, and had something in common with Madrid's relations with the Basque regions. The intricacies of Belgian provincial politics cannot be pursued very far in a book on economic and social history, but they are integral to Belgian development after 1945. The Netherlands, unlike Belgium and Luxembourg, had almost no natural resources. Its great era of maritime success in the sixteenth and seventeenth centuries had been followed by economic stagnation in the eighteenth. Dutch industrialisation did not begin until the 1880s with textiles, leather and other small enterprises. The major transformation was not launched until the heavily capital-intensive engineering and shipbuilding industries got under way after 1890 (Van Zanden and Griffiths, 1989, 6). Textiles, chemicals and engineering were the leading industries by 1939, while agriculture had begun to concentrate on specialised, high-value crops with a big export potential, and on livestock. Provincial specialisation, dating back to the Dutch golden age in the seventeenth century, was reinforced from the mid-nineteenth century as the railways improved what was already an excellent transport system. Growing Dutch imports of raw materials, and exports to its colonies, reinforced the system of well-equipped seaports, Amsterdam and Rotterdam at their head, with smaller ports in the hinterland on the branches of the Rhine delta and the Ijssel, and on the broad drains created for land reclamation since the seventeenth century. The rich business environment in the big cities fostered various types of refining, brewing, distillery, precision industries, and insurance, many of which dated back to the sixteenth century and could grow on the basis of expertise and confidence. The population of the Netherlands was much the same as Belgium's, with just over 8.5 million people in 1938.

Luxembourg had a rich agriculture but the bulk of its exports were iron and steel. Its tiny population of 270,000 required it to cooperate closely with its neighbours and after it had opted for continuing independence at a referendum in 1919, it had established an economic union, known as the BLEU (Belgium-Luxembourg Economic Union), with Belgium in 1922. Its economic influence on Belgium was small but it would come into its own as a fully-fledged member of the EEC in 1958, when its role of honest broker would be often appreciated.

The origins of cooperation

During the discussions between Belgian, Dutch and Luxembourg ministers-in-exile in London during the war, it was readily agreed that the Low Countries could never defend themselves against concerted military attack. This recognition led them on to discuss European political integration and the prevention of further wars. A parallel series of discussions on economic issues took place, and here scope was detected for close cooperation between Dutch and Belgian economies which differed markedly in their products but whose GDPs per capita were very similar. As a result, each had been a strong exporter to the other before the war, and in 1932 they had joined with Luxembourg in a tariff reduction treaty designed to ward off the effects of growing world protectionism at that time.

The ministers recognised that, however Europe's trading affairs were handled after the war, the cooperation of Belgium/ Luxembourg and the Netherlands was bound to continue. With the USA hoping for spontaneous reductions of barriers to trade, regional customs unions would be welcome. Tariffs between Belgium and the Netherlands would not be a big problem, as they had already been very low before the war. In 1948, year of the Benelux customs union, 15.6 per cent of Dutch exports went to Belgium and Luxembourg, and 14.7 per cent of Dutch imports came from there (Van Zanden and Griffiths, 1989, 249). However, both countries, together with Luxembourg, exported an unusually high proportion of their output by European standards. Netherlands merchandise exports in 1950 amounted to 26.9 per cent of GDP. This was much the highest proportion among the OECD countries. The equivalent Belgian figure was 20.3 per cent (Maddison, 1989, 143). The three countries consequently had a strong interest in free trade on a world scale, and a Benelux customs union was more likely to negotiate favourable terms with other countries than could the individual members acting on their own. Especially important were relations with Germany, which was likely to be the main purchaser and the main supplier for the three Benelux countries after the war.

In October 1943 the exchange rates of the Dutch guilder and the Belgian franc (which was also the currency used by Luxembourg) were agreed in London, and the establishment of the Benelux association was announced in September 1944, on the eve of liberation (Mommen, 1994, 74). A period of confusion then ensued and little progress could be made towards implementation for a few years. The creation of the Benelux customs union in 1948, on the basis of an agreement signed in 1947, was a hurried step designed to establish an economic union in advance of any European arrangements which the Marshall plan might bring about. Agriculture was completely excluded, foreshadowing EEC difficulties. Part of the delay had been due to the fact that the Netherlands had detected a number of complications, notably in its important trading links with Germany, and in its close cooperation with Britain, both of which dated back to before the war. The Dutch were much happier with the Schuman plan in 1950, which they saw as leading to the expansion of their important German market, as a result of French acceptance of a normal political and economic role for Germany within western Europe (Van Zanden and Griffiths, 1989, 199). These and other difficulties meant that the full economic potential of the Benelux association would not be achieved until its incorporation in the EEC.

The Benelux nevertheless played a central role in post-war European integration. The three countries joined in the Brussels Pact (Britain, France, Benelux) of March 1948. This was a pre-cursor of NATO, which would be established in 1949. It incorporated the Benelux into the alliance (Treaty of Dunkirk, 1947) set up by Britain and France, the two main European powers, to protect north-west Europe against a future German invasion. The Benelux agreement also simplified the negotiation of the Schuman plan in 1950. Belgium and Luxembourg, heavily committed to the production of coal and steel, were bound to want to join the European Coal and Steel Community (ECSC) once the basic understanding between France and Germany had been reached. The Netherlands, of course, produced very little coal and steel, but this divergence was part of the basis on which Benelux had been negotiated. With Belgian coal and steel already flowing into the Netherlands virtually without restraint, the Netherlands was certain to want to join the ECSC in its turn. The adhesion of the Benelux, together with Italy, prevented the Schuman plan from producing a Franco-German cartel which might have become a barrier to European integration.

The final Benelux agreement was signed in 1958 in the wake of the Treaty of Rome, after a number of practical difficulties had delayed the creation of the association envisaged in 1948. It

allowed the Benelux to continue to function within the EEC but,
in practice, relations between the three countries did not diverge
much after 1958 from their relations as EEC members. However,
the Benelux countries were acknowledged as the pioneers of
European economic integration and their expertise and influence
remained of great value to the EEC.

The Benelux strategy developed in London during the war was
for a further industrialisation of the Netherlands, drawing on Belgian
coal, iron and steel, other semi-finished goods, and engineering.
Belgium and Luxembourg would be able to draw in their turn on
Dutch agricultural products, including the butter and eggs in
which the Netherlands rivalled Denmark. The customs union was
also intended to neutralise the small size of the Benelux countries.
At the end of the war, Belgium had a population of only 8.5
million, and the Netherlands was only a little larger, at 9.5
million. Luxembourg, with only 290,000 people, was almost in the
Monaco and Andorra class. This distribution recalled that of the
Nordic countries, which did not make the same formal progress
towards association at this time, but their experiences in two wars
were very different from those of the Benelux and their trading
interests in 1945 were much more complex.

In fact, the economic features and interests of the Benelux
countries did more to associate them than did their formal agreements. All three countries were affected by a wartime experience
in which they had made an important net contribution to the
German war effort, and had suffered serious internal tensions as a
result. Belgium's coal reserves and heavy industries had been
especially important to Germany and, as in France, certain
ministers and many industrial firms had cooperated with the
Germans to an extent which went beyond the arrangements
reluctantly agreed by the Belgian government in Brussels. Meanwhile, the Left had emerged as the main opposition to the
invaders and armed resistance movements had grown up, notably
in Belgium. Promises of social reform from the governments-in-
exile in London created confusion, especially towards the end of
the war. The Roman Catholic Church, which dominated the
religious life of all three countries, lost respect.

There were important differences between the countries,
however. The Netherlands suffered much the greatest physical
damage. Belgium's potential in war materials generated the
greatest degree of collaboration. The Germans detected a semi-
Aryan political and social potential in the Netherlands, and to a

lesser extent in Flanders. They encouraged pre-war Fascist organisations in those areas and tried to influence education. In the Netherlands, Reichskommissar A Seyss-Inquart made strenuous efforts to reconstruct Dutch society on Nazi lines, making much play of Hitler's desire to merge the Dutch and German economies, and to give the Dutch a living standard comparable to Germany's (Van Zanden and Griffiths, 1989, 167). Compared to the living standard promised by Hitler to what was left of Poland (the most abject peasant or unskilled worker in Germany would earn at least 10 per cent more than the highest-earning Pole), this was an attractive prospect, but with British bombers thundering overhead almost nightly on their way to German targets from as early as 1940, a long-term German presence in the Netherlands was always in doubt. In any case, not all the Dutch people were offered the Führer's manna. Jewish owners and managers, as in the other occupied countries, were removed early on from their enterprises and subjected to growing horrors as time passed. These and other activities earned Seyss-Inquart a death sentence at Nuremberg.

Belgium's quick surrender in 1940 allowed it to retain its own government. As in France, a Communist-led resistance movement opposed the occupiers but there was no De Gaulle to liberate Belgium and impose his own post-war settlement. The government-in-exile in London was not fully confident of its own authority and when it returned to Brussels in September 1944 it faced the additional problem of King Leopold III who, like Pétain, had been taken off to imprisonment in Germany after D-Day. Released in May 1945, Leopold was too compromised by his wartime stance to return to Belgium and a series of temporary arrangements had to be made. It was not until 1950 that Leopold abdicated in favour of his son, Baudouin I. These challenges to a foreign monarchy which had existed only since 1831 recalled the post-war problems of the Greek Crown. In Belgium they were exacerbated by the growing linguistic and political split between Wallonia and Flanders, and even the king's marriage to a Spanish Roman Catholic, Queen Fabiola, in 1960, brought out the full range of deep-seated Belgian divisions.

Dutch problems were more economic than political at the end of the war. Like Belgium, the Netherlands had retained its own government. The royal family's courage and independence had won it universal respect. The growth of reformist thinking on socialist lines, which had much in common with British developments, minimised post-war divisions and created the foundations of a government stability which has typified the Netherlands ever since. However, with considerably heavier war damage than Belgium, the Netherlands found it much harder to move to a peacetime economy. In Belgium, the presence of Allied troops and the use of Antwerp as a distribution point for supplies created a serious danger of inflation and black market operations, but the legendary action of Camille Gut, the first post-war Finance Minister, in freezing all deposits of liquid funds, kept the situation well under control.

Post-war Belgium

Belgian post-war politics had much in common with France. The Communists were admitted to the early governments but left in 1947. The issue of the monarchy had complicated efforts to form a stable coalition of the Left, and it was not until the 'Great Coalition' of Christian Democrats and Socialists was formed in 1947 under the Socialist, Paul-Henri Spaak, that a stable settlement could be secured. Spaak had been a member of the London government in exile, and had been involved in the reform proposals which issued from London towards the end of the war. As the Germans withdrew from Belgium in late 1944, the London ministers and the Belgian parties and unions reached agreement on a basis for reform after the war. This was the Social Pact, finalised in December 1944. It set up a full social security system for manual workers and established a number of consultative mechanisms involving the State, the employers, and organised labour. Wages, hours and working conditions were determined by these means in the early post-war years. Social and industrial conflicts were not completely eradicated, but the government could always draw on these institutions to prevent the kind of disruptive struggles which affected France in the later 1940s (Mommen, 1994, 80). This understanding between the employers, the government, and labour lasted into the 1950s. In 1954, for instance, they signed a Joint Declaration on Productivity urging the achievement of higher productivity by humane and expansionist means (Mommen, 1994, 81). With rapid economic growth now beginning, such agreements encouraged the flexible use of labour while creating trade union confidence in the future of industry. Like developments in the Nordic countries, they helped build up a harmony of interests (nowadays alarmingly dubbed 'corporatist' by some younger American economic historians) which Britain still lacked.

Belgium's participation in the Benelux customs union was helped by its rapid removal of rationing and controls after the war. This process, virtually complete by 1949, was eased by the structure of Belgian industry, with a few firms dominating large-scale manufacturing, cartels operating without restraint, and the large part played in Belgian exports by steel and other semi-finished products (Mommen, 1994, 84). Able to make a quick start in its contribution to western European reconstruction, Belgium had reached its pre-war export level by 1950, and with its exports amounting to 20.3 per cent of its GDP it was, in proportionate terms, western Europe's biggest exporter after the Netherlands and Denmark (Maddison, 1989, 143). Belgium was spared serious foreign currency problems as much of its exported output was purchased in US dollars, and shortages were few, even of consumer goods. There was no nationalisation programme after the war, in contrast to France and Britain, and the structure of ownership and cartels remained much the same as before 1940. Oil refining was the only important new industry to be organised on lines determined by the State. The State made no attempt to direct industrial production. However, the government launched a 'battle for coal' in 1945 and its heavy investment in the more antiquated parts of the mining industry, in association with the owners, was extended to become a broader programme subsidising investment in electricity, coke, textiles, metals and other areas. This broader programme was largely defined under the government of 1947–49 led by Paul-Henri Spaak, with Gaston Eyskens as Finance Minister. Most of the investment, which continued into the late 1950s, was directed into traditional Belgian industries, with mining at their head (Mommen, 1994, 87).

The Belgian post-war settlement had been generous to organised labour and the big drive to develop the mines gave the miners great influence, at least until the 1950s. The Conseil National des Charbonnages (CNC), set up in 1947, grouped the owners and the workforce, and made recommendations on the mining investment programme and, in the 1950s, closure priorities. The mines became a powerful interest, with the workforce totalling 153,000 miners in 1947. The political and regional implications were very important, with, for instance, the bulk of the older, declining mines concentrated in the French-speaking region of Wallonia. The bargaining strength of the miners, of whom there was a big shortage after the war, as in France and the Ruhr, helped them to improve their pay and conditions. Another traditional industry, textiles, was also favoured by government capital, again with disappointing results. However, similar decisions were made elsewhere in industrial Europe, with Britain's over-commitment to coal the closest parallel.

The new trading conditions within the ECSC from 1952 were a big challenge to Belgian industry, which had already been affected by the revival of German production from as early as 1949. Coal output stagnated from 1952, and strenuous efforts to increase productivity had almost no effect, owing mainly to geological constraints in Wallonia. Belgian resistance to employment in the mines led to the large-scale recruitment of foreign workers, notably from Italy and Spain. By 1957, some 60 per cent of the mining workforce came from outside Belgium (Mommen, 1994, 89). Some of the older mines had to close and a national plan for this was agreed in 1956.

The steel industry did better. It had the chance to grow and re-equip with more efficient machinery to meet demand for a range of steels in Belgium and later the ECSC. The replacement of the traditional Gilchrist-Thomas blast furnaces and the con-struction of strip mills to supply the motor and household industries improved quality and productivity. A number of mergers allowed individual steelworks to be used more efficiently and investment to be concentrated at key points. With somewhat better working conditions than mining, the moderate steel workforce of around 45,000 could be maintained without major recourse to foreign recruitment (Mommen, 1994, 90–1). Luxembourg, on the other hand, recognised the need to diversify from steel and looked for foreign firms. The opening of a Goodyear tyre factory in 1950 marked the beginning of this process. In 1959 the government set up a development office and a number of multinationals started production in the 1960s (Piquet Marchal, 1985, 323).

In the early 1950s some 10 per cent of the Belgian workforce were unemployed or on short time (Mommen, 1994, 86). However, redundant miners were retrained or paid off by the ECSC. Cyclical unemployment was a bigger problem owing to Belgium's over-commitment to a few industries.

The cyclical downturn of 1957 hit Belgium especially hard. Predictably, the economic policies followed since the war had produced an economy of low productivity and the narrow range of traditional exports found it increasingly hard to compete with expanding economies such as Germany, France and Italy. Belgian labour costs were as high as Britain's. Consumer goods had been neglected. The rate of investment was very low, and much investment in the older industries was designed simply to prevent firms running at a loss (defensive investment, as it was known in Belgium), which resulted in a very low rate of profit. The rate of economic growth was seen to be very low, at 2.9 per cent per annum between 1953 and 1960, and the slow growth of the home market was a major discouragement (Mommen, 1994, 100). These problems were similar to those of Britain. With limited means of protecting its home market, Belgium was very open to competition from imports and its weakness in consumer industries made it very vulnerable in this growing sector of the market.

By the mid-1950s the Belgian trade unions, worried by high unemployment, were campaigning for a programme of structural reforms to be carried through by the government and the two hundred or so families which were deemed to control the bulk of the country's industry. Their demands were taken up by the Christian Democratic Party which formed a government in 1958. In 1959, measures to stimulate investment and to help declining regions were passed. Drawing on post-war example, the Christian Democrats called together the employers' associations and the trade unions. In 1960, these joined with the government in agreeing on the principle of economic and social planning, including an incomes policy. A new Social Pact was signed. The Comité National d'Expansion Economique was set up to oversee the preparation of a five-year plan designed to secure a growth rate of 4 per cent (Mommen, 1994, 108). Taxes were increased to reduce the government deficit.

The defeat of a general strike in 1960–61, and the decolon-isation of the Belgian Congo in 1960, were painful episodes but they cleared the way for economic growth in the 1960s at around the growth rate foreseen in the plan. There was heavy investment in new industries such as motors, petrochemicals and electronics, and in services. For the first time in over a century, Belgium left Britain trailing in its wake. However, linguistic divisions, which had been exacerbated after the war by the relative decline of industry in French-speaking Wallonia, to the south, became more serious in the 1960s as new investment and the growth of new industries, including multinationals, favoured Dutch-speaking Flanders to the north. At the turn of the century the numbers of French speakers and Flemish speakers in Belgium had been roughly equal, but by

1944 the population of Flanders totalled 4.2 millions compared to 2.9 millions in Wallonia (de Meeüs, 1962, 363). An officially bilingual population of 1.3 millions in the Brussels district did not help to prevent a growing concern among the Walloons that they were losing control of the country which they had long claimed to direct. Meanwhile, the Flemings grew increasingly confident of their ability to secure their own interests as enterprise and investment flooded into their province. Foreign investors, in particular, preferred the country areas around Antwerp, which had sea access and which were made the object of a ten-year State development programme in 1956. Wallonia, with its long tradition of old industries and a workforce that was set in its ways, sensed a plot by Flemish politicians to put it in the background, with the support of the Belgian state.

Belgium's success in the 1960s was unable to survive the oil-related problems of the 1970s. Belgium was harder hit from 1973 than most other OECD countries. With Flanders reliant on foreign investment, and Wallonia in industrial decline, the linguistic hostilities became chronic. The Belgian balance of trade went into deficit from 1974 for the first time since the war. Ironically, the mining industry was too far advanced on the path of total closure to take advantage of the demand for alternative fuels, and production dropped by one-third between 1974 and 1979, despite huge government subsidies (Mommen, 1994, 164). The high cost of domestic coal was a big problem and the charges for electricity and other energy, as borne by business and domestic users, were among the highest in western Europe. In addition, the established role of the trade unions weakened the position of the government when it tried to set up an agreed incomes and employment policy. The national political parties divided into linguistic groups, producing numerous coalition governments.

Multinationals, which had produced much of the growth of the 1960s, especially in Flanders, were generally hard hit and a number left Belgium altogether (Mommen, 1994, 169–71). Motor production was a major victim. It was hard to develop policies and programmes which affected the whole country equally, but any differential was likely to generate provincial opposition. With exports still making up a huge proportion of Belgian GDP (49.9 per cent in 1973, and 55 per cent in 1980), the economy was very vulnerable to changes on world markets. Belgium's proportion of exports to GDP was now far higher than that of any other OECD country, and the predominance of a few staples meant that sharp falls in aggregate exports were a big danger as competition grew, especially as several export industries had very high energy costs. Steel, which had greatly expanded between the late 1950s and 1974 while remaining entirely in private hands and indifferent to government attempts to negotiate a national programme of development, was hard hit by the oil crisis in 1973 and contracted sharply thereafter. The State now intervened to prevent the complete collapse of overcommitted firms like Cockerill Sambre and to plan a rational programme of closures.

Between 1974 and 1981 a series of coalition governments based on an alliance between the Christian Democrats and the Left struggled with problems similar to Britain's. Working-class discontent was seen as a major threat and the State tended to pursue a policy of mollifying the trade unions. As in Britain, the main aim was to maintain employment without creating excessive inflation, but Belgian export constraints made this very difficult. With wages rising automatically in step with the cost of living, there was little chance of reducing labour costs. Domestic employment support schemes, combined with early retirement programmes, were very costly, and by the end of the 1970s Belgian government borrowing was equal to 9.5 per cent of GNP. Public expenditure reached more than 50 per cent of GNP by 1980 (Mommen, 1994, 150, 156). Employment creation schemes favoured jobs in the public sector and by 1979 28.5 per cent of Belgian employees were working for the State (Mommen, 1994, 156).

In 1981 the last of the four Christian Democrat/Socialist governments under Gaston Eyskens was brought down over an issue of regional preference typical of those which had plagued Belgian politics since the early 1970s. The result of the subsequent general election reflected the general movement of opinion in the industrialised world against the idea of defending employment at the expense of monetary and fiscal stability, and in favour of courageous steps to reconstruct the economy. With Margaret Thatcher in power in Britain since 1979, and Ronald Reagan elected as US President in 1981, the loss of a number of Flemish Christian Democrat seats in the 1981 election led Wilfried Martens (Flemish Christian Democrat) to form a Centre-Right government which would stay in power until 1985, and in a reconstituted form, until 1987.

Martens secured full support from parliament for a fiscal and monetary stabilisation programme. Social security costs had risen massively since 1974. Support for the unemployed had cost 15 billion francs in 1974; by 1983 it had risen to 175 billion francs (Piquet Marchal, 1985, 341). Martens took forceful steps, including the limitation of social security benefits, to reduce public expenditure and the national debt, which were among the highest in Europe. He used the powerful post-war machinery to control wages. In February 1982 he devalued the Belgian franc for the first time since the British-induced devaluation of 1949. The rate of the devaluation, 8.5 per cent, was carefully chosen to enhance industrial competitiveness. The devaluation took the Belgian franc well below its agreed level in the European Monetary System but the government defended the new parity and Belgium's reputation for currency stability survived. Martens maintained the post-1973 employment policies but ensured that any improvements in benefits and working conditions were paid for by higher productivity. In March 1983 the unemployment rate in Belgium was 12.2 per cent. The power of the big trade unions was reduced by the break-up of their alliances. Inefficient firms now started to go out of business. A wage freeze and other deflationary measures reduced the purchasing power of Belgian wages by 10 per cent between 1981 and 1985 (Mommen, 1994, 179). Company profits, meanwhile, began to increase and the corporate investment ratio had reached the respectable level of 5 per cent by 1985. New export products, and new markets outside the EEC, permitted a revaluation of the currency by 1.5 per cent in 1983. By 1986, Belgian exports amounted to 61.4 per cent of GDP, far surpassing even the Netherlands (45.3 per cent) (Maddison, 1989, 143).

By the time a further general election took place in 1987, the country still faced a big public deficit. The regional problem, more serious than ever, was now tackled by a political and economic regionalisation amounting to a devolution of powers from Brussels. Company rationalisation, encouraged by the government, had produced a number of efficient, competitive sectors by the mid-1980s, led by the chemical industry. With industrial ownership still in a few hands, the government was able to negotiate rationalisation effectively and despite great difficulties it was able to bring about the reorganisation of the ailing steel industry in the 1980s.

The world cyclical depression of the early 1990s was bound to affect a trading economy like Belgium's very seriously. In the trough year of 1993, Belgium's real GDP *fell* by 1.25 per cent. The long-running problems of high unemployment and government deficits now began to affect interest rates and the disruption of the workings of the ERM put pressure on the Belgian franc. However, the government responded with a 'global plan' in November 1993 to tackle the problems of competitiveness, unemployment, and the social security system. The plan, which included another wage freeze, was well received and a recovery was under way by 1995. The OECD predicted a growth rate of just over 2.5 per cent in 1995–96, with unemployment continuing at the level of 11–12 per cent which it had reached in 1993. Domestic demand was intended to replace overseas demand as the main dynamic of the economy. By 1995 the effective value of the Belgian franc was appreciating, and the threat of serious inflation was receding. The budget deficit and interest rates were expected to decline slowly, with some improvement in unemployment (OECD, **57**, 1995, 84). This situation was typical for an EU industrial country in the mid-1990s, but once again Belgium found itself aspiring to a situation enjoyed by Britain.

The Netherlands post-war

After the war, Dutch industrial development proceeded on a basis of private initiative, investment from abroad, and government guidance. With hardly any coal, and that of a poor quality, the Netherlands was heavily dependent on imported energy. Nuclear and tide power were investigated in the 1950s, but the biggest leap forward occurred in 1959 when a rich source of natural gas was discovered at Slochteren. As in Belgium and Luxembourg, nationalisation was eschewed, but a programme of social welfare was built up, partly with a view to eradicating social inequalities. The socialist movement remained very influential after the war, creating a policy climate similar to that of Sweden. The long-lived Schermerhorn-Drees government, formed in June 1945, saw economic recovery as its prime task and its social reforms never threatened economic stability. The population accepted these priorities in part because of their experiences in the war. The involvement of Queen Wilhelmina as a unifying and modernising influence was also encouraging, and a happy contrast with the Belgian royal complications after the war. The Dutch programme of rationing, allocation of raw materials and wage control was a product of wartime conditions which had been much worse than those endured in Belgium, including the starvation conditions in 1944–45 when the retreating German forces cut off supplies from the Netherlands (to the considerable embarrassment of Seyss-

Inquart). The social welfare programme became increasingly costly, however. A big housing programme was also necessary to cater for a rapidly growing population. Most new housing was provided or subsidised by the State. These facilities, combined with the heavy taxation needed to pay for them, promoted social equality to an even greater extent than in Belgium, reinforcing the parallel with Sweden.

As in Belgium, consultation between employers and workers expanded after 1945 on foundations which had first been established in the nineteenth century. The Dutch economy had been more seriously damaged during the war than almost any other in western Europe. Capital losses in 1945 amounted to 40 per cent of the total Dutch capital stock in 1939 (Van Zanden and Griffiths, 1989, 186). Rigid wage restrictions were agreed by all the parties from 1945 as part of a strenuous recovery package. A Central Economic Plan was launched in late 1946. With an unfavourable balance of trade, the Netherlands encountered a serious balance of payments crisis in 1947. However, a number of countries were in that position, or were approaching it, and the Marshall plan provided much of the help that was needed. Dutch exports to the dollar area rose sharply between 1947 and the early 1950s, while dollar imports declined, solving part of the country's hard currency problems. Meanwhile, trade with Germany grew markedly from 1949, with the balance of the exchange remaining in favour of the Dutch. Recent work by P van der Eng and other Dutch economic historians has built up a picture of yet another European country which would have been set back several years if Marshall aid had not been available, and Dutch historiography now forms an important part of the developing critique of Alan Milward's revisionism (Van Zanden and Griffiths, 1989, 195).

The Dutch decision to decolonise rapidly probably helped the revival of the domestic economy in that capital and skills were urgently needed at home in the early post-war years. The Netherlands' colonies in the Indian Ocean had fallen easy victims to Japanese occupation and the Dutch government in exile had feared the problems of reestablishing control and carrying out reconstruction there, given the impoverishment of the mother country during the war. Encouraged by the USA, the Dutch launched a decolonisation programme at the end of the war, beginning with the independence of the huge territory of Indonesia in 1945. Belgium did not take the same step until 1960, when its only colony of any consequence, the Belgian Congo, was made independent as the new republic of Zaire. The Congo had never been of great economic benefit to Belgium and both its post-war retention, and the abrupt departure of the Belgians in 1960, were partly the product of the unique complications of Belgian domestic politics. When Zaire quickly sank into brutal anarchy, Belgium was widely blamed for lack of foresight and indifference. The Zaire episode, which dragged on through a decade of civil war, damaged Belgium's international reputation at a time when its internal issues of ethnic exploitation were building up to a peak. Meanwhile, UN cocktail-party criticisms of the Netherlands that it had abandoned Indonesia too abruptly, allowing dictatorship to take root there a few years later, aroused little interest. With the Netherlands drawing in large numbers of immigrants from its former colonies, and assimilating them with a tolerance and generosity unique in Europe, the Dutch built up an internationalist reputation on German and Swedish lines. Such reputations were very helpful in world trade.

In 1950 a law on economic organisation was passed. It included the creation of a national Economic and Social Council, with representatives of the employers, labour, and a number of independent members named by the queen. The Council took part in the application of the tough wages policy set up in 1945 and in force, though with increasing flexibility, until it broke down in 1963. In 1967 the government adopted more of a free-market approach to wages, though the consultative bodies survived. In the early 1980s the government threatened to revert to wage controls, but the employers and the unions offered to show restraint and this proved adequate.

Netherlands businesses took advantage of the expansion of European trade after the war. Its agriculture was less seriously affected by the war than that of most occupied countries and its processing industries prospered. Its exports, which had been only 19.9 per cent of national income in 1938, at the end of the protection-ridden 1930s, had risen from virtually nil in 1945 to 16.9 per cent in 1947, shadowing the British export success of the time. A steady increase thereafter led to exports amounting to 35.9 per cent of national income in 1951 (Van Zanden and Griffiths, 1989, 191). GATT, the Marshall plan, and the EPU favoured Dutch trade and the government was a strong supporter of these initiatives. Like Belgium, the Netherlands was keen to develop the Benelux customs union and also to promote trade liberalisation across Europe.

Western Europe's developing role as a great exporter, and as an importer of raw materials, allowed the Netherlands to take advantage of its position at the mouth of the Rhine to develop Rotterdam and other ports for very large ships, and to channel smaller cargoes down the Rhine and its tributaries and canals into the heart of industrial Germany, Belgium and France. Large-scale processing industries grew up near these ports, much as industry grew up in the hinterland of Antwerp. However, the Dutch government acted to avoid a big concentration of labour and capital near the coast at a time when inland farming was shedding labour. Following the British example of industrial location and planning after the war, it drew up a territorial plan based on the principle of the *Randstad* (the circular arrangement of the country's main cities) and encouraged the creation of light industrial and service employment across the country, in step with cooperative and subsidised housing. The resulting annular rail network, operated by electric semi-fast trains whose frequency and punctuality rivalled Japanese National Railways operations in the Tokyo region, held the country together in a way to which Belgium could not aspire until its motorway network was completed in the 1970s, by which time the cultural separation of Flanders and Wallonia was irrevocable. There is more to all this than railways, of course, but Belgian Railways, still using a lot of steam into the 1960s to take advantage of local coal, and with a network composed of multiple local sections rather than through-routes, were trapped with speed standards similar to those of the East German *Reichsbahn.*

The years 1951 to 1973 were a period of brilliant economic success for the Netherlands. J L Van Zanden has pointed out that not only the rate of growth, but its great length and its stability, made it stand out in the economic history of the Netherlands (Van Zanden and Griffiths, 1989, 210). The upward trend was broken only once, in 1958. Between 1951 and 1963, the economic growth of the Netherlands was much the fastest of the three Benelux countries, averaging 4.4 per cent of GNP annually (*ibid.*, 212). Unemployment dropped to well below 3 per cent from 1954 and remained at a very low level until the 1970s. From around 1960, however, the Dutch economy entered a phase of over-investment and this became a liability when world trade contracted after 1973. The Dutch annual rate of increase of GNP averaged 5.5 per cent between 1963 and 1973 (Van Zanden and Griffiths, 1989, 212, 221).

The average annual rate of growth of GNP over the whole period from 1951 to 1973 was 4.9 per cent. This was high by western European standards, though by no means exceptional, and a number of contextual factors produced a growth inertia in the Netherlands from 1945 onwards. The rapid growth of the national population, from 8,685,000 in 1938 to 13,439,000 in 1973, made the Netherlands one of the few countries in western Europe with an expanding labour force. For a trading nation like the Netherlands, the growth in the world economy in the 1950s and 1960s was bound to generate an expansion of output. In addition, the Europe-wide phenomenon of 'catching-up' on American technology especially favoured the Netherlands with its huge investment effort in post-war reconstruction. The liberal Dutch policy on immigration, and not just from the old Dutch colonies, contributed much skill and enterprise to the workforce. The industrial development plans of 1949–57 ensured that investment went into industries with a high export potential, and their success prolonged an investment boom which maintained full employment and rising earnings. Dutch products were thus able to remain competitive on world markets into the early 1970s. Food products continued to be in great demand abroad, and in the 1980s they still amounted to one-fifth of total Dutch exports. The result was a long, export-led boom in the 1950s and 1960s. Dutch exports approached the astronomical Belgian level by the late 1970s, with 42.5 per cent of GNP exported over the years 1975–80 (Piquet Marchal, 1985, 331).

The OPEC interventions between 1973 and 1979 were a serious problem for the Netherlands owing to the shortage of natural resources there. The aggregate Dutch growth rate dropped to an average of 2.7 per cent per annum over the years 1973–79 when western economies were trying to maintain consumption even at the risk of inflation, and it plummeted to 0.7 per cent between 1979 and 1985 when deflationary strategies became the norm, protectionism reared its head again, and overseas demand crumpled. During the first period the Dutch growth rate was a little higher than the OECD average, but in the second period it was very much lower. These figures were of course inflated by the high rate of population increase in the Netherlands. The rate of increase of GDP per capita declined virtually to nil in 1980 and there were big absolute declines in 1981 and 1982. The fall in the price of oil in 1981 was only a partial cause for rejoicing as it dragged down the value of Dutch natural gas. Per capita growth rates remained disappointing, and cumulatively below Belgium's, until 1989, when the Dutch economy at last grew by an impressive figure, 3.4 per cent (OECD, 1991, Historical statistics, 48).

Unemployment was less than the European average until 1980 but it then soared to 15.4 per cent in 1983, with women's unemployment becoming an especially serious problem (Van Zanden and Griffiths, 1989, 255–61). In March 1983, the monthly unemployment rate in the Netherlands reached a peak of 16.5 per cent. In the early 1980s the Dutch government threatened wage controls but the employers and the employees agreed, through the existing wage negotiating structures, to exercise restraint.

The Netherlands was less seriously affected than Belgium by the cyclical depression of the early 1990s, but in GDP terms it followed a very similar path, with growth sinking almost to nil in 1993 and recovering to around 2–3 per cent by 1995/96. The OECD predictions for the Netherlands in mid-1995 were so much like those for the other European industrial economies that they do not need close attention here, except that the Netherlands, like Belgium, was expected to see a growth of domestic consumption, and a relative decline in exports, in the later 1990s (OECD **57**, 1995, 97–8). The OECD did not say so, but here as elsewhere in western Europe there was plenty of evidence to suggest that national average growth rates would not exceed 2–3 per cent until the end of the millennium.

Achievements of cooperation

At the end of our period, Belgium and the Netherlands had a similar GDP per capita. In 1991, Belgium's was $19,295. The Netherlands, at $18,565, may seem slightly less productive but allowing for the various adjustments regularly made to world GDP figures, the two countries were effectively of equal productivity (*The Economist*, 1993, 24). Belgium's post-war condition as a very old industrial country contrasted with that of the Netherlands, with its greater scope for the development of new industries. This contrast is borne out by the development of their populations. Belgium's population of 8.5 million at the end of the war had increased to only 10 million by 1995. Starting from much the same level, the population of the Netherlands had risen to 15 million by 1995. This massive increase reflected a rise in the number of jobs and living standards as industrialisation surged ahead.

The Belgian performance was nevertheless impressive given the problems of economic restructuring and internal conflicts which the country had encountered since the war. Belgium's internal dissensions were the worst in Europe, and they got worse during the period. Despite these unique problems, Belgium was able to catch up on the Netherlands from a position in 1950 where its per capita GDP had been around 90 per cent of the Dutch level (Maddison, 1989, 19). This suggested that the Benelux customs union, and later the ECSC and the EEC, had helped associate two economies which had long worked closely together, but which could now jointly achieve their full potential.

Like Sweden, the Netherlands was marked by political stability, financial probity, price stability, and by a high rate of growth which had originated at the beginning of the century. For Van Zanden and Griffiths, however, the main parallel for the Netherlands was Switzerland (Van Zanden and Griffiths, 1989, 15–16). These comparisons do full justice to the achievement of one of the most civilised, gentle and hospitable peoples in Europe. However, it is also a compliment to the Benelux and the European vision which the Dutch, the Belgians and the Luxemburgers have done so much to promote that Belgium, for all its difficulties, enjoyed a living standard similar to that of the Netherlands throughout the years 1945–95, together with a civilised, comfortable lifestyle which remains one of Europe's best-kept secrets. In the Benelux countries, a unique experiment in international cooperation has secured its just reward.

CHAPTER TEN

Progress and Problems on the Western European Fringe since the 1960s

With one exception, the countries which signed the Treaty of Rome in 1957 were members of the western European industrial core. That exception was Italy. Italy was the most advanced member of the southern fringe. Her northern manufacturing regions centred on Turin and Milan were among Europe's most productive, but the problem of her backward South (*Mezzogiorno*) had not yet been resolved. Italy became a founder member of the EEC because, like the other members of the Six who had founded the European Coal and Steel Community in 1952, she wanted to extend that successful but clearly delimited initiative to broader spheres of European integration. Italy's search for rehabilitation after the war had led her governments and leaders of opinion to support a number of efforts to associate the countries of Europe. These respected aspirations, together with Italy's post-war efforts to develop a specialised steel industry, secured her admission to the ECSC, despite her being the least industrialised member and the one with the least to offer in terms of natural resources and skilled labour. In 1957, in a stronger economic and political position, Italy wanted to reinforce her contact with the core as a means of accelerating her internal development. Like West Germany, Italy moved from the extremes of pre-war Fascist autarky to an internationalist and integrationist position which set an example to Europe.

That the other fringe countries did not join the EEC in 1957 is understandable. The other three countries of the southern fringe were chronically backward, and two of them were governed by Right-wing regimes which would have not been welcome in integrationist circles. The Nordic countries, trading extensively among themselves and with Britain, and wary of the Soviet Union, decided to stay clear. Norway and Denmark were members of NATO, but Sweden's established neutrality, and Finland's restrictive agreements with the Soviet Union, not only discouraged them from joining the EEC, but acted as a constraint on Norway and Denmark as well (Malmström, 1965, 21–30). However, by 1995 all these fringe countries, in both North and South, would have achieved a higher level of industrialisation and would have become become EEC members.

This progressive incorporation of the fringe into the integrationist institutions of the core after 1957 was partly the product of political changes. The collapse of Right-wing regimes in the South played its part, as did the collapse of Communism in the East. However, the inexorable movement towards industrialisation in both North and South in such a small, densely-populated continent produced a progressive economic, social and cultural integration. With the countries of the industrial core now closely associated in the EEC, it was natural that the fringe countries should see their own industrial integration with the core in terms of joining the EEC. In this regard, we can note that neither fringe, whether it be the North or the South, generated a regional economic association of any consequence after 1945. The Nordic Council of 1952, and the Common Nordic Labour Market of 1954, were the closest equivalents, but the latter acted slowly even within its narrow range of functions and allowed Britain to take the lead in economic association in the North. This meant that both the North and the South had eventually to adapt to the EEC, rather than developing their own arrangements. For the South, the main task was to shed authoritarian political arrangements and to modernise their economies up to the point where they could follow Italy into the EEC without weakening the organisation or themselves. In the North, political and cultural attitudes had to change, and this meant not only the attitudes of ministers and elected representatives, but of ordinary people who were asked to pronounce on EEC membership at a number of national referenda. These referenda revealed deep-seated attitudes of national independence, deep-lying party-political differences, and cultural individuality. Ironically, southern governments were spared these complications in their efforts to join the EEC as their limited democratic traditions did not generate a strong demand for plebiscites.

The Nordic countries

The Nordic countries retained an important advantage into the 1960s and beyond. This was their very high living standards, which derived mainly from their considerable natural resources in relation to their low populations. Although high labour costs were a deterrent to industrialisation, the Nordic countries were in the vanguard of mechanised techniques, design, and production engineering. For instance, shipbuilding in Sweden and Norway soon surpassed Britain's backward yards in the 1950s and 1960s. In 1965, the Nordic countries built 16 per cent of the world's shipping. Their industrialisation drive in the 1960s was based on the most advanced industries and techniques. The high average value of their quality industrial exports soon dealt with any remaining balance-of-payments problems, as in Denmark. A highly educated labour force helped the technological industries. In Sweden, Volvo and Saab motors produced a very high quality vehicle, suitable for the hard, northern winters, which found ready export markets to the south from the late 1950s. These cars were very expensive because of their solid construction, exacerbated by high labour costs, but as personal incomes rose in northern Europe in the 1960s, they secured growing sales abroad. Non-European immigrant workers were brought in from Turkey and other countries favoured by Germany. Saab also produced aircraft, mainly military types, to sustain Sweden's neutrality. NATO forces were unable to buy them, but they sold well in other neutral countries. Traditional industries also prospered; in 1965 the Nordic countries produced 18.3 per cent of the world's wood pulp and 13.1 per cent of its newsprint. They also caught 9.4 per cent of the world's fish (nearly half of it herring). Finally, 14.5 per cent of the world's merchant fleet was registered in the Nordic countries (Alexandersson, 1971, 8). Education and welfare facilities were improving everywhere, following the example of Sweden.

The Nordic countries were sufficiently confident in their own economic strength, both in the present and in the future, to avoid being greatly disturbed by the creation of the EEC in 1957 or by Britain's manoeuvres after 1959. They welcomed EFTA, as it reflected their existing trading relationships while enhancing their bargaining power in dealing with the EEC. The formal link with Britain which EFTA offered was very valuable. The long delay before Britain (and Denmark) could gain access to the EEC in

1973 was not a problem because the importance of their exports of raw materials and high-quality, highly-specialised manufactured exports helped them to secure adequate access to EEC markets via EFTA negotiations or bilateral agreements.

Even the oil crisis of 1973 was less damaging to Nordic Europe than elsewhere. Norway was already prospecting for oil and gas in the North Sea in the early 1970s and by the end of the decade it was deriving a bigger income from this source than Britain would at its peak in the early 1980s. With a population of only 4 million people, Norway had to export almost all of this oil. The other Nordic countries were prime beneficiaries. Meanwhile, Denmark was able to join the EEC with Britain in 1973. This secured Denmark's major current markets for the export of food products, and opened up the possibility of more in southern Europe. There was no doubt that her expanding industries, nearly all of which had been set up since the war and were based on advanced technology, with secure markets, could compete within the EEC despite their high labour costs.

Sweden

Sweden was in a strong position by 1960 with its advanced industries, mainly centred in the various branches of engineering, supplementing its established forestry and minerals activities. Rather like western Germany, it exported widely outside Europe and its neutral status gave it a brilliant reputation in the Third World as a peaceful arbiter in Cold War disputes.

The oil crisis of 1973 hit Sweden hard and output stagnated in the later 1970s, with a reduction of as much as 1.9 per cent in 1977. Growth continued slowly into the early 1980s. From 1984 there was some improvement overall and Sweden joined in the speculative boom which affected most of Europe, though exports stagnated. The collapse of the boom began to have its effects at the end of the decade and the international recession, together with the internal reforms of the Centre-Right government, hit it especially hard between 1991 and 1993. This was Sweden's worst recession since the 1930s. Sweden's foreign trade account was in surplus in the early 1990s, thanks partly to an effective depreciation of the currency of 20 per cent in 1992–93, but her total foreign payments were in deficit. The home market was acutely depressed. Sweden's unemployment rate was a mere 1.7

per cent in 1990 but the effects of the recession had pushed it up to 8.2 per cent in 1993 and to 13 per cent by 1995. Sweden's GDP contracted by 4.5 per cent between 1991 and 1993, by which time her budget deficit, as a proportion of her GDP, was nearly the largest among the OECD countries.

The Swedish government responded with fiscal and monetary methods. By 1995 the rate of inflation, traditionally high in Sweden, had been reduced but the contrast between the vigour of the export sector and depressed domestic conditions was accentuated. The OECD predicted that the basic imbalance in the Swedish economy would continue for some years to come, preventing a fall in unemployment (OECD, *Sweden*, 1995, 1).

These difficulties, together with the growing tensions within the Soviet bloc, formed the background for Sweden's move towards the EEC. The decision was made in 1990 by a government formed by the Social Democratic Labour Party (SAP) which had guided Sweden along the broad path of neutrality and welfarism since the 1930s. However, when a Centre-Right coalition took power in 1991, displacing the SAP for only the second time since 1932, the link between stabilising policies at home, and formal integration into western Europe, became clear. The new government promised to review the 'Swedish model' and bring about a 'freedom of choice revolution' (Boje and Hort, 1993, 71). Negotiations began in 1991, at the same time as Norway and Finland, and Sweden joined the EU in 1995, after a referendum. Sweden retained its high living standards, but its major difficulties in the early 1990s marked the end of the exemplary period which had begun after the war. Like the other Nordic countries, Sweden now needed stronger economic links outside the North, and beyond EFTA. A specialised, highly productive economy with an educated workforce was no longer enough to avoid serious imbalances, while expensive welfare arrangements needed careful review. The result was Sweden's membership of the EU in 1995. Economically, this was a major gain for Sweden, but the great national ideal of a socialist society was bound to be subject to some change in the years to come.

Denmark

Denmark was seriously affected by the oil crisis. It resumed its traditional position as a country which had to pay dearly for its raw materials imports, while its new industrial exports suffered from reduced world demand. Changes in government and government policy in the mid-1970s did little to help the economy or confidence (Johansen, 1987, 167–8). Oil-saving measures had little effect until the end of the decade. Denmark seemed to have restored its position by 1982, when the growth rate reached 3.1 per cent. A serious deterioration then set in in 1987. However, in the early 1990s a new revival took place in conditions of impressive stability. Denmark was now in the strongest position among the Nordic countries. Fiscal and monetary policies kept the rate of inflation down. By 1993 Denmark had reduced its official discount rate to 6.25 per cent, and in 1994 the rate dropped as low as 5.5 per cent. It paid a price in the shape of high unemployment, which reached 12.3 per cent in 1993, though this was generally in line with unemployment rates elsewhere in Europe, which hovered around 10 per cent (OECD, *Denmark*, 1994).

As a member of the EEC since 1973, Denmark was not affected by the big movement of opinion elsewhere in the North in the late 1980s and 1990s in favour of European integration. On the contrary, when Denmark held a referendum on the Maastricht treaty in 1992, the result was a narrow majority *against*. The debate had revolved mainly around questions of national sovereignty and the government was able to secure a reversal of the result in a referendum in 1993, after it had negotiated a number of opt-outs. This embarrassing episode was exceptional, however. Ever since 1973, Denmark's example as an active EEC member helped influence opinion elsewhere in the North and Denmark was able to help the other Nordic applicants during their negotiations in the early 1990s. By 1995, Denmark was once again a strong influence; in particular, it had become a strong advocate of the incorporation of eastern Europe into the EU (*The European*, 7–13 December 1995).

Norway

In Nordic terms, Norway was a big economic success once a long-term basis for the economy had been established in the early 1950s. Output grew at a rate of 4.2 per cent between 1950 and 1970, with virtually full employment. The merchant fleet expanded from 5.7 million gross tons in 1950 to 25.8 million gross tons in 1975. Most of the ships acquired were built abroad, but Norwegian shipbuilding expanded rapidly, especially in the 1960s. Foreign trade increased by about 10 per cent per year as Norway joined enthusiastically in the European movement towards trade liberalisation (Hodne, 1983, 180). Business mergers multiplied in the 1960s as the economy adapted to more open trading conditions (ibid., 218–21). The country's huge oil reserves under the North Sea made it virtually indifferent to OPEC measures after 1973. Norway's main problem by the later 1970s was the embarrassing inflow of foreign currency generated by its oil exports. Costs were so high that other Norwegian exports ceased to be competitive. High welfare payments could be financed easily enough but unemployment reached unprecedented levels and various social problems were in the offing. The government set up educational and retraining schemes, and encouraged capital exports. Norway had rejected membership of the EEC at a referendum in 1972. The electorate was persuaded that Norwegian social policies and culture would be threatened by Brussels. In the following year, the big rise in the world oil price appeared to justify the decision.

With oil and gas making up half Norway's exports, the country was very vulnerable to price changes on the world energy market. Economic growth was much reduced in the early 1980s when the oil price dropped, and after a brief revival growth slumped again at the end of the decade. However, the growth rate increased substantially from the early 1990s, in contrast to Sweden. In 1994 it was nearly 4 per cent, the highest for a decade. Oil and gas exports were buoyant in the late 1980s and they continued to grow into the 1990s. Norway's merchant fleet was the fifth-largest in the world, and the biggest in western Europe, in 1992. Norway still ran a balance of payments surplus in the 1990s and inflation was around 2 per cent per annum. Its unemployment level remained in the region of 5–6 per cent. Its average working week was 36.8 hours in 1991 (OECD, *Norway*, 1995).

This situation was preferable to Sweden's but the need to integrate more closely with the continental economy of western Europe was increasingly obvious. In 1991 Norway made a second application to join the EEC. Together with Finland and Sweden, it joined the EU in 1995.

Finland

Finland was hit very hard by the recession of the early 1990s, combined with dislocation in Russia. Unemployment, which was at

3.5 per cent in 1990, increased to 17.9 per cent in 1993. In 1994 it was approaching 20 per cent. The Finnish balance of payments was in deficit.

As elsewhere in the North, a strong movement occurred in favour of joining the EEC from the late 1980s. In the case of Finland, the collapse of the Soviet Union in 1991 and the signing of new friendship agreements with the CIS allowed Finland to look towards Brussels. Finland joined the EU in 1995.

The year 1995 saw the formal integration of the Nordic fringe (except distant Iceland) into the western European economy. The referenda which confirmed the legislative decisions of Norway, Finland and Sweden in 1994 showed how far popular opinion had warmed to formal European integration since the 1970s. Joining the EEC completed the symmetrical process whereby both the southern and the northern fringes had joined the industrial core. Both had industrialised in order to do so, with primary products forming a declining proportion of their exports from the very high levels of the 1940s. The North, however, always had a strong foundation in natural resources and its high wage costs had required it to develop specialised, high productivity manufacturing with high added value. The economic history of the North since the war was one of the success stories of western Europe. The South was a very different story. Chronically short of natural resources, and with very low wages, its path to industrialisation was bound to be very different and the success story, in its case, is still ambiguous and incomplete.

The transformation of southern Europe

In 1960 the southern European countries remained a disparate group marked mainly by economic backwardness and social tensions. Only Italy showed clear signs of modernisation. By 1995 Italy and Spain were fully industrialised, but Portugal and Greece now formed a 'fringe of a fringe' in the South. Their signs of modernisation were outweighed by backward features and, worst of all, progress was slow. Meanwhile, the problem of the Italian South remained unresolved. The old contrast between northern and southern Europe had not disappeared.

Italy

Italy's participation in the EEC from 1958 took place on the favourable terms which her respected membership of the ECSC had allowed her to negotiate. Sufficiently modernised now to take full advantage of the opportunity, Italy's GNP increased by 71 per cent between 1958 and 1968, an average annual growth rate of 5.5 per cent. Trade with EEC countries increased more than five times (Willis, 1971, 72).

There was, however, a price to pay – corruption. The injection of new money, new men, and new methods into a conservative and backward society produced a rich and corrupt elite of politicians, businessmen and professional advisers under the protection of a series of Centre-Right governments which in their turn depended on the complex networks of client support built up since the war by the Christian Democrats. This combination of new and old rich, new and old power, kept control over both the ill-paid urban masses and the declining peasantry. American involvement in reform, which in any case declined after 1948, ultimately failed to produce changes in national institutions and attitudes on the lines achieved in Germany (Harper, 1986, 166). Even the government's creation of the *Cassa per il Mezzogiorno* to modernise the South in 1950, with a big loan from the World Bank, followed by the tardy beginnings of southern land reform in the early 1950s, had unpleasant side-effects, with organised crime in the shape of the Mafia and its outliers which were drawn into the heart of the modern Italian economy and northern politics. The insidious implications of this system were not fully appreciated at the time but the socially-aware film director, Federico Fellini, portrayed the life of the new rich in *La dolce vita* in 1960. However, international audiences tended to admire the style and elegance of life in the new Italy rather than understand the underlying criticism. The 'Italian miracle' would carry on for a few years more, until the 1970s brought more intractable problems.

Though all the components of Italian modernisation were in place by 1960, only the 'northern industrial triangle', the area bounded by Milan, Genoa and Turin – long established as a centre of engineering and textiles – bore comparison with the industrial and business regions of northern Europe. Agrarian reform, even in the North, had not advanced very far and heavy emigration to the Americas, Australia and northern Europe was still going on (Ginsburg, 1990, 211).

It was in the 1960s, though, that Italy's post-war commitment to international trade produced its return. A number of large north-western firms proved competitive in technology and price on European markets. Fiat in motors and Zanussi in electricals exported heavily, first in southern Europe where their combination of low price and tried-and-tested technology gave them an advantage over north European producers, but increasingly in the mass markets of northern Europe as well. Their combination of cheap labour and advanced production techniques was well suited to the expanding trading system of the EEC, while the much slower development of Spain, Portugal and Greece meant that Italy could thrive as the only cheap-labour advanced manufacturer in western Europe. Italy achieved stable and rapid growth in the 1960s, averaging 6 per cent per annum. The great success of Italian exports meant that the balance of payments current account was in surplus every year except 1963, and the surplus became large and stable from 1965. The danger of inflation was offset by overseas investment, and by the fact that the Italian economy retained substantial unused resources even at the end of the decade. Inflation was moderate by European standards except in 1962–63 and 1968–69. The lira was never under threat and its parity was not altered (OECD, *Monetary Policy in Italy*, 1973, 9). Much of this would change for the worse in 1969, but in successful Italy, above all, the impending world difficulties of the 1970s were hard to anticipate.

By 1967 Italy was the third-largest producer of refrigerators in the world, after the United States and Japan. It had also become the largest European producer of washing-machines and dish-washers (Ginsburg, 1990, 215). The Italian steel industry was now one of the largest in Europe, led by the Finsider consortium. The State continued to provide stability on the basis of post-war understandings, and trade union activity remained minimal until the late 1960s. The agrarian problem was resolved, after a fashion, by migration to the industrial areas, though the accumulation of unskilled workers from the South in the slums and shanty towns of Milan, Turin and other northern cities was a serious social problem. There was little public housing and the private sector did not begin to provide significant quantities of cheap housing – and that to a very low standard – until the later 1960s (Ginsburg, 1990, 225–7).

State investment and planning in the South began to make clear progress in the early 1960s. Public infrastructural schemes and inducements to expanding northern firms helped attract enterprises like Alfa-Romeo, whose large factory near Naples launched the Alfasud onto European export markets in the mid-1960s. This combination of style and economy sought to emulate the Renault Dauphine of the late 1950s though, as with Ford's Escort, made at a new plant in Liverpool from the early 1960s, a combination of cheap engineering and a new labour force caused difficulties. Generally, government inducements favoured heavy industry in order to soak up as much labour as possible, and the resulting giant plants in steel and chemicals were soon pilloried as 'cathedrals in the desert' (Dyker, 1992 [2], 83).

The early 1960s, however, saw the beginnings of political and social tensions. These reflected a combination of old and new problems. The Centre-Left victory in the elections of 1963 began a period of indecisive government, especially associated with the coalition administrations of the ineffectual Christian Democrat, Aldo Moro. The expanding trade unions made their presence felt for the first time since the war and a wave of industrial unrest built up to a peak in the 'hot autumn' of 1969 and lasted into the early 1970s. Industrial wages soared, especially after 1969, and the decline of the labour reserve in the countryside weakened the negotiating position of the employers (Dyker, 1992 [2], 72–75). Industrial competition from cheap-labour countries in the Third World and from technically more advanced countries began to bite in the early 1960s (Graham, 1990, 110–11). The failure to set up an effective planning system to prevent speculation and a poor urban environment exposed the hold which corruption had established over the rapidly growing industrial cities. The public sector continued in deficit, emphasising the contrast between the enterprising private industrial sector and political weakness.

Underlying these events was the fear that anti-democratic forces were massing to both Left and Right and that modernisation had produced new versions of the old tensions which in the past had disrupted Italian society or had encouraged a conservative defence. The Italian student demonstrations of 1967–68 brought these issues to a head. Italian universities, which were a path to secure careers for the children of the middle classes, had been left to cope with growing demand without additional funds, rather like the other Italian social services. Student protest against their conditions of study was therefore combined with criticism of a mean State and the combination of materialism and corruption which lay behind it. An inflexible State response led to the proliferation in Italy of Communist and anarchist ideas, and the emergence of mainly Left-wing groups prepared to use violence against both celebrities and ordinary people.

The Red Brigades and other groups were just part of the wave of political violence which swept western Europe from the later 1960s, but Italy's rapid post-war transformation made it the most fragile society of its day. Political fragmentation and the opportunism of the new business class could no longer be held together by the Church and the urban masses seemed open to extremist influence, notably from the Left. Mass protest of all sorts proliferated between 1968 and 1975, contributing to the country's slow economic growth until the new world economic conditions created a tougher climate (Jacquemin and De Jong, 1977, 15). With wage costs rising faster than those of other countries from 1969, exports now came to depend on productivity improvements and devaluations of the lira (Dyker, 1992 [2], 69).

Italian politics had already been moving to the Right in the early 1970s, mainly in reaction to the excesses of the Left. The oil crisis of 1973 concentrated attention on a more basic problem of economic adjustment. Italy's rapid industrialisation without significant natural resources made it uniquely vulnerable to the oil embargo and price increases of the years 1973–79. The new industries of the South were especially hard hit. Italy passed though the crisis but only at the expense of a very high rate of inflation and the growth of the 'black' economy. Also influential was the growth of small firms ('the Third Italy') which followed the 'hot autumn' of 1969. They were less affected by the generous wage legislation enacted during the industrial crisis and they were also encouraged by fiscal changes designed to offset the effects of inflation. Many of them supplied components and services to the larger firms and their lower costs and high productivity partly offset the problems of the big firms. By 1980, in many industries, some of these versatile 'satellite' firms had replaced their former clients who were no longer able to compete. Their success was widely welcomed on social grounds. Their spatial diffusion was seen as keeping labour in the countryside and small towns, and boosting local pride in a manner seen as representative of traditional Italy where towns competed for regional pre-eminence.

High inflation persisted into the early 1980s but a rapid economic recovery occurred from the middle of the decade. Trade union influence declined after the defeat of the big Fiat strike in 1980, and conservative government maintained financial and social stability. The decline in oil prices and the falling dollar drove the terms of trade decisively in Italy's favour, and the country's industrial strengths could again be brought fully into play. When, in 1986, OECD figures suggested that Italy's GDP had overtaken Britain's, a country of similar population, a big government and media celebration took place of *il sorpasso* – the 'overtaking'. This effort to portray Italy as the fifth-richest country in the world soon ran into difficulties arising from the Italian figures, and especially the measurement of the 'black' economy. However, the episode symbolised Italy's post-war achievement.

From 1989, Italy was again affected by a contraction of European demand. A further move to quality products based on advanced techniques was seen as the solution, but the continuing world recession of the early 1990s was a serious handicap. So was the large public sector deficit, which had been inflated since the early 1970s by government concessions to the labour unrest of 1969. In 1993, Italy's GDP fell for the first time since 1975. Unemployment hovered around 10 per cent or a little more throughout the early 1990s. As an economy of export-led growth since the war, Italy was still dependent on developments abroad. In 1994, Italy had an unemployment rate of more than 11 per cent. Its balance of payments was in deficit throughout the first half of the 1990s. Efforts to privatise part of the large Italian nationalised sector produced a series of difficulties, culminating (as this book went to press) in the disappointing launch of ENI, the State oil conglomerate, in December 1995.

Despite the efforts since the war, the South remained clearly more backward than the Centre and the North. In 1989, the standard of living in the South was 70 per cent of that of the Centre and North, while per capita income was only 60 per cent of the national average. Even these low levels had to be sustained by big fiscal transfers. The South was also socially and culturally backward (Zamagni, 1993, 376). Its per capita incomes were only half those of the industrial North and levels of skill and motivation were very low.

Spain

Spain took its first significant steps towards convergence with the rest of western Europe in 1958–59, when a balance of payments crisis and a French-influenced Stabilisation Programme (1959) began a shift from an economy directed on Fascist lines to a more liberal, outward-looking structure. In particular, the programme sought to attract foreign capital to Spain. Changes within the government, beginning with Franco's new administration of 1957, weakened the influence of Fascist ideology. US aid of various sorts continued, on the strength of the mutual defence treaty of 1953. Funds were provided at a lower level than in the 1950s, and they were partly linked to military purchases. However, they continued to finance the import of the raw materials of which Spain had an endemic lack and further undermined the old Spanish obsession with self-sufficiency. Spain joined the IMF, the OEEC and the World Bank in 1958. Monetary stabilisation was promoted using more conventional fiscal and financing methods, and a series of laws were passed encouraging foreign investment. Wages were virtually frozen between 1957 and 1961 and the rate of inflation was reduced to around 5 per cent by the early 1960s. These were convincing measures but for a few years they failed to generate much economic growth. Then, Spain's First Development Plan was launched in 1964, not only following the fashionable French example of 'indicative planning', but emulating the French planning structure in even the smallest details (Harrison, 1978, 155). Among other ends, the government wanted to secure international respect in this way, and to make up for the EEC's rejection in 1964 of the application which Spain had made to join in 1962. The main obstacle to Spain's membership, though, was lack of democracy in Spain.

Over the 1960s as a whole, the Spanish economy grew at a rate of 7.4 per cent per year. Planning may have played a part, but it was the big growth of tourism which, by offsetting a large part of the balance of payments deficit, in association with foreign investment, released the country's productive potential (Harrison, 1978, 156). In 1959 just over 4 million tourists visited Spain, but nearly 35 million did so in 1973. Receipts from foreign tourists increased more than twenty times between 1959 and 1975 (Harrison, 1978, 156). With cheaper credit and more abundant capital, Spanish manufacturing was released from previous constraints. The import of scarce raw materials now became easier to finance and industrial production increased at a rate of 7.9 per cent per annum between 1959 and 1972 (Harrison, 1978, 163). This rapid growth generated renewed inflation and payments problems in the 1960s, including the devaluation of the peseta in 1967. The achievement of targets in the Second (1967–71) and Third

(1972–75) Plans was upset, especially in respect of their social objectives. The Spanish economic growth rate averaged only 5.6 per cent per annum between 1966 and 1971 (Payne, 1987, 477). However, inflation stayed under control at around 6.5 per cent per annum during the 1960s.

Spanish GDP nevertheless doubled in real terms in the 1960s, and growth continued at an annual average rate of around 7 per cent until the mid-1970s. Spain's average growth rate between 1960 and 1975 was the highest in Europe, at 7.2 per cent per annum (Lopez-Claros, 1988, 1). This progress produced striking results. For instance, in 1953, Spanish GDP had been only 14 per cent of that of France. By 1965 it had risen to risen to 22 per cent and it rose to 23 per cent by 1974. Given that French GDP was expanding rapidly over this period, this was a big achievement. Agriculture's share of the workforce declined. Between 1940 and 1975 it fell from 50.52 per cent to 22.91 per cent of the active labour force, with the sharpest reduction occurring after 1960 (Harrison, 1978, 150). Even in backward Andalucia, less than 40 per cent of the workforce was in the primary sector by 1970. Large cities flourished, and by 1975, 50 per cent of the population lived in cities of 100,000 or more (Payne, 1987, 479).

The government began to designate regional development poles from the 1960s, at a time when they were a fashionable form of economic planning throughout Europe. State intervention in industrial affairs continued, while the structure of agriculture was very little altered. Tariffs were still used to protect Spanish industries. Above all, the Franco regime continued to prevent the development of a lively political and intellectual life (Salmon, 1992, 36–7).

The years 1960–73 had something in common with the Italian experience in the 1950s, including the much slower pace of social than of economic change. Emigration continued, mainly to Latin America before 1960 but thereafter mainly to other countries in western Europe as rapid growth in the industrial areas soaked up any remaining labour surplus there. The Stabilisation Programme of 1958–59 encouraged emigration in order to reduce unemployment and to increase the volume of remittances in foreign currencies; according to government estimates, Spanish migrant workers sent home the equivalent of more than $700 million in 1975 (Harrison, 1978, 151–2). Spanish women were slow to enter employment (though 1 million were estimated to have done so in the 1960s). Regional variations in economic development remained acute, and the localised development planning and the fashionable, French-inspired 'growth poles' designated in the 1960s produced uneven results similar to Italy (Harrison, 1978, 166–7). The continuing influence of Fascist institutions and the Church were a brake on change, with the government taking care that higher earnings and mobility did not engender a political threat. In contrast to Italy, however, Spain achieved a big reduction in the rate of inflation after 1959, and the emergence of technocratic planning on French lines in 1964 may have helped sustain the high rate of economic growth during the decade. Seen as a whole, Spain reverted to liberal economic policies during the decade and this prepared the way for a return to democracy once Franco had gone, and to participation in the economic and social life of western Europe.

The oil crisis of 1973 created major problems for Spain. Thanks to its good relations with the Arab states, Spain was exempted from the initial boycott but she had to pay the higher prices (Harrison, 1985, 171). Like Italy, it was heavily dependent on oil imports, and a resurgence of overseas payments difficulties, made worse by a sharp drop in foreign tourism, revived some of the old problems of the 1950s, except that the export of labour was no longer a palliative as there was little demand for Spanish labour elsewhere in Europe. The emigration of migrant workers had slowed sharply from 1972, and growing unemployment abroad forced many of them to return to Spain. Manufactured goods, which had been the leading sector in Spain's expansion, proved hard to sell, especially as much of the growth had occurred in energy-intensive industries such as steel, chemicals and shipbuilding. The transition to democracy and the emergence of a trade union movement made it hard to resist wage claims and inflation set in in 1974. The National Energy Plan of 1975 (PEN–75) did little to reduce energy requirements or to develop new sources of energy in the form of nuclear power and gas (Harrison, 1993, 54–55). The years 1975–78 were a period of recession. The rate of inflation reached 37 per cent in 1977, while GDP increased at an average rate of less than 2 per cent between 1975 and 1979 (Lopez-Claros, 1988, 1). Recovery began in 1978 when the peseta was devalued by 20 per cent, but a new recession followed the OPEC price rise of 1979.

Spain's fundamental balance of payments problem, obscured in the 1960s by capital imports, remittances from emigrants and income from the expanding tourist industry of the 'Costas', emerged with renewed force. The total emigrating in 1976 was a mere 15 per cent of what it had been in 1970 (Harrison, 1978, 152). Formal national planning was abandoned in 1975, having helped achieve an average annual growth rate of 6 per cent since 1964 (Dyker, 1992 [2], 201). A return to high inflation helped push up the unemployment rate, and conditions tended to become worse for the rest of the decade, partly as a result of government concessions to the developing trade unions after Franco's death. Growth rates slumped, partly because the post-Franco administrations gave priority to establishing a social pact with the Spanish people.

Although it was widely assumed that Franco's death in 1975 would lead to a move towards democracy, the government wanted to secure continuity and stability, fearing a disruptive return of the Spanish Communist Party leadership from exile. The first general election, in 1977, produced a government whose first task was to deal with the growing financial problems of the day. Devaluation and a package of institutional reforms (the Moncloa agreements, agreed by the government and the opposition parties in 1977) were used to postpone a concerted strategy, and nothing had been done to resolve the basic problem of the balance of payments by the time of the further oil price increase in 1979. The Moncloa agreements made some progress towards a more open economy, though the context of controls, government intervention, and a protected economy remained in place. Between 1975 and 1984 the Spanish growth rate averaged only 1.5 per cent, and unemployment rose from 8.8 per cent in 1979 to 22 per cent in 1985 (Salmon, 1992, 38–9). However, the National Energy Plan of 1979 helped greatly to reduce dependence on imported oil, partly by expanding Spanish coal production, hydroelectric generation, and nuclear energy.

The election of a Socialist government in 1982 produced a shift towards economic orthodoxy, linked to the long-term aim of political and social stability. This was due in part to Spain's entry into the EEC in 1986, which boosted foreign investment in Spain and encouraged domestic producers to modernise their plant, methods and products. The rate of investment rose to nearly three times the OECD average (OECD, *Spain*, 1994, 85). The new government made a start on dispersing some of the State's huge accumulation of industrial holdings. This was a big problem as INI, the largest public industrial enterprise, had been required to absorb a large number of bankrupt enterprises in the 1970s and was making huge losses in consequence. By the later 1980s, though, INI activities were being progressively reduced, as were its losses (Lopez-Claros, 1988, 20). The annual growth rate accelerated from 1987, making Spain the most dynamic economy in Europe. Between 1987 and 1990 the growth rate hovered in the region of 4–5 per cent. The liberalisation of government policies continued. Spain was able to enter the EMS in 1989. Foreign investment grew, coming chiefly now from other EEC countries rather than the USA as it had in the 1950s and 1960s. Spain now became the fourth-largest recipient of foreign investment, after the USA, UK, and France. Nevertheless, by early 1990 unemployment was still running at 16 per cent.

Organised labour recognised the need for restraint and it contributed to a big reduction in unemployment by the end of the decade. However, wage costs increased rapidly and Spain could not escape its underlying inflationary tendency. State-controlled firms, still a big feature of the Spanish economy, were difficult to control and they remained wasteful. Labour mobility and the flexible use of labour were still hampered by the *Ordenanzas Laborales*, an inheritance from Franquist corporatism. By 1991 Spain had developed a big balance of payments deficit and budget deficit. The arrival of the European downturn in that year hit Spain especially hard (OECD, *Spain*, 1994, 85–90).

By the end of 1993 unemployment had reached 24 per cent and the peseta had been devalued three times. A big drop in domestic demand allowed exports to increase but inflation, at nearly 5 per cent, was nearly double the OECD average. With an initial fall in GDP, and then very low GDP growth, unemployment remained very high into the middle of the decade. Only a big revival of the European economy could bring about a change in the country's fortunes but, as elsewhere in southern Europe, a change in Germany's fortunes, in the context of a revival of the world economy, was the big requirement.

Meanwhile, the Spanish brought in a tough budget in 1994, the main features of which were a wage freeze, sharp controls on central and provincial government expenditure, and more efficient tax collection. Steps were being taken to remove the old-style corporatist labour regulations.

Greece

The Greek economy began to make a degree of progress after 1960, with the government programmes of the 1950s beginning to have an effect. The proportion of the workforce employed in industry rose to 22.9 per cent in 1968 and to 27.8 per cent in 1974 (OECD, *Hist.Stat.*, 1991, 40). GDP increased at an annual average of 7.7 per cent between 1963 and 1973. However, Greece experienced a high rate of emigration in the 1960s as demand for labour expanded elsewhere in Europe, especially in Germany. The elderly increased as a proportion of the population. In 1960 the total active population in Greece was 43.3 per cent of the total population, a figure very close to the EEC average of 44.2 per cent, but it fell thereafter and in 1989 it was 39.5 per cent, the lowest level in Europe apart from Ireland and Spain (OECD, *Hist.Stat.*, 1991, 36). Of course, the figures may have been distorted by the 'black economy' phenomenon so common in southern Europe, but the fiscal implications of such evasion would also have been a burden for the Greek economy.

The impact of the oil crisis on Greece will be entirely predictable for readers who have penetrated this far, but Greece suffered an additional blow in that its merchant fleet, most of which was composed of oil tankers, experienced a disastrous fall in demand. Many Greek tankers were laid up, and ultimately scrapped. By 1992 the Greek merchant fleet was only the eleventh-largest in the world (though its capacity was still slightly larger than that of the British merchant fleet (*Economist*, 1993, 60)). With foreign demand for additional Greek labour, which had gone mainly to Germany, greatly cut back, the industrial proportion of the workforce *dropped* in the 1980s. By 1989 it was only 27.5 per cent. The average working week in Greece in 1992 was 41.1 hours, suggesting a low level of equipment.

However, industrial exports grew as a proportion of total exports, from 7.7 per cent in the years 1962–66 to 46 per cent in 1980. (Piquet Marchal, 1985, 350). Meanwhile, the proportion engaged in agriculture dropped sharply, from 57.1 per cent in 1960 to 25.3 per cent in 1989. The residue was absorbed by service employment, which increased from 25.5 per cent in 1960 to 47.1 per cent in 1989 (OECD, *Hist.Stat.*, 1991, 40–1). An increase in service employment of this magnitude was general throughout western Europe during this period, including the South, but in a country as poor as Greece it was hard to sustain without creating balance of payments problems. Political problems did not help. The civil war ended with government in the hands of the conservatives. The Right-wing ES (later ERE) held power from 1952 to 1963. In 1963 the Centre-Left EK, led by Giorgios Papandreou, took power after a general election. After a disagreement with the new king, Constantine II, Papandreou was dismissed in 1965. In 1967, a military regime took over, suspending all democratic rights. This regime of the 'colonels' collapsed in 1974 and a new, democratic constitution was adopted in 1975.

The EEC allowed Greece to join the Community in 1981, ahead of Spain and Portugal which were economically better qualified but which needed time to harmonise their economies so that they could join at the same time. Moreover, Greece had been an associate member of the EEC since 1962. The EEC also wanted to encourage the return of democracy to Greece. However, the regime of the 'colonels' had been marked by economic incompetence and little foreign investment had been attracted. The demise of the 'colonels' had coincided with the oil crisis and the climate of development had been a poor one into the later 1980s. Inflation reached a peak of 24.9 per cent in 1980 and did not drop below 20 per cent until 1984. Growth picked up a little in the late 1980s but inflation remained around 15 per cent. In 1993, with the Greek economy again in recession, Papandreou returned to power and committed Greece to fiscal discipline. The government adopted a 'convergence programme' (1994–99), designed to eliminate the budget deficit and to bring inflation down to average EEC levels (OECD *Economic Outlook*, **57**, 1995, 89). A new tax structure, introduced in 1994, was expected to reduce tax evasion. Papandreou also promised a move towards economic deregulation and privatisation on the lines favoured by the IMF for backward countries with big foreign payments deficits. Inflation dropped to 9.5 per cent in 1995. Greece thus came into line with Portugal, reflecting the economic similarity of the two countries. Nevertheless, there had been little improvement in the growth rate by 1995, owing largely to the world recession.

The Greek holiday industry enjoyed a moderate success. In 1974 it attracted 1,956,000 visitors, making it thirteenth in the western European national rankings. By 1985 its annual total had risen to 6,574,000, and it had risen to ninth. In 1991 it attracted 8,036,000 visitors. This kept it at ninth in the west European rankings, just after Portugal. The growth was impressive but overall this was a moderate performance for a country with so little to export and more sun and ruins than most. Only the Netherlands, Ireland, Belgium, Portugal and the Nordic countries did worse, while Spain (35,347,000) and Italy (26,840,000) showed what could be done (*Economist*, 1993, 61). In terms of visitors per head of population, Greece did better than Italy and as well as Spain, but these large, developed economies were not strictly comparable. The reputation of Greece as a holiday host suffered in 1995 when the British press detected an agreement to raise prices by the association of Greek hotel owners. This permitted the diffusion of complaints about poor hotels, poor transport, and cheating by traders (*Independent*, 30 August 1995). With Greece attracting many fewer tourists than usual in 1995 owing to the recession, the defects of the Greek holiday industry were only too obvious.

Portugal

In the 1960s Portugal began to benefit from the high rate of growth in western Europe. Investment from abroad increased as the tourist industry expanded and a number of modern industrial enterprises were set up. Between 1969 and 1973 the growth rate averaged 7.4 per cent. Exports increased, especially in manufactured products. Portuguese workers continued to migrate to take up employment elsewhere in Europe, with an increase in the rate of emigration in the mid-1960s, and their remittances to their families kept the overseas account in surplus. They also helped to keep unemployment in Portugal down to around 2 per cent. The government was able to maintain external equilibrium on a permanent basis. Portugal now seemed to be on the Spanish path of development. The proportion of the workforce employed in manufacturing increased from 22.6 per cent in 1960 to 24.9 per cent in 1974. This was rather less than in Spain, which increased from 23.0 per cent to 26.3 per cent over the same period, but the trend has to be taken in association with the fall in employment in agriculture. Whereas in 1960, 43.9 per cent of the Portuguese labour force worked on the land, only 34.9 per cent did so in 1974. Again, the Spanish reduction was more pronounced, ending with an agricultural workforce of 23.2 per cent in 1974 (OECD, *Hist.Stat.*, 1991, 40–1). However, Portugal's progress from a lower base was impressive enough.

As elsewhere in the South, industrial expansion drew people into the cities but created a shortage of capital for housing. As in northern Italy in the 1950s, the virtual absence of a public housing programme prevented the provision of accommodation even on social grounds. Even as late as the mid-1970s, only one new dwelling out of twenty built in Lisbon was in the public sector. Portugal's maritime geography and big rivers meant that most of the urban population was concentrated in the two big seaports of Lisbon and Oporto, and the chronic housing shortage here led to the building of large shanty towns. At the same time, higher industrial wages were partly devalued by soaring rents. With Portuguese social services still organised on corporatist lines, favouring particular industries and social groups, the growing social problems of the 1960s could not be tackled effectively. This accumulation of problems and discontent, far worse than those generated in Spain by the movement into the industrial cities since the later 1950s, would help explain the unique course of events in Portugal after the oil shock of 1973.

As in Spain, the death or departure of the ageing Fascist dictator Salazar was awaited as a chance to bring about reforms in Portugal. Salazar retired in 1968, at the age of seventy-nine, having failed to introduce modernising reforms on the lines of those favoured by Franco. His departure had been less well prepared than Franco's would prove to be. His nominated successor, Marcelo Caetano, proved less decisive than his Roman-sounding name might suggest, and he was removed in a bloodless army coup in April 1974 after the early effects of the oil crisis – principally a huge balance of payments deficit – had proved too much for him at a time of high inflation and high economic growth resulting from the previous boom. The country was now plunged into a disruptive struggle for power and influence between interests ranging from the Fascists and the Catholics to extreme Communists and anarchists, most of which were represented in the army as well as in the civil population. Portugal's defence of its African colonies had meant not only a very demanding system of national service, but a wide distribution of weapons and knowledge of how to use them.

With Portuguese dissidents, many of them Communists with political experience in France, returning from exile, extremist ideas flourished, while the army oscillated between keeping order and planning to take over power completely. Labour organisations formed their ranks almost overnight, and workers' control and mass democracy theories, formulated in Paris, Frankfurt and other centres of revolutionary Marxism, spread like a virus. These events had much of the Paris student uprising of 1968, which had influenced the younger leaders. The workers' basic grievance was that their wages had not kept up with growth and inflation since the later 1960s. If they had been allowed a free trade union system they would have no doubt resolved this problem much earlier, but it became a major factor in the revolution of 1974 and led on to a variety of demands which had scarcely been in the workers' minds before 1974. To sustain the rise in living standards even after 1974, a large part of the economy was brought under State control.

The colonies were made independent immediately, which allowed some funds to be channelled into domestic spending, but Portugal lost an important source of cheap raw materials and a market for its inefficiently produced manufactures. Portuguese emigrants returned to Portugal from the colonies and many needed support. Left-wing military men and politicians were in absolute control for a while in 1975 and much money was wasted in various welfare schemes and experiments in cooperative pro-duction. Income was redistributed in favour of manual workers in town and country, and the result was a rise in imports and a fall in the rate of economic growth. Socialist parties and trade unions discouraged the foreign investment and productivity gains that Portugal badly needed, and the country was affected by instability into the late 1970s. Inflation was especially serious after 1974, together with external deficits. Economic growth slowed to 1 per cent in 1974 and went into absolute decline in 1975. The European post-1973 recession slashed the demand for Portuguese workers and cut the flow of remittances into Portugal. In 1976 the government decided to burst out of their predicament by bold reflation but this, predictably, produced a chronic balance of payments deficit by 1977. A hurried devaluation only made matters worse. In 1977 Portugal had to ask for support from the IMF and negotiate a stabilisation plan (Schmitt, 1981, 2–5).

IMF involvement proved to be very beneficial. It allowed the government to introduce a series of austerity measures which culminated in May 1978 in a stabilisation programme funded by the IMF. The Portuguese escudo was progressively devalued to reduce costs, while interest rates were increased pro rata in order to increase savings and investment at home. This programme made rapid progress towards the almost complete elimination of the foreign deficit as early as 1978 (Schmitt, 1981, 1). The rate of economic growth, which had been running at an inflationary rate of over 4 per cent, fell to 2.1 per cent in 1978, but by 1979 it was back to its previous level (OECD, *Hist.Stat.*, 1991).

As elsewhere in southern Europe, adjustments painfully made after the oil crisis of 1973 did not exempt a country from even more intractable problems after the new increase in the oil price in 1979. The decision of the industrial nations to counter OPEC by deflation caused acute difficulties for countries which, like Portugal, were progressing painfully towards industrialisation on the assumption that adequate markets would be open to them elsewhere in Europe. In the 1980s those markets no longer developed at the same rate, while expansion of the home market would only bring back inflation and make exports uncompetitive.

Portuguese GDP per capita started to grow more slowly in 1980 and in 1983 and 1984 it dropped sharply overall. There was a revival in the later 1980s with a growth rate of 5.2 per cent reached in 1989, but there was a further reduction in the early 1990s. Portugal's EEC membership, secured at the same time as Spain in 1986, was a great stimulus, both in terms of achieving the necessary standards in advance of membership, and in joining the Common Market at a time of rapid growth throughout Europe. As a less developed country, Portugal qualified for some generous EEC development schemes and it took full advantage of these.

By 1995 Portugal was showing only slow progress towards fundamental improvement, however. Agricultural employment had dropped sharply to 11.6 per cent of the labour force, but agricultural productivity remained low. Real GDP dropped in 1993, in common with much of southern Europe, but Portugal was especially hard hit. Unemployment was high, reaching 5.6 per cent in 1993, but the decline in the value of the escudo produced a high rate of inflation. There was a persistent balance of payments deficit, though inflation was low by 1995. The export performance was impressive, with a very high proportion of manufactures. However, the uneven nature of the Portuguese economy drew in an even greater volume of imports. In 1993, the value of imports was one-third greater than that of exports. In the mid-1990s, Portugal was still struggling to achieve living standards equivalent to those of Spain and Italy. In 1995, Portugal's GDP per capita was only 60 per cent of Spain's and 50 per cent of Italy's. Among the economies of the southern fringe, it had most in common with Greece, as a country with a weak agriculture and slow development in manufacturing. Indeed, both countries had a very similar level of GDP per capita – around $9000 in 1995 (compared to $22,500 in Sweden). In these two countries, the southern fringe appeared to have developed its own fringe, where more problems remained to be solved than anywhere else in Europe. And with southern Italy retaining much in common with Portugal and Greece, the South still harboured, in 1995, a large area of resistance to modernisation.

CHAPTER ELEVEN

Western European Society Since 1970

Social change in an era of slower growth

The early 1970s are a climacteric in the economic history of western Europe. In its social history, no such clear turning point can be discerned. Most of the trends identified in Chapter 5 continued after 1970, albeit at different rates in some cases. Above all, living standards continued to improve.

Figure 11.1 shows the growth of output between 1974 and 1990. The figures are based on current prices and reflect the generally high rates of inflation after 1974. Convergence is the main feature here. In 1974, for instance, West Germany's GNP per capita was 3.03 times that of Spain. In 1991, German GDP per capita was only 1.7 times larger than Spain's. In 1974, West Germany's GNP per capita was 1.76 times that of Britain. By 1991 it was only 1.26 times larger. This convergence reflected the integration of the west European economy which resulted from the extension of the EEC and the broader tariff reductions brought about by GATT and bilateral agreements. Only Greece and Portugal still lagged. Italy was a leading industrial nation and Spain, though starting from a very low base, was moving rapidly towards full industrial status.

To give a clearer impression of variations in living standards, adjustments are normally made to take account of exchange rates. In 1990, per capita purchasing power was highest in the USA, which appears as 100 in Figure 11.2. According to these estimates, eleven western European countries lay within a band ranging from 73.2 per cent to 84.9 per cent of the US standard. Two small countries lay well above this level, and four countries on the southern and western fringes lay well below. The eleven inter-

FIGURE 11.1 *The growth of national output (in US dollars), 1974–90.*

	GNP per head, 1974	GDP per head, 1991
Switzerland	6,340	33,515
Sweden	6,151	25,487
USA	5,941	22,560
West Germany	5,462	21,248 (Germany)
Denmark	5,403	23,676
Belgium	5,044	19,295
Norway	4,912	24,151
Netherlands	4,693	18,565
France	4,486	20,603
Finland	4,184	24,396
Austria	3,917	20,379
UK	3,094	16,748
Italy	2,442	18,576
Greece	2,090	6,498
Ireland	2,042	10,782
Spain	1,800	12,461
Portugal	1,400	5,626

Source: derived from Showers, 1973; *Economist*, 1993.

FIGURE 11.2 *Relative purchasing power per head, 1990.*

USA	100
Switzerland	97.3
Luxembourg	89.7
Germany	84.9
France	81.2
Sweden	79.3
Denmark	78.2
Austria	77.0
Finland	76.7
Belgium	76.4
Norway	74.7
Italy	74.1
Britain	73.7
Netherlands	73.2
Spain	54.7
Ireland	49.4
Portugal	40.9
Greece	34.3

Source: based on *Economist*, 1993, 25.

mediate countries included the whole of the core and the northern fringe. With their purchasing power equal to just over three-quarters of that of the world's richest country, they formed a large area of prosperity covering most of western Europe within which national differences were no longer of great significance. Instead, a great, largely homogeneous society of prosperity and common customs had emerged in western Europe. Only the South (including southern Italy) had not yet been fully incorporated into it.

This convergence means that it becomes increasingly possible after 1970 to generalise about western Europe. For instance, we can detect a general decline in the rate of natural increase, especially in the North, as Europeans came to value material benefits and leisure more and children less. Of the twenty slowest-growing national populations in the world in 1980–91, thirteen were in western Europe (*Economist*, 1993, 15). Physical mobility increased everywhere in the form of activities such as travel to work, visiting friends, relatives, and distant boy- and girl-friends, theatre and concert visits, holidays, second homes, and changes of domicile arising from new employment and retirement. Mobility substitution, mainly in the form of the telephone, developed even faster. These western European trends tended to bring the same products and services onto the market at the same time, and changes in practices and attitudes also took place everywhere at much the same time.

Educational standards rose as young people spent more time in formal education. Formal religious observance declined, especially in northern Europe. Crime tended to increase, and a world of security precautions was created with mobile police, security guards, dogs and cameras. There was a surge of political violence. Public dishonesty and political crime became more common. Standards of sexual morality appeared to drop, though this is hard to measure and may be a product of media interest. Homosexuality became more widely tolerated and even fashionable.

Population

Changing social attitudes in western Europe were directly reflected in changes in population size. Until the later 1960s western Europe had registered a high rate of natural increase. Southern Europe joined this trend very late, and in the North the rate of increase was starting to slow down, but the overall movement conformed to the trend in economic growth. After 1970 the trend was downwards, with the North seeing a shift from consumption through children to consumption through goods and services. In the South, the same effect was visible but the decline in the economic growth rate probably played a bigger part as people found that they could not afford as many children.

In 1960 the future Twelve countries of the EEC had a total population of 296.8 million. Between 1960 and 1975 their annual average population growth rate was 0.7 per cent, and by 1975 the total population of the Twelve had risen to 328.9 million. Between 1975 and 1990 the growth rate averaged only 0.3 per cent, and by 1990 the population of the Twelve had risen to 344.3 million. In the 1980s, the rate of natural increase in the EEC was the lowest of any major world region. It was considerably lower than that of North America, and by 1995 some of the more advanced countries such as Sweden and Denmark were recording a negative rate of natural increase. Indeed, if the trend in the rate of natural increase detected among the Twelve since 1985 were to continue until the end of the century, the EEC would be depending on immigration to prevent its population dropping into overall decline.

FIGURE 11.3 *Population of the Twelve, 1960–90.*

	Population (in millions)			Average annual percentage increase	
	1960	*1975*	*1990*	*1960–75*	*1975–90*
Germany	72.4	77.2	79.4	0.43	0.18
Belgium	9.15	9.8	9.96	0.45	0.1
France	45.7	52.7	56.42	0.96	0.45
Luxembourg	0.31	0.36	0.38	0.95	0.36
Netherlands	11.5	13.8	14.95	1.23	0.54
UK	52.6	56.0	57.4	0.43	0.16
Denmark	4.58	5.06	5.14	0.67	0.1
Spain	30.3	35.6	38.96	1.08	0.6
Greece	8.33	9.05	10.12	0.24	0.74
Ireland	2.83	3.21	3.5	0.83	0.58
Italy	50.2	55.8	57.66	0.71	0.22
Portugal	8.83	9.43	10.39	0.44	0.65
EEC	296.8	328.9	344.3	0.7	0.3

Source: Féron and Thoraval, 1992, 43.

As the table shows, only Portugal and Greece, late developers of the South, had a rising rate of population increase. Taken as a whole, however, the South retained a high rate of population increase into the second half of the period, while the North became a region of low population increase. The decline in immigration into the countries of the North after 1973 was partly responsible for the trend there, but the main cause was a combination of high personal incomes and a high level of education, which depressed the birth rate.

The family

The 1970s saw an acceleration of the trend away from the nuclear family, especially in northern Europe. The divorce rate increased but even more striking was the growth in the number of legal separations. Trends in women's employment were partly responsible. The growth in female employment, and especially part-time employment, contributed to the growth in the number of unmarried couples.

The nuclear family became smaller, with the two-child family becoming the norm (Ambrosius and Hubbard, 1989, 23–4). Teenage and adult children, on the other hand, lived at home in greater numbers owing to the spread of higher education and the high rate of unemployment. They could not afford to establish their own households, even though the living standards of young people in employment continued to improve and such people moved away earlier than before.

Class structure

Most western European countries reached full industrialisation after 1945. This meant that their social structures converged on the British and Belgian models, with a small agricultural sector employing some 5–10 per cent of the total workforce, around 40 per cent working in industry (including about 30 per cent in manufacturing), and upwards of 50 per cent in service employment.

Once this degree of maturity had been reached, the main structural change was an increase in the size of the service sector.

FIGURE 11.4 *Service employment as a percentage of total employment in selected European countries.*

	1950	1980
Austria	31	49
Belgium	43	64
Denmark	42	64
Finland	26	53
France	37	57
Germany	35	51
Italy	36	49
Netherlands	46	64
Norway	37	62
Sweden	39	62
Switzerland	37	53
UK	48	60

Source: drawn from Maddison, 1989, 134.

Male service workers were generally better paid than workers in industry and the growth in their numbers boosted demand for consumer goods, housing, and leisure provision. They had an increasing influence on the composition of demand. The service workforce included a high proportion of women who were less well paid than the men, and more frequently in part-time employment; their effective demand had less effect on supply, except in clothing, cosmetics, and reading materials.

Class conflict

These developments in employment tended to reduce the severity of class conflict after 1945. Full employment and rising manual earnings, together with improved working conditions, education, better welfare facilities and subsidised housing produced a greater understanding between the social classes and the State. The Second World War contributed to this feeling of common interest. Mass entertainment, and especially television, allowed experiences to be shared across the social classes. The rise of Christian Democracy after the war, and the limited influence of Communism, generated a philosophy of cooperation which increasingly replaced class perspectives. Europe's biggest economy, western Germany, had moved away from class mentalities during the Third Reich, and in the new Germany after 1945 no regression was allowed by the Allied occupiers or by the new German leaders.

Not all countries, however, enjoyed the productivity of Germany and several governments found that the policies they pursued to encourage class harmony were inflationary. Only Britain, with its persistently low growth rate, was seriously afflicted before 1970, but the general inflationary spiral of the 1970s affected most countries and caused serious social tensions in some cases. After 1979, a common intention to control inflation led to a reduction of benefits and the growth of unemployment which affected more manual than non-manual workers. These measures tended to encourage competition and individualism. Youth protests and violence, which were often associated with immigrant tensions, became more common, for it was here that unemployment hit hardest, but class protest remained subdued.

The influence of slower growth

From the later 1970s the rate of improvement in living standards slowed down. At the same time, unemployment began to change from the temporary or marginal companion of full employment to a long-term condition suffered by proportions of the workforce which at times recalled the 1930s. Slower economic growth had a diffuse impact on society. The rate of innovation and the growth of supply in consumer goods and services was slower than in the 1960s. The Concorde airliner which in the 1960s was going to fly us all round the world at twice the speed of sound was reduced to a spectre in the 1970s by OPEC oil prices, conservationist pressures in the USA, and the world depression. In 1995, most long-range international passengers are carried by the subsonic Boeing 747, brought into service in 1970, and will be until 2015 or even later. We are not all going to the moon, not now. On the other hand, mass sales fostered by the standardisation of demand allowed reductions in the price of many goods and services. Video recorders, for instance, halved in price in Britain between 1985 and 1990 as the television-viewing public suddenly made them a requirement. If you keep making the same things, they can often get much cheaper, especially if you start making them in the Far East.

During the later 1970s, and even more from the early 1980s, public expenditure was restrained in order to control inflation, and public facilities were cut back. In Britain, the public toilet was the most visible victim of these economies. Private and voluntary action was encouraged to fill the gaps (though in Britain the accessible toilet shortfall remained chronic in 1995). The 'privatisation' of public services and even of the public heritage, a policy in which Britain gave the lead from the 1980s, encouraged the belief that everything had its price. By 1995, even cathedrals and university colleges were levying entry charges in Britain. The former were not well equipped in toilets, either, though the colleges had a glut of them.

Overall, the years after 1970 were a time of greater uncertainty. The fear of nuclear war was reduced, but the previous security of employment was undermined. Confidence in future gains and advancement was replaced by an atmosphere of doubt and competition. Great thinkers and gurus of various types no longer excited or convinced the public. Germaine Greer, the most famous feminist of the 1960s, appeared on television in 1995 as a vaguely comic chat-show turn. Louis Althusser's reputation as a revolutionary philosopher of the Left, already in decline in the 1980s, did not survive his tragic murder of his wife in his apartment at the Collège de France. Performance was tested, appraised and evaluated *ad nauseam*. In-service training and refresher courses abounded. The fall in the marriage and birth rates partly reflected a questioning of the value of commitment to the future. In England and Wales, the proportion of illegitimate births was rising towards 10 per cent in the later 1980s. In Scotland, it was 12 per cent at the end of the decade (Thompson, ed., 1990, 2, 35). In France, for all its Roman Catholic traditions, the annual number of divorces per 100 marriages rose from 13.1 in 1972 to 29.1 in 1984 (ADA, 1986, 238).

Meanwhile, confidence in the future was replaced by a hankering after security in the past. The historic heritage of western Europe was protected even more than in the past, and interest in the conservation of nature increased. Not only did interest grow in the heritage of the distant past, including the Parthenon and Chartres cathedral, it also encompassed efforts to create or honour the past of the industrial era.

In Barcelona, the fantastic, organic, historicist architecture of Antonio Gaudí, kept alive for many years by democratic and nationalistic aspirations in Catalonia, began to gain a wider respect in the 1960s. The buildings were refurbished, new guides were printed, and ambitious plans to complete Gaudí's biggest church, the Sagrada Familia, were set in train. A decade later, the work of a more neglected architect, Charles Rennie Mackintosh, was resurrected in Glasgow by a group of enthusiasts, backed by funds from the City of Glasgow and the Strathclyde Regional Council. As industrial Glasgow declined and was converted into a centre of services and leisure with the help of public funds, Mackintosh emerged as the symbol of an ideal Glasgow. An unbuilt design of 1901 by Mackintosh, the *Haus eines Kunstfreundes*, was built from scratch in a Glasgow park, complete with conforming furniture.

Yet neither Gaudí nor Mackintosh came from a distant past. Both had flourished around 1900, and their achievement was to create an alternative to industrialism in the midst of the industrialisation process. Both created images which already dwelt in the mind of the beholder – the bedtime story, the child's illustrated book, Snow White, the seaside holiday, the coloured lantern. Meanwhile, the modernist images which had excited the 1960s – the tower block of flats, or the Concorde airliner – faded or disturbed. One symbol of the transition must suffice. In the late 1970s Jaguar cars started to produce a big sports car, the styling of which was *not* intended to look modern. It did not look very elegant either, but it conveyed a feeling of solidity and durability. Expensive cars, it implied, would have to last longer than in the past, so the design should not go out of date too quickly. In 1995, the Rover car company, now owned by BMW, relaunched the nostalgic MG sports car which had gone out of production in 1980. In the 1980s this 'retro' taste was developed in many fields of design. The word 'modern' almost went out of use, to be partially replaced by 'post-industrial', 'post-modern', 'post-Fordist' and other terms expressive of the uncertainty of the day.

Urban life and housing

The deceleration of economic growth from the 1970s coincided with the virtual completion of urbanisation across most of western Europe. Most urban development since the war had taken place in and around the larger cities. The middle classes had been able to acquire 'second homes' in the countryside, taking over the cottages vacated by rural people migrating to the cities. This phenomenon had been especially marked in France, where a quaint usage, 'gîte rural', was revived to describe cottages let to holidaymakers. However, the three-quarters of the urban populations who worked in manual or low-paid service jobs were trapped in the cities for almost the whole year.

Most of their housing was either pre-1914 stock with limited facilities and dimensions, or flats built in the various areas of the public sector (local authority, cooperative, trade union, self-build) in the 1950s and 1960s. The standards of these dwellings were low, generally because so much investment was being directed into industrial production at the time, while generous public subsidies were seen as inflationary. Much high-rise housing in northern Europe could no longer attract the lower middle classes and skilled workers, and some came to be occupied exclusively by people of non-European origin.

Traditionally Europe's urban masses had lived in flats, and urbanisation in southern Europe from the 1950s had taken this form almost exclusively. Only in England and adjoining Belgium, the Netherlands, and parts of northern France and Germany had single-family housing predominated. Public opinion polls in France had shown a preference for single-family housing as early as the 1950s, but building and land costs were too high to allow a general move in this direction.

During the 1970s, however, the balance of demand and supply turned in favour of single-family housing. In Stockholm, for instance, 70 per cent of new dwellings were in apartments in the 1960s. By 1977, 70 per cent were in single-family houses. In the Paris New Towns there had been a restriction on the number of new single-family houses built to 30 per cent of the total, but this limit was abolished in 1976–77 and developers were subsequently *encouraged* to build single-family houses (White, 1984, 51–2).

In southern Europe, on the other hand, rapid urbanisation meant tall blocks of flats everywhere, continuing an established tradition which dated back to the Middle Ages. With effective residential planning generally absent, the blocks were often huddled together at very high densities. The flats were usually very small, and overcrowding was much greater in southern Europe than in the North (White, 1984, 54). Private builders produced most of the housing, and speculation and economising together depressed the standard of the housing provided. Paradoxically, perhaps the biggest environmental disaster of all occurred on the 'Costas', the Mediterranean coast of Spain, where the aptly named 'urbanización' phenomenon, beginning in the mid-1960s as foreign capital was drawn into Spain, produced an arid belt of apartments and villas, virtually devoid of careful planning.

Mobility and mobility substitution

The spread of the telephone made a massive, and largely unacknowledged, contribution to European social life. In West Germany, the proportion of households with a telephone soared from a mere 12.5 per cent in 1968 to 69.3 per cent ten years later (Leaman, 1988, 205). The British trend was similar (Bowden and Offer, 1994, 744). In Spain, there were 59 telephones per thousand population in 1960 and 135 in 1970 (Payne, 1987, 485). This transformation was partly the result of national policy which ensured the necessary investment in lines and exchanges.

A similar revolution took place in France in the 1970s and 1980s, when long-distance public telephone cabins sprouted in even the smallest villages and nearly every call got through at last. As late as the 1960s, to make a public telephone call had usually meant going into a bar and buying a drink, together with an over-priced token with a groove on one side, or a larger, thinner token without a groove. This system, which was often known as the 'Taxiphone', condemned the client to making his call from the toilets. Long-distance calls involved lengthy queueing at a post office or at a large cafe with an *Interurbain* service run by harassed telephonists. By 1991, France had one telephone for every 1.7 people, compared to 1.0 in Sweden and the USA, 1.3 in Britain and Norway, and 1.7 in Germany (*Economist*, 1993, 74).

In the South, a more subdued telephonic revolution occurred in the 1980s and 1990s. In Italy, there was one telephone for 1.9 people by 1991, and in Spain there was one for 2.3 people. In some cases, as in Greece, where there was one telephone for every 2.2 people by 1991, the spread of cabins and domestic connections put a big strain on the trunk lines and exchanges, but social relations were transformed by these revolutions, so often neglected by social historians.

The motor car nevertheless remained a key creator of mobility after 1970. Already well under way by 1970, the process of motorisation continued thereafter. In northern Europe, where there had been extensive car ownership by 1970, the motor revolution had already taken place and growth thereafter simply produced a saturation effect. The rate of growth in the number of private cars was lower after 1970 but the provision of new roads and parking now reached maturity in the North, allowing a more efficient use of motor vehicles in urban areas. This brought about a marked change in their spatial structure towards lower densities, the emergence of functionally specialised districts, and the growth of smaller towns within reach of the big cities and conurbations. In West Germany, 79.8 per cent of households had a car in 1978, compared to only 43.3 per cent ten years before (Leaman, 1988, 204). In 1990, 122.4 million private cars were in use in western Europe, compared to 64.8 million in 1970 and 6.1 million in 1950 (Clout, 1994, 173).

In southern Europe, however, lower living standards and very high population densities in the big cities (which restricted parking space) kept car ownership much lower than in the North. For instance, the rate of private car ownership in the south in 1980 was only half that of northern Europe (Ambrosius and Hubbard, 1989, 76). In about 1985, the level of car ownership in Italy was nearly as high as in West Germany, but in Portugal and Greece the level was about one-third that of West Germany (*Economist*, 1987, 23). In Spain, the number of cars per thousand people increased by more than seven times in the 1960s but it was still no more than seventy in 1970 (Payne, 1987, 485. By 1988–91 it had risen to 320 per thousand people, but this ranked it only fourteenth in western Europe, and compared to 490 in Germany (*Economist*, 1993, 56).

FIGURE 11.5 *Number of cars per 100 people, 1988–91.*

USA	57
Luxembourg	50
Germany	49
Italy	46
Switzerland	46
France	42
Sweden	42
Austria	39
Belgium	39
Finland	38
Netherlands	37
Norway	35
UK	35
Denmark	32
Spain	32

Source: based on *Economist*, 1994, 56.

Newspapers

Newspaper sales, which had climbed almost everywhere in western Europe after the war, stabilised in the 1960s. Britain's home delivery system was not emulated elsewhere, and while two working-class daily newspapers in Britain had a circulation of over 4 million, the biggest German equivalent sold only 2.5 million copies to a much bigger population. Competition from television and radio became a growing threat from the 1960s. Some newspapers closed, and ownership increasingly fell into the hands of a small number of 'press barons', such as Lord Beaverbrook in Britain and Axel Springer in Germany (Ambrosius and Hubbard, 1989, 112–13).

In the 1970s, Rupert Murdoch, a forceful Australian entrepreneur, started to buy up British newspapers. He also launched a new working-class paper, *The Sun*, which aimed at the least educated section of the British population and soon achieved a record circulation. In the 1990s he developed growing interests in television with his Sky satellite network. Murdoch's main English rival, Robert Maxwell, owned a daily newspaper of socialist allegiance, a popular paper in New York, a weekly concentrating on news from the whole of western Europe, *The European*, and an English football club. His efforts to buy other clubs were thwarted by the Football League.

Maxwell's mysterious death in 1991 left his business operations under such a cloud of suspicion that the wide range of his interests was forgotten. However, his football club ambitions struck a chord in Italy, where the media magnate, Silvio Berlusconi, who built up a newspaper and television empire in Italy and France by the early 1980s, also owned Inter, the leading Italian football club, based in Milan. In 1994 Berlusconi entered the Italian parliamentary elections at the head of a loose coalition of business-friendly parties. Entitled *Forza Italia*, a football-related slogan, Berlusconi's movement claimed to want to remove the corruption from Italian politics, and to govern efficiently. Berlusconi became Prime Minister, but within a year he was forced to resign because of his own earlier corruption. This link between the mass media, the masses of sporting supporters, corruption, and political ambitions, was disturbing.

By 1995 western Europe had not developed a common media structure. This was partly due to language differences. Robert Maxwell's attempt at an English-language European weekly newspaper, *The European*, founded in 1990 largely as an expensive integrationist gesture, survived his death. Ironically, it was little read in Britain despite its mainly British editorial staff, but the quality of its coverage of news and opinion across Europe secured it a growing readership at an informed level throughout the continent. By 1995 it had a big business section, in which the English language could function to full effect. Its 'Letters to the Editor', a quintessentially English feature, attracted letters from non-anglophones and anglophones in equal numbers. In the last issue of June 1995, for instance, 'Letters to the Editor' included eight letters from correspondents with English names, and six from people with non-English names. Even more striking was the spread of addresses, which did not coincide with the supposed nationality of the names. Three of the English names wrote from France, one wrote from Germany, and a Russian wrote from Switzerland.

It was clear that any successful European weekly or daily would have to be published in English. A number of serious weeklies had built up wide circulations in Europe since before the war, and could be regarded in effect as European publications. They included a number of American titles with European editions, such as *Time*, and the British *The Economist*. The close link between business and the English language ruled out the emergence of rivals in other languages.

Britain, despite its long traditions of professional sport and newspapers, did not support major sporting newspapers. The big contrast here was with southern Europe. In 1991 the three sporting dailies in Italy had a total circulation of over a million, and the French *L'Equipe* sold nearly 300,000. Spain and Greece had four sporting dailies between them, and even Portugal had one (Féron and Thoraval, 1992, 286). *L'Equipe*'s longstanding success probably reflected the regional structure of the French provincial dailies, which hindered national reporting of sport. In the four Mediterranean countries, there may be a connection with the Fascist encouragement of sport in earlier years. Overall, however, professional sport, which had developed on a large scale in the 1950s and 1960s, became increasingly linked to television.

The growth of the electronic media had not greatly undermined the daily newspaper press by 1995. In northern Europe, the press increasingly divided into a middle-class segment composed of papers dealing with politics and business, and a mass circulation press dealing with sex and violence. *Bild*, the German popular paper, had a circulation of 5.4 million in 1991. The even more lurid *Sun*, Robert Murdoch's crude British 'tabloid', had a circulation of 3.8 million. An intermediate group of newspapers aimed at the lower middle class, such as the British *Daily Mail* and the French *Libération*. In southern Europe, sensational tabloids had not developed, with big national and regional newspapers predominating, full of factual news and reports of humdrum events. A big home of regional newspapers was France, reflecting its great area and non-industrial tradition. In 1991, 77 regional dailies were published in France, the biggest being *Ouest France*, with a circulation of 775,000. None of the German regional dailies reached this size, but this was because there were so many of them – 375 or, if the separate editions are counted as independent newspapers, 1260 (Féron and Thoraval, 1992, 286).

Radio and television broadcasting

Cultural changes are always difficult to locate precisely in historical time, but the saturation of western Europe by radio and television broadcasting was clearly under way in the 1960s. Transistor radios, the beginnings of colour television in the mid-1960s, and mass ownership of television sets (and, in Britain, rental arrangements), flooded the whole of western Europe, including the relatively impoverished South. Indoor toilets and showers were the unattainable luxury of this era for many people. Thanks to mass production of the receivers, and the very low cost of radio wave transmission, radio and television could enrich the life of even the poorest home. By 1995, some 98 per cent of homes in the developed world had a television set (Smith, 1995, 2). A similar saturation level for radios had been reached in the 1960s.

Radio, the great communications innovation of the inter-war years, had emerged at a time when governments feared popular unrest fomented by mass communications. Cinema censorship is the best-known result of this fear, but radio was also affected. By the mid-1920s national and regional stations dominated the scene, exemplified by the BBC, which broadcast from 1926 under the terms of a 'charter'. Presented as the independent purveyor of 'truth', the BBC became, under its first Director-General, John Reith, a strongly conservative and elitist force.

Towards the end of the 1930s commercial radio began to emerge as a serious challenge to the national systems. Radio

Luxembourg, a private challenge to the BBC and a specialist in the popular music which Reith abhorred, dates from 1929. It soon began to broadcast directly to England with its pulse transmitter which produced a distinctive, and annoying, sound undulation on reception in England. Tolerably audible only at night, Radio Luxembourg was an adventure in listening which indicated a very large popular demand for entertainment based on popular music.

After the Second World War, there was a movement towards the rationalisation of radio broadcasting over most of western Europe. In France, the private radio stations, which had broadcast alongside those of the postal authorities between 1923 and 1941, were not revived after the Liberation. Instead, a State broadcasting system, Radiodiffusion et Télévision Française (RTF), came into existence in 1945 (Paulu, 1967, 59). In western Germany, the Allied stations were replaced from the later 1940s by nine *Land*-based stations set up between 1948 and 1959, the last of these, predictably, being in the Saar (Paulu, 1967, 64). The Italian broadcasting company changed its name to RAI (Radio Audizioni Italia) in 1944, but otherwise retained the features of the State corporation set up under the Fascists in 1927. In 1952 a new charter incorporated television (Paulu, 1967, 76). All this left little room for private commercial stations. Only four were operating in western Europe in the 1960s.

The new British youth culture of the 1960s had a radical effect on radio. During and after the war, the BBC had adopted a more popular pattern of entertainment with music on 'Workers' Playtime' and 'Semprini Serenade' lines. By 1960 this fare was out of touch with rock 'n' roll, other American imports, and skiffle, and interests in the record and advertising worlds set up a number of 'pirate' radio stations, most of them based on tethered ships in the North Sea (Paulu, 1967, 21). From here, Radio Caroline and several others could broadcast pop music into the London area with impunity. Execrated at first by the BBC, the pirate stations built up a huge audience including large numbers of workers. Radio London acquired a weekly audience of over 10 million. Garage repair shops, laundries, and warehouses all over the South-east throbbed to the crudest sounds, emitted by transistor radios. From now on, silent manual work was a virtual impossibility.

The BBC eventually came to tolerate its commercial rivals. Between 1967 and 1970 Parliament outlawed the pirate stations on the understanding that the BBC would begin to feature popular music on a new channel, Radio 1. A system of BBC local radio stations was authorised, with local BBC stations competing with authorised private local stations playing almost continuous popular music.

This new stability in Britain was followed by a surge of private radio stations on the continent after the student and youth disturbances of 1968. Italy (1975), France (1977), Belgium (1978) and Spain (1979) went down this path. The south of Europe quickly became a sea of sound, illicit at first but soon legalised. By 1992, Italy had twenty private radio networks and some 3,000 local stations. Bi-lingual Belgium had 650 private stations. In the former Fascist countries, the collapse of the big official stations led to a rapid growth of independent radios, notably in Spain. Where the system was already partially in private hands under national legislation, further proliferation was more difficult (Féron and Thoraval, 1992, 288–9). In Britain with its competing but regulated local radio networks, 'pirate' stations were unable to operate except as brief publicity stunts, campaigning for greater freedom. This shoestring radio contrasted with capital-intensive, big-business television.

When television broadcasting resumed in the late 1940s and early 1950s, it was based almost everywhere on the existing radio structures. The BBC relaunched its pre-war service in 1946. In Belgium, government control was essential to ensure that the needs of the Walloon and Flemish populations were clearly and fairly met. In France, however, criticisms of excessive State control of broadcasting, which had multiplied under De Gaulle, were met by the creation in 1964 of the ORTF (Office de Radiodiffusion-Télévision Française) (Paulu, 1967, 58–9). This was an independent body modelled partly on the BBC. The British experiment with a rival, 'commercial' system (Independent Television Authority – ITA), set up in 1955, was not generally followed until after 1984, when Germany, France and Denmark set up private systems operating alongside the State stations in line with current enthusiasm for privatisation and competition. In Luxembourg, television was set up from scratch by a private company, also in 1955, following pre-war radio traditions in that small country. In Spain and Portugal, governments were especially favourable to State television which was seen as a cheap means of securing popular acquiescence for authoritarian regimes.

In western Germany, 74 per cent of households had a television by 1969; by 1972, 95 per cent were equipped (Materialien, 1974, 253). By the 1980s the equipment of households with television sets was at its practical maximum almost everywhere. In 1991, 99.2 per cent of households in Italy had a television. Even Ireland had 95.3 per cent. Depending on the country, the average spectator watched on average for between two and four hours a day. In Britain, the average daily viewing time, over the period 1960–83, was two hours and fourteen minutes per day, compared to a US average of two hours and two minutes (Bowden and Offer, 1994, 736–7). Almost everywhere, the evening news programme was a rare occasion in the day when all the members of the family came together (Féron and Thoraval, 1992, 295). However, from around 1985 the increasingly competitive nature of the national television systems produced a gradual reduction in the hours devoted to serious programmes, and an expansion of entertainment programmes.

Europe-wide broadcasting was complicated by the variety of languages, but sport and musical entertainment were a big success from the early 1950s. Eurovision, an association of national television systems, was established in 1954. Television relays of football matches began in 1955, in step with the European Cup. The Eurovision Song Contest was set up shortly afterwards, teaching the European masses a little basic French and English ('deux points'). Most successful of all was the inter-town competition, *Jeux sans frontières*, launched in the 1960s. The title was of linguistic interest because, whereas nearly all the participating countries used the continental title or a direct translation of it, Britain clung to its own domestic title of *It's a Knockout*. The national comperes were a rumbustious and polyglot lot and the game appealed to a 'holiday camp' audience which proved to be a large one throughout Europe.

The 1980s and 1990s saw the rapid proliferation of two advanced transmission methods, partially linked to new production companies. Cable television, originating in the 1960s, was the less revolutionary, as the cables were normally used to carry the programmes of existing companies, though these could be multiplied almost to infinity by access to foreign stations. Satellite transmission, available to existing companies for a rental payment from 1983, and carrying more than eighty programmes in Europe by 1990, was also not necessarily a transforming force, but Britain's biggest media entrepreneur, Rupert Murdoch, broke through into a new world when he set up a multinational production and broadcasting company, BSkyB, in 1989 (Smith, 1995, 163). Although watched mainly in Britain, and broadcasting in English, it was available elsewhere in Europe via the Luxembourg-based Astra satellite, or by cable. Other stations with European aspirations included the English-language Eurosport, Screensport, and the American-owned MTV Europe, the francophone TV5 Europe, and the German Eins Plus. CNN, the round-the-clock American news station, founded in 1981, built up a big satellite audience in Europe by the 1990s.

Sky TV was widely watched throughout Europe from its beginnings in 1991, strengthening the role of the English language outside countries such as Sweden and the Netherlands, whose television programmes had long included English material, often without subtitles. Sky TV broadcast little apart from news and old cinema films, in order to limit production costs, but the potential for a European television was clearly visible, along with the European newspaper press foreshadowed by *The European*. Also visible was a partial privatisation of European television, in line with both the developing potential of technology, and contemporary economic orthodoxy.

The cinema

As a barometer of mass leisure, the cinema had been affected by the rise of television and the growth of new leisure pursuits in the 1950s and 1960s. Even in southern Europe it was eventually affected by the rise of television.

The European decline in cinema attendances began in the later 1950s. Cinemas began to close in rural areas and in the industrialised North. In West Germany, attendances fell from a peak of 818 million in 1956 to 144 million in 1980, when only half the number of cinemas were open as in the peak year of 1959 (Ambrosius and Hubbard, 1989, 114). In the 1980s, however, it made a strong revival, with an audience mainly of young people. Multiple cinemas were now built outside the towns on American lines, often by American companies like National Amusements. Hollywood output became more prolific, swamping the European industry except in France. The films were intended to be purely entertaining but this was what the young audience required. Indeed, their subjects were mainly youth, adventure, and modern life, with some of the more intelligent films, such as Woody Allen's portrayals of neurotic young intellectuals in New York, holding a mirror up to the life of the audience.

The French cinema industry was still the biggest in Europe but the demise of the *nouvelle vague* in the later 1960s threw it back into the arms of American influence. A number of historical and romantic films were made in collaboration with Italian production companies in order to compete with the more expensive American productions but the result, inevitably, was American in character. Foreign directors, including Joseph Losey, were invited to make films in France but the results were often uneasy, neither French nor international. Luis Bunuel was the most successful of them, but he was allowed to pursue his perennial theme of an aimless and cynical bourgeoisie. His *Le charme discret de la bourgeoisie*, a French/Spanish/Italian co-production of 1972, recalled Sartre's *Huis clos* as a group of idle, bored bourgeois wander about a mysterious Paris, unable to situate themselves in time or space.

Younger directors, aiming for the growing audience of prosperous young people in the new suburbs, followed the American example by telling stories about dynamic but rather shiftless young people, with an emphasis on beauty. Luc Besson's *Subway* (1985) showed its athletic young heroes evading the police in the Paris metro. His *Nikita* (1990) dealt with a nihilistic young girl criminal. *Les amants du Pont-Neuf* (1991), by Léos Carax, a story of two young Paris tramps, featured the largest outdoor set ever built in France. However, Carax's romantic emphasis on his huge 'Paris' set and his sentimental treatment of his main characters echoed the parallel growth of a renewed 'cinéma de qualité', stressing traditional and historic themes drawn from French history and literature, after about 1985. Gérard Depardieu emerged as the leading star of films of this type. They reflected the interest in the historical heritage which emerged throughout Europe in the 1980s and 1990s. Meanwhile, the French realist tradition disappeared almost completely, to be replaced by television reportage. Susan Hayward has described the French cinema of the 1980s and early 1990s as 'pastiche culture' (Hayward, 1993, 283). A daring judgment, this, but if French culture can succumb to the conservatism and caution of the European arts at the end of the century, what hope is there for the rest of Europe?

British films also exploited the national heritage and a warm, historical past, both in terms of sets and stories. The main milestone was the spectacular historical romance, *The Charge of the Light Brigade* (1968). The director, Tony Richardson, had scored a huge success with his picaresque romp, *Tom Jones*, in the wildly swinging England of 1963. Now, he portrayed a glorious event from Britain's imperial past in a sober, careful manner stressing historical experience. Some films made extensive use of historic or landscape locations. Others made use of the country's huge collections of antique cars and historic railway lines to create a sentimental atmosphere. The beautiful English countryside was used to calm and reassure rather than to excite.

In Germany, history now played, if not a reassuring role, then one through which a nation could share in recent historical experiences which otherwise would have lurked in the individual mind. Ever since the war, the reeducation of Germany and the quest for international recognition and responsibility had produced an ambivalent attitude towards German national traditions. From the late 1960s, however, creative confidence grew and direct portrayals of German experience, including the Third Reich, began to appear. One symbol of the change was the occasional appearance of Hitler's portrait on the front cover of *Der Spiegel* after years in which his deteriorating physiognomy had been kept well out of the way. In the cinema, stories of working-class life were common, but country tales, like *Mathias Kneissl* (1971), were especially popular, portraying as they did fundamental human relationships in an environment untainted by industrialisation and National Socialism. The film director, Wim Wenders, made several films dealing with the German past. Other directors made films directly for television but released versions of them for cinema showing. Some of these stressed the strengths of German society in the long run. *Das Boot* (1981), the most expensive German production up to that time, and *Stalingrad* (1993) portrayed Nazi Germany as a horror which devoured decent people. Implicitly, nothing was left behind. However, most films on post-war Germany were pessimistic in their interpretation, implying that no escape from the Nazi past was possible, either in western or eastern Germany.

For the average viewer, the most popular solution to the conflict of benign tradition and perverted nationalism was the *Heimat* (heritage) film, which originated in the late 1960s. This genre culminated in *Heimat* (1980–84), a multi-part television production (mini-series) by Edgar Reisz, which took the viewer at the gentlest of paces through the history of a small village in the obscure Hunsrück region from the First World War to the present day in the mid-1980s. The story stressed human values in the context of an eternal Germany. History now rescued Germany from its past, but the future, in the cinema as elsewhere, secured little attention.

Largely undisturbed by war and brutal industrialisation, the Nordic cinema maintained a long tradition of interest in human values and relationships set in respected national societies. Drawing on the theatre of Ibsen, Kaj Munk and others, Nordic directors such as the Swedish Gustaf Molander pursued themes of self-perception and human interaction within close family environments. The veteran Danish director, Carl Dreyer, liked to pursue these issues within historical settings, as in his influential *Vredens dag* (Dies irae) (1943). Ingmar Bergman, the leading Swedish director of the 1950s and 1960s, valued this tradition, as he showed in *The Seventh Seal* (1956), but he became preoccupied with very close personal relationships which developed, or sometimes did not develop, in claustrophobic interiors redolent of life in the long northern winters. *The Silence* (1963) and *Persona* (1966) rather overdid this subject. Meanwhile, the more modest film industries of Norway and Finland retained an interest in the development of popular life in two countries which had no tradition of distortion or caricature. Honesty, modesty and realism characterised their work, with sensitive issues such as the occupation of Norway by German forces, and Finland's successful efforts to defend its national independence, treated with care and perception.

Outsiders are often tempted to believe that Nordic films, and especially those of Sweden, provide an insight into life in a confusing world of gloomy winters and sunny summer nights. Nordic people try to disabuse them of this.

Sex: image and reality

A revolution in the understanding and portrayal of sex occurred in the late 1960s and the early 1970s (and the Swedish cinema definitely played a part here). Homosexuality, a quite common phenomenon in the media and the arts, got a good press in the late 1970s and even more in the 1990s, once the AIDS scare of the 1980s had largely died down. Pornography flourished in the 1970s after becoming the latest New York elite fad in 1973, with generous Dutch laws on sexual entertainment allowing Amsterdam to become the European capital of this business. 'Sex shops' multiplied throughout most of urban Europe and even in Britain the police became more tolerant of them, at any rate in the 1970s and the early 1980s. In France, where Giscard d'Estaing made a point of relaxing censorship in 1974, pornographic films made up half the total screenings between 1975 and 1979 (Hayward, 1993, 244). *Emmanuelle* (1974) was the first successful semi-pornographic film on the main circuits. It was a huge success in France and throughout Europe, and became the model for many more such films. It topped the box office returns in France in 1974, and it attracted more than 2 million spectators in Paris (Hayward, 1993, 245). This type of film carried on into the 1990s, if increasingly on late night television and on commercial video, but the more daring pornography was restrained by the police in the more censorious 1980s and 1990s. Largely untroubled by the law, meanwhile, was the healthy, fun-loving photographic nude like the 'Page Three girls' launched by Rupert Murdoch's new British daily, *The Sun*, in 1970. This type of naturistic illustration had been common in the mass German press much earlier, with even *Der Spiegel*, a serious news magazine, managing to justify including one nude photograph in *every* issue by the later 1960s.

Prostitution became more widespread, especially in countries like Britain where welfare benefits were reduced in the 1980s. Rising average incomes and increased car ownership were probably the main factors in this trend. Toleration of street prostitution in Britain in the 1960s was replaced by a tougher police stance from the 1970s and much prostitution moved to saunas and massage parlours. Urban renewal was sometimes aimed at 'red light districts'; some of the tougher areas of central Barcelona, for instance, were gutted in preparation for the Olympic Games of 1992. In Germany, municipally controlled 'Eros centres', set up from the later 1950s, catered especially for immigrant workers. Mobile prostitutes and home visits multiplied in the 1980s as the girls became as motorised as their clients. In France, the Minitel computer/television system was a big vehicle for random contacts, especially in the Paris area. Free advertising newspapers served a similar purpose. In 1990s Britain most prostitutes were in their early twenties. Many had children, two being the usual number. A boyfriend, who was not necessarily the father of the children, helped out with the children and the telephone when the mother was 'working', but he did not usually live in, partly for social security reasons. This was, of course, a peripheral form of family living but it provides an extreme indication of the fragmentation of the traditional, nuclear family which was coming about in the 1990s, especially among the working classes and parts of the immigrant population. Difficult to observe scientifically because of the dearth of tax and social security information relating to the individuals concerned, it was a symptom of the fluid community of the public housing estate and the multi-occupied slum.

Education

Education was directly affected by the gloomier economic climate after about 1970. Young people leaving education found it especially hard to find jobs as unemployment increased. At times, and in certain countries, the schools were used to keep youngsters out of the labour market for a year or two. A bigger element of training for employment was introduced into the syllabus. The general tendency was for young people to spend longer in school, though there were important national variations. In Britain, the population aged 15–64 in 1950 had spent an average of 9.4 years in formal education. In 1980, the equivalent average figure was 10.66 years. The equivalent French figure in 1980 was 10.3 years. This was a big advance for France, which had recorded only 8.18 years in 1950, but the increase was probably associated mainly with the big shift in population from the countryside, with its limited provision for secondary education, to the town. Education had played a big part in the 'national renewal' reforms favoured by De Gaulle after 1944, but the actual changes had not been very great (Shennan, 1989, 169–87). The German figure in 1950 was 8.51 years, and this had risen only to 9.41 by 1980, somewhat belying the myth of Germany as a well educated country (Maddison, 1989, 136).

Meanwhile, as a huge area of public expenditure, education was subject to budgetary pressure from the early 1970s, and cuts became serious after 1979 as governments pursued tough anti-inflationary policies. Increased State scrutiny of education led to an emphasis on visible savings and practical objectives. School-children and students, worried by the prospect of unemployment, responded well to new training courses and schemes. Education, meanwhile, moved away from the critical, liberating experience which it had become between 1945 and the 1960s. It became an important part of the creation of a more materialistic, conservative but practical mentality which marked western Europe after about 1980.

Rural life

By 1995 agriculture in northern Europe had become the work of a small minority. In Germany, for instance, two-thirds of the agricultural workforce disappeared between 1950 and 1975; as a proportion of the national workforce it fell from 34 per cent to 7 per cent (Borchardt, 1991, 109). In southern Europe many more people worked in agriculture, but the trend was in the same direction. By 1989, agricultural workers made up only 13 per cent of the workforce in Spain, and in Portugal the proportion was 19 per cent. This move away from the land destroyed the myth of rural life as a national ideal, which it had been in Germany in the 1930s, and to some extent also in France. However, it allowed the creation of a new myth based on a romanticised, protected but virtually deserted countryside dotted with holiday cottages.

Nature and conservation

Urbanisation and economic growth were a threat to western Europe's natural and historic inheritance. Rising incomes, on the other hand, could make funds available to restore and protect the historic heritage, and to conserve the natural heritage. In northern Europe in particular, opinion moved strongly in favour of conservation in the 1960s. The trend was reinforced from the 1970s as slower growth and uncertainty made people value the past, and as more leisure time was available to them to enjoy the heritage.

In southern Europe, nature was less valued and some of it succumbed to the worst effects of industrialisation and urbanisation. Italy's post-war ambitions in oil refining did untold damage to the Mediterranean. By the 1960s the water lapping on the beaches of Rapallo and other resorts of the Italian Riviera was covered by a permanent layer of oil, while the foundations of Venice were gnawed by a noxious cocktail of damaging pollutants. The lack of a tide in the Mediterranean made it very difficult to keep the beaches clean.

The urban heritage of southern Europe, on the other hand, was very well protected, especially in Italy where historic and artistic monuments had been carefully preserved since the nineteenth century. There were some horrors, like the spreading working-class flats and power cables of eastern and southern Rome which encroached on ancient remains unique in Europe, but the South generally knew how to hold on to its greatest resource. It was, however, Britain that led Europe in public conservation after 1945. The countryside around her towns was statutorily protected by green belts from 1955. A network of national parks was set up in 1949. The Civic Amenities Act of 1967 extended protection to entire urban districts, mainly by the designation of conservation areas in which even minor changes required approval and funds were available for enhancement or the recreation of original features. By 1991 over 1,600 conservation areas were in existence (Cullingworth and Nadin, 1994, 160). The Countryside Act of 1968 was comparable in its purpose, allowing the creation of country parks where suitable forms of recreation could be encouraged, and helping to prevent jarring intrusions into the rural scene. The Landmark Trust, a private organisation devoted to the restoration of historic buildings of the second rank, was founded by a rich benefactor, (Sir) John Smith, in 1965. The Landmark Trust acquired buildings which were usually not of sufficient interest to command the involvement of the State or the National Trust (founded 1895). When restored, the buildings were made available as holiday homes, thus broadening the concept of historic preservation from an exhibit to a living experience. In the 1980s, the National Trust also began to rent cottages on its estates to holidaymakers.

In France, towns were similarly protected, by legislation dating back to 1837. Under the Fifth Republic, in 1962, the 'Malraux Law' extended De Gaulle's reforming ideal to historic protection, partly with a view to strengthening the national heritage in order to reinforce the foundations of De Gaulle's strongly patriotic regime. The new powers permitted the enhancement of very large urban areas, using the principle of the *secteur sauvegardé*. As in Italy, where civic efforts to conserve some of the older districts of historic towns had become effective in the 1960s, the restoration work was so expensive that private funds had to be attracted. Rents rose as a result, and many of the original, low-income tenants had to leave or were not replaced. The resulting phenomenon of *embourgeoisement*, a term of almost universal European currency by the later 1960s, was detected in the Marais, in Paris, by 1970. In the Marais, an almost undisturbed area of seventeenth- and eighteenth-century mansions, the process of environmental renewal went on into the 1990s, turning it into a byword for the ultra-chic. This equation of history, success and wealth – much of it distinctly *nouveau* – had a political implication, with wealth seeking legitimation in a partially artificial past, as it had done in the nineteenth century (see Dellheim, 1982, 24–46). Meanwhile, Presidents Pompidou and Mitterrand added new monuments like the Pompidou Centre and the Bastille opera house to the old, associating their personal power with national tradition.

In western Germany, the conservation campaign took on a party-political character which took it beyond environmental interests. The Greens, who grew up in the later 1970s, were mainly a youth movement protesting against what they saw as the materialism and philistinism of German society. In 1979 they obtained seats in the state parliament of Bremen (Laqueur, 1985, 57). With its small electorate and Left-wing university, Bremen had been an easy target for extremism since the late 1960s. By 1983, however, the Greens had seats in the Bundestag. Normally they secured only 5–7 per cent of the votes, but they often had enough seats to disrupt normal government and this encouraged some of their anarchic and socialistic members. Many of the issues they adopted were only remotely related to the environment. In the later 1980s their sinister, semi-revolutionary side became clearer and, after some major scandals, they weakened in the early 1990s.

Elite culture

After 1945, elite culture responded to the perceived needs and opportunities of the day and contributed extensively to the comprehension of the post-war world, and to the creation of further change. After 1970, its nature and role changed. Like so much of western European life, it looked to the past, reminiscing and reviving old successes, and returning to an old romanticism and whimsy. The Marxist philosophers of the university world, like Louis Althusser, lost much of their influence among students who now wanted a job-securing qualification rather than the chance to change the world. Novelists increasingly aimed at segments of the population, such as women, homosexuals, non-European immigrants, and the young middle class, rather than the reading public as a whole. It was more a time of special interests than of universality.

Even Paris, the cultural paradigm of Europe, fell victim to the post-1970 mood. At a time of doubt and frustration, Paris returned to the past. Tried-and-tested formulae were used in plays, operas and art exhibitions. The avant-garde of the 1940s, 1950s and

1960s, which all Europe had emulated, died away. Modernism was often replaced by a decadent but harmless rococo. Sometimes known as 'le post-moderne', this tendency failed to provide a model for the age (Larkin, 1988, 220). All over Europe, the theatre ceased to provide an insight into a rapidly changing world as it had after 1945. It was a refined, minority entertainment, without the 'kitchen sink'. The surge of interest in opera from the later 1980s had some of the features of a mass European movement, but it was, as opera had always been, an entertainment rather than a provoker of thought.

Broader audiences drew great pleasure from a new type of musical show pioneered in Britain, and exported to the USA and the continent of Europe, on a heavily capitalised basis more reminiscent of the cinema than the theatre. The pioneers here were (Sir) Andrew Lloyd Webber and Tim Rice, whose fast-moving, song-packed *Joseph and the Amazing Technicolor Dreamcoat* became a standard production in the 1970s, like a new *Messiah* of the later twentieth century. Lloyd Webber's success in managing and financing multiple, simultaneous productions led on to the unprecedented world-wide success of his *Cats* in the 1980s. His business company, formed in 1977 and floated on the London Stock Exchange in 1986 during the speculative boom, was hard hit by the world stock market crash of 1987, but he bought the company back in 1990 and by the mid-1990s was expanding into theatre acquisition and construction world-wide. By 1995, over a hundred million people had seen Webber shows across the world, and his company had a payroll of over 4,000 (*Voyager*, July/August 1995, 13–14). Lloyd Webber must have brought more new spectators into the theatre than any other impresario of his era. Not surprisingly, the entertainment provided was, on the whole, cheerful and sentimental. Here was no Angry Young Man. Instead, here was one of the richest men in England, still only forty-seven in 1995, yet able to buy Great Masters to hang in State art galleries. Some historians claim that the Italian Renaissance was the result of rich businessmen switching their investment into culture at a time of low economic growth. With the Lloyd Webbers, the Palumbos and the Sugars shaping British culture in the 1990s, a new age of the Medici had come about.

Youth culture

The idea of a youth culture no longer appeared so innocent and attractive as in the 1960s. An even more prosperous youth seemed to develop some unpleasant characteristics. In 1981, young people were responsible for over half of all violent crimes in the OECD countries (Dahrendorf, 1982, 4). The 'hooligan' emerged as a violent, conformist, young man in the early 1970s. Violence at British soccer matches, which had become a major problem from the later 1960s, spread throughout Europe in the later 1970s, fanned by television and growing travel by supporters to international Cup matches. The Heysel stadium disaster at Brussels in 1985, where rioting by Liverpool fans led to the deaths of dozens of peaceful Italians, was the climax of this anarchic behaviour, in that police controls gradually became more effective in the 1990s. Drunkenness and violence among the young also became a problem in Spanish holiday resorts by the 1980s, where the cheapest sunny holidays in Europe were available.

On a more positive note, American interest in personal fitness and health began to influence Europe in the 1970s. France took the lead and in 1975 fitness clubs were taking root there. They probably reflected, more than anything else, France's high-density cities. Jogging was very rare there because of the pressure of traffic. Elsewhere, jogging and cycling became increasingly common from the 1970s, as did a general interest in personal health and diet. The South, however, lagged in these areas, enjoying unhealthy, uncomfortable living, smoking and drinking to its heart's content while avoiding many of the neuroses of the North. This was one of the advantages of backwardness and in 1995 the South was still holding on to it tenaciously.

Rock concerts became even more frequent and more ambitious after 1970, and an underground sub-culture of drugs and caravanning built up around them. These communal occasions attracted much media interest. Perhaps more than any other mass phenomenon, they were completely classless, with young members of royal and aristocratic families participating as enthusiastically as the most mobile of 'new age travellers'. At the same time, the individual enjoyment of music took a huge step forward with the invention of the Sony Walkman in Japan and its launch in Europe in 1980. The Walkman allowed music to issue from the listener into the environment, thus incorporating the environment into the music even when the listener was mobile. As it also cut off the listener from the noises of the environment, it encouraged individualism, as did so much of post-1970 Europe. This contradiction between the individual, isolated soul and the continuing groupie existence of the 1960s was one of the complex features of the late twentieth century. The simple youth culture of the 1960s, so revolutionary in its day, had given way to something much more puzzling.

Indoor pastimes

Shorter working hours continued to have a big impact on leisure from the 1970s. Slower growth and work sharing after the oil crisis of 1973 tended to reduce the number of hours worked. In France, for instance, the average working week fell from 44.7 hours in 1970 to 40.8 hours in 1980 (Commission du Bilan, *Forces et faiblesses*, 1982, 198). Television, of course, took up most of the slack but higher education levels meant that indoor pastimes, which increasingly acquired a continental character through extensive marketing, continued to evolve. The letter-board game, Scrabble, copyrighted by the English firm of J.W. Spear and Sons in 1948, was developed in a large number of foreign language versions which swept Europe in the 1970s. Playable by adults and children at the same time, it was one of the few games which could persuade middle class families to turn off the television. A portable version for use during travel was developed for addicts.

Chess remained a minority pastime, except in Spain where it had long been a national pursuit, involving working people for the most part. Requiring quiet (except in Spain), it had a limited role as a social pastime and was more of an intellectual pursuit. The classic game of the upper and middle class, bridge, remained popular, especially in France where it often accompanied after-dinner conversation. Indeed, formal conversation after meals, and the uncomfortable, antique chairs that went with it, proved surprisingly persistent among the French middle classes. In southern Europe, the custom of sitting for long hours in cafes had not been disturbed by 1995, with the Greeks probably the European record-holders in this form of activity. Low activity rates in Greece probably contributed to this result, but at the same time the Greeks may have had a secret which had escaped the North. There may also have been a connection with Greece's only statistical world record, that of being the leading smoking nation (7.8 cigarettes per person per day in 1990, compared to 4.6 in Britain).

Holidays

The only depressive factor affecting holidays was the slower economic growth which set in from the mid-1970s. The real incomes of most people did not rise as fast as before and average per capita outlay on holidays increased more slowly. At the same time, the huge currency fluctuations which tended to occur between the early 1970s and the mid-1980s could cheapen holidays in certain countries for a few years, attracting a large new clientele. In the mid-1970s, a time of sub-tropical weather in Britain, foreign tourists flooded in, the intrepid Germans at their head, to take advantage of the cheap pound sterling. By 1980, the new British petro-pound was so valuable that droves of miners started to spend their summer holiday in Florida. In the 1990s, exotic Third World destinations such as India and the Caribbean were attracting working-class holidaymakers whose predecessors in the 1950s would have looked no further than Travemünde or Southend.

High unemployment did not threaten the holidays of those in employment, and high inflation from the early 1970s in industrialised Europe sometimes improved the terms of trade for the long-distance holiday-maker. The position of the unemployed was less clear, but in many cases their benefits were high enough to allow them to take a traditional summer holiday, especially when they had young children. Efforts to reduce the number of jobs through redundancies affected employees older than fifty-five for the most part, and many of these people had already stopped taking a traditional family holiday. There were, however, certain times when the trend towards very distant holidays was reversed in countries like Britain where currency depreciation could sometimes discourage foreign travel. At these times, domestic holidays again became customary and frustrated British tourists gasped once again at the Cotswolds and other beauties of their own country. In southern Europe, low living standards and currency exchange problems discouraged foreign holidays until the 1980s, except for single young people.

By the 1980s, most of Germany's organised labour had six weeks of paid holiday a year. Once the Stakhanovite 1950s were over, the

Germans used their strong mark to travel more widely than any other European people, rivalling the Americans in their ambitious destinations and active exploitation of their holiday investment. With Germany too expensive and not sufficiently attractive to draw many foreign tourists, the tourism account was heavily in deficit for Germany. The scale of that deficit indicates the progress of German foreign tourism; in 1980 it totalled DM26 billion.

In 1965 the Club Méditerrannée started to use the slogan, 'Sun, sea and sex'. By this time, however, its 1950s clientele of office staff and shop assistants seemed too limited and the Club started to open up more exotic 'villages' and sought to attract the middle classes through a higher standard of comfort and more stimulating activities. With French employees now enjoying four weeks of statutory paid holiday, investment in holiday facilities was very attractive. In the 1980s the Club opened many new sites, some of them thousands of miles away. The Club formula, which was very much like what a British holiday camp might be if it had a middle-class clientele, could appear dated but as time passed the average age of the holidaymakers increased, with addicts returning year after year. In 1995 the Club had to close a number of 'villages' but it was not clear whether a change in fashion, or over-extension in a period of recession, was to blame.

European languages

As western European countries ceded increasing powers to the EU, there was a growing scope for the development of regional societies and cultures. The discouragement of regional dialects and languages in the interests of national unity, which had reached its peak at the end of the nineteenth century, was no longer necessary. This regional diversity, as in Wales and Brittany for instance, was accompanied by the growing use of English as a common European language. This sprang largely from the American presence after the war, and a move towards English as first language in the schools. American and British mass culture also had an effect.

France was the main opponent of this trend. With its credentials as the language of diplomacy unchallenged after the war, French had been seen as the potential common language of the EU since the 1950s. In 1993 the French Minister of Culture, Jacques Toutbon, had a law passed requiring the use of French in scientific meetings in France, but this had little effect. As the number of member countries increased, the working language of the EU came increasingly to be English, even though each country had the right to use its own language in official business. The triumph of English could seem ironic and even unfair in the light of the notorious indifference of the British people towards learning foreign languages. However, it was logical enough. The British and the Americans owed the dominance of their language to the commercial prowess of their forebears in the nineteenth century. They bequeathed a great asset to their descendants, a universal language. As student travellers move across Europe in the summer, using their cheap rail passes, they can be heard communicating in English. To hear a Greek, a Portuguese, and a Belgian, say, in discussion on a station platform in Germany using a language generated in a once obscure north-western island is a moving experience and as potent a symbol of European integration as any Brussels circular.

Feminism and other special interests

After about 1970 special-interest movements became more common. Although they had a national basis, their minority character often led them to organise on a European scale. There were so many of these movements by the 1990s, backed by the media which increasingly sought news in the doings of minorities, that no attempt can be made to review them all here.

Typical of this tendency was feminism. Simone de Beauvoir's, *The Second Sex*, the basic text of the movement, was published in 1949, after the war had strengthened the position of women. Simone de Beauvoir was widely regarded as the model independent woman of the day. The book was widely read and admired by women and men, but did not spark off a women's movement. Women's vocal assertion of their rights did not begin until after 1968, in the wake of the student riots. Moreover, the basic ideology came from America, where feminism had started early in the 1960s. In Britain, feminism partially replaced the fashionable New Left position of the 1960s, which had united a large part of the young, socialist intelligentsia but which had sought general change. Its main impact was in the Nordic countries, where the social services backed women's independence, but Britain and the Netherlands were also affected

(Urwin, 1989, 242–3). France, and the South, were less affected, owing to Roman Catholic values and more traditional family structures. In May 1974, a referendum on divorce was held in Italy, and the pro-divorce tendency won a majority, but in 1981 an anti-abortion motion was defeated at a referendum in Italy.

What this meant was that until the 1970s, advocates of social change and people's rights pursued their aims via the reform of society as a whole. From the 1970s, increasingly, a fragmentation occurred. The old structures of social class, convention and national character were in decline, while associations linked to age, status and leisure interests were growing up. This sometimes produced alliances, for instance of male homosexuals and lesbians, or of anti-motorway campaigners and nature conservancy enthusiasts. However, the decline of most of the European Green parties in the 1990s showed that alliances of convenience could not always convince a broader public.

Corruption

In the early 1990s a great wave of corruption cases surfaced. In most cases they linked politics and business, and went back well into the past. Italy, as so often, was in the vanguard. Links between the Mafia and senior politicians reached up to the Prime Minister, in the case of Giulio Andreotti, who in 1994 was charged with illegal links with the Mafia over almost the whole of his career. A former Foreign Minister, Gianni De Michelis, was sentenced to four years in prison on corruption charges in 1995. In 1994 a number of senior politicians and businessmen were involved in corruption charges all over Europe. Magazines like *L'Express* liked to group their portraits, superimposed on a map of western Europe, to suggest a universal malaise. There were links with privatisation, football, Brussels, and television but, looking at these cases as a whole, one senses that the boundary between honesty and dishonesty, never very clear in public life, had become even more blurred since the 1960s. The Rice-Davies Principle now applied more strongly than ever.

Political violence

During the 1960s, new radical thinking and mass protest had welled up, especially among university students. By the early 1970s the emphasis of protest had switched to small groups which were prepared to make their point through violence. Some of their members were elderly students, veterans of the street demonstrations, but others were a motley of activists and malcontents drawn from a variety of backgrounds, including crime. Women were prominent in these groups. Ideology was confused but virulent. Some of the groups sought regional or ethnic independence.

When the impressive Paris student riots of 1968 failed to bring down the government of De Gaulle (though he resigned in the following year), the idea of radical social change, backed by the masses, was dispersed. The Leftist views of the students, which were sincere as well as convoluted, did not divert them from their career aim of securing well-paid white-collar positions in administration or education, and their vision of an ideal society, as voiced in the exciting public debates in the Odéon theatre in Paris in 1968, soon faded once the authorities restored order in the summer and autumn of that year. The German disturbances, however, went on into 1969, and their violent character pointed the way to a more sinister form of protest which would be carried on by a group of revolutionary fanatics rather than by students. A similar tendency occurred in Italy.

The common Axis experience of Germany and Italy had some connection with what now happened. The wiping out of a guilty Fascist past had made room for Communism and anarchism among a small minority of young people who could feel no respect for the recent history of their countries. The Christian Democrat compromise which had created political stability in their countries since the late 1940s, and the improvement in living standards, had largely deprived their ideas of political influence. They blamed the United States for repressing other views, and detected a world capitalist plot which could defend both imperialism in the Third World and conservative forces in western Europe. With no chance of electoral success, they were prepared to launch into campaigns of violence.

The main German groups were the RAF (Rote Armee Fraktion) and the Baader-Meinhof gang. Their Italian equivalents were the Red Brigades and a secret masonic lodge, P2. In Italy, left-wing and right-wing groups simultaneously engaged in indiscriminate violence. The first bomb exploded in Milan in December 1969. Their actions created a police crackdown in the late 1960s and early 1970s, but results were slow. In Italy, the kidnap and murder of Aldo Moro, the Christian Democrat leader and former Prime

Minister, by the Red Brigades in 1978 at last turned public opinion against the outrages and allowed the authorities to gain control.

In Spain, the Basque separatist group, ETA (Basque Homeland and Liberty), launched a campaign for political and cultural independence in the 1960s. It used terrorist techniques and did not begin to decline until the post-Franco government of Spain began to make concessions in the late 1970s.

In Britain a small number of extremists followed the continental example, but the most active, the Angry Brigade (their name recalling, probably unconsciously, the Angry Young Men of the 1950s), was soon stamped out. Britain, however, had an older protest movement. In 1968, Catholic activists in Ulster started to campaign for 'civil rights' with a view to securing better access to housing and employment. In the following year, the venerable IRA (Irish Republican Army), whose main aim was the achievement of a united Ireland, split into two wings, the Official IRA and the Provisional IRA (Provos). During 1968, both began a campaign of violence in support of their case for a united Ireland.

The IRA had run a bombing campaign in England in 1939, but there had been little violence after 1945. Between 1956 and 1962 the IRA had launched a number of raids from southern Ireland on installations along the Ulster border, but they presented these as military operations and were hesitant to encourage Catholic and Protestant hostility in Northern Ireland. However, in the new climate of civil unrest in Ulster after 1968, and with British troops present to keep order there from the same year, the Provos stirred up Catholic feeling in Ulster against the Protestant majority, and against the British presence which they presented as 'imperialist' and pro-Protestant. The result was a new form of conflict in Ulster, with incidents and contrived civil clashes replacing the 'military' tactics. The light and versatile weapons used by other terrorists and obtainable in some cases from sources in eastern Europe allowed IRA weapons to be stored in the North. The bombings and assassinations now used by the Provos were comparable to the continental extremist groups and the IRA kept in touch with them, and later with extremist groups in the Middle East, in order to obtain arms, tactical advice and moral support. Some IRA members underwent joint training with terrorists from other countries. Their new strategy, they found, made it possible to use bombs in towns without undermining their case, even when fatalities occurred.

In the towns and country of Northern Ireland, tens of

thousands were drawn into the conflict on both sides. A mentality and culture of violence grew up which seriously affected young people and children. The resulting atavism ran strongly counter to social trends in the west of Europe. It recalled the atmosphere in Sicily, though here, of course, there was no religious conflict. The resulting struggle, which would last until a truce halted the violence in 1994, would make Britain, together with Spain, Europe's longest-running centre of terrorist violence.

The late 1960s thus saw a resurgence of violence across Europe, recalling the Fascist struggles of the 1920s and 1930s, except that the new insurgents claimed allegiance to the Left, not the Right. At the turn of the decade, western Europe was moving towards the suspicious, neurotic climate which recalled parts of the 1920s. However, terrorism reached a peak in the mid-1970s and then entered a sharp decline, except in Ireland. Governments took firmer action to capture and punish the terrorists. Continuing atrocities, which tended to become more murderous as the terrorists strove to capture public attention, deprived them of popular sympathy. The student protests, which had encouraged the terrorists, if indirectly, died down, and the whole climate of anarchy which had built up at the end of the 1960s died away in the depressing economic climate which had emerged by the mid-1970s.

European convergence

Looking back over the years since 1945, a convergence of national and regional lifestyles can be seen throughout western Europe. It is based on rising, converging living standards and the emergence of a common array of consumer goods and leisure activities. Basic expenditure, on food, clothing and housing, declined as a proportion of household budgets. In most European countries after the war, basic expenditure absorbed at least half the average budget; in France the proportion was an extraordinary 64 per cent. By 1995, this head of expenditure had fallen to around one-quarter over most of western Europe (Féron and Thoraval, 1992, 48). The reduction in basic expenditure allowed a shift of demand towards consumer goods, services, and leisure which were increasingly available on a Europe-wide scale.

Nevertheless, it was in the area of basic expenditure that regional tastes and customs proved most tenacious. North-western

Europe's pattern of small houses made a marked contrast with the tenement houses and the newer, high-rise blocks of the Mediterranean regions. New building, at any rate until the 1980s, tended to reinforce this divergence. Eating habits also persisted. In northern Europe cooking was done mainly with fats. In the South, olive oil was preferred, even when cheap fats became available through EEC trading. The northerners consumed large quantities of potatoes, cakes, and sweet desserts. Their main alcoholic drink was beer. The southerners ate pasta and rice as their main carbohydrate, drank wine, and obtained much of their sugar from fresh fruit (Féron and Thoraval, 1992, 49). The most visible continental trends were the universal diffusion of American-style 'fast food' from the later 1960s, and the provision in northern Europe of exotic and 'spicy' food by southern and oriental restaurateurs from the late 1950s. Restaurants of the latter type were often associated with immigration from outside Europe, not because the immigrants were rich enough to eat there, but because they were poor enough to work there. By the 1990s many of these places were providing 'take-away' (i.e. fast) food, and the spreading availability of free delivery suggested that popular lifestyles in western Europe were at last approaching American standards. In this as in many respects, though, an apparent Europeanisation was part of a much broader Americanisation occurring on a world scale. Like most cherished goals, the continental mass culture, once achieved, has turned out to be something else.

Non-material belief systems, such as religion and folk custom, have declined. The move to urban areas has played a large part in this trend. However, even in remote rural areas of mountain or marsh, where a remnant of the traditional population survived, old beliefs and practices faded or were converted into tourist attractions. Everything now had its price, while the product had to be dressed up in new clothes. The rough side of rural life was hidden, to allow the tourist and holidaymaker to view traditional Europe as though it were on colour television.

Tradition thus merged into the society of consumption, backed by the media, especially television. Advertising was the most obvious means of directing behaviour across Europe but the news and entertainment content of the media had an indirect impact, because advertising was such an important source of revenue for them. The main linguistic medium of this convergence was the English language. As the main medium of trade, English achieved a growing currency after the war owing mainly to its use by the Americans. English culture also made a contribution, as its European character made it in some respects more acceptable to the rest of Europe. As time passed, however, the mass culture of western Europe was increasingly a continental one, in whatever language it was expressed.

CHAPTER TWELVE

Conclusion

Economic and social history in a contemporary context

François Bédarida, the social historian, brought the study of contemporary history to prominence in France in the 1970s and 1980s with his Institut d'Histoire du Temps Présent. He chose the title 'history of the present' partly because, in France, 'contemporary history' had come to mean 'since 1789'.

This book is an example of 'contemporary history' in the British sense, in that it deals with events that lie within the memory of people alive today (see Barraclough, 1964), and seeks to bring past and present together (Gaddis, 1995, 16–17). However, there is a world of difference between the history of the early post-war years, already upholstered with historical scholarship and debate, and the years 1991–95 which this book strives to cover without the benefit of historical perspective in the customary sense. Indeed, even the middle years between 1952 and 1990 have not greatly attracted historians, except in respect of the creation of the EEC and related aspects of European integration. Perhaps we need to amend Bédarida's concept of a 'history of the present day' in order to describe the historian's efforts to handle recent events which may not prove to be of historical significance in the longer term.

The historian studying the very recent past is tempted to project history forward into an imaginary future, to create an artificial perspective on the present. In 1995, he asks above all what effects the collapse of the Communist system in the Soviet Union and eastern Europe will have on the rest of the world. In a book like this, which has detected, following John Stuart Mill, 'a tendency toward a better and happier state' in post-1945 western Europe, and has accounted for that improvement principally on the basis of greater international trade, the temptation is to assume that the happy state will continue into the future, and will include those eastern European countries which are now more open to trade with the West than they were before 1989–91, and where democracy is under gradual construction (we hope).

The historical period

This volume has adopted a conventional periodisation of fifty years. It is conventional in such surveys to compare the half-century under study with the preceding fifty-year period, and sometimes with other fifty-year periods which may help set the study-period in context. The years 1945–95 in the history of western Europe make a striking contrast with the years 1895–1945. The absence of major wars involving the continent, the rapid rate of economic growth, the progress of international cooperation, high and rising living standards, and the considerable degree of social and political stability, made western Europe the world's leading example of multi-national success within the capitalist system. Compared with the years 1895–1945 it is a period in which 'great' events such as wars, revolutions, and depressions hardly ever occur. The economic deceleration after the early 1970s is the main discontinuity but the general direction of change is unaltered into the 1990s. The ideological context of activity has more of the confident later nineteenth century than it does of the competitive first half of the twentieth. Indeed, the emphasis on international trade and secure currencies as the way forward after 1945 recalls the nineteenth-century vision of a world of independent but cooperating countries. That vision collapsed in 1914. In 1995 a much stronger version of it not only remained in full vigour in western Europe, but was probably being adopted in the formerly Communist East (or so we hope).

Geography

By 1989 the twelve countries of the EEC had a population of 325 million and a population density of 144 people per square kilometre. This compared to a population of 249 million in the

USA, and a much lower population density of 27 per square kilometre. Although productivity was still about one-third higher in the USA than in western Europe, the compact distribution of a huge population in western Europe was a big economic asset, especially as it was based on a close-knit structure of urban areas. In these ways, western Europe was a powerful economic space, more dependent on primary imports than the USA, but partly in consequence of this a more prolific exporter. The potential of this region looked very high in 1995, especially in anticipation of a world economic recovery resulting from adjustment to the collapse of the Communist system (we hope). [These repetitive qualifications were added on 20 December 1995, two days after the Russian elections which made the Communists the biggest party in the Duma. Such are the perils of the 'history of the present'.]

Population

The completion of European industrialisation after 1945, with its huge increase in output and rise in living standards, was accompanied at first by a rise in the rate of population increase in comparison with the inter-war years, but this was followed from the 1960s by a long-term trend towards the stabilisation of population. In 1940 the population of western Europe was 264 million. In 1992 it was 440 million. This increase was slow in comparison with the other advanced continents, with the population of the USA and Canada combined rising from 141,928,000 in 1938 to 284,046,000 in 1992, and Australia from 6,904,000 in 1938 to 17,529,000 in 1992. Western Europe was much less affected by immigration than North America and Australia, and there was an underlying movement in western Europe towards a demographic balance with the number of deaths equalling the number of births. Prosperous countries such as Sweden and West Germany led the way towards the world of the single-child or childless married couple. Also proliferating there was the unmarried couple which in the middle classes often did not have children (the same could not be said of working-class unmarried couples, ironically enough). In Germany the result was an overall decline of population from the mid-1970s, as the oil crisis and its aftermath discouraged the immigration which previously had made up for the decline in natural increase. The fastest growth occurred in southern Europe and among the immigrants from outside Europe.

The result was a stabilisation of population growth among the natives of the more advanced areas of Europe, a gradual decline in birth rates in the modernising South, and persistent high rates among the non-European immigrants and their children in their northern settlement areas. Overall, Europeans were not letting traditional parenthood norms detract from the prosperity achieved since the war. This tendency allowed women to achieve greater qualifications, freedom and independence, and, in some cases to enjoy a higher quality of life. In some countries, such as Switzerland, Sweden and Germany, natives were beginning to feel that immigrant children were present in such large numbers that they were beginning to take over their country's future, but in 1995 their numbers did not really justify this concern. In any case, there was no sign that the natives were sufficiently concerned about the takeover threat to start having more children.

FIGURE 12.1 *Population of selected western European countries, 1938–87 (in thousands).*

	1938	1950	1965	1973	1980	1987
Belgium	8,374	8,640	9,464	9,739	9,847	9,862
France	41,960	41,836	48,758	52,118	53,880	55,685
Germany	46,376	49,983	58,619	61,976	61,566	60,858
Italy	43,004	46,769	51,526	54,462	56,157	57,094
Netherlands	8,685	10,114	12,295	13,439	14,150	14,616
Sweden	6,310	7,042	7,734	8,137	8,311	8,366
UK	47,494	50,363	54,350	56,210	56,314	56,687

Source: Maddison, 1989, 128.

The common growth path

Economic growth is now the badge of capitalism, partly because post-war capitalism has generated so much growth, and partly because, given that it is assumed that the increase in resources generated by growth benefits all social groups, the redistribution of income and wealth appears less necessary than socialist theory would require.

The acceleration of economic progress after 1945 is most often expressed in terms of the annual per capita rate of growth in GDP. The techniques of national accounting which make these comparisons possible were largely the product of the work of Simon

Kuznets, Colin Clark, and others (Maddison, 1982, 21). Comparative figures for western European countries are calculated by the OECD and reliable pre-1950 estimates are available. National accounting is now the main basis of the work of economic historians on long-run change (e.g. Aldcroft, 1993).

Since 1945, the per capita growth of GDP on an annual basis in western Europe has been much higher than at any previous period in the economic history of the continent. It has taken place in the context of an even higher rate of growth for the industrialised world as a whole. However, the rate of growth slowed markedly after the early 1970s, dividing the period into a quarter century of extremely rapid growth, followed by a quarter century in which the rate of growth dropped by about half. With floods of data to describe this unique, and very welcome, growth phenomenon, refined statistical representations for Europe and the world are legion. One of the most striking is Angus Maddison's evolving world dataset. Based on a sample of thirty-two countries, representing four-fifths of the world economy, it shows an annual per capita growth rate of 1.1 per cent from 1900 to 1950, and 2.5 per cent between 1950 and 1987 (Maddison, 1989, 14). Bairoch's estimates for nineteenth-century Europe suggest a compound rate of growth in GNP per capita of just under 1 per cent between 1800 and 1913 (Bairoch, 1976, 298–9). Between 1900 and 1950, the growth of GDP per capita in the countries of the OECD (most countries of western Europe, together with the USA, Canada and Japan) was only 1.3 per cent, most of this growth occurring between 1900 and 1914, and between 1919 and 1929. Between 1950 and 1987, the rate of increase more than doubled, at 3.0 per cent, with a very high rate of increase between 1950 and 1973 (3.8 per cent), and a lower rate after 1973 (1.9 per cent) (Maddison, 1989, 15, 35). The European countries of the OECD followed a similar path. Between 1960 and 1968 their GDP per capita increased at an average rate of 3.7 per cent per annum. Their growth accelerated to 4.0 per cent per annum between 1968 and 1973. Between 1973 and 1979 it dropped to 2.0 per cent per annum, and between 1979 and 1989 it was a mere 1.7 per cent (OECD, *Hist.Stat.*, 1991, 48).

The period of slower growth, though contrasting markedly with the first period, did not mark a complete return to the low growth rates before 1950, and in this book it is seen as a continuation of the post-war growth tendency. However, being associated with policies, experiences and attitudes which to some degree recall the

1930s, it diverges historically from the years before 1973, a year which frequently figures as a turning point in this book. The issue of petrol coupons in Britain in 1973 was as much a milestone as the issue of gas masks in 1938. For many Europeans, things never have been the same again since 1973.

It has often been noted that the economic growth of the industrialised countries followed a generally similar path after 1945, and this appears to cause some surprise to observers (e.g. Graham, 1990, 2). However, in a world of greater exchange and mobility, convergence is to be expected. Western Europe, as the world's biggest concentration of industrial countries, has clearly followed a narrowing growth path since 1950, while converging on the USA (Maddison, 1991, 160–4).

FIGURE 12.2 *GDP per capita in international dollars, 1929–87 (1980 prices).*

	1929	1950	1973	1987
Austria	2,118	2,123	6,434	8,792
Belgium	2,882	3,114	6,937	8,769
Denmark	2,913	3,895	7,845	9,949
Finland	1,667	2,610	6,804	9,500
France	2,629	2,941	7,462	9,475
W.Germany	2,153	2,508	7,595	9,964
Italy	2,089	2,323	6,824	9,023
Netherlands	3,373	3,554	7,754	9,197
Norway	2,184	3,436	7,071	11,653
Sweden	2,242	3,898	8,288	10,328
Switzerland	3,672	5,256	10,556	11,907
UK	3,200	4,171	7,413	9,178
USA	4,909	6,697	10,977	13,550
Canada	3,286	4,822	9,350	12,702
Bangladesh	372	331	281	375
India	403	359	513	662
Japan	1,162	1,116	6,622	9,756
S.Korea	749	564	1,790	4,143
Argentina	2,036	2,324	3,713	3,302
Mexico	835	1,169	2,349	2,667

Source: data drawn from Maddison, 1989, 19.

The above table shows most of the countries of western Europe converging into a narrow income band, clearly differentiated from North America, and the Third World. We know that convergence is also taking place across the world as a whole, but the European pattern is clearly linked to rapid economic growth within a very active regional trading system. In effect, a single western European economy was well on the way to achievement by 1995, and by this time the economic performance of most countries in western Europe reflected continental conditions as well as national conditions.

Rapid economic growth since the last war is commonly attributed to the following factors, which are based largely on the perceptions of Angus Maddison (Maddison, 1989, 65):

1. the creation at the end of the war of a rational economic order in the West, resulting in a harmony of interest between the capitalist countries
2. replacement of colonialism by deliberate policies of 'development' designed to improve output and increase consumption, together with better education
3. greater international exchange and movement (more trade, specialisation, flows of capital and technology, international migration)
4. increased investment, and development and diffusion of technology
5. the security and stimulus provided by a world of growth, without deflationary shocks.

There were, of course, some deflationary shocks after 1973. The collapse of stock market values after the OPEC intervention in 1973 was worse than in 1929. Another stock market collapse in 1987 also recalled 1929. However, the economic climate was much more stable after 1945 than it had been in the 1920s and 1930s. The events of 20 October 1987, for instance, looked potentially disastrous at first because technology and the opening of the London Stock Exchange to new traders ('the big bang') had created a volatile world market. The drop in values was more immediate because the world trading floors were linked electronically and the panic was more frightening. Values dropped by about 35 per cent on the European markets. Only Tokyo escaped. For once the world media did not seem to be exaggerating the danger of a serious recession, and a return to 1929–32 seemed at least possible, if not likely.

In the event, the world recession did not occur. It did not do so because most of the inbuilt elements of instability which had caused so much trouble in 1929 were no longer present. For instance, the use of bank credit to speculate in shares which had pushed Wall Street prices so high in the late 1920s was no longer permitted on any of the world's stock markets because it was obviously so dangerous. Governments were willing to take quick action to reflate their economies to maintain demand and to protect employment (Roberts and Kynaston, 1995, 148). They did so partly because they had been accustomed since the war to conferring through international organisations like the OECD and the IMF and sometimes to accepting advice or even instructions from these sources. Additionally, their experience since the war had so convinced them of the importance of quick intervention in their economies at a time of crisis that they could take action even without international approval.

The decline in the rate of growth after about 1973 needs some explanation, however. It was due to:

1. the low income elasticity of demand for manufactured goods in the industrial countries, owing partly to the initial equipment of most European households with cars and major consumer durables by 1970
2. the completion of western Europe's 'catching up' on American technology
3. the lack of productivity-raising innovation in the expanding tertiary sector (until the general introduction of computers in the 1980s)
4. OPEC policies on oil prices and production between 1973 and the early 1980s
5. government deflationary policies designed to control global inflation after the OPEC price increases of 1979
6. reduced Third World demand caused by restricted purchases of their products by the industrial world
7. protective restrictions on trade by countries and customs unions
8. serious economic difficulties in the USA arising mainly from the continuing external payments deficit
9. slow reconstruction by the formerly Communist countries after 1991
10. lack of investor confidence arising from persistence of lower growth.

The debate on growth and deceleration

This summary of a complex causation does not, however, do justice to a debate among economists and economic historians which has been going on since the 1950s. It would not be helpful to try to analyse the whole debate here, but some of the emphases are worth noting.

The rapid growth until the mid-1970s is often explained in terms of a 'catching-up' process, with national rates of growth varying in inverse proportion to post-war levels of productivity (Feinstein, 1990, 20–1). The USA and Canada, already much more productive than western Europe before the war, had built up a big lead in innovation by 1945. Given the post-war conditions of economic cooperation between the two continents, together with the growth of world trade in an expanding Western economy, western European producers were able to adopt these innovations rapidly in the 1950s and the 1960s (e.g. Maddison, 1991, 23). The more 'backward' the country, the quicker it 'caught up'. The result was a western European convergence towards the US level of output by 1973 (Feinstein, 1990, 21). Resource allocation improved greatly in comparison with the protectionist 1930s, and the European need for US dollars concentrated the minds of exporters and governments. The result was 'supergrowth', as Kindleberger and Shonfield termed it in 1971 (Kindleberger and Shonfield, 1971, 1–2). Boltho attributes the rapid growth after the war to new economic policies, and new entrepreneurial confidence. He sees growth as a self-fulfilling process. It has a momentum which can produce rapid progress for a while, but which is bound to come to an end (Boltho, 1982, 36–7). Milward perceives a completion of western European industrialisation in favourable conditions (Milward, 'Germany', 1992).

The end of 'supergrowth' around 1970 generally conforms to these explanations. There is evidence that the innovations of the 1960s were less significant than their predecessors. The OPEC oil price increases of 1973 reversed the terms of trade until the early 1980s. The achievement of full employment in the 1960s allowed labour to exploit its position. Investment could have countered this threat but a decline in profitability discouraged it. Investment continued to rise nevertheless in the late 1960s and the early 1970s, but inflation now became an obstacle. Entrepreneurial confidence was completely undermined by the oil crisis (Boltho,

1982, 36–7). 'Convergence' and 'catching-up' continued, with Britain now a major beneficiary.

International integration

All the main explanations of rapid growth after 1945 include an element based on closer links between the national economies of western Europe and the world as a whole. Admittedly, the development of these links continues after 1970 without having a visible effect on the growth rate, but the growth of non-tariff barriers to trade outside the EEC may have had an effect. Integration within the EEC has continued, allowing growing specialisation since 1970 despite the low growth rate. International cooperation and integration have been the key theme of western European history since 1945 and they merit full review here.

The increasingly integrated economic experience of western Europe is best viewed in the framework of an increasingly consolidated Western world economy, made possible by the post-war arrangements for international payments; the growing freedom of capital flows; the gradual removal of quantitative and qualitative impediments to trade; the spread of the multi-national firm; the standardisation of technology; the convergence of purchasing power; the standardisation of consumer tastes; international labour migration, and the spread of the English language. High economic growth rates have been widely linked to high trade growth rates (e.g. Maddison, 1962), and the growth of trade in manufactured products has generally been higher than the growth of output in primary products (Graham, 1990, 9–10). Exchange allows specialisation, with countries producing commodities in which they have a comparative advantage. Their range of output narrows, but their productivity increases. Technology developed by the more advanced countries and firms is widely adopted abroad, producing rapid increases in productivity. Agricultural employment declines as food is imported, and the rural workforce moves into the cities where it finds more productive employment. Labour-saving technology in the home, most of it originating in the USA, and the growth of tertiary employment resulting from rising living standards, encourage women to move into paid jobs.

Seen from the end of the twentieth century, the 1930s stand out as a period in which the industrial countries interfered with healthy competititon by setting up tariffs, preferences and quotas to protect their industries, and to reinforce their deflationary policies. These policies reversed the heroic free trade movement of 1840–1914. After 1945 western Europe and the USA turned back towards the nineteenth-century ideal.

Western Europe's efforts to remove its barriers to trade have to be seen in the context of the world movement of trade liberalisation, mainly under the GATT arrangements, but also as the result of regional free trade associations, customs unions, and friendship agreements. GATT, as a treaty rather than an organisation, led to a series of 'rounds' of negotiations intended progressively to reduce tariffs and other restrictions on trade. These were:

1950–51	Torquay
1955–56	Geneva
1960–62	'Dillon Round'
1964–67	'Kennedy Round'
1973–79	'Tokyo Round'
1986–94	'Uruguay Round'

The slower rate of economic growth after the early 1970s does not discredit these connections. Trade within the EEC continued to expand faster than output, in contrast to world trade which by 1979–85 was growing at the same rate as world GDP, suggesting that greater national restrictions on trade were having their effect, and also slowing down the growth of world output (Boltho and Allsopp, 1987, iii). Protective barriers to trade (including the growing phenomenon of non-tariff barriers) probably restrained exports from the EEC, but progress towards integration continued within the EEC, while membership expanded, producing an increase in the volume of trade between the EEC countries. Between 1970 and 1990, trade between EEC countries increased from 51.8 per cent to 60.0 per cent of the total trade of the EEC countries (Williams, 1994, 66). Average tariffs between the industrial countries dropped below 10 per cent from the later 1970s thanks to the progress of GATT and other negotiations, including progressive reductions within the customs unions (principally EEC, EFTA, USA/Canada, Carecon) (Page, 1987, 37–9). In fact, tariffs were directed mainly against the developing countries by the industrial countries, penalising the cheap food and cheap manufactures of the Third World (Boltho and Allsopp, 1987, iv). So, as a giant customs union, the EEC was able to protect itself from the worst effects of slow world growth.

Figure 12.3 indicates the growing importance of trade to the national economies of western Europe.

FIGURE 12.3 *Commodity exports as a percentage of GDP at current market prices.*

	1929	1950	1973	1986
Belgium	39.9	20.3	49.9	61.4
Denmark	26.7	21.3	21.9	25.8
Finland	24.0	16.6	20.5	23.2
France	13.3	10.6	14.4	17.3
Germany	15.3	8.5	19.7	27.3
Italy	10.4	7.0	12.5	16.3
Netherlands	30.7	26.9	37.3	45.3
Norway	18.4	18.2	24.4	26.5
Sweden	18.8	17.8	23.5	28.6
Switzerland	19.4	20.0	23.2	27.7
UK	15.6	14.4	16.4	19.5

Source: data drawn from Maddison, 1989, 143.

In value terms exports increased substantially. The value of exports by the OECD countries at constant prices increased nearly ten times between 1950 and 1986. German exports increased over twenty-five times, and UK exports increased nearly four times. The French multiple was nearly ten (Maddison, 1989, 142).

Seen from 1995, this process justifies the American vision of a prosperous world economy after the war. Most of the Third World has not shared in it, and the Communist world has stood apart. The industrialised West, however, has developed along the lines implicit in the Bretton Woods and GATT concepts, and of the Atlantic Charter of 1941–42. This means that it has developed along lines established according to the Anglo-American concept of the freedom of the individual and private property rights, and the British concept of free trade. The first of these concepts goes back to the seventeenth and eighteenth centuries with the English and American revolutions against tyranny, and the second to Adam Smith in the late eighteenth-century context of the Enlightenment. That the Americans, the British, and the Canadians could agree on these principles during the testing years of the war when their values were threatened by a contrasting approach to human existence, National Socialism, is not surprising. Nor is it surprising that they should believe that by an association of the sterling area, and of the dollar area, they could draw the whole of the post-war world into an economic system based on these principles.

Within this system, national economic policies in western Europe were not likely to have the same impact or independence as before the war. Increasingly, countries would seek adjustments within the general economic tendency. In times of general difficulty, governments would consult through bodies such as the IMF and the OECD, and more specialised groups like the Club of Rome and the Group of Ten. This was a very different world from that before 1939, and in western Europe it produced a very different economic history.

The future seen from the present

When the Soviet and and East European Communist system collapsed in 1989–91, a debate developed among intellectuals and journalists in Germany about what they described as the 'end of history', a state of affairs in which the great strategic and ideological conflicts had at last come to an end, leaving the world to look forward to a peaceful life on the 'broad, sunlit uplands' of Churchill's wartime dream. The 'end of history' debate spread beyond Germany but it soon became a bore. Wars in Iraq, Africa and the former Yugoslavia allowed the media to return to their normal concerns and the historians stopped worrying about their future role. However, as western Europe approached the end of the millennium which it had done so much to shape, it did seem to stand on a Churchillian upland. The problems feared in 1945 had to a large extent been solved. Western Europe was prosperous, calm and stable.

This result was not fortuitous, even though the role of the State was in decline in 1995 and individual choice was cherished to a degree which recalled Victorian England, Leonardo's Florence, or Periclean Athens. The secure prosperity which western Europe had achieved was the product of a formula which had guided its affairs since 1945. This formula was based on the defence of the rights of the individual, and the idea of free trade between nations, supplemented by the creation of a common purpose and conduct among the nations of western Europe. Exchange and specialisation would increase incomes across the continent, and national jealousies would fade away, leaving western Europe as a haven of peace and prosperity.

This formula had three main components. The oldest was the British free trade ideal, which had contributed to world prosperity in the nineteenth century but which had been swept away in the 1920s and 1930s as countries struggled for the biggest share of a reduced output. The most visible was the widespread desire to avoid a further European war. This ambition can seem so obvious that British economic and social historians often undervalue it. It emerged at the end of the war as primarily a political programme, with economic integration emerging in the 1950s as the most practical means of preventing new forms of national extremism and military conflicts. No economic history of contemporary Europe can ignore this fundamental role of political history. The third, and most important, was the contribution of the United States to the rebuilding of Europe in the context of a new world of prosperity and individual freedom. That new world embodied the principle of free trade, but it could not be created without money. The United States provided that money in a variety of ways, most of it in the form of a military effort designed to resist the threat of domination by an alternative system, Communism.

Nevertheless, the economic future remained unclear in 1995. Perceptions varied. For some observers, western Europe was trapped in a period of low growth which had begun in the mid-1970s. Others stressed the exceptional nature of the growth registered in the twenty-five years after the war and were not disturbed by the return to 'normal' growth. Within this growth phase, the business cycle could produce significant fluctuations but these were not a cause of concern. They were known to optimistic commentators and public advisory bodies such as the OECD as 'downturns' or 'recessions'.

In 1995 western Europe was recovering weakly from a recession which had begun in 1991 within the world economy. The OECD detected the beginnings of a European recovery from 1994 and hailed a general expansion of output in 1995, but the strength and persistence of the upturn remained uncertain. In the short term, growth was predicted by the OECD to be around 2.5 per cent in 1994 and nearly 3 per cent in 1995 and 1996. Inflation was well under control but unemployment was persistently high (OECD, *Economic Outlook*, **55**, ix; **57**, xi, 1, 2). The OECD was optimistic, but this was a worrying state of affairs.

Low growth had been a feature of the European and world

economies for twenty years. The collapse of the Communist bloc between 1989 and 1991 had appeared at first to offer the opportunity for a European revival, but it had not come about. The absorption of East Germany alone had put a severe strain on the West German economy and, less directly, on western Europe as a whole. The former Soviet Union and, to a lesser extent, the former eastern satellite countries, were restrained by low demand, backward technology, and institutions and attitudes which discouraged growth on capitalist lines.

By the mid-1990s, the West had done little to invest in eastern Europe, discouraged by its own economic weakness after 1991 and the lack of assurance that its funds would be put to effective use. The only exception was Germany, which had poured money into East Germany from 1989. This profligate action, which so contrasted with the sober domestic policies pursued in the Federal Republic since 1948, turned East Germany from a country cousin into a giant cuckoo in the nest. Western Germany, for its part, changed almost overnight from Europe's biggest lender to Europe's biggest borrower. Committed to maintaining the value of the Deutschmark, on which the ERM and the future European currency relied, Germany increased its short-term interest rates, drawing in funds additional to those required for the East German operation. High costs, combined with a declining rate of productivity growth and low productive investment, undermined German exports. In short, Germany was no longer the powerhouse of western Europe but a heavy burden on it.

A new 'Marshall plan'?

Although an OECD growth rate of around 2.5 per cent in the mid-1990s was respectable in long-run historical terms, the persistence of a high rate of unemployment in a Europe which had made full use of its human resources soon after the war, indicated a potential capacity which remained unused. In 1994, the proportion unemployed in the EU, 11.5 per cent, contrasted with the US average of 6.0 per cent, suggesting that job-saving policies and generous unemployment pay in Europe were restricting the labour supply. In 1992 the OECD Ministers commissioned a study to establish the reasons for the limited progress in dealing with unemployment and to suggest remedies (OECD, *Economic Outlook*, **55**, xi). The OECD published the results in June 1994 in its

Economic Outlook. It made a strong plea for faster growth in order to make the OECD countries once again into 'high-employment societies with steadily-rising national living standards'. Policy intervention on macro-economic and structural levels should increase the 'supply potential' of national economies. In particular, 'growth-inhibiting rigidities' should be reduced, in order to reduce the tendency of any recovery to generate inflation. This, among other things, would mean reviewing the social security system which most countries had expanded since the mid-1970s when unemployment became serious. Faster growth and a reduction of unemployment would generate greater social cohesion and would make it easier to achieve social goals (OECD, *Economic Outlook*, **55**, ix). This orthodoxy generated little disagreement. However, the process of growth seemed likely to be slow.

Particularly intractable was the relative backwardness of the western European South. The Mediterranean fringe countries, Italy excluded, but including Ireland on the western fringe, recorded a per capita GDP which, in 1990, remained well below the EEC average. There had been a gradual improvement in each of them since the establishment of the EEC, and there was every sign that a gradual convergence on the average would continue. Ireland, for instance, had broken free from its dependence on the United Kingdom as the purchaser of nearly all its manufactures. By 1985, nearly half Ireland's expanding exports of manufactured goods went to non-UK destinations (Kennedy, et al., 1988, 194–5). Nevertheless, a process of several decades seemed to be in prospect. Moreover, with the Italian *Mezzogiorno* retaining many of the backward features of the rest of the Mediterranean fringe, quite a large area of southern Europe still seemed to be resistant to continental modernisation processes in 1995.

The northern fringe, meanwhile, had adapted fully. Of course, the North had much greater natural resources than the South, and the South had social structures, customs and mentalities which, as Francesco Galassi has shown, tended to produce mass emigration and an enervating family control of local enterprise. In southern Italy, the extreme result of these structures was the Mafia, which remained endemic in 1995 because it was rooted so deeply in society (Dye and Galassi, 1995). So, as in the USA, there seemed to be 'something different about the South', and the differences had social rather than economic origins. It remained to be seen whether the successful economic logic of the EU could be applied there as it had been in the North.

In 1995 the delayed development of southern Europe was a matter of growing concern. Although national incomes there were beginning to catch up those of the North, the rate of convergence had slowed during the period of slower growth since 1970. Low demand in the South restrained the growth of output in western Europe, which in turn slowed down the development of the South. Without faster growth, this divergence could not easily be resolved and there was a clear danger that it might be built into the economy of the EU on a long-term basis.

A similar concern, though more remote, was the backwardness of the East. Until the East could be brought up to the same economic level as the EU, its potential as a market and as an area of specialised production could not be achieved. This left the North as a highly integrated, heavily industrialised region, unable to compete effectively with the growth industries of the Far East, and constrained by trade barriers outside Europe. With talk of a two-speed Europe echoing down the Brussels corridors and in a thousand television interviews, the nightmare sprang up of a return to the Schuman plan of 1950, with a cluster of countries in north-west Europe trying to recreate the anti-war spirit of the European Coal and Steel Community, and Britain turning out to sea again in the *Revenge* with its Viking galleys in its wake. But this is the nightmare. What about the vision?

Historical surveys of this type often look for symmetries. Early on in this book we assigned considerable importance to the Marshall plan of 1947, which helped launch western Europe into an era of unprecedented prosperity. Now, at the very end of the book, we look for a new Marshall plan to modernise eastern Europe. Expertise and guidance, as well as money, will be needed. The plan will need to transform attitudes and institutions warped by decades of Communism. There will be implications for western aid to the Third World. Western Europe will need to supply a large share of the funds. Europe's history, however, may yet offer a guide to the future.

Bibliography

Unless otherwise stated, place of publication is the UK.

ABELSHAUSER W 1983 *Wirtschaftsgeschichte der Bundesrepublik Deutschland, 1945–1980.* Suhrkamp, Frankfurt-am-Main

ABRAMS R K et al. 1990 *The impact of the European community's internal market on the EFTA.* International Monetary Fund, Washington

ADA 1986 *Bilan de la France.* Table Ronde, Paris

AERTS E, MILWARD A (eds) 1990 *Economic planning in the post-1945 period.* Leuven University Press, Leuven

ALDCROFT D H 1978 *The European economy 1914–1980.* Croom Helm

ALDCROFT D H 1993 *The European economy 1914–1990* 3rd edn. Routledge

ALEXANDERSSON G 1971 *Les pays du Nord.* Presses Universitaires de France, Paris

ALFORD B W E 1988 *British economic performance 1945–1975.* Macmillan

AMBROSI C and A 1981 *La France 1870–1981.* Masson, Paris

AMBROSIUS G, HUBBARD W H 1989 *A social and economic history of twentieth-century Europe.* Harvard University Press, Cambridge, Mass.

ARDAGH J 1968 *The new French revolution: a social and economic survey of France 1945–1967.* Secker and Warburg

ARDAGH J 1982 *France in the 1980s.* Secker and Warburg

ARDAGH J 1990 *France today.* Penguin

ASHWORTH W 1987 *A short history of the international economy since 1850* 4th edn. Longman

BAIROCH P 1976 Europe's gross national product, 1800–1975. *The Journal of European Economic History,* **5**, 1976, 273–340

BALASSA B (ed.) 1975 *European economic integration.* North-Holland, Amsterdam

BARNOUIN B 1986 *The European labour movement and European integration.* Frances Pinter

BARRACLOUGH G 1964 *An introduction to contemporary history.* Watts

BECK E 1986 *Under the Bombs: The German Home Front, 1942–1945.* University Press of Kentucky, Lexington

BECKERMAN W (ed.) 1972 *The Labour government's economic record: 1964–1970.* Duckworth

BEREND I, RANKI G 1974 *Economic development in east-central Europe in the 19th and 20th centuries.* Columbia University Press, New York

BERGHAHN V 1986 *The Americanisation of West German industry 1945–1973.* Berg

BARSTEIN S 1989 *La France de l'expansion. 1. La république gaullienne, 1958–1969.* Seuil, Paris

BEVERIDGE W H 1942 *Social insurance and allied services.* HMSO

BEVERIDGE W H 1944 *Full employment in a free society: a report.* Allen and Unwin

BIRKE A M 1987 *Britain and Germany: historical patterns of a relationship.* German Historical Institute

BÖHME H 1978 *An introduction to the social and economic history of Germany: politics and economic change in the nineteenth and twentieth centuries.* Basil Blackwell

BOJE T, HORT S, (eds) 1993 *Scandinavia in a new Europe.* Scandinavian University Press, Oslo

BOLT R 1995 *The xenophobe's guide to the Dutch.* Ravette Books

BOLTHO A (ed.) 1982 *The European economy: growth and crisis.* Oxford University Press

BOLTHO A, ALLSOPP C 1987 The assessment: trade and trade policy. *Oxford Review of Economic Policy* **3** (1) 1–19

BORCHARDT K 1991 *Perspectives on modern German economic history and policy.* Cambridge University Press

BORNE D 1992 *Histoire de la société française depuis 1945.* Armand Colin, Paris

BOSSUAT G 1992 *La France, l'aide américaine et la construction européenne, 1944–1954* 2 vols. Comité pour l'histoire économique et financière de la France, Paris

BOURGUIGNON F, GALLAIS-HAMONNO 1977 *International labour migrations and economic choices: the European case.* OECD, Paris

BOWDEN S, OFFER A 1994 Household appliances and the use of time: the United States and Britain since the 1920s. *Economic History Review* **47** (4), 725–48.

BRAUN H J 1990 *The German economy in the twentieth century.* Routledge

BRINKLEY D, HACKETT C (eds) 1991 *Jean Monnet: the path to European unity.* Macmillan

BROWDER D A 1993 The GI dollar and the Wirtschaftswunder, *Journal of European Economic History* **22** (3) 601–12

BUACHE F 1988 *Le cinéma français des années 60.* 5 Continents, Renens

Building peace out of war: studies in international reconstruction. 1944 PEP

BURK K 1990 The international environment. In Graham A, *Government and economics in the postwar world: economic policies and comparative performance 1945–85.* Routledge

CAIRNCROSS A 1985 *Years of recovery: British economic policy 1945–51.* Methuen

CAIRNCROSS A 1988 *The price of war: British policy on German reparations 1941–1949.* Basil Blackwell

CAIRNCROSS A 1992 *The British economy since 1945: economic policy and performance 1945–1990.* Blackwell

CALVET H 1956 *La société française contemporaine.* Fernard Nathan, Paris

CALVOCORESSI P 1991 *World politics since 1945* 6th edn. Longman

Le Capital **35** August 1994

CAREW A 1987 *Labour under the Marshall plan: the politics of productivity and the marketing of management science.* Manchester University Press

CARON F 1979 *An economic history of modern France.* Methuen

CARRÉ J J et al. 1975 *French economic growth.* Stanford University Press, Stanford

CHARDONNET J 1958 *L'économie française: étude géographique d'une décadence et des possibilités de redressement,* tome 1. Dalloz, Paris

CHELES L et al. 1991 *Neo-fascism in Europe.* Longman

CHURCH R 1994 *The rise and decline of the British motor industry.* Macmillan

CIPOLLA C M (ed.) 1976 *The Fontana economic history of Europe. Contemporary economies part 1.* Collins

CIPOLLA C M (ed.) 1976 *The Fontana economic history of Europe. Contemporary economies part 2.* Collins

CIPOLLA C (ed.) 1976 *The Fontana economic history of Europe: the twentieth century part 2.* Fontana

CLOUT H et al. 1994 *Western Europe: geographical perspectives* 3rd edn. Longman

COFFEY P 1973 *The social economy of France.* Macmillan

COLLINS D 1975a *The European communities: the social policy of the first phase* vol 1 *The European coal and steel community 1951–70.* Martin Robertson

COLLINS D 1975b *The European communities: the social policy of the first phase* vol 2 *The European economic community 1958–72.* Martin Robertson

COMMISSION DU BILAN 1982 *La France en mai 1981: force et faiblesses.* La documentation française, Paris

COMMISSION EUROPÉENNE 1994 *Croissance, compétivité, emploi: les défis et les pistes pour entrer dans le XXI siècle. Livre blanc.* Office des publications officielles des Communautés européennes, Luxembourg

COOK M (ed.) 1993 *French culture since 1945.* Longman

COPPOLANI R, GARDAIR J M 1976 *La France de 1945 à 1976 à travers un choix d'articles du Monde 1.* Hatier, Paris

CRAFTS N F R, WOODWARD N W C 1991 *The British economy since 1945: introduction and overview.* Oxford University Press

CRAWFORD I 1963 *The Profumo Affair: a crisis in contemporary society.* White Lodge Books

CRESPY G (ed.) 1990 *Marché unique, marché multiple: stratégies européennes des acteurs industriels.* Economica, Paris

CROSSICK G (ed.) 1977 *The lower middle class in Britain, 1870–1914.* Croom Helm

CROUZET M 1970 *The European renaissance since 1945.* Thames and Hudson

CULLINGWORTH J B 1975 *Environmental planning, 1939–1969,* vol 1 *reconstruction and land use planning, 1939–1947.* HMSO

CULLINGWORTH J B, NADIN V 1994 *Town and country planning in Britain* 11th edn. Routledge

DE MEEÜS A 1962 *History of the Belgians.* Thames and Hudson

DAHRENDORF R 1982 Drifting between helplessness and patent cures. In Dahrendorf R *Europe's economy in crisis.* Holmes and Meier, New York

DAHRENDORF R 1982 *Europe's economy in crisis.* Holmes and Meier, New York

DE GAULLE C 1970 *Discours et messages, 4: Pour l'effort, août 1962 – décembre 1965.* Plon, Paris

DE JOUVENEL B 1948 *L'Amérique en Europe: le plan Marshall et la coopération intercontinentale.* Plon, Paris

DELL E 1995 *The Schuman plan and the British abdication of leadership in Europe.* Oxford University Press

DELLHEIM C 1982 *The face of the past: the preservation of the medieval inheritance in Victorian England.* Cambridge University Press

DENISON E F 1967 *Why growth rates differ: postwar experience in nine western countries.* Brookings Institution, Washington

D'HÉROUVILLE H 1949 *L'économie européenne.* Presses Universitaires de France, Paris

D'HÉROUVILLE H 1964 *La communauté économique atlantique.* Presses Universitaires de France, Paris

DI NOLFO E (ed.) 1992 *Power in Europe? II. Great Britain, France, Germany and Italy and the origins of the EEC 1952–1957.* Walter de Gruyter, Berlin

DIEFENDORF J M et al. 1993 *American policy and the reconstruction of West Germany 1945–55.* Cambridge University Press

DINTENFASS M 1992 *The decline of industrial Britain 1879–1980.* Routledge

Director's guide to Europe: a companion for the businessman visiting and trading with Europe 3rd edn. 1973 Gower Press

DROST H 1995 *What's what and who's who in Europe.* Cassell

DUCHÊNE F 1994 *Jean Monnet: the first statesman of interdependence.* Norton, New York

DUPUY G 1995 *Les territoires de l'automobile.* Anthropos, Paris

DURTH W, GUTSCHOW N 1993 *Träume in Trümmern: Stadtplanung 1940–1950.* Deutscher Taschenbuch Verlag, Munich

DYE A, GALASSI F 1995 Paternalism and protection: the institutional response of the European periphery to industrialisation in Martin A P, Simpson J (eds) *The economic development of Spain.* E. Elgon, Madrid

DYKER D A 1992 *The European economy.* Longman

DYKER D A (ed.) 1992 *The national economies of Europe.* Longman

The Economist 1976 *The world in figures.* The Economist Newspaper Limited

The Economist 1987 *The world in figures* 5th edn. Hodder and Stoughton

The Economist 1991 *The Economist Atlas.* The Economist Books Ltd

The Economist 1992 *Pocket Europe.* The Economist Books Ltd

The Economist 1993 *The world in figures* (pocket edn). Penguin

ECK J-F 1994 *Histoire de l'économie française depuis 1945.* Armand Colin, Paris

EDGERTON D E H 1994 British industrial R and D 1900–1970. *Journal of European Economic History* **23**(1) 49–68

EICHENGREEN B 1993 *Reconstructing Europe's trade and payments: the European payments union.* Manchester University Press

ELLWOOD D W 1992 *Rebuilding Europe: western Europe, America and post-war reconstruction.* Longman

ELLWOOD D W 1993 The Marshall plan. *Rassegna* 15(54/2)

EMERSON M et al. 1988 *1992: la nouvelle économie européenne: une évaluation par la Commission de la C E des effets économiques de l'achèvement du marché intérieur.* CECA CEE CEEA, Brussels

ERHARD L 1958 *Prosperity through competition.* Thames and Hudson

L'ESPAGNE À L'HEURE DU DÉVELOPPEMENT. 1967 *Revue Tiers-Monde* 8(32)

FEINSTEIN, C 1990 British economic growth: international and historical perspectives. *Economic Review* 7(5) 19–26

FÉRON F, THORAVAL A 1992 *L'état de l'Europe.* La Découverte, Paris

FITOUSSI J P, PHELPS E S 1988 *The slump in Europe: reconstructing open economic theory.* Basil Blackwell

FOREMAN-PECK J 1983 *A history of the world economy: international economic relations since 1950.* Wheatsheaf Books, New Jersey

FOURASTIÉ J 1979 *Les trente glorieuses ou la révolution invisible de 1946 à 1975.* Fayard, Paris

FRERIS A 1986 *The Greek economy in the twentieth century.* Croom Helm

GADDIS J 1995 *On contemporary history.* Clarendon Press

GALASSI F, COHEN J 1994 The economics of tenancy in early twentieth-century southern Italy. *Economic History Review* 47 (3) 585–600

GALBRAITH J 1994 *The world economy since the wars.* Sinclair-Stevenson

GALY M et al. 1993 *Spain: converging with the European community.* International Monetary Fund, Washington

GAMBLE A 1985 *Britain in decline* 2nd edn. Macmillan

GAVAGHAN J 1991 Britain and the Marshall plan: the British press, 5th June 1947–31st December 1959. Salford University MSc dissertation

GEORGE S 1991 *Britain and European integration since 1945.* Blackwell

GEORGE S 1994 *An awkward partner: Britain in the European community* 2nd edn. Oxford University Press

GIERSCH H, PAQUÉ K H, SCHMIEDING H 1992 *The fading miracle: four decades of market economy in Germany.* Cambridge University Press

GILES F 1991 *The locust years: the story of the fourth French republic 1946–1958.* Secker and Warburg

GIMBEL J 1968 *The American occupation of Germany: politics and the military.* Stanford University Press, Stanford

GINSBURG P 1990 *A history of contemporary Italy: society and politics 1943–1988.* Penguin

GIRAULT R 1993 Politique et économie internationales 1947–1948: rapport introductif. In Girault R, Lévy-Leboyer M (eds) *Le plan Marshall et le relèvement économique de l'Europe.* Comité pour l'histoire économique et financière, Ministère des Finances, Paris

GIRAULT R, LÉVY-LEBOYER M (eds) 1993 *Le plan Marshall et le relèvement économique de l'Europe.* Comité pour l'histoire économique et financière, Ministère des Finances, Paris

GISCARD D'ESTAING E 1954 *La France et l'unification économique de l'Europe.* Editions Génin, Paris

GRAHAM A (ed.) 1990 *Government and economics in the postwar world: economic policies and comparative performance 1945–85.* Routledge

GREBING H 1985 *The history of the German labour movement: a survey.* Berg Publishers

GUESLIN A 1992 *L'état, l'économie et la société française, XIXe–XXe siècle.* Hachette, Paris

HALLETT G 1973 *The social economy of West Germany.* Macmillan

HALLETT G 1990 West Germany. In Graham A, *Government and economics in the postwar world: economic policies and comparative performance 1945–85.* Routledge

HANCOCK W K, GOWING M M 1949 *British war economy.* HMSO

HANSEN A H 1945 *America's rule in the world economy.* Norton, New York

HARBORD J, WRIGHT B 1994 *40 years of British television.* Index

HARDACH G 1994 *Der Marshall plan: Auslandshilfe und Wiederaufbau in Westdeutschland 1948–1952.* Deutscher Taschenbuch Verlag, Munich

HARDACH K 1990 *The political economy of Germany in the twentieth century.* University of California Press, Berkeley

HARGREAVES A G 1987 *Immigration in post-war France: a documentary anthology.* Methuen Educational

HARPER J L 1986 *America and the reconstruction of Italy 1945–1948.* Cambridge University Press

HARRISON J 1978 *An economic history of modern Spain.* Holmes and Maier, New York

HARRISON J 1985 *The Spanish economy in the twentieth century.* Croom Helm

HARRISON J 1993 *The Spanish economy: from the civil war to the European Community.* Macmillan

HARVIE C 1994 *The rise of regional Europe.* Routledge

HASELER S 1989 *The battle for Britain: Thatcher and the new liberals.* Tauris

HAYCRAFT J 1987 *Italian labyrinth.* Penguin
HAYES J P 1993 *Making trade policy in the European community.* Macmillan
HAYWARD S 1993 *French national cinema.* Routledge
HEWISON R 1981 *In anger: culture in the cold war 1945–60.* Weidenfeld and Nicolson
HODNE F 1983 *The Norwegian economy, 1920–1980.* Croom Helm
HOGAN M J 1987 *The Marshall plan: America, Britain and the reconstruction of western Europe 1947–1952.* Cambridge University Press
HOHENBERG P 1968 *A primer on the economic history of Europe.* Random House, New York
HOHLBEIN H 1985 *Hamburg 1945: Kriegsende Not und Neubeginn.* Landeszentrale für politische Bildung, Hamburg
HOLLAND S 1980 *Uncommon market: capital, class and power in the European community.* St Martin's Press
HUGGETT F 1969 *Modern Belgium.* Pall Mall Press
INTERNATIONAL LABOUR OFFICE 1969 *Manpower aspects of recent economic developments in Europe.* International Labour Office, Geneva
ISENBERG I 1970 *The outlook for western Europe.* H W Wilson Co., New York
JACQUEMIN A P, DE JONG H W 1977 *European industrial organisation.* Macmillan
JACQUEMIN A P, SAPIR A 1989 *The European internal market: trade and competition. Selected readings.* Oxford University Press, New York
JOACHIMIDES C M et al. 1985 *German art in the twentieth century: painting and sculpture 1905–1985.* Royal Academy of Arts
JOHANSEN H 1987 *The Danish economy in the twentieth century.* Croom Helm
JOHNSON P (ed.) 1994 *Twentieth-century Britain: economic, social and cultural change.* Longman
JONES A 1994 *The new Germany: a human geography.* Witney, Chichester
JONES K, SMITH A D 1970 *The economic impact of commonwealth immigration.* Cambridge University Press
KAELBLE H 1989 *A social history of western Europe 1880–1980.* Gill and Macmillan, Dublin
KAVANAGH D 1987 *Thatcherism and British politics: the end of consensus?* Oxford University Press
KENNEDY K et al. 1988 *The economic development of Ireland in the twentieth century.* Routledge

KENWOOD A G, LOUGHEED A C 1992 *The growth of the international economy 1820–1990* 3rd edn. Routledge

KINDLEBERGER C 1967 *Europe's post-war growth: the role of labor supply.* Harvard University Press, Cambridge, Massachusetts

KINDLEBERGER C P, SHONFIELD A 1971 *North American and western European economic policies.* Macmillan

KOFAS J V 1989 *Intervention and underdevelopment: Greece during the cold war.* Pennsylvania State University, University Park

KOSLOWSKI P (ed.) 1992 *Imaginer l'Europe: le marché intérieur européen, tâche culturelle et économique.* Editions du Cerf, Paris

KOVRIG B 1991 *Of walls and bridges: the United States and eastern Europe.* New York University Press, New York

KRAMER A 1991 *Die britische Demontagepolitik am Beispiel Hamburg 1945–1950.* Verlag Verein für Hamburgische Geschichte, Hamburg

KUISEL R F 1981 *Capitalism and the state in modern France: renovation and economic management in the twentieth century.* Cambridge University Press

LAQUEUR W 1972 *Europa since Hitler: the rebirth of Europe.* Penguin

LAQUEUR W 1985 *Germany today: a personal report.* Little, Brown and Co., Boston

LANE P 1987 *The post-war world: an introduction.* Batsford

LARKIN M 1988 *France since the popular front: government and people, 1936–1968.* Clarendon Press

LE ROY P 1994 *La politique agricole commune.* Economica, Paris

LEAMAN J 1988 *The political economy of West Germany 1945–1985: an introduction.* Macmillan

LEE S J 1982 *Aspects of European history 1789–1980.* Methuen

LEIWIG H 1988 *Deutschland Stunde null: historische Luftaufnahmen 1945.* Motorbuch Verlag, Stuttgart

LINDBERG L N, Scheingold S A 1970 *Europe's would-be policy.* Prentice-Hall, Englewood Cliffs

LIPSCHITZ L et al. 1989 *The Federal Republic of Germany: adjustment in a surplus country.* International Monetary Fund, Washington

LIPSCHITZ L, MCDONALD D (eds) 1990 *German unification: economic issues.* International Monetary Fund, Washington

LOPEZ-CLAROS A 1988 *The search for efficiency in the adjustment process: Spain in the 1980s.* International Monetary Fund, Washington

LOVELL A (ed.) 1967 *Art of the cinema in ten European countries.* Council for Cultural Co-operation of the Council of Europe, Strasbourg

LOWE R 1994 The Welfare State in Britain since 1945. *Refresh* **18** 1.4

LYNCH F 1984 Resolving the paradox of the Monnet Plan: national and international planning in French reconstruction. *Economic History Review* **37** (2) 229–43

LYNCH F 1990 France. In Graham A (ed.) *Government and economics in the postwar world: economic policies and comparative performance 1945–85.* Routledge

MCCLELLAND C E, SCHER S P 1974 *Postwar German culture: an anthology.* E P Dutton and Co., New York

MCMILLAN J F 1992 *Twentieth-century France: politics and society 1898–1991.* Edward Arnold

MADDISON A 1962 Growth and fluctuations in the world economy 1870–1960. *Banca Nazionale del Lavoro Quarterly Review,* **61**, 3–71

MADDISON A 1964 *Economic growth in the West: comparative experience in Europe and North America.* Twentieth Century Fund, New York

MADDISON A 1982 *Phases of capitalist development.* Oxford University Press

MADDISON A 1989 *The world economy in the 20th century.* OECD, Paris

MADDISON A 1991 *Dynamic forces in capitalist development: a long-run comparative view.* Oxford University Press

MAIER C S 1987 *In search of stability: explorations in historical political economy.* Cambridge University Press

MAIER C S (ed.) 1991 *The Marshall plan and Germany: West German development within the framework of the European recovery program.* Berg, New York

MAIER C S 1993 Premises of the recovery program. In Girault R *Le plan Marshall et le relèvement économique de l'Europe.* Comité pour l'histoire économique et financière, Ministère des Finances, Paris

MALMSTRÖM V 1965 *Norden: crossroads of destiny and progress.* Van Nostrand, Princeton, NJ

1969 *Manpower aspects of recent economic developments in Europe.* International Labour Office, Geneva

MANVELL R 1966 *New cinema in Europe.* Studio Vista

MARMARAS E 1989 The privately-built multi-storey apartment building: the case of inter-war Athens. *Planning Perspectives* **4** (1) 45–78

MARWICK A 1974 *War and social change in the twentieth century.* Macmillan

MARWICK A 1982 *British society since 1945.* Penguin

MASON A 1995 *The xenophobe's guide to the Belgians.* Ravette Books

1974 *Materialien zum Bericht zur Lage der Nation.* Bundesministerium für innerdeutsche Beziehungen, Berlin

MATHIAS P, POSTAN M (eds) 1978 *The Cambridge economic history of Europe* vol 7 *The industrial economies: capital, labour and enterprise. Part 1 Britain, France, Germany and Scandinavia.* Cambridge University Press

MATHIEU G 1965 *Peut-on loger les Français?* Seuil, Paris

MATTHEWS R 1993 Political and economic causes of the economic slowdown *Scottish Journal of Political Economy* **40** (2) 129–42

MAURO F 1971 *Histoire de l'économie mondiale.* Editeurs Sirey, Paris

MEAD W 1958 *An economic geography of the Scandinavian states and Finland.* University of London Press

MEENAN J 1970 *The Irish economy since 1922.* Liverpool University Press

MILLER J E 1986 *The United States and Italy 1940–1950: the politics and diplomacy of stabilization.* University of North Carolina Press, Chapel Hill

MILLWARD R, SINGLETON J (eds) 1995 *The political economy of nationalisation in Britain 1920–1950.* Cambridge University Press

MILWARD A S 1970a *The economic effects of the two world wars on Britain.* Macmillan

MILWARD A S 1970b *The New Order and the French economy.* Clarendon Press

MILWARD A S 1977 *War economy and society 1939–1945.* Allen Lane

MILWARD A S 1984 *The reconstruction of western Europe 1945–51.* Methuen

MILWARD A S 1989 Was the Marshall plan necessary? *Diplomatic History* **13** (2) 231–53

MILWARD A S 1992 *The European rescue of the nation-state.* Routledge

MILWARD A S 1992 Germany and European integration 1949–66. Lecture at German Historical Institute, London, 3 November

MILWARD A S et al. 1993 *The frontier of national sovereignty: history and theory 1945–1992.* Routledge

MINC A 1989 *La grande illusion.* Bernard Crasset, Paris

MITCHELL B 1978 *European historical statistics 1750–1970* (abridged edn). Macmillan

MOLLE W 1990 *The economics of European integration: theory, practice, policy.* Dartmouth

MOMMEN A 1994 *The Belgian economy in the twentieth century.* Routledge

MONNET J 1976 *Mémoires.* Fayard, Paris

MORGAN K O 1990 *The people's peace: British history 1945–1990.* Oxford University Press

MORIN F, DUPUY C 1993 *Le coeur financier européen.* Economica, Paris

MUNTING R, HOLDERNESS B 1991 *Crisis, recovery and war: an economic history of continental Europe 1918–1945.* Philip Allan

NEVIN E 1990 *The economics of Europe.* Macmillan

NICHOLLS A J 1994 *Freedom with responsibility: the social market economy in Germany 1918–1963.* Clarendon Press

NOIN D, WOODS R (eds) 1993 *The changing population of Europe.* Blackwell

OECD 55 1994 *Economic outlook, June 1994.* OECD, Paris

OECD 57 1995 *Economic outlook, June 1995.* OECD, Paris

OECD 1994 *OECD economic surveys 1993–1994: Denmark.* OECD, Paris

OECD 1994 *OECD economic surveys: 1993–1994: Germany.* OECD, Paris

OECD 1995 *OECD economic surveys 1994–1995: Norway.* OECD, Paris

OECD 1994 *OECD economic surveys 1993–1994: Spain.* OECD, Paris

OECD 1995 *OECD economic surveys 1994–1995: Sweden.* OECD, Paris

OECD 1994 *OECD economic surveys 1993–1994: United Kingdom.* OECD, Paris

OECD 1963 *France (economic surveys).* OECD, Paris

OECD 1970 *France (economic surveys).* OECD, Paris

OECD 1970 *Germany (economic surveys).* OECD, Paris

OECD 1978 *Germany (economic surveys).* OECD, Paris

OECD 1991 *Historical statistics 1960–1989.* OECD, Paris

OECD 1994 *Main economic indicators.* OECD, Paris

OECD 1974 *Monetary policy in France.* OECD, Paris

OECD 1973 *Monetary policy in Germany.* OECD, Paris

OECD 1973 *Monetary policy in Italy.* OECD, Paris

OECD 1994 *OECD economic surveys 1993–1994; France.* OECD, Paris

OEEC 1956 *Economic conditions in the federal republic of Germany.* OEEC, Paris

PAGE S 1987 The rise in protection since 1974. *Oxford Review of Economic Policy* 3(1) 37–51

PANAYI P 1993 *Racial violence in Britain 1840–1950.* Leicester University Press

PAULU B 1967 *Radio and television on the broadcasting continent.* University of Minnesota Press, Minneapolis

PAYNE S 1973 *A history of Spain and Portugal* vol 2. University of Wisconsin Press, Madison

PAYNE S 1987 *The Franco regime 1936–1975.* University of Wisconsin Press, Madison

PEDEN G C 1988 *Keynes, the treasury and British economic policy*. Macmillan

PERLMAN M 1993 In search of monetary union. *Journal of European Economic History* **22**(2) 313–32

PETSCH W and J 1983 *Bundesrepublik – eine neue Heimat? Städtebau und Architektur nach '45*. Elefanten Press, Berlin

PFLAUM H 1990 *Germany on film: theme and content in the cinema of the Federal Republic of Germany*. Wayne State University Press, Detroit

PIQUET MARCHAL O 1985 *Histoire économique de l'Europe des dix: de la seconde guerre mondiale à aujourd'hui*. Librairie des Techniques, Paris

PIMLOTT B 1992 *Harold Wilson*. Harper Collins

POLLARD S 1974 *European economic integration 1815–1970*. Thames and Hudson

POLLARD S. 1981 *Peaceful conquest: the industrialization of Europe 1760–1870*. Oxford University Press

POLLARD S 1983 *The development of the British economy* 1914–1980 3rd edn. Edward Arnold

POLLARD S 1992a *The development of the British economy 1914–1990* 4th edn. Edward Arnold

POLLARD, S. 1992b *The wasting of the British economy: British economic policy 1945 to the present*. St Martin's Press, New York

PORTER B 1987 *Britain, Europe and the world 1850–1986: delusions of grandeur* 2nd edn. Unwin Hyman

POSTAN M M 1967 *An economic history of western Europe 1945–1964* Methuen

PRESSNELL L S 1986 *External economic policy since the war* vol 1: *The post-war financial settlement*. HMSO

PRESTON P 1990 Spain. In Graham A (ed.) *Government and economics in the postwar world: economic policies and comparative performance 1945–85*. Routledge

1991 *Reconstructions et modernisation: la France après les ruines 1918–1945*. Archives Nationales, Paris

REX J, MOORE R 1967 *Race, community and conflict: a study of Sparkbrook*. Oxford University Press

RIBHEGGE W, SCHÖNBACH E M, WITT M 1991 *Hamm: Geschichte der Stadt und Region im 19 und 20 Jahrhundert*. Patmos Verlag, Düsseldorf

RIOUX J P 1980 *La France de la quatrième république: 1 L'ardeur et la nécessité 1944–1952*. Editions du Seuil, Paris

RIOUX J P 1983 *La France de la quatrième république: 2 L'expansion et l'impuissance 1952–1958*. Editions du Seuil, Paris

ROBBINS K 1994 *The eclipse of a great power: modern Britain 1870–1992* 2nd edn. Longman

ROBERTS J M 1980 *The Pelican history of the world.* Penguin

ROBERTS R, KYNASTON D 1995 *The Bank of England: money, power and influence, 1694–1994.* Clarendon Press

RÖPKE W 1959 *L'économie mondiale aux XIXe et XXe siècles.* Droz, Geneva

ROSEMAN M 1992 *Recasting the Ruhr 1945–1958: manpower, economic recovery and labour relations.* Oxford; Berg; New York

ROSSI N, TONIOLO G 1992 Catching up or falling behind? Italy's economic growth 1895–1947. *Economic History Review* 45(3) 537–63

ROSTOW W 1978 *The world economy: history and prospect.* University of Texas Press, Austin

RUBINSTEIN W 1993 *Capitalism, culture and decline in Britain, 1750–1990.* Routledge

SALMON K 1992 *Andalucia: an emerging regional economy in Europe.* Junta de Andalucia, Seville

SALMON P 1990 Scandinavia. In Graham A (ed.) *Government and economics in the postwar world: economic policies and comparative performance 1945–85.* Routledge

SASSOON D 1990 Italy. In Graham A (ed.) *Government and economics in the postwar world: economic policies and comparative performance 1945–85.* Routledge

SCAMMELL W M 1980 *The international economy since 1945.* Macmillan

SCHILDT A, SYWOTTEK A (eds) 1993 *Modernisierung im Wiederaufbau: die Westdeutsche Gesellschaft der 50er Jahre.* Dietz, Bonn

SCHMITT H O 1981 *Economic stabilization and growth in Portugal* (occasional paper no 2). International Monetary Fund, Washington

SCHULZ G 1991a Wohnungspolitik und soziale Sicherung nach 1945: das ende der Arbeiterwohnungsfrage. In Tenfelde K (ed.) *Arbeiter im 20 Jahrhundert.* Klett-cotta, Berlin 483–506

SCHULZ G 1991b Wohnungspolitik und Wirtschaftsordnung: die Auseinandersetzungen um die Integration der Wohnungspolitik in der Marktwirtschaft 1945–1960. In Petzina, D (ed.) *Ordnungspolitische Weichenstellungen nach dem Zweiten Weltkrieg.* Duncker und Humblot, Berlin 123–43

SCHULZ G 1993 Perspektiven europäischer Wohnungspolitik 1918 bis 1960. In Schulz (ed.) *Wohnungspolitik im Sozialstaat: Deutscher und Europäische Lösungen 1918–1960.* Droste, Düsseldorf

SEERS D, VAITSOS C 1982 *The second enlargement of the EEC: the integration of unequal partners.* Macmillan

SERVAN-SCHREIBER J J 1967 *Le défi américain.* Denoël, Paris

SHENNAN A 1989 *Rethinking France: plans for renewal 1940–1946.* Clarendon Press

SHEPHERD G, DUCHÊNE F, SAUNDERS C 1983 *Europe's industries: public and private strategies for change.* Pinter

SHOWERS V 1973 *The world in figures.* John Wiley

SMITH A (ed.) 1995 *Television: an international history.* Oxford University Press

STETTINIUS E R Jr. 1944 *Lend-lease: weapon for victory* Macmillan, New York

STOKES R G 1988 *Divide and prosper: the heirs of I G Farben under Allied authority 1945–1951.* University of California Press, Berkeley

STOLPER G et al. 1967 *The German economy, 1870 to the present.* Weidenfeld and Nicolson

SUPPLE B 1994 Fear of failing: economic history and the decline of Britain. *Economic History Review* **47**(3) 441–58

SUTCLIFFE A, SMITH R 1974 *Birmingham 1939–1970.* Clarendon Press

TEMIN P 1995 The 'Koreaboom' in West Germany: fact or fiction? *Economic History Review* **48**(4): 737–53

THATCHER M 1993 *The Downing street years.* Harper Collins

THOMPSON E P 1970 *Warwick University limited: industry, management and the universities.* Penguin

THOMPSON F (ed.) 1990 *The Cambridge social history of Britain 1750–1950* vol 2 *People and their environment.* Cambridge University Press

THURLOW D 1992 *Profumo: the hate factor.* Robert Hale

TIPTON F B, ALDRICH R 1987 *An economic and social history of Europe from 1939 to the present.* Macmillan Education

TODD E 1991 *The making of modern France: politics, ideology and culture.* Basil Blackwell

TONER M, WHITE C 1995 *Bluff your way in the European Union.* Ravette Books

TORTELLA G 1994 Patterns of economic retardation and recovery in south-western Europe in the nineteenth and twentieth centuries. *Economic History Review* **47**(1) 1–21

TSOUKALIS L (ed.) 1986 *Europe, America and the world economy.* Blackwell

TURNER H A 1987 *The two Germanies since 1945.* Yale University Press, New Haven

TURNER I D (ed.) 1989 *Reconstruction in post-war Germany: British occupation policy and the western zones 1945–55.* Berg

UNGERER H et al. 1986 *The European monetary system: recent developments.* International Monetary Fund, Washington

URWIN D W 1989 *Western Europe since 1945: a political history* 4th edn. Longman

URWIN D W 1995 *The community of Europe: a history of European integration since 1945* 2nd edn. Longman

VAN DEN BEMPT P, QUINTYN M 1989 *Espace financier européen et coopération monétaire.* Economica, Paris

VAN ZANDEN J, GRIFFITHS R 1989 *Economische geschiedenis van Nederland in de 20e eeuw.* Aula, Utrecht

VERMILYE J 1994 *Great Italian films.* Citadel Press, New York

WALL IRWIN M 1991 *The United States and the making of post-war France 1945–1954.* Cambridge University Press

WALLERSTEIN I 1974 *The modern world system, 1. Capitalist agriculture and the origins of the European world-economy in the sixteenth century.* Academic Press, New York

WALVIN J 1984 *Passage to Britain: immigration in British history and politics.* Penguin

WARD S (ed.) 1992 *The garden city: past, present and future.* Spon

WERTH A 1966 *France 1940–1955.* Beacon Press, Boston

WHITE P 1884 *The west European city: a social geography.* Longman

WHITNAH D R, ERICKSON E L 1985 *The American occupation of Austria: planning and early years.* Greenwood Press, Westport, Conn

WICKHAM S 1969 *L'éspace industriel européen.* Calmann-Lévy, Paris

WIENER M J 1985 *English culture and the decline of the industrial spirit 1850–1980.* Penguin

WILLETT R 1989 *The Americanization of Germany 1945–1949.* Routledge

WILLIAMS A M 1994 *The European community: the contradictions of integration* 2nd edn. Blackwell

WILLIAMS R H (ed.) 1984 *Planning in Europe: urban and regional planning in the EEC.* Allen and Unwin

WILLIS F R 1962 *The French in Germany 1945–1949.* Stanford University Press, Stanford

WILLIS F R 1965 *France, Germany and the new Europe 1945–1963.* Stanford University Press, Stanford

WILLIS F R 1971 *Italy chooses Europe.* Oxford University Press, New York

WISKEMANN E 1971 *Italy since 1945.* Macmillan

WOOLF S 1972 *The rebirth of Italy 1943–50.* Longman

WOOLF S 1991 *Napoleon's integration of Europe.* Routledge

WORSWICK G D N, ADY P H 1962 *The British economy in the nineteen-fifties.* Clarendon Press

WRIGHT J F 1979 *Britain in the age of economic management: an economic history since 1939.* Oxford University Press

WURM C (ed.) 1995 *Western Europe and Germany: the beginnings of European integration 1945–1960.* Berg

YOUNG J W 1984 *Britain, France and the unity of Europe 1945–51.* Leicester University Press

YOUNG J W 1990 *France, the cold war and the western alliance: 1944–1949 – French foreign policy and post-war Europe.* Leicester University Press

YOUNG J W 1991 *Cold war Europe 1945–1989: a political history.* Edward Arnold

YOUNG J W 1993 *Britain and European unity 1945–1992.* Macmillan

YOUNG W 1963 *The Profumo affair: aspects of conservatism.* Penguin

ZAMAGNI V 1993 *The economic history of Italy 1860–1990: recovery after decline.* Clarendon Press

ZINK H 1957 *The United States in Germany 1944–1955.* Greenwood Press, Westport

Index

Greece, 82; holidays, 159, 325; hours of
work, 147; housing and urban
reconstruction, 25–6, 34–5, 37, 139, 143,
182, 184; immigration, 181–4, 191–2, 196;
imports, 235, 238; incomes policies, 238–9;
industrial unrest, 234, 243; industry, 24,
32–4, 35, 36–7, 233, 234, 238, 239–41, 242,
244, 246; inflation, 204, 238, 242, 248;
investment, 133, 244, 245; living standards,
143, 232, 236, 249; manufacturing, 24, 32,
233, 234, 239–41, 242, 246; military
deaths, 137; motor industry, 32, 36–7, 233,
238, 239, 244; nationalisation, 23, 33–4;
newspapers, 307; population, 198, 298,
337; privatisation, 35, 242, 244, 245;
purchasing power, 296; radio
broadcasting, 309, 310–11; rationing, 30,
31, 33, 35, 143; regional planning, 33;
road building, 37–8, 144; service sector,
240, 300; social reform, 9–10, 29–30, 33,
34–5, 138; student protest, 172; taxation,
244, 247; telephones, 305; television, 147,
311, 312; theatre, 149, 155, 156, 167–8;
trade unions, 34, 234–5, 242–3, 245, 246;
unemployment, 234, 242, 248; wages, 239,
243; youth culture, 150, 151
British Airways, 245
British Steel, 240
Brown, George, 130, 234
Brussels Pact (1948), 107, 253
Bunuel, Luis, 314
Byron Price Report, 54–5

Calvin Hoover Report, 54
Camus, Albert, 160–1
Canada, 336, 339, 342
car industry *see* motor industry
car ownership, 143–4, 145–6, 213, 305–6
Carax, L, 314
Caetano, Marcelo, 291
cartels, 60, 61, 117
Castle, Barbara, 234
catching-up, process of, 38, 341, 342
Cecchini Report, 128
censorship, 155–6, 309
Chabrol, Claude, 165
Chirac, Jacques, 230
Christian Democracy, 63, 211, 300
church attendance, 144
Churchill, Winston, 6, 89, 110
cigarettes, 148
cinema, 164–6, 313–16; British, 156, 164,
314–15; French, 141–2, 164–6, 314;
German, 162, 166, 315; internationalist,
118; Nordic, 316; realist, 148–9, 164–6
Civic Amenities Act (1967), 320
civil service, France, 43
class, 299–301; middle, 144–5; working,
144–5, 146–50
Clay, Lucius D, 54, 55
Clément, René, 165
Club Méditerranée, 158–9, 326
coal, 28; Belgium, 257–8, 260; Britain, 32,

204, 238, 243; France, 45, 48, 107, 108,
111; Germany, 204, 215–16; Spain, 286, *see
also* European Coal and Steel Community,
the Ruhr, Schuman Plan
Cobden, Richard, 101
Coca-Cola Company, 141, 142
Cohn-Bendit, Daniel, 170
Colbert, Jean-Baptiste, 100
collaborators, 41
colonial empires: Belgian, 180, 259, 264–5;
British, 12–13, 179, 180; Dutch, 180,
264–5; French, 12, 179, 180, 225;
Portuguese, 95, 292; as sources of labour,
179–81
Comité National d'Expansion Economique,
259
Committee for European Economic
Cooperation *see* Organisation for
European Economic Cooperation
Common Agricultural Policy (CAP), 116,
118, 120–2, 124, 125, 126, 129, 224
Common Market *see* European Economic
Community
Common Nordic Labour Market, 80, 271
Commonwealth Immigration Act (1962), 183
Communism, 6, 16, 22, 81–2, 329; collapse
of, 200–1, 206–9, 348
Communists: Belgium, 256; France, 42, 170;
Italy, 85, 281
Confédération Française Démocratique du
Travail (CFDT), 170
Confédération Générale du Travail (CGT),
170, 171
Congress of Europe (1948), 110
Conseil National des Charbonnages (CNC),
257
conservation, 302–3, 319–21
Constantine II, King of Greece, 289
contraception, 156–7
corruption, 278, 280, 328
Council of Europe, 107, 110
Council on Foreign Relations, 7
Council of Ministers, 130–1
Council for Mutual Economic Assistance
(Comecon), 133, 178
counterpart funds, 20, 21, 47–8
Countryside Act (1968), 320
crime and impropriety, 172–4, 297
Cuban missiles crisis, 207
culture, 160–4, 321–2, *see also* art, cinema,
literature, theatre
currency, 11–12; Belgium, 252, 262; Britain,
31, 237; devaluation of, 22, 48, 83, 201,
226, 237, 262; dollar convertibility of, 31,
68, 109–10; European, 129, 135; flotation,
202; France, 48, 222–3, 226; Germany, 62,
68; Greece, 83; revaluation of, 202
customs union, 107–8; Benelux countries,
104, 252–3; Franco-Italian, 108, *see also*
European Coal and Steel Community,
European Economic Community

deaths, 137, 336

Federal Republic, 62; and France, 111,
124, 241; holidays, 159–60, 325–6; hours
of work, 145, 147; housing, 68–9;
immigration, 187–91, 192–3, 195, 196–7,
216–17; imports, 66, 69–70, 214, 216, 217;
industry, 24, 36, 51, 55–6, 57–8, 60–1,
65–8, 119, 213, 215–16, 217, 218, 219;
inflation, 204, 213, 216, 217; investment,
53, 70, 133, 213, 216; literature, 162–3;
living standards, 213; manufacturing, 24,
65, 66, 217, 219; and Marshall aid, 70;
military deaths, 137; motor industry, 36;
National Democratic Party, 192; National
Socialist ideology and policies, 2–4; and
Netherlands, 253, 264; nuclear power,
216; occupation zones, 53–4, 55–7;
political parties, 58–9, 62, 192–3, 216, 321;
population, 52, 53, 198, 222, 298, 337;
purchasing power, 296; radio
broadcasting, 310; rearmament, 71;
refugees in, 55, 57, 67, 190–1; reparations,
56–7; Die Republikaner, 192–3;
reunification of, 219–20; Roman Catholic
Church, 58; service employment, 240, 300;
Social Democrats, 62, 216; student protest,
171, 329; telephones, 305; television, 311;
terrorism, 281, 329; theatre, 167; trade,
69–70; trade unions, 58, 59, 67, 234;
unemployment, 67, 145, 190, 215, 216,
217–18, 221; urban reconstruction, 25, 26;
wages, 145, 213; works councils, 67; youth
culture, 152
Germany, East, 64, 209, 219–22, 348
Ghana, 180
Giscard d'Estaing, V, 228
GNP, 2, 22, 51, 66, 214, 266, 267, 278, 295,
296, 338
Godard, Jean-Luc, 165
gold standard, 102
Gorbachev, Mikhail, 207
Government and Relief in Occupied Areas
(GARIOA), 14–15
Grass, Günter, 163
Greece, 11, 40, 81, 82–3, 95, 126, 146, 277,
288–90, 295, 296, 298, 305, 306, 324–5
Greek immigrants, 187, 188, 190
Greek Orthodox Church, 81
Green parties, 216, 321, 328
Greer, Germaine, 302
Group 47, 162–3
Guitry, Sacha, 164
Gut, Camille, 256

Hamer, Robert, 164
Havana Charter, 12
health and fitness, 323
Heath, Edward, 127, 237–8
Heffner, Hugh, 173
Heldt, Werner, 164
hire-purchase credit, Italy, 87
Hitler, Adolf, 4
Hoffman, Paul, 21
Hoggart, Richard, 148

holidays, 157–60, 325–6, *see also* tourism
homosexuality, 157, 297, 316
hours of work, 145, 146, 147, 228, 276, 288,
324
housing, 24–7, 34–5, 37, 303–4, 332; Britain,
25–6, 34–5, 37, 139, 143, 182, 184; France,
185, 224, 304; Germany, 68–9; Italy, 279;
Netherlands, 264; Portugal, 291; Spain,
304; Sweden, 77
Howard, Ebenezer, 26, 119
Howe, Sir Geoffrey, 247
Hull, Cordell, 9
Hungary, 179, 188
hydro-electricity, 80, 286

IG Farbenindustrie, 60
immigration, 81, 176–98, 216–17, 225, 265,
267, 299, 336
imperial preference, 102
import substitution, Spain, 92, 93
imports, 131, 336; agricultural products, 118,
119; Britain, 235, 238; France, 51, 227;
Germany, 66, 69–70, 214, 216, 217;
Netherlands, 251, 252, 264; Nordic
countries, 75; Portugal, 293; Spain, 91
incomes policies, 205; Britain, 238–9
Independent Television Authority (ITA), 311
India, 180, 339; immigrants from, 179, 181,
182
Indochina (Vietnam), 169, 180, 235
Indonesia, 180, 264, 265
indoor pastimes, 324–5
industrial unrest: Britain, 234, 243; France,
42–3; Italy, 280
industry, 119, 134, 157, 271, 299; Belgium,
24, 250, 257–9, 260, 261, 262; Britain, 24,
32–4, 35, 36–7, 233, 234, 238, 239–41, 242,
244, 246; France, 24, 37, 44–5, 47–51, 223,
229; Germany, 24, 36, 51, 55–6, 57–8,
60–1, 65–8, 119, 213, 215–16, 217, 218,
219; Greece, 83, 288; Italy, 24, 37, 84–9,
113, 278, 279, 280, 281; Netherlands, 251,
265–6, 267; Nordic countries, 74, 76–80,
272, 275; Portugal, 96, 290, 291, 293;
Spain, 90, 92, 94, 283, *see also*
manufacturing industry
inflation, 205, 206, 211, 301, 342, 347;
Britain, 204, 238, 242, 248; France, 204,
222, 224, 226, 227; Germany, 204, 213,
216, 217; Greece, 289; Italy, 84, 88, 204,
279; Portugal, 292, 293; Spain, 93, 283,
284, 285, 286, 287; Sweden, 274
innovation, 341, 342
Institute for Industrial Reconstruction (IRI),
86
integration, 100–35; international, 343–6;
origins of, 100–2, *see also* economic
integration
International Bank for Reconstruction and
Development (IBRD) *see* World Bank
International Monetary Fund (IMF), 11,
127, 203, 283, 292
International Steel Cartel, 111

Index

373

International Trade Organisation (ITO), 12
investment, 342; Belgium, 257, 259; Britain,
133, 244, 245; EEC in US, 133; France,
47–8, 51, 223; Germany, 53, 70, 213, 216;
Netherlands, 267; Norway, 78; Portugal,
290; Spain, 93, 283, 286, 287; US in
Europe, 133, 245
IRA, 330
Iran, 188, 205
Ireland, 40, 73, 123, 125, 296, 298, 312, 349
Ireland, Northern, 330–1
iron and steel see steel
irrigation schemes, Spain, 93–4
Italian immigrants, 187, 190, 196
Italy, 11, 14, 16, 21, 81, 83–9, 106, 108, 111,
137, 153, 270, 277, 278–82, 295, 307, 345,
349; agriculture, 89, 278; Americanisation,
140; car ownership, 146, 306; colonies,
180; Communists, 85, 281; conservation,
319–20; corruption, 278, 280, 328; and
customs union, 108; divorce, 328;
economy, 40, 84–9, 212, 240, 249, 278–80,
281–2, 296, 339; and the EEC, 278;
emigration, 278; exports, 36, 85, 87, 241,
246, 279, 281; holidays, 159; hours of
work, 147; housing, 279; immigration, 191,
194; industrial unrest, 280; industry, 24,
37, 84–9, 113, 278, 279, 280, 281; inflation,
84, 88, 204, 279; land reform, 86;
manufacturing, 24, 84, 85, 86, 87, 89, 279;
Marshall plan, 85–6, 88; motor industry,
37; nationalisation, 23; political tension,
169, 171–2, 278, 280–1, 329–30;
population, 298, 337; privatisation, 282;
purchasing power, 296; radio
broadcasting, 310, 311; service
employment, 300; steel industry, 87–8,
113; student protest, 169, 171–2, 280–1,
329; telephones, 305; television, 312;
terrorism, 329; tourism, 290; trade unions,
88, 280, 281; unemployment, 88, 282; and
the US, 84–6, 88, 89; wages, 88, 280, 281;
youth culture, 152

Jamaica, 181
Japan, 6, 13, 52, 127, 131, 240, 339
Jews, 176, 192
job creation, 129, 261

Keeler, Christine, 72
Keith, Max, 142
Keynes, J M, 10, 29
Khruschev, Nikita, 207
Kluge, Alexander, 166
Kohl, Helmut, 218
Korea, South, 339
Korean War, 65
Kray twins, 173–4

labour, immigrants as source of, 176–98, 215
Labour Party, 29, 30
land reform, 86, 223–4
Landmark Trust, 320

languages, 326–7, 332–3
Lawrence, D H, 155
Lawson, Nigel, 247
Lean, David, 164
leisure, 144, 145, 147–8, 324–5, see also
cinema, sport, television
Lelouch, Claude, 165
Lend-Lease agreement, 6, 9, 14, 31, 104
Leopold III (King of Belgium), 255
Le Pen, Jean-Marie, 193, 194
Ley, Robert, 59
literature, 148, 155–6, 161–3
Littlewood, Joan, 168
living standards, 113, 139–40, 145–6, 206,
211, 295–7; Belgium, 269; Britain, 143,
232, 236, 249; France, 226; Germany, 213;
Nordic countries, 272; rural, 119–20; USA,
139–40, 295
Lloyd Webber, Andrew, 322
Losey, Joseph, 314
Louis, Joe, 142
Luxembourg, 40, 236, 250, 251, 252, 254,
258, 296, 298, 306, 311

McCloy, John ('Jack'), 11, 112
Mackintosh, Charles Rennie, 303
Macmillan, Harold, 37, 39, 232, 233
Mafia, 278, 328, 349
magazines, 144, 152, 153, 156
Major, John, 247–8
Malraux, André, 162
Mansholt, Sicco, 121
manufacturing industry, 24, 131, 134, 204–5,
299, 343; Britain, 24, 32, 233, 234, 239–41,
242, 246; Germany, 24, 65, 66, 145, 217,
219; Greece, 83; Italy, 24, 84, 85, 86, 87,
89, 279; Portugal, 96, 290, 293; Spain, 91,
283, 285, see also aircraft industry, motor
industry
Marshall, George C, 17, 18, 23
Marshall plan, 15, 17–23, 47, 70, 75, 78–9,
82, 83, 85–6, 88, 95, 107–9, 264
Martens, Wilfried, 261–2
materialism, 68
Maxwell, Robert, 307
meat production, 2
Mercantilism, 100
mergers, international, 134
Mexico, 339
middle class, 144–5
migration see emigration, immigration
Mill, John Stuart, 63, 334
Mitterrand, François, 205, 209, 227
mobility and mobility substitution, 297,
305–6
Moncloa agreements, 286
monetarism, 242
monetary union, 125, 129
Monnet, Jean, 21, 43–4, 45, 103, 104, 105,
110–11, 112, 114–15, 124, 132
Monnet plan, 46–7, 48, 49
morality, 172–3, 297
Morgenthau, Henry, 54, 57